Sample Pages

Illustrations of Organization and Research Techniques in West's

Key Number Digests
National Reporter System
U.S.C.A. and Other West Statutes
Corpus Juris Secundum
Words and Phrases
Black's Law Dictionary
WESTLAW

Designed for Classroom Use
in All Courses on Legal Research

Reprinted from copyrighted publications
of the West Publishing Company,
Copyright © 1986

Third Edition

By
The Publisher's Edit

D1502182

St. Paul, Minn.
WEST PUBLISHING CO.
1986

Outline of Legal Reference Material

Primary Sources

Statutes

Constitutions
Treaties
Federal Statutes ⟶

> Statutes at Large
> U.S. Code (and WESTLAW)
> U.S. Code Annotated
> U.S. Code Service

State Statutes ⟶

> Session Laws, etc.
> Compiled Statutes, Revised Statutes
> Codes, etc.
> WESTLAW

Municipal Ordinances
Rules of Administrative Bodies
Rules of Court
Executive Orders and Promulgations

Decisions

United States ⟶
    Supreme Court Reports

> Government Series
> Lawyer's Edition
> Supreme Court Reporter
>   (National Reporter System)
> WESTLAW

Federal Cases (to 1880)
Federal Reporter (1880 to date) (National Reporter System) and WESTLAW
Federal Supplement (1932 to date) (National Reporter System) and WESTLAW
Federal Rules Decisions (National Reporter System) and WESTLAW
State Reports and WESTLAW

National Reporter System ⟶

> Supreme Court Reporter
> Federal Reporter
> Federal Supplement
> Federal Rules Decisions
> Atlantic Reporter
> North Eastern Reporter
> North Western Reporter
> Pacific Reporter
> South Eastern Reporter
> Southern Reporter
> South Western Reporter
> California Reporter
> New York Supplement
> Military Justice Reporter
> WESTLAW

Selected Reports

> American Law Reports, 4th
>   ALR Federal

Subject or Special Reports ⟶

> American Bankruptcy Reports
> American Maritime Cases
> West's Bankruptcy Reporter
> Education Law Reporter
> Social Security Reporter
> WESTLAW

Decisions of Administrative Bodies

> Interstate Commerce Commission
> Federal Trade Commission
> WESTLAW

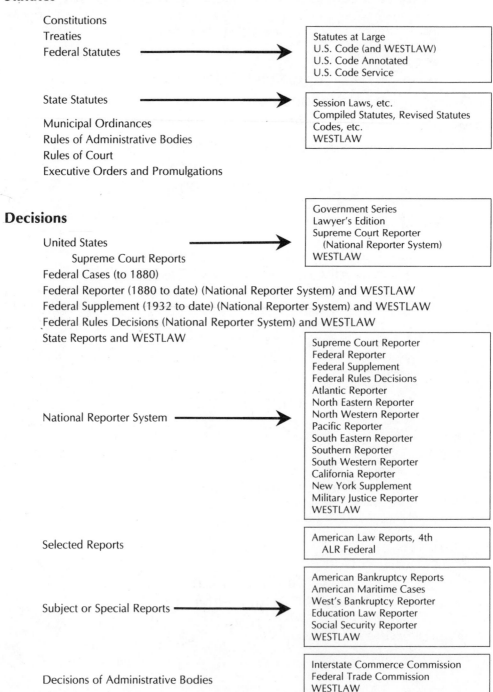

Secondary Sources

Encyclopedia   →   Corpus Juris Secundum
American Jurisprudence, 3rd

Words and Phrases
Textbooks
Treatises
Practitioner's Handbooks
Loose Leaf Services
Legal Dictionaries
Citation Books
Legal Thesauruses
Law Reviews
WESTLAW

Finding Tools

Digests

American Digest System

Century Digest	1658 to 1896
First Decennial Digest	1897 to 1906
Second Decennial Digest	1907 to 1916
Third Decennial Digest	1916 to 1926
Fourth Decennial Digest	1926 to 1936
Fifth Decennial Digest	1936 to 1946
Sixth Decennial Digest	1946 to 1956
Seventh Decennial Digest	1956 to 1966
Eighth Decennial Digest	1966 to 1976
Ninth Decennial, Part I	1976 to 1981
General Digest	1981 to present

Other Digests

Supreme Court Digest
Federal Practice Digest
State and Reporter Digests
Selected Case Series Digests
Subject or Special Reports Digest
WESTLAW

Tables of

Cases Reported
Cases Digested, Plaintiff
Cases Digested, Defendant
Cases Affirmed, Reversed, or Modified
Cases Cited by Popular Name
Cases Cited
Parallel Citations
Statutes Construed

Other

Indexes to Legal Periodicals

Computer Assisted Legal Research

WESTLAW
LEXIS
VERALEX

Contents

Introduction

This pamphlet provides pages from major West publications and screens from WESTLAW along with problems to illustrate the use of these research tools.

If this is your first experience with legal research, the following pages provide you with helpful information.

"How to Analyze Fact Situations" (pg vii) is a suggested framework for you to use to analyze facts and isolate words or concepts important to your research.

The Outline of Legal Reference Material (pgs ii–iii) indicates the organization of reference sources into three main categories. They are: **Primary Sources**—materials containing the text of the law such as cases from federal or state courts or statutes passed by legislatures, **Secondary Sources**—books such as encyclopedias, dictionaries and treatises which explain and comment on the law and **Finding Tools**—such as digests which help you find material pertinent to your research problem.

WESTLAW—our computer assisted legal research service—can act as a primary, secondary or finding source, depending on how it is used.

When you research legal issues you are often confronted with a multitude of facts but minimal direction. In order to successfully complete your research you need to sift through the facts and concepts and decide which are most important to your research. The technique suggested below is one many researchers use successfully. It can be used for the sample problems in the chapters on Digests, USCA and CJS. A similar technique is used for WESTLAW research.

How to Analyze Facts

When analyzing your fact situation for the purpose of searching for cases or statutes on point, it is a good plan to ask yourself "What words describe the parties concerned; the places or things involved; the basis of action or issue; the possible defenses and the relief sought."

Parties

Parties should be understood to be persons of a particular class, occupation or relation; e.g. children, collectors, heirs, or any person who is either directly or indirectly necessary to a proper determination of the action.

Places and Things

Places and things should be understood as being objects which necessarily must exist before any cause of action or dispute can arise; objects perceptible through the senses; e.g. automobiles, sidewalks, derricks or garages are words describing the places or things which must exist before a cause of action alleging negligent use or defective condition can arise regarding them.

Basis of Action or Issue

Basis of action or issue should be understood as being some wrong suffered by reason of another's neglect of duty; e.g. loss (of goods); some affirmative wrong—boycott, ejection, assault; some legal obligation ignored—stop, look and listen or the infraction of some statutory or constitutional provision—eight-hour law, the Sherman Act.

Defense

Defense should be understood as being some reason in law or fact why plaintiff should not recover; e.g. failure of consideration, act of God, assumption of risk, infancy.

Relief Sought

Relief sought should be understood as being the legal remedy sought; e.g. restraining order, restoration damages, annulment.

West's Federal Practice Digest 3d

West Digests

The Digest chapter illustrates the use of West's indexing system to find cases dealing with your legal issue. You will use the important words from your worksheet, consult the descriptive-word index and find key numbers which lead you to digests of case law.

Digest Problem

Government agents observed a person buying chemicals which could be used to make an illegal drug. Without a warrant, they placed an electronic tracking device on his vehicle. They followed him and made an arrest at the warehouse where the illegal drug was made. The attorney for the defendant wishes to make a motion to exclude evidence seized as a result of the placement of the beeper on his clients' auto without a warrant. What case law discusses the issue of warrantless use of beepers in this situation?

Worksheet

Parties:

Places and Things:

Basis of Action or Issue:

Defense:

Relief Sought:

WEST'S
FEDERAL PRACTICE
DIGEST 3d

Volume 1

ABANDONED AND LOST PROPERTY — ADMIRALTY

ST. PAUL, MINN.
WEST PUBLISHING CO.

PREFACE

The continuing rapid growth of Federal case law reflects the increase in the volume of litigation in the Federal Courts.

To insure that the Federal Digest remains a functional indexing service to Federal case law all of the material accumulated since publication of Federal Digest 2d has been recompiled into a set of convenient, uniform bound volumes.

These new volumes will comprise Federal Digest 3d. Federal Digest 2d will continue to provide coverage of Federal case law from 1961 to November, 1975. Case law subsequent to November, 1975 is indexed in Federal Digest 3d.

The Modern Federal Practice Digest remains the reference work for Federal cases reported from 1939 to 1961.

The Federal Digest is the reference index for reported cases prior to 1939.

In the third edition are found updated and expanded topic headings, revised topics and expanded key lines within topics. These will enhance research of today's Federal case law.

THE PUBLISHER

January, 1984

*

WEST'S
FEDERAL PRACTICE
DIGEST 2d

Volume 88

DESCRIPTIVE – WORD INDEX
A – C

ST. PAUL, MINN.

WEST PUBLISHING CO.

BEAUTICIANS—Cont'd
UNFAIR trade practices—
Price fixing. **Trade Reg 876**

BEAUTY CONTESTS
MISS America service mark, protecting by forbidding registration of Little Miss America. **Trade Reg 197**

BEAUTY PAGEANTS
NUDITY, registered marks. **Trade Reg 350, 648**

BEAUTY PARLORS
REIMBURSEMENT for cost of advertising salon and seller's products, price discrimination. **Trade Reg 918**
RES IPSA LOQUITUR—
Dermatitis after permanent wave. **Mast & S 66**
TIPS, internal revenue withholding provisions, challenging constitutionality. **Int Rev 1892**
WAGES and hours regulations—
Suppliers. **Labor 1212**

BEAUTY PRODUCTS
FRANCHISE, manufacturer terminating, preliminary injunction against refusal to deal with distributor. **Monop 24(7)**

BEAVER
BLUE Sky Laws, investment contracts, live beaver sales for breeding purposes. **Licens 18½(43)**
BREEDING beaver, contracts for sale, etc., anti-fraud provisions of federal securities laws. **Licens 18½ (43)**
RANCH securities and sellers introducing many wild beaver into herd, rescission. **Sec Reg 117**

BED SHEETS
MOTELS—
Income tax, gross receipts, reconstruction from used bed sheets count. **Int Rev 1288.1**

BEDDING PRODUCTS
MANUFACTURER, discontinuance of sales to retailer for transshipping goods to sister state. **Monop 17(1.3)**

BEDRIDDEN
DISABILITY benefits—
Social Security Act. **Social S 242**
PROSECUTRIX in rape trial, testimony in home. **Crim Law 635**

BEDROOMS
COTENANT's separate bedroom, tenant's authority to consent to entry. **Searches 7(26)**
FAMILY dwelling, permission given by mother to police search of son's bedroom. **Searches 7(27)**

BEDS
DEATH, sofa bed closing, seller's negligence. **Fed Civ Proc 2515**
HOSPITAL bed—
Collapse, patient's action against physician's malpractice insurer. **Torts 26(1)**
Implied warranty, breach. **Sales 445(4)**
SANITIZATION for new convicts. **Crim Law 1213**
WATERS and water courses, see this index Submerged Lands

BEE KEEPERS
APPLICATION for permit to import bees, validity of requirement of certificate of inspection. **Anim 31**

BEE PIN
COPYING expression of idea of jeweled bee pin. **Copyr 53**

BEEF
GRADING standards, regulations revising, deficiency in inflation impact statement. **U S 28**
PRICE ceiling, permissibility—
Const Law 298(1)
War 111

BEEFEATER
TRADE—MARKS and trade names—
Secondary meaning—
Infringement. **Trade Reg 587**

BEEPERS
AIRPLANE, attachment of device. **Searches 1**
AIRPLANE installation authorization warrant, termination date lacking. **Searches 3.4**
BATTERY—OPERATED device attached to suspect's van—
Crim Law 394.4(2)
Searches 1
BUMPER attachment, extortion, plan endangering unknown person's life. **Searches 3.3(7)**
INTERNATIONAL package, beeper inserted to signal government agent of opening. **Searches 1**
PACKAGES, warrantless insertion of beeper—
Crim Law 394.4(2)
Cust Dut 126
Searches 7(20)
VEHICLE, installation. **Searches 7(10)**

BEER
Generally, see also this index Intoxicating Liquors
CABARET tax—
Juke box dancing, retailer furnishing. **Int Rev 1112**
CUSTOMS duties—
United States tax free purchases, manifest, inclusion with imports. **Cust Dut 129, 130(9)**
INTOXICATING liquor in general, see this index Intoxicating Liquors
THREATS, brewer, refusal to sell. **Threats 10**
TRADE—MARKS and trade-names—
Infringement, evidence. **Trade Reg 583, 587**
Secondary meaning. **Trade Reg 587**

BEGGING
VAGRANTS, see this index Vagrancy

BEHAVIOR
See this index Conduct

BEHAVIOR DEFECTS
MEDICAL or psychiatric condition, disability. **Armed S 13.5(5)**

BEHAVIOR OF PUPILS
CORPORAL punishment to modify, prerequisites. **Schools 176**

BEHAVIORAL PROBLEMS
CHILDREN, special education right—
Const Law 253(2)
Schools 148
POLICE, membership discrimination against Negroes, five-man-veto rule. **Civil R 13.16**
PRESIDENT, letters about official capacity to other members, privilege. **Libel 45(1)**

BELATED APPEAL
NOTICE of appeal, filing incorrectly announced. **Crim Law 1069(6)**

BELIEF
See, also, this index—
Opinions
Opinions of courts or judges
Opinions of jurors

ELECTRONIC EAVESDROPPING—Cont'd

TAPE recorded telephone conversations—

Admissibility. Crim Law 394.3

Consent—

Induction coil, placing on extension. Crim Law 394.3

Voluntariness, government's special employee giving. Crim Law 680(1)

Interrogation without counsel. Crim Law 412.2(1)

Order of proof, voluntariness of consent. Crim Law 680(1)

Self-incrimination, compelling. Crim Law 393(1)

TAPE recordings—

Copies, admissibility. Crim Law 398(2)

Foreign language, playing to jury, interpreter translating. Crim Law 663

Government agent's telephone conversation with defendant, admissibility with agent's consent. Crim Law 394.3

Long distance telephone calls, placing without charge, investigating device for circumventing toll equipment. Crim Law 394.5(2)

Taking without taxpayer's knowledge, interviews with treasury agents. Crim Law 438

Transcripts for jury—

Convenience. Crim Law 663

Purpose, identification of speakers during deliberation. Crim Law 673(2)

TAX evasion case, transcripts containing attorney-client conversation, grand jury presentation warranting new trial. Crim Law 1189

TAX evasion prosecution, monitored conversations used in evidence. Crim Law 394.5(1)

TECHNICAL trespass—

Violating federal eavesdropping rule. Tel 491

TELEPHONE booth. Const Law 266

Conversation, violating privacy. Searches 7(10)

TELEPHONE company, monitoring own employees. Tel 495

TELEPHONE conversations—

Magnetic pickup device, sender's consent to use. Tel 495

Mother and daughter, separated husband recording. Tel 498

Party's consent, admissibility. Crim Law 394.3

TELEPHONE service—

Installation request not consent. Tel 495

TRANSMITTER planted on body of undercover agent, conversation between defendant and undercover agent—

Crim Law 394.3

Searches 7(10)

UNDERCOVER agent's conversation with illegal whiskey seller, admissibility. Crim Law 394.3

UNITED States courts—

State laws prohibiting, affect. Crim Law 394

UNREASONABLE search or seizure. Searches 7(1)

VENTILATING shaft by sheriff. Searches 7(1)

ELECTRONIC EAVESDROPPING DEVICES

LIBEL, article caption that divorce litigant got assistant of spouse's employee to sell out. Libel 50½

ELECTRONIC EQUIPMENT

PRINTED circuits, patents. Pat 323

RAIL shipments—

Character and value of goods, shipper's statement. Carr 110

ELECTRONIC FUNDS TRANSFER SYSTEMS

SAVINGS and loan association accounts, access of holders, status of systems as branch. B & L Assoc 24

ELECTRONIC LOCATION DEVICES

AIRCRAFT, attachment of device. Searches 1

ELECTRONIC MONITORING

HARMLESS error in admitting conversations overheard by. Crim Law 1169(1)

ELECTRONIC RECORDING DEVICES

DISCOVERY, make, model, and serial numbers. Crim Law 627.6(3)

ELECTRONIC SCANNED POSITIVES

SECONDARY boycott to persuade supplier to substitute photo-engraving method in printing industry, evidence. Labor 578

ELECTRONIC SURVEILLANCE

ACTING assistant attorney general, authorization of application before senate confirmation. Tel 496

AFFIDAVIT—

Wiretap denial, effectiveness as denial of illegal use of pen register. Gr Jury 36

AGGRIEVED person's right to suppress content of wire or oral communication illegally intercepted. Crim Law 394.5(2)

ASSERTION of possible illegal surveillance, sufficiency to require government to reply. Tel 496

ASSISTANT attorney general designated ad hoc to authorize application, wiretap evidence suppressed—

Crim Law 394.3

Tel 496

ATTORNEY general, good faith, omnibus crime control. Tel 498

ATTORNEY General authorizing in interest of national security. Searches 7(1)

BAD faith, application not identifying person other than suspect—

Crim Law 394.3

Tel 496

BEEPERS, placement on vehicle. Searches 7(10)

BERGER decision, applicability to cases pending when Mapp case was decided. Courts 100(1)

BUSINESS premises, forcible entry to install wiretap—

Searches 7(10)

Tel 496

COMPELLING disclosure to defendants of records of. Crim Law 627.8(1)

CONTEMPT, grand jury witness, representation not discussed over tapped line—

Crim Law 641.12(1)

Gr Jury 36

CONTINUOUS listening for thirty days, validity of statute authorizing—

Searches 7(1)

Tel 492

CONTRABAND, monitor installed after lawful seizure. Searches 7(10)

CONVERSATIONS overheard as inadmissible against owner of premises whether present or not. Crim Law 394.3

CONVERSATIONS recorded illegally, examining government logs to determine relevancy. Crim Law 627.7(4), 627.8(4)

COURT not to assume that statute prohibiting would be disregarded. Crim Law 322

COURT order, person authorizing application, government not truthfully identifying—

Crim Law 394.3

Tel 496

DEFENSE counsel's conversation, bail pending appeal from civil contempt commitment. Contempt 56

DEPOSITIONS, F.B.I. agent supervising surveillance. Fed Civ Proc 1415

DISCLOSURE motion, search of files and affidavit denying request for surveillance. Crim Law 627.8(1)

ELECTRONIC SURVEILLANCE—Cont'd

DISCOVERY—

Post-trial, government claiming full disclosure. **Crim Law 394.6(3)**

DOMESTIC organization not agent of foreign power, necessity for warrant, national security. **Tel 496**

EQUIPMENT supplier's brochure using the word secret, promotion of surreptitious interception of communications. **Tel 491**

EVIDENCE obtained by. **Searches 7(10)**

EXAMINATION of logs by defense. **Crim Law 997(11)**

FORCIBLE entry without explicit authority, devices installed. **Crim Law 394.3**

FORMAL denial, sufficiency, scan of law firm's offices detecting positive response. **Gr Jury 36**

GOVERNMENT acknowledgment or denial, motion requesting, letters in another case denying. **Crim Law 394.6(4)**

GRAND jury, surveillance contents incorporated in search warrant in record, suppression. **Gr Jury 36**

GRAND jury witnesses—

Affidavit, search to determine any surveillance, sufficiency. **Gr Jury 36**

Affidavits denying illegal taps. **Gr Jury 36**

Contempt, sufficiency of denial of surveillance of witnesses and attorneys. **Gr Jury 36**

Information leading to subpoena, questioning legality of obtaining—

Gr Jury 36

Searches 7(26)

Special attorney concluding no surveillance, sufficiency. **Gr Jury 36**

HABITUAL violations, illegal surveillance disclosing, evidence of later violations. **Crim Law 394.1(3)**

HEADQUARTERS, organization demonstrating against Soviet policy, necessity for judicial authorization. **Searches 7(10)**

HEARING—

Motion not made before trial. **Crim Law 394.6(3)**

Truth on averments in affidavit. **Crim Law 394.6(5)**

IDEA first voiced by witness' attorney. **Crim Law 394.3**

ILLEGAL interception, disclosure—

Crim Law 627.7(2)

Tel 496

IMPEACHMENT of witness, bargain over sentence, defense not allowed to call federal attorney. **Witn 67**

IMPLIED authority, secret entry to install or remove bugs. **Tel 496**

IN camera inspection of records as proper procedure for ascertaining identification of accused's voice. **Crim Law 627.8(4)**

INCOME tax evasion—

Evidence. **Crim Law 394.5(1)**

INCOME tax violation, copies of conversations. **Crim Law 627.6(1)**

INFORMATION and belief, allegation, sufficiency of denial without checking three agencies. **Crim Law 394.5(1)**

JUDGE, disqualification for bias after authorizing wiretap. **Judges 49(1)**

MEETING, illegality of surveillance, burden of proof. **Const Law 266(7)**

MICROPHONE used on premises with owner's consent, accused not entitled to disclosure—

Crim Law 627.6(1)

Searches 7(27)

MINIMIZATION, evidentiary hearing. **Crim Law 394.6(5)**

MOOTNESS, motions to disclose, affidavits denying surveillance filed. **Crim Law 627.5(5)**

NARCOTICS violations, remand. **Crim law 1189**

ELECTRONIC SURVEILLANCE—Cont'd

NATIONAL security—

Confidential information, injunction—

Inj 89(2)

U S 23(5)

Warranty requirement, retroactivity. **Courts 100(1)**

NEW trial, claim of surveillance order without attorney general's authorization, affirmance without prejudice. **Crim Law 1182**

NONFEDERAL government agency, affirmance or denial of surveillance, compulsion. **Tel 496**

OVERSEAS citizens or organizations, surveillance by army, necessity for prior judicial authorization. **Tel 496**

PEN registers, facilities and technology, providing to police. **Fed Cts 10**

PRESIDENT of United States, power to authorize warrantless wiretap to gather foreign intelligence—

Searches 3.2

Tel 496

PRIOR illegal and relevant surveillance, just cause for refusing to testify before grand jury. **Gr Jury 36**

PROBABLE cause for eavesdropping and wiretapping—

Searches 3.2

Tel 496

PROTECTIVE order, government sued for damages admitting surveillance without order. **Stip 14(10)**

RECORDS, disclosure necessity, contempt evidence concerning only courtroom behavior. **Contempt 61(1)**

RETROACTIVE operation of decision that search and seizure of speech requires some trespass or actual penetration of particular enclosure. **Courts 100(1)**

REVIEW, witness in contempt seeking additional review, inspection of documents. **Crim Law 627.6(2)**

SPECIAL agents, validity of order indicating authorization to carry out surveillance. **Tel 496**

SPECIFICATION in application and orders, validity of statutory provisions. **Tel 492**

SURREPTITIOUS entry, device installation, authorizing any manner. **Tel 496**

TELEPHONE booth. **Searches 7(10)**

TELEPHONE company, investigation whether subscriber bypassing billing equipment—

Searches 7(10)

Tel 495

TRANSCRIPTS produced by, request for inspection by defendant. **Crim Law 627.6(5), 1166(1)**

TRANSMITTER, extortion victim carrying at restaurant parking lot meeting. **Crim Law 394.6(5)**

UNION organizer's motel room, employer timely repudiating. **Labor 734**

VACATING conviction, retroactive application of decision, device used by consent of one party to conversation. **Courts 100(1)**

WITNESSES, contempt for not answering, tapes from unlawful surveillance destroyed. **Witn 21**

ELECTRONIC TRACKING DEVICES

AIRPLANE, installation authorization warrant, termination date lacking. **Searches 3.4**

AUTOMOBILES, attachment of device to vehicle, status as search. **Searches 1**

CAFFEINE drum—

Device implanted without court approval, preservation of evidence not in issue. **Drugs & N 182**

Government agent placing device inside, privacy expectation. **Searches 7(1)**

ELECTRONIC TRANSMITTING DEVICE

EVIDENCE, conversation between government agent and defendant transmitted to other agents through use of device. **Crim Law 394.3**

NARCOTICS transaction, government informant wearing device, Fourth Amendment rights violation. **Searches 7(1)**

West's
FEDERAL PRACTICE
DIGEST 2d

Vol. 88

Descriptive-Word Index
A — C

1985
Cumulative Annual Pocket Part

All Federal Case Law of
The Modern Era

The ⌘ symbol, WEST's, and Federal Practice Digest are registered trademarks of West
Publishing Co. Registered in U.S. Patent and Trademark Office.

ST. PAUL, MINN.

WEST PUBLISHING CO.

Closing with Cases Reported in

COPYRIGHT © 1978 through 1984 WEST PUBLISHING CO.

COPYRIGHT © 1985
By
WEST PUBLISHING CO.

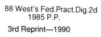
88 West's Fed.Pract.Dig.2d
1985 P.P.
3rd Reprint—1990

BAR

TRIAL—
  Requirements for admission to—
    Constitutionality of court rules establishing—
      Atty & C 4
      Const Law 287.2(5)

BAR ASSOCIATION

AGENCY of state, Civil Rights Act. Civil R 13.7
CONSPIRACY claim against—
  Immunity. Consp 13
EXCISE tax imposed on employers, liability for. Int Rev 4370
IMMUNITY—
  Civil rights claims. Civil R 13.8(1)

BAR EXAMINATION

TITLE VII of Civil Rights Act of 1964, applicability of to.
  Civil R 9.10

BAR EXAMINERS

IMMUNITY—
  Actions relating to application. Atty & C 7

BAREBOAT CHARTER

ALL possession and control of ship surrendered by owner to charterer. Ship 39(1)

BARGAIN

DUTY to—
  After debtor in possession rejects collective bargaining agreement. Labor 177

BARGES

DAMAGE to caused by improper loading of a cargo of petroleum products. Ship 110
DAMAGED by improper loading of cargo—
  Damages for demurrage. Ship 131
USED as crane platform, repairs on vessels, assessment of duty. Cust Dut 23

BARRATRY

SMUGGLING, chartered vessel. Ship 71

BASEBALL

ACCOUNTING principles—
  Use in determining profit or loss of club—
    For tax purposes. Int Rev 3315
CONTRACTS—
  Cost of acquiring—
    Depreciable over useful lives. Int Rev 3480
COPYRIGHT—
  Microwave transmission of television broadcasts. Copyr 67.1
  Retransmitting copyright owned by professional baseball team. Copyr 67.1
GROUP boycott in violation of Sherman Act—
  Horizontal stifling of competition on part of city and team—
    Use of stadium. Monop 12(10)

BASEBALL CARDS

AGREEMENT between players association and manufacturer. Monop 12(6)
SINGLE manufacturer, licensing agreements with all players, restraint of trade. Monop 12(6)

BASKETBALL

ATHLETIC association prohibiting wearing of headgear.
  Const Law 254(4)
COACH at state university—
  "Limited public figure"—
    For purposes of libel. Libel 48(1)
GIRL'S right to try out for boys' teams. Schools 164

BASKETBALL—Cont'd

HIGH school association rule prohibiting wearing of hats.
  Const Law 84
HIGH schools, equal protection, girls—
  Const Law 224(2)
  Schools 164
INJURIES—
  Employee while playing for employer-sponsored team—
    Arising out of and in course of employment—
      For purposes of worker's compensation. Work Comp 664
REFUSAL to allow girl to try out for boys basketball team, discrimination, justification, burden of proof.
  Civil R 13.13(1)
SCHOOL Board refusing to allow girl to try out for boys' team, equal protection. Const Law 224(2)
YARMULKES while playing, athletic association's rule prohibiting—
  Const Law 84
  Schools 164

BEARDS

CIVIL rights, employer's "no-beard" policy as actionable.
  Civil R 9.10
EMPLOYMENT discrimination. Civil R 9.10
  Evidence, prima facie discrimination. Civil R 44(1)

BEEF

DIETHYSTILBESTROL—
  Implanting steers with—
    Evidence, sufficiency—
      In statutory seizure action. Food 24(3)
IMPORT—
  Privilege to—
    Withdrawing. Food 3

BEEF COUNCIL

OUT-OF-STATE beef processors—
  Requiring to support—
    Equal protection—
      Const Law 230.3(6)
      Food 1.10

BEEF PROCESSORS

TAX on out-of-state—
  Discrimination against interstate commerce. Commerce 74.10

BEEPER

INSTALLATION—
  Effect of consent. Tel 495, 511
  Time limitation on—
    In court order authorizing attachment and maintenance. Tel 519
MONITORING signals of—
  As driver transported chemical to owner's property.
    Searches 7(1, 10)
SURVEILLANCE of citizen. Tel 494
WARRANTLESS installation, reasonable suspicion as adequate to support. Searches 7(1)
WARRANTLESS use of—
  To monitor location of noncontraband withdrawn from public view—
    Unconstitutional search or seizure. Tel 511

BEFORE AND AFTER RULE

PARTIAL taking, just compensation. Em Dom 136

BEGIN

CIVIL rights, comments on Israeli Prime Minister not constituting disparagements of Judaism. Civil R 9.10

BENCH TRIAL

Generally, see this index Summary Trial
EXCLUDING relevant evidence. Evid 146

WEST'S
FEDERAL PRACTICE
DIGEST 2d

Volume 69

SEARCHES AND SEIZURES—
SECURED TRANSACTIONS

ST. PAUL, MINN.

WEST PUBLISHING CO.

SEARCHES AND SEIZURES

SUBJECTS INCLUDED

Examination of persons or places for discovery of property stolen or otherwise unlawfully obtained or held, or of evidence of the commission of an offense

Taking into legal custody such property or proofs, or property forfeited for violation of law

Nature and scope of such remedies in general

Constitutional and statutory provisions relating to such searches and seizures

In what cases and to and against whom and in respect of what property they are allowed

Jurisdiction over and proceedings to obtain searches or seizures

Issuance, requisites and validity of search warrants and warrants for seizure, etc.

Execution of warrants, making searches and seizures, proceedings to enforce seizures, and disposition of property seized

Liabilities for wrongfully procuring or making searches or seizures

SUBJECTS EXCLUDED AND COVERED BY OTHER TOPICS

Arrest, searches incidental to, see ARREST

Evidence wrongfully obtained, see CRIMINAL LAW

Forfeiture for crime, grounds, see FORFEITURES and specific topics involving forfeitures

International law, operation as to seizures, see INTERNATIONAL LAW

Particular subjects, searches and seizures for enforcement of laws relating to, see CUSTOMS DUTIES, DRUGS AND NARCOTICS, GAMING, INTERNAL REVENUE, INTOXICATING LIQUORS, LOTTERIES

For detailed references to other topics, see Descriptive-Word Index

---

Analysis

For detailed references to other topics, see Descriptive-Word Index

ing, owner of film was entitled to have it returned, and prosecutors were not entitled to show the film to other public officials or selected citizens. U.S.C.A.Const. Amends. 1, 14.

Abrams & Parisi, Inc. v. Canale, 309 F.Supp. 1360.

D.C.W.Va. 1976. When individual has been released from criminal jeopardy and indictment against him expires, he is entitled to return of his papers and other materials as matter of course, and that includes any photostats and other forms of copy made from them.

U. S. v. Moore, 423 F.Supp. 858.

D.C.Wis. 1973. Where theater operator was not given any notice, and there was no adversary hearing held, prior to issuance of search warrant pursuant to which film was seized from the theater, and where the film was scheduled to be shown for some future time, and the theater had not displayed such film or any other since the seizure, theater operator's likelihood of prevailing on merits in its action seeking declaratory or injunctive relief and alleging that the seizure violated its First Amendment rights and that Wisconsin statute proscribing exhibiting of obscene picture or film was unconstitutional as interpreted by the Wisconsin Supreme Court was so great as to compel return of the film. W.S.A. 944.21(1)(a); U.S.C.A.Const. Amend. 1.

Detco, Inc. v. Neelen, 356 F.Supp. 289.

D.C.Wis. 1971. Cash taken by agents while executing search warrants would not be treated differently from other materials seized pursuant to search warrant and would not be returned to defendants, in prosecution for conspiracy to carry on interstate gambling activities. 18 U.S.C.A. § 1952.

U. S. v. Machi, 324 F.Supp. 153.

D.C.Wis. 1970. Where seizure of books and documents was blatantly unlawful, government was not entitled to retain either originals or any copies which might have been made from such originals, and all photocopies and microfilm copies of seized records and documents would be ordered returned.

U. S. v. Le Clair, 315 F.Supp. 853.

7. Unreasonable searches and seizures.

Library references

C.J.S. Searches and Seizures § 8 et seq.

7(1). Constitutional rights and violation thereof in general.

U.S. 1976. While standing in doorway of her house, defendant was in a "public place" for purposes of the Fourth Amendment, since she was not in an area where she had any expectation of privacy and was not merely visible to the public but was as exposed to pub-

lic view, speech, hearing, and touch as if she had been standing completely outside her house; thus, when the police, who concededly had probable cause to do so, sought to arrest her, they merely intended to make a warrantless arrest in a public place upon probable cause and did not violate the Fourth Amendment. U.S.C.A.Const. Amend. 4.

U. S. v. Santana, 96 S.Ct. 2406, 427 U.S. 38, 49 L.Ed.2d 300.

U.S.Cal. 1976. To accommodate public and private interests, some quantum of individualized suspicion is usually prerequisite to constitutional search or seizure, but Fourth Amendment imposes no irreducible requirement of such suspicion. U.S.C.A.Const. Amend. 4.

U. S. v. Martinez-Fuerte, 96 S.Ct. 3074, 428 U.S. 543, 49 L.Ed.2d 1116, on remand 538 F.2d 858.

In delineating constitutional safeguards applicable in particular contexts, court weighs public interest against Fourth Amendment interest of the individual. U.S.C.A.Const. Amend. 4.

U. S. v. Martinez-Fuerte, 96 S.Ct. 3074, 428 U.S. 543, 49 L.Ed.2d 1116, on remand 538 F.2d 858.

Fourth Amendment imposes limits on search and seizure power in order to prevent arbitrary and oppressive interference by enforcement officials with privacy and personal security of individuals. U.S.C.A.Const. Amend. 4.

U. S. v. Martinez-Fuerte, 96 S.Ct. 3074, 428 U.S. 543, 49 L.Ed.2d 1116, on remand 538 F.2d 858.

U.S.Cal. 1975. The central concern of the Fourth Amendment is to protect liberty and privacy from arbitrary and oppressive interference by government officials. U.S.C.A. Const. Amend. 4.

U. S. v. Ortiz, 95 S.Ct. 2585, 422 U.S. 891, 45 L.Ed.2d 623.

The Fourth Amendment's requirement that searches and seizures be reasonable also may limit police use of unnecessarily frightening or offensive methods of surveillance and investigation. U.S.C.A.Const. Amend. 4.

U. S. v. Ortiz, 95 S.Ct. 2585, 422 U.S. 891, 45 L.Ed.2d 623.

U.S.Cal. 1975. The Fourth Amendment applies to all seizures of the person, including seizures that involve only a brief detention short of traditional arrest. U.S.C.A.Const. Amend. 4.

U. S. v. Brignoni-Ponce, 95 S.Ct. 2574, 422 U.S. 873, 45 L.Ed.2d 607.

Whenever a police officer accosts an individual and restrains his freedom to walk

see United States Code Annotated

len articles therein were in plain view, and where plaintiff's wife consented to their seizure, search and seizure were not unreasonable, and defendants were not liable for damages. 42 U.S.C.A. § 1983; U.S.C.A.Const. Amend. 4.

> Robbins v. Bryant, 349 F.Supp. 94, affirmed 474 F.2d 1342.

⚷7(10). **Persons, places, and possessions protected from searches and seizures without warrant.**

U.S.Cal. 1976. Sanctity of private dwellings is ordinarily afforded the most stringent Fourth Amendment protection; one's expectation of privacy in automobile and of freedom in its operation is significantly different from traditional expectation of privacy and freedom in one's residence. U.S.C.A.Const. Amend. 4.

> U. S. v. Martinez-Fuerte, 96 S.Ct. 3074, 428 U.S. 543, 49 L.Ed.2d 1116, on remand 538 F.2d 858.

Decision of border patrol to locate checkpoint at San Clemente was reasonable in view of needs of law enforcement furthered by such location, high absolute number of apprehensions at such checkpoint, and fact that San Clemente was selected as location where San Diego-to-Los Angeles traffic was lightest, thereby minimizing interference with legitimate traffic. U.S.C.A.Const. Amend. 4.

> U. S. v. Martinez-Fuerte, 96 S.Ct. 3074, 428 U.S. 543, 49 L.Ed.2d 1116, on remand 538 F.2d 858.

Principal protection of Fourth Amendment rights at checkpoints lies in appropriate limitations on scope of stop. U.S.C.A.Const. Amend. 4.

> U. S. v. Martinez-Fuerte, 96 S.Ct. 3074, 428 U.S. 543, 49 L.Ed.2d 1116, on remand 538 F.2d 858.

U.S.Cal. 1974. Bank's keeping records of its customers pursuant to the Bank Secrecy Act does not constitute a "seizure," and inasmuch as access to the records is to be controlled by legal process, the record-keeping provisions did not give rise to an illegal search and seizure. U.S.C.A.Const. Amend. 4; 12 U.S.C.A. §§ 1730d, 1829b, 1951–1959.

> California Bankers Ass'n v. Shultz, 94 S.Ct. 1494, 416 U.S. 21, 39 L.Ed.2d 812.

Regulations of Secretary of Treasury implementing the domestic reporting requirements of the Bank Secrecy Act abridge no Fourth Amendment right of the bank itself inasmuch as bank is a party to the transaction, and requirements for reporting information with respect to abnormally large transactions in currency were not unreasonable. U.S. C.A.Const. Amend. 5; Currency and Foreign Transactions Reporting Act, §§ 206, 222, 31 U.S.C.A. §§ 1055, 1082.

> California Bankers Ass'n v. Shultz, 94 S.Ct. 1494, 416 U.S. 21, 39 L.Ed.2d 812.

U.S.Cal. 1967. What a person seeks to preserve as private, even in an area accessible to the public, may be constitutionally protected under Fourth Amendment. U.S.C.A.Const. Amend. 4.

> Katz v. U. S., 88 S.Ct. 507, 389 U.S. 347, 19 L.Ed.2d 576.

A person in a telephone booth may rely upon protection of Fourth Amendment, and is entitled to assume that words he utters into mouthpiece will not be broadcast to the world. U.S.C.A.Const. Amend. 4.

> Katz v. U. S., 88 S.Ct. 507, 389 U.S. 347, 19 L.Ed.2d 576.

Government's activities in electronically listening to and recording defendant's words spoken into telephone receiver in public telephone booth violated the privacy upon which defendant justifiably relied while using the telephone booth and thus constituted a "search and seizure" within Fourth Amendment, and fact that electronic device employed to achieve that end did not happen to penetrate the wall of the booth could have no constitutional significance. U.S.C.A.Const. Amend. 4.

> Katz v. U. S., 88 S.Ct. 507, 389 U.S. 347, 19 L.Ed.2d 576.

Search and seizure, without prior judicial sanction and attendant safeguards, conducted by electronic surveillance by way of an electronic listening and recording device attached to outside of public telephone booth from which defendant had placed calls did not comply with constitutional standards, although, accepting account of government's actions as accurate, magistrate could constitutionally have authorized with appropriate safeguards the very limited search and seizure that government asserted in fact took place and although it was apparent that agents had acted with restraint. U.S.C.A.Const. Amend. 4.

> Katz v. U. S., 88 S.Ct. 507, 389 U.S. 347, 19 L.Ed.2d 576.

U.S.Cal. 1967. Except in carefully defined classes of cases, search of private property without proper consent is unreasonable unless it has been authorized by valid search warrant. U.S.C.A.Const. Amend. 4.

> Camara v. Municipal Court of City and County of San Francisco, 87 S.Ct. 1727, 387 U.S. 523, 18 L.Ed.2d 930.

Lessee of ground floor of apartment building had constitutional right to insist that city housing inspector obtain warrant to search his premises and could not constitutionally be convicted of violating city housing code by refusing to consent to warrantless inspection. U.S.C.A.Const. Amend. 4.

> Camara v. Municipal Court of City and County of San Francisco, 87 S.Ct. 1727, 387 U.S. 523, 18 L.Ed.2d 930.

see United States Code Annotated

For references to other topics, see Descriptive-Word Index

to prevent removal of any instruments or fruits of the crime which might be found therein, or to photograph the automobile, or both. 18 U.S.C.A. § 2113.

> U. S. v. Radford, 361 F.2d 777, certiorari denied 87 S.Ct. 158, 385 U.S. 877, 17 L.Ed.2d 105.

C.A.Md. 1965. Search of a state court defendant's room and bureau without a warrant even if with consent of defendant's mother was in violation of the Fourth Amendment, and a note discovered in the bureau and seized as a result of such search was the fruit thereof and was constitutionally objectionable.

> Reeves v. Warden, Md. Penitentiary, 346 F.2d 915.

C.A.Md. 1963. Search of apartment and seizure of property therein were illegal, and use at trial of evidence so obtained violated state prisoner's constitutional rights, despite Maryland law to the contrary, where police officers did not have warrant or permission from anyone to enter apartment in which state prisoner was living with a woman, but searched the apartment and seized the evidence while no one was in apartment, and arrested state prisoner on nearby street following search. U.S.C.A.Const. Amends. 4, 14.

> Walker v. Pepersack, 316 F.2d 119.

C.A.Md. 1963. A person's hotel room is protected against unreasonable search. U.S. C.A.Const. Amends. 4, 14.

> Hall v. Warden, Md. Penitentiary, 313 F.2d 483, certiorari denied Pepersack v. Hall, 83 S.Ct. 1693, 374 U.S. 809, 10 L.Ed.2d 1032.

C.A.Md. 1962. The word "effects," within meaning of Fourth Amendment's protection against unreasonable searches and seizures of effects, encompasses automobiles and books. U.S.C.A.Const. Amend. 4.

> U. S. v. Peisner, 311 F.2d 94, 5 A.L.R.3d 1196.

Fourth Amendment provision precluding unreasonable searches and seizures of persons, their houses, papers and effects is sufficiently broad to afford protection against unreasonable searches and seizures to all types of property even though contraband of any type or obscene in nature. U.S.C.A.Const. Amend. 4.

> U. S. v. Peisner, 311 F.2d 94, 5 A.L.R.3d 1196.

C.A.Mass. 1977. Though concealment of electronic beepers in contraband substances has been upheld on theory that possessors of such articles have no legitimate expectancy of privacy with respect thereto, such principle cannot be extended to insertion of a beeper in legally possessed noncontraband substances whose probable use is to make an illegal drug.

> U. S. v. Moore, 562 F.2d 106.

While intrusion involved in surveillance of a vehicle by electronic beeper, whether or not technical trespass was involved in its placement, is considerably lessened by the fact that one driving on the public roads knows that he is subject to public scrutiny, intrusion on reasonable privacy expectations cannot be written off as nonexistent, and use of beepers to trace motor vehicles without a warrant is justified only if officers have probable cause at the time. U.S.C.A.Const. Amend. 4.

> U. S. v. Moore, 562 F.2d 106.

Call from drug company with respect to chemicals purchased by one defendant, discovery that address given was not one where a chemical manufacturer would operate, nature of chemicals purchased, and agents' familiarity with the manufacture of controlled substances created sufficient basis for believing that a criminal enterprise was underway, and thus use of electronic beepers to monitor defendants' vehicles for a limted period of time, during delivery of chemicals to place of manufacture, did not violate the Fourth Amendment even though no warrant was obtained. U.S.C.A.Const. Amend. 4.

> U. S. v. Moore, 562 F.2d 106.

Where chemicals containing transmitter were not contraband or otherwise wrongfully in defendants' possession, Government had no right to determine their continued presence in house by use of warrantless electronic surveillance, even by use of beeper which did not transmit defendants' conversations. U.S.C.A. Const. Amend. 4.

> U. S. v. Moore, 562 F.2d 106.

C.A.Mass. 1976. Even if the Fourth Amendment was applicable to request made by police commissioner that police officers fill out a questionnaire listing sources of income, significant assets held by them, and copies of their federal and state income tax returns, the order was not so lacking in justification as to be an unreasonable invasion of the policemen's legitimate expectations of privacy. U.S.C.A.Const. Amend. 4.

> O'Brien v. DiGrazia, 544 F.2d 543, certiorari denied 97 S.Ct. 2173.

C.A.Mass. 1976. Whatever can be said for a theory that allows warrantless searches of luggage for contraband upon individual officer's determination of probable cause, it has not received sufficient recognition by Supreme Court, outside automobile area, or generally, for the First Circuit Court of Appeals to recognize it as a valid exception to Fourth Amendment warrant requirement. U.S.C.A. Const. Amend. 4.

> U. S. v. Chadwick, 532 F.2d 773, certiorari granted 97 S.Ct. 54, 429 U.S. 814, 50 L.Ed.2d 74, affirmed 97 S.Ct. 2476.

see United States Code Annotated

West's
FEDERAL PRACTICE
DIGEST 2d

Vol. 69

Searches and Seizures — Secured Transactions

1985

Cumulative Pamphlet Supplementing
Vol. 69 Federal Practice Digest 2d

THE WEST DIGEST TOPIC NUMBERS WHICH CAN BE
USED FOR WESTLAW SEARCHES ARE LISTED ON
PAGE III OF THIS POCKET PART.

All Federal Case Law of
The Modern Era

Up-Dated Weekly by West's
Federal Reporter Advance Sheets

The ⚷ symbol, WEST's, and Federal Practice Digest are registered trademarks of West
Publishing Co.   Registered in U.S. Patent and Trademark Office.

ST. PAUL, MINN.

WEST PUBLISHING CO.

Closing with Cases Reported in

COPYRIGHT © 1978 through 1984 WEST PUBLISHING CO.

COPYRIGHT © 1985
By
WEST PUBLISHING CO.

69 West's Fed.Pract.Dig.2d
1985 Pamph.

41, 18 U.S.C.A.; U.S.C.A.Const. Amend. 4.—U. S. v. Benford, 457 F.Supp. 589.

D.C.N.Y. 1983. Seizure of items during course of search, where the particular items were not specified in warrant, is per se unreasonable under Fourth Amendment, subject only to a few specifically established and well-delineated exceptions, including the plain view doctrine. U.S.C.A. Const. Amend. 4.—U.S. v. Santarsiero, 566 F.Supp. 536.

D.C.Pa. 1979. Fact that police made two entries into defendants' automobile pursuant to single search warrant did not require finding that they violated defendants' Fourth Amendment rights inasmuch as second search was merely continuation of initial intrusion. U.S.C.A.Const. Amend. 4.—U. S. v. Huslage, 480 F.Supp. 870.

7(10). Persons, places, and possessions protected from searches and seizures without warrant.

U.S. 1985. Although defendant's mobile motor home possessed some attributes of a home, it was readily mobile, and there was a reduced expectation of privacy stemming from pervasive regulation of vehicles capable of traveling on highways; thus, warrantless search of mobile motor home did not violate Fourth Amendment. U.S.C.A. Const.Amend. 4.—California v. Carney, 105 S.Ct. 2066, 85 L.Ed.2d 406.

U.S. 1979. Requirement that pretrial detainees remain outside their rooms during routine "shakedown" inspections by prison officials did not violate Fourth or Fifth Amendments, but simply facilitated safe and effective performance of searches. U.S.C.A.Const. Amends. 4, 5.—Bell v. Wolfish, 99 S.Ct. 1861, 441 U.S. 520, 60 L.Ed.2d 447.

Practice of visual body-cavity searches of pretrial detainees following contact visits did not violate Fourth or Fifth Amendments, in that balancing significant and legitimate security interests of institution against inmate's privacy interests, such searches could be conducted on less than probable cause and were not unreasonable. U.S. C.A.Const. Amends. 4, 5.—Id.

U.S.Ariz. 1978. Even though investigating homicide detectives knew that one officer had been seriously injured and began search of apartment where shooting occurred promptly upon their arrival at the apartment and searched only for evidence either establishing the circumstances of the death or relevant to motive or intent or knowledge, their four-day warrantless search of the apartment could not be justified under any so-called "murder scene exception" to the Fourth and Fourteenth Amendments. U.S.C.A.Const. Amends. 4, 14.—Mincey v. Arizona, 98 S.Ct. 2408, 437 U.S. 385, 57 L.Ed.2d 290.

U.S.Ark. 1979. A lawful search of luggage generally may be performed only pursuant to a warrant. U.S.C.A.Const. Amends. 4, 14.—Arkansas v. Sanders, 99 S.Ct. 2586, 442 U.S. 753, 61 L.Ed.2d 235.

In the absence of exigent circumstances, police are required to obtain a warrant before searching luggage taken from an automobile properly stopped and searched for contraband. U.S.C.A. Const. Amends. 4, 14.—Id.

U.S.Cal. 1985. Having presented herself at the border for admission, and having subjected herself to criminal enforcement powers of federal Government, defendant was entitled to be free from unreasonable search and seizure. 19 U.S. C.A. § 482; U.S.C.A. Const.Amend. 4.—U.S. v. Montoya de Hernandez, 105 S.Ct. 3304.

Not only is expectation of privacy less at border than in interior, Fourth Amendment [U.S.C.A. Const.Amend. 4] balance between interests of government and privacy right of individual is struck much more favorably to government at the border.—Id.

U.S.Cal. 1981. A closed piece of luggage found in a lawfully searched car is constitutionally protected to the same extent as are closed pieces of luggage found anywhere else. (Per Justice Stewart with three Justices concurring and the Chief Justice and one Justice concurring in the judgment.) U.S.C.A.Const. Amend. 4.—Robbins v. California, 101 S.Ct. 2841, 453 U.S. 420, 69 L.Ed.2d 744, on remand People v. Robbins, 178 Cal.Rptr. 672, 125 C.A.3d 818.

The Fourth Amendment protects people's effects whether they are "personal" or "impersonal," and thus, once placed within a closed, opaque container, a diary and a dishpan are equally protected by the Fourth Amendment. (Per Justice Stewart with three Justices concurring and the Chief Justice and one Justice concurring in the judgment.) U.S.C.A.Const. Amend. 4.—Id.

Unless the container or package found by the police during course of a search is such that its contents may be said to be in plain view, those contents are fully protected by the Fourth Amendment; in order to fall within exception to rule, a container must so clearly announce its contents, whether by distinctive configuration, transparency or otherwise, that its contents are obvious to an observer. (Per Justice Stewart with three Justices concurring and the Chief Justice and one Justice concurring in the judgment.) U.S.C.A.Const. Amend. 4.—Id.

A closed opaque container may not be opened without a warrant, even if found during course of a lawful search of an automobile, and thus opening of two packages, which were wrapped in green opaque plastic and which contained bricks of marihuana, without a search warrant during lawful search of defendant's automobile violated the Fourth and Fourteenth Amendments. (Per Justice Stewart with three Justices concurring and the Chief Justice and one Justice concurring in result.) U.S.C.A.Const. Amends. 4, 14.—Id.

U.S.Cal. 1978. Although university student newspaper was not suspect of any wrongdoing in connection with clash between demonstrators and police at university hospital, Fourth Amendment did not forbid issuance of warrant to search newspaper offices for photographs and negatives revealing identities of demonstrators who assaulted the officers. U.S.C.A.Const. Amends. 1, 4, 14.— Zurcher v. Stanford Daily, 98 S.Ct. 1970, 436 U.S. 547, 56 L.Ed.2d 525, rehearing denied 99 S.Ct. 231, 439 U.S. 885, 58 L.Ed.2d 200 and Bergna v. Stanford Daily, 99 S.Ct. 232, 439 U.S. 885, 58 L.Ed.2d 200.

Presumptively protected materials are not necessarily immune from seizure under warrant for use at a criminal trial. U.S.C.A.Const. Amends. 1, 4, 14.—Id.

U.S.Dist.Col. 1982. A lawful search of fixed premises generally extends to the entire area in which the object of the search may be found and is not limited by the possibility that separate acts of entry or opening may be required to complete the search. U.S.C.A.Const.Amend. 4.—U. S. v. Ross, 102 S.Ct. 2157, 456 U.S. 798, 72 L.Ed.2d 572.

When a legitimate search is under way, and when its purpose and its limits have been precisely defined, nice distinctions between closets, drawers, and containers, in the case of a home, or between glove compartments, upholstered seats, trunks and wrapped packages, in the case of a vehicle, must give way to the interest in prompt and efficient completion of task at hand. U.S.C.A. Const.Amend. 4.—Id.

Fourth Amendment provides protection to the owner of every container that conceals its contents from plain view, but the protection afforded by the Amendment varies in different settings. U.S.C.A.Const.Amend. 4.—Id.

Individual's expectation of privacy in vehicle and its contents may not survive if probable cause quirement that searches be based on probable cause to believe that subject of search has violated or is violating the law; rather, legality of search of student should depend simply on reasonableness, under all the circumstances, of the search. U.S. C.A. Const.Amend. 4.—Id.

Under ordinary circumstances, search of student by teacher or other school official will be justified at its inception when there are reasonable grounds for suspecting that search will turn up evidence that student has violated or is violating either the law or rules of school. U.S.C.A. Const.Amend. 4.—Id.

Search of student by teacher or other school official would be permissible in its scope when measures adopted are reasonably related to objectives of search and not excessively intrusive in light of sex of student and nature of infraction. U.S.C.A. Const.Amend. 4.—Id.

Initial search of student's purse by assistant vice principal for cigarettes was reasonable where report had been given to assistant vice principal that student had been smoking in violation of school rule, warranting reasonable suspicion that she had cigarettes in her purse, despite fact that cigarettes, if found, would constitute "mere evidence" of violation of no-smoking rule. U.S.C.A. Const. Amend. 4.—Id.

U.S.N.M. 1984. Where ten cans of ether had been ordered from government informant, mere installation of electronic beeper by Drug Enforcement Administration into can of its own to be included as part of shipment by such government informant did not violate any one's Fourth Amendment rights, but, rather, any impairment of privacy interests that might have occurred was occasioned by monitoring of the beeper. U.S.C.A. Const.Amend. 4; Comprehensive Drug Abuse Prevention and Control Act of 1970, §§ 401(a)(1), 406, 21 U.S.C.A. §§ 841(a)(1), 846.—U.S. v. Karo, 104 S.Ct. 3296, rehearing denied 105 S.Ct. 51.

Government is not completely free from constraints of Fourth Amendment to determine by means of electric device, without warrant and without probable cause or reasonable suspicion, whether particular article, or person for that matter, is in an individual's home at particular time. U.S.C.A. Const.Amend. 4.—Id.

U.S.N.Y. 1980. Physical entry of home is chief evil against which wording of Fourth Amendment is directed. U.S.C.A.Const. Amend. 4.—Payton v. New York, 100 S.Ct. 1371, 445 U.S. 573, 63 L.Ed.2d 639, on remand 433 N.Y.S.2d 61, 51 N.Y.2d 169, 412 N.E.2d 1288.

It is basic principle of Fourth Amendment law that searches and seizures inside home without warrant are presumptively unreasonable, and that search or seizure carried out on suspect's premises without warrant is per se unreasonable unless police can show that it falls within one of carefully designed set of exceptions based on presence of "exigent circumstances." U.S.C.A.Const. Amend. 4.—Id.

Area that may legally be searched is broader when executing search warrant than when executing arrest warrant in home, but zone of privacy is nowhere more clearly defined than when bounded by unambiguous physical dimensions of individual's home, and at very core of Fourth Amendment stands right of man to retreat into his own home and there be free from unreasonable government intrusion, and this is true as against seizures of property and seizures of person. U.S. C.A.Const. Amend. 4.—Id.

Category of property that may be seized with warrant, consistent with Fourth Amendment, includes mere evidence. U.S.C.A.Const. Amend. 4. —Id.

Prohibitions of Fourth Amendment protect against invasion, by electronic eavesdropping, of individual's privacy in phone booth not owned by him. U.S.C.A.Const. Amend. 4.—Id.

If there is sufficient evidence of citizen's participation in felony to persuade judicial officer that his arrest is justified, it is constitutionally reasonable to require him to open his doors to officers of the law, and thus for Fourth Amendment purposes arrest warrant founded on probable cause implicitly carries with it limited authority to open dwelling in which suspect lives when there is reason to believe suspect is within. U.S.C.A.Const. Amend. 4.—Id.

U.S.N.D. 1984. Entry into public lobby of motel-restaurant for purpose of serving an administrative subpoena is not the sort of governmental act forbidden by the Fourth Amendment and, hence, entry into public lobby of motel-restaurant by agent of Secretary of Labor to serve administrative subpoena requesting production of documents, to be produced at another location, in connection with wages and hours investigation under Fair Labor Standards Act did not violate Fourth Amendment, notwithstanding lack of judicial warrant, as the subpoena did not authorize entry or inspection of premises and no nonconsensual entry into areas not open to the public was made. Fair Labor Standards Act of 1938, §§ 9, 11(a), 29 U.S.C.A. §§ 209, 211(a); U.S.C.A. Const.Amend. 4.—Donovan v. Lone Steer, Inc., 104 S.Ct. 769.

U.S.Pa. 1977. Where police officers on routine patrol observed defendant driving an automobile with an expired license plate and lawfully stopped vehicle for purpose of issuing a traffic summons, order of one of officers that defendant get out of automobile was reasonable and thus permissible under Fourth Amendment, notwithstanding that officers had no reason to suspect foul play from defendant at time of the stop since there had been nothing unusual or suspicious about his behavior. U.S.C.A.Const. Amends. 4, 14.—Pennsylvania v. Mimms, 98 S.Ct. 330, 434 U.S. 106, 54 L.Ed.2d 331, on remand Com. v. Mimms, 385 A.2d 334, 477 Pa. 553.

Once a motor vehicle has been lawfully detained for a traffic violation, the police officer may order the driver to get out of the vehicle without violating the Fourth Amendment's proscription of unreasonable searches and seizures. U.S.C.A.Const. Amends. 4, 14.—Id.

U.S.S.C. 1985. Authority and limits of Fourth Amendment apply to investigative stops of vehicles. U.S.C.A. Const.Amend. 4.—U.S. v. Sharpe, 105 S.Ct. 1568, 84 L.Ed.2d 605.

U.S.Tex. 1983. Action of police officer in shining his flashlight to illuminate interior of driver's car, stopped for routine license check, trenched upon no right secured to latter by Fourth Amendment. (Per Justice Rehnquist, with the Chief Justice and two Justices concurring and five Justices concurring in the judgment). U.S.C.A. Const. Amend. 4.—Texas v. Brown, 103 S.Ct. 1535, 460 U.S. 730, 75 L.Ed.2d 502, on remand Brown v. State, 657 S.W.2d 797.

U.S.Tex. 1976. Sanctity of private dwellings is ordinarily afforded the most stringent Fourth Amendment protection; one's expectation of privacy in automobile and of freedom in its operation is significantly different from traditional expectation of privacy and freedom in one's residence. U.S.C.A.Const. Amend. 4.—Sifuentes v. U. S., 96 S.Ct. 3074, 428 U.S. 543, 49 L.Ed.2d 1116.

Decision of border patrol to locate checkpoint at San Clemente was reasonable in view of needs of law enforcement furthered by such location, high absolute number of apprehensions at such checkpoint, and fact that San Clemente was selected as location where San Diego-to-Los Angeles traffic was lightest, thereby minimizing interference with legitimate traffic. U.S.C.A.Const. Amend. 4.—Id.

C.A.Canal Zone 1978. Where police officers had reasonable suspicion to approach vehicle for investigatory purposes and briefly question suspects about possible criminal activity, such intrusion upon suspects' liberties as resulted from officers' order to step out of vehicle did not violate Fourth Amendment's proscription of unreasonable searches and seizures. U.S.C.A.Const. Amend. 4.—Government of Canal Zone v. Bender, 573 F.2d 1329.

C.A.Colo. 1981. Defendants had no reasonable expectation of privacy in millyard of their lumber company, surrounded by nothing more than barbed wire fence. U.S.C.A.Const. Amend. 4.—U. S. v. Rucinski, 658 F.2d 741, certiorari denied 102 S.Ct. 1430, 455 U.S. 939, 71 L.Ed.2d 649.

C.A.Colo. 1980. What a person knowingly exposes is not constitutionally protected from observation, nor are activities or objects which are exposed, regardless of subjective intent, in a matter inconsistent with reasonable expectations of privacy. U.S.C.A.Const. Amend. 4.—U. S. v. Burns, 624 F.2d 95, certiorari denied Reynolds v. U. S., 101 S.Ct. 361, 449 U.S. 954, 66 L.Ed.2d 219.

C.A.Colo. 1978. Where federal agents lost contact with electronic tracking device, which had been attached to a container of ether, following its movement from house and independent effort was necessary to reestablish contact, contact through which clandestine laboratory where amphetamines were being produced was discovered was not tainted by surveillance within the house based on warrantless use of device.—U. S. v. Clayborne, 584 F.2d 346.

Where agents, who lost contact with electronic tracking device that had been attached to container of ether after its movement from one defendant's house, had to use airplane to pick up beeper signal and locate clandestine laboratory, which was located in commercial building with windows covered to protect against viewing of materials inside, slight intrusion resulting from use of device was not per se in violation of the Fourth Amendment and its warrantless use by agents was therefore not invalid. U.S.C.A.Const. Amend. 4.—Id.

C.A.Colo. 1978. Utilization of electronic tracking device, without prior court approval, may be justified by probable cause and exigent circumstances. U.S.C.A.Const. Amend. 4.—U. S. v. Shovea, 580 F.2d 1382, certiorari denied Gaias v. U. S., 99 S.Ct. 581, 439 U.S. 986, 58 L.Ed.2d 659 and 99 S.Ct. 1216, 440 U.S. 908, 59 L.Ed.2d 456.

Federal agents had sufficient probable cause to attach electronic tracking device to defendant's car without first acquiring court order and did not violate defendant's Fourth Amendment rights in so doing, where agents knew that codefendant had purchased chemicals, a primary precursor of methamphetamine, and agents observed codefendant leave residence, carrying suitcase in careful manner, drive to airport in elusive manner, fly to another city where he was met by defendant and drive to defendant's residence. 18 U.S.C.A. § 2; Comprehensive Drug Abuse Prevention and Control Act of 1970, § 401(a)(1), 21 U.S.C.A. § 841(a)(1); U.S.C.A.Const. Amend. 4.—Id.

C.A.Conn. 1984. A defendant cannot invoke Fourth Amendment's protections unless he has a legitimate expectation of privacy against government's intrusion. U.S.C.A. Const.Amend. 4.—U.S. v. Roy, 734 F.2d 108.

Test for determining whether a legitimate expectation of privacy exists is that a person have exhibited an actual subjective expectation of privacy and that the expectation be one that society is prepared to recognize as "reasonable." U.S.C.A. Const.Amend. 4.—Id.

C.A.Conn. 1980. Though containers not inevitably used for the storage of private effects may benefit from an expectation of privacy under some circumstances, this generally requires that the owner take some additional positive step objectively signalling to others an expectation that the privacy of the container's contents will be respected.—U. S. v. Markland, 635 F.2d 174, certiorari denied 101 S.Ct. 2332, 451 U.S. 991, 68 L.Ed.2d 851.

Fact that plastic thermal beverage container was zipped shut, as it would ordinarily be in the course of normal use for storing food or drink, was not sufficient to give objective notice of an expectation of privacy, in view of the nature of container, which was a bag designed to store and transport food and drink.—Id.

C.A.Conn. 1980. There is no reasonable expectation of privacy with regard to the outside of a letter. U.S.C.A.Const. Amend. 4.—U. S. v. DePoli, 628 F.2d 779.

C.A.11 (Fla.) 1985. Fourth Amendment does not protect subjective expectations of privacy that are unreasonable or otherwise illegitimate. U.S. C.A. Const.Amend. 4.—U.S. v. Lopez, 761 F.2d 632.

To receive protection of the Fourth Amendment, expectation of privacy must be one society is prepared to recognize as legitimate. U.S.C.A. Const.Amend. 4.—Id.

Requirement for a justifiable expectation of privacy in order to receive protection of the Fourth Amendment is twofold, namely, defendant must show an actual or subjective expectation of privacy in area searched and expectation must be one that society is prepared to recognize as reasonable. U.S.C.A. Const.Amend. 4.—Id.

It is not sufficient that a sailor have the right to exclude others from his ship in order to have legitimate expectation of privacy for Fourth Amendment purposes, because a coast guard officer may without permission conduct a safety and document search and gain access to all common areas of boat. U.S.C.A. Const.Amend. 4.—Id.

Defendants did not have a reasonable expectation of privacy in secret compartment constructed within confines of hull of ship which contained marijuana, and thus they had no standing to challenge Coast Guard's search of compartment. U.S.C.A. Const.Amend. 4.—Id.

Once Coast Guard officers had probable cause to search vessel, it was not unreasonable to take it to Islamorada for subsequent investigation, with or without consent of crew members. U.S.C.A. Const.Amend. 4.—Id.

Search conducted once vessel arrived at Islamorada was in no respect unreasonable, where further structural alterations, such as a false water line and fiberglass work, were observed by agent, who then used an axe to gain access to secret compartment. U.S.C.A. Const.Amend. 4.—Id.

C.A.11 (Fla.) 1985. Border searches are not subject to constitutional probable cause and warrant requirements; however, the broad authority to conduct border searches is circumscribed by the reasonableness requirement of the Fourth Amendment. U.S.C.A. Const.Amend. 4.—U.S. v. Sarda-Villa, 760 F.2d 1232.

C.A.Fla. 1984. Legitimacy of a defendant's privacy claim as to areas searched is determined by totality of circumstances.—U.S. v. Baron-Mantilla, 743 F.2d 868.

Although defendant did not own premises searched, nor did he rent them, and telephone in premises was not listed in his name, defendant could have nonetheless established legitimate expectation of privacy in premises by demonstrating an unrestricted right of occupancy or custody and control of premises as distinguished from occasional presence on premises as a mere guest or invitee.—Id.

Defendant who did not own or rent premises searched, did not have telephone in premises listed in his name, and failed to produce any neighbor or building employee who could have

D.C.Mich. 1979. Search warrant was necessary to place electronic beeper in drum of chemical which defendant purchased from undercover agent allegedly for purpose of illegally manufacturing phencyclidine where drum was not contraband per se, beeper not only enabled federal authorities to trace and locate the container but also had potential to enable them to trace the private movements of persons in possession of the container, even into their homes. Comprehensive Drug Abuse Prevention and Control Act of 1970, §§ 401(a)(1), 406, 21 U.S.C.A. §§ 841(a)(1), 846; U.S.C.A.Const. Amend. 4.—U. S. v. Bailey, 465 F.Supp. 1138, affirmed 628 F.2d 938.

Since exact procedure anticipated in criminal rule governing search warrants does not fit pen registers, card drops or electronic beepers, it is necessary for the judge or magistrate authorizing use of such devices to interpolate so that the "warrant" will satisfy constitutional standards and other standards, if any, imposed by law for issuance of warrants. Fed.Rules Crim.Proc. rules 41, 41(b, c), 18 U.S.C.A.—Id.

Warrant authorizing placement of electronic beeper in drum of chemicals which defendant purchased from undercover federal agent for alleged purpose of manufacturing phencyclidine was void where no time limitation was specified and none, not even a reasonable time, could be inferred and warrant purported to authorize surveillance as long as the beeper functioned; hence, delivery of drum to defendant was a violation of her privacy and, likewise, continued use of beeper at codefendant's premises was a violation of his Fourth Amendment rights. Comprehensive Drug Abuse Prevention and Control Act of 1970, §§ 401(a)(1), 406, 21 U.S.C.A. §§ 841(a)(1), 846; U.S.C.A.Const. Amend. 4.—Id.

D.C.Mich. 1977. An automobile has a lesser privacy interest than a business establishment. U.S.C.A.Const. Amend. 4.—U. S. v. Giacalone, 455 F.Supp. 26.

D.C.Minn. 1984. Absent reasonable, articulable suspicion of unlawful conduct, law enforcement officials cannot use roving patrols to stop vehicles randomly at discretion of police; potential for abuse of officers' discretion makes such stops unconstitutional. U.S.C.A. Const.Amend. 4.—Stark v. Perpich, 590 F.Supp. 1057.

Use of fixed checkpoints to stop all passing vehicles or portion of all vehicles on systematic basis is permissible when used to further important state interest. U.S.C.A. Const.Amends. 4, 14.—Id.

Legality of plan for police stops of vehicles involves considerations of whether plan incorporates safeguards to minimize discretion of officers making stops and whether asserted state interests in making such stops justify intrusion on motorists' Fourth Amendment rights. U.S.C.A. Const. Amend. 4.—Id.

D.C.Minn. 1984. In order for intrusion to reach constitutional dimensions, person must have exhibited actual, subjective reasonable expectation of privacy in area searched.—Avenson v. Zegart, 577 F.Supp. 958.

It was reasonable for deputy sheriff and humane society director, upon receiving no answer at house to which they went to inform owners that humane society had received complaints about owners' dog-breeding business and upon viewing a lighted and open barn, to go to the barn to seek owners, and actions did not violate any constitutional rights of owners. 42 U.S.C.A. § 1983.—Id.

D.C.Minn. 1982. Initial intrusion into the enclosed camper of pickup truck was an illegal inventory search under the *Wilson* decision, in which the Court of Appeals held that the routine search of a locked automobile trunk is unreasonable under the Fourth Amendment. U.S.C.A.

Const.Amend. 4.—U.S. v. Maier, 553 F.Supp. 438, reversed 691 F.2d 421, certiorari denied 103 S.Ct. 1524, appeal after remand 720 F.2d 978, certiorari denied 104 S.Ct. 2342.

D.C.Minn. 1979. Questioned document was not obtained by Internal Revenue Service by violation of Fourth Amendment where document, though written material, was not composed or intended for public consumption and where IRS involvement was not subject to being characterized as official involvement in either quality or persistence. U.S.C.A. Const. Amend. 4.—U. S. v. Bonnell, 483 F.Supp. 1070.

D.C.Mont. 1983. Where intrusion of which water customer complained did not involve entry of his home or his business, but, rather, entry by water and sewage department employees upon unfenced portion of customer's property, located immediately adjacent to driveway/parking lot, appurtenant to customer's commercial business building, and entry was made during working day in open and unobtrusive manner for sole purpose of terminating water service to customer's property, entry upon property was not violative of Fourth Amendment. U.S.C.A. Const.Amend. 4.—Frates v. City of Great Falls, 568 F.Supp. 1330, affirmed in part, remanded in part 732 F.2d 163.

D.C.N.J. 1985. Except in certain carefully limited classes of cases, search of private property or person without consent is "unreasonable" unless it has been authorized by a valid search warrant. U.S.C.A. Const.Amend. 4.—Shoemaker v. Handel, 608 F.Supp. 1151.

D.C.N.J. 1981. Warrantless administrative investigation of licensee's premises by Nuclear Regulatory Commission inspectors did not contravene any constitutional restraint against unreasonable searches and seizures. U.S.C.A.Const. Amend. 4.—U. S. Nuclear Regulatory Commission v. Radiation Technology, Inc., 519 F.Supp. 1266.

D.C.N.J. 1980. Search warrants may authorize seizure of materials arguably within the orbit of protection of the First Amendment. U.S.C.A. Const. Amends. 1, 4.—U. S. v. Nilsen, 482 F.Supp. 1335.

D.C.N.J. 1978. Fourth Amendment's protections extend to items in the mail and thus letters and packages may only be opened and examined pursuant to proper warrant, as if items were to be searched in one's household. U.S.C.A.Const. Amend. 4.—Paton v. La Prade, 469 F.Supp. 773.

D.C.N.J. 1976. U. S. v. Mirmelli, 421 F.Supp. 684, affirmed 556 F.2d 569, certiorari denied 98 S.Ct. 115, 434 U.S. 832, 54 L.Ed.2d 92.

D.C.N.J. 1976. U. S. v. Speights, 413 F.Supp. 1221, reversed 557 F.2d 362.

D.C.N.M. 1983. Reasonable expectation of privacy is determined in light of facts and circumstances of each case, and relevant factors include precautions customarily taken by those seeking privacy, the way a location is used, history of the Fourth Amendment and society's recognition of permissible conduct in particular places as reflected by property rights. U.S.C.A. Const.Amend. 4.—U.S. v. Obregon, 573 F.Supp. 876.

As matter of law, there is much lower expectation of privacy associated with car than with one's person or personal residence, and although cars are within scope of Fourth Amendment, the privacy that person reasonably may expect in their use is limited, and passengers have even lesser expectation. U.S.C.A. Const.Amend. 4.—Id.

Discretionary spot check of driver and his car is contrary to Fourth Amendment unless there is articulable and reasonable suspicion that driver is not licensed or that car is not registered or that either car or an occupant is otherwise subject to seizure for violating the law, but state police may attempt to stop all oncoming traffic to check driver's licenses and car registrations, without

COLORADO DIGEST

VOLUME 12A
SEARCHES AND SEIZURES — SUICIDE

COVERING CASES FROM
STATE AND FEDERAL COURTS

ST. PAUL, MINN.
WEST PUBLISHING CO.

reasonable search and seizure. U.S.C.A. Const. Amend. 4; Const. art. 2, § 7.

> Hernandez v. People, 385 P.2d 996, 153 Colo. 316.

⚷7(10). Persons, places, and possessions protected from searches and seizures without warrant.

U.S.Colo. 1969. The Fourth Amendment protects reasonable expectations of privacy and does not protect persons engaged in crime from the risk that those with whom they associate or converse will cooperate with the government. U.S.C.A.Const. Amend. 4.

> Alderman v. U. S., 89 S.Ct. 961, 394 U.S. 165, 22 L.Ed.2d 176, rehearing denied Ivanov v. U. S., 89 S.Ct. 1177, 394 U.S. 939, 22 L.Ed.2d 475, appeal after remand U. S. v. Alderisio, 424 F.2d 20.

C.A.Colo. 1962. Evidence obtained by intentional eavesdropping of government agents, unaccompanied by physical trespass on constitutionally protected premises and unaided by use of electronic or mechanical device, is admissible in federal prosecutions, and its reception does not violate the Fourth Amendment. U.S.C.A.Const. Amend. 4; Communications Act of 1934, § 1 et seq. as amended 47 U.S.C.A. § 151 et seq.

> Anspach v. U. S., 305 F.2d 48, certiorari denied 83 S.Ct. 46, 371 U.S. 826, 9 L. Ed.2d 65, rehearing denied 83 S.Ct. 252, 371 U.S. 917, 9 L.Ed.2d 176.

Colo. 1965. Belief, however well founded, that article sought is concealed in dwelling house furnishes no justification for search of that place without a warrant, and such searches are constitutionally unlawful notwithstanding facts unquestionably showing probable cause. U.S.C.A.Const. Amend. 4; Const. art. 2, § 7.

> Wilson v. People, 398 P.2d 35, 156 Colo. 243.

Colo. 1967. Constitutional right to be free from unreasonable search and seizure did not require that police officer, who suspected that part of stolen goods had been thrown in public alley the night before, obtain a search warrant before searching alley.

> Martinez v. People, 425 P.2d 299, 162 Colo. 195.

Colo. 1967. State constitution does not require a more restrictive rule with respect to search of automobiles than that applied under federal constitutional standards as determined by United States Supreme Court.

> Stewart v. People, 426 P.2d 545, 162 Colo. 117.

Colo. 1968. Inspection of an unoccupied automobile which was parked about one-half block from scene of crime and which conformed to description of automobile seen by eyewitness was reasonable, and billfolds found in process of checking automobile for identification of owner were admissible in prosecution for larceny and burglary.

> Scott v. People, 444 P.2d 388, 166 Colo. 432.

Colo. 1970. Consent of defendant charged with causing injury while driving under influence of intoxicating liquor was not constitutionally required under Fourth Amendment in order to administer breathalyzer test. U.S.C.A.Const. Amend. 4.

> People v. Sanchez, 476 P.2d 980.

Colo. 1971. Defendant who claimed that police acted improperly in conducting surveillance of backyard of apartment where he lived from position outside property failed to establish that backyard was area where he was entitled to reasonable expectation of privacy free from visual intrusions.

> People v. Ortega, 485 P.2d 894.

Colo. 1971. Withdrawal of blood sample at hospital where defendant had been taken following automobile accident did not violate defendant's constitutional rights, and was in compliance with applicable constitutional standards.

> People v. Smith, 486 P.2d 8.

Consent of defendant, who was hospitalized following automobile accident, was not required for taking of blood sample.

> People v. Smith, 486 P.2d 8.

Colo. 1971. Neither Fourth Amendment to United States Constitution nor art. II, § 7 of the Colorado Constitution protects an individual in a place where he has no reasonable expectation of privacy. U.S.C.A.Const. Amend. 4; Const. art. 2, § 7.

> Zamora v. People, 487 P.2d 1116.

Colo. 1972. Where there was commission of felony-murder at scene of burglary, and automobile which brought burglars to scene of crime and in which they had intended to effect their escape was abandoned at scene by burglars, who fled from scene on foot into night and remained at large for some time, search of automobile by law enforcement authorities though without warrant, was reasonable as part of investigation. Colo.R.Crim.P. rule 41(e); U.S.C.A. Const. Amend. 4.

> Kurtz v. People, 494 P.2d 97.

West's
COLORADO DIGEST

CONSOLIDATED EDITION

Vol. 12A

Searches and Seizures — Suicide

1986
Cumulative Annual Pocket Part

THE WEST DIGEST TOPIC NUMBERS WHICH CAN BE
USED FOR WESTLAW SEARCHES ARE LISTED ON
PAGE III OF THIS POCKET PART.

Up-Dated Weekly by West's
Pacific 2d Reporter Advance Sheets

The ⟐ symbol and WEST's are registered trademarks of West Publishing Co. Registered in U.S.
Patent and Trademark Office. Colorado Digest is a trademark of West Publishing Co.

ST. PAUL, MINN.

WEST PUBLISHING CO.

Closing with Cases Reported in

COPYRIGHT © 1972 through 1985 WEST PUBLISHING CO.

_____

COPYRIGHT © 1986
By
WEST PUBLISHING CO.

12A Colo.Dig.
1986 P.P.

ment is that affidavits for search warrants must be treated by courts in commonsense and realistic manner, and warrants issued pursuant thereto are not to be given hypertechnical interpretation. U.S.C.A.Const. Amend. 4; Fed.Rules Crim.Proc. rule 41, 18 U.S.C.A.—Matter of Carlson, 580 F.2d 1365.

Colo. 1982. Fourth Amendment mandates excision of erroneous statement in affidavit for search warrant if defendant can show by preponderance of evidence that such error was caused by officer affiant's perjury or reckless disregard for the truth. U.S.C.A.Const.Amend. 4.—People v. Dailey, 639 P.2d 1068.

Colo. 1975. Fourth Amendment does not deny to law enforcement officers the support of usual inferences which reasonable men may draw from sworn statements and testimony; so long as inference is drawn from information set forth in affidavit for search warrant inference is permissible. U.S.C.A.Const. Amend. 4.—People v. Fike, 539 P.2d 125, 189 Colo. 238.

☞7(8). —— Description.

D.C.Colo. 1977. Even if representations in affidavit for search warrants sought to seize property for administrative collection of taxes established probable cause, requested order would violate Fourth Amendment where it did not describe things to be seized and only limitation was that entry should be made during business hours or in daytime and within ten days of order. 26 U.S.C.A. (I.R.C.1954) § 6331; U.S.C.A.Const. Amend. 4.— Matter of Carlson, 434 F.Supp. 554, reversed 580 F.2d 1365.

Colo. 1982. Any search of law office for client files and materials must be precisely limited and restricted to prevent an exploratory search; confidentiality of attorney-client relationship must be preserved by protecting the communications, documents, and materials which client has made available to his lawyer in order to obtain legal advice.—Law Offices of Bernard D. Morley, P. C. v. MacFarlane, 647 P.2d 1215.

Colo. 1974. By virtue of reasonableness requirement of Fourth Amendment, not only must officer executing search warrant be able to reasonably ascertain place to be searched, there must also be no reasonable probability that another place might be mistakenly searched. U.S.C.A. Const. Amend. 4.—People v. Ragulsky, 518 P.2d 286, 184 Colo. 86.

☞7(9). —— Execution of warrants.

C.A.Colo. 1980. Seizure of unlisted money when probable cause was otherwise present represented no undue exercise of police discretion and no abuse of Fourth Amendment safeguards. U.S. C.A.Const. Amend. 4.—U. S. v. Burns, 624 F.2d 95, certiorari denied Reynolds v. U. S., 101 S.Ct. 361, 449 U.S. 954, 66 L.Ed.2d 219.

Colo. 1978. Where police officers in executing an arrest warrant for defendant in his apartment observed some items of stolen clothing, secured apartment and obtained a search warrant, search, pursuant to warrant, which extended only to those areas of apartment where the stolen items described in search warrant might be secreted was reasonable and police could seize marijuana discovered during course of such search and marijuana seized was admissible in prosecution for possession with intent to dispense dangerous drug, cannibas over one ounce. C.R.S. '73, 12–22–404, 12–22–412.—People v. Garcia, 579 P.2d 1150, 195 Colo. 547.

Colo. 1972. Where officers arrived at premises which had been under surveillance and were admitted by defendant who, upon reading search warrant, stated that the address was wrong, officer who had conducted the surveillance instructed the other officers to "hold it right there" and to remain at premises while he returned to county

judge who had issued the warrant, and warrant as subsequently corrected was then served on defendant and executed by search which resulted in seizure of narcotics, such entry into premises pursuant to the original warrant and service of such warrant did not constitute execution of warrant so as to render subsequent seizure illegal; rather, procedure followed conformed to requirements of Fourth Amendment and of state constitutional provision governing search warrant, and thus seized narcotics were admissible. Const. art. 2, § 7; Colo.R.Crim.P. rule 41(c); U.S.C.A.Const. Amend. 4.—Mayorga v. People, 496 P.2d 304, 178 Colo. 106.

Colo.App. 1984. Although a search warrant must be directed to an officer authorized by law to execute it in county where the property is located, where proper authorities are contacted to assist in executing a warrant directed to an officer from another county, the execution of such warrant, if the warrant is based on probable cause, does not violate a defendant's Fourth Amendment rights. C.R.S. 16–3–305; U.S.C.A. Const.Amend. 4.—People v. Hamer, 689 P.2d 1147.

☞7(10). **Persons, places, and possessions protected from searches and seizures without warrant.**

U.S.Colo. 1974. State health inspector who entered outdoor premises without knowledge or consent of occupier of premises to observe, and make opacity test of, smoke plumes emitted from chimneys did not violate Fourth Amendment rights of occupier. U.S.C.A.Const. Amend. 4.—Air Pollution Variance Bd. of Colorado v. Western Alfalfa Corp., 94 S.Ct. 2114, 416 U.S. 861, 40 L.Ed.2d 607, on remand 534 P.2d 796, 35 Colo.App. 207, affirmed 553 P.2d 811, 191 Colo. 455.

U.S.Colo. 1969. Alderman v. U. S., 89 S.Ct. 961, 394 U.S. 165, 22 L.Ed.2d 176, appeal after remand U. S. v. Alderisio, 424 F.2d 20.

C.A.10 (Colo.) 1985. Once agents were justified in seizing defendant's audiotape, playing of tape, that was labeled "Confidential, Do Not Play," did not violate Fourth Amendment [U.S.C.A. Const. Amend. 4], where tape was not locked away, hidden or sealed.—U.S. v. Falcon, 766 F.2d 1469.

C.A.Colo. 1981. Defendants had no reasonable expectation of privacy in millyard of their lumber company, surrounded by nothing more than barbed wire fence. U.S.C.A.Const. Amend. 4.—U. S. v. Rucinski, 658 F.2d 741, certiorari denied 102 S.Ct. 1430, 455 U.S. 939, 71 L.Ed.2d 649.

C.A.Colo. 1980. What a person knowingly exposes is not constitutionally protected from observation, nor are activities or objects which are exposed, regardless of subjective intent, in a matter inconsistent with reasonable expectations of privacy. U.S.C.A.Const. Amend. 4.—U. S. v. Burns, 624 F.2d 95, certiorari denied Reynolds v. U. S., 101 S.Ct. 361, 449 U.S. 954, 66 L.Ed.2d 219.

C.A.Colo. 1978. Where federal agents lost contact with electronic tracking device, which had been attached to a container of ether, following its movement from house and independent effort was necessary to reestablish contact, contact through which clandestine laboratory where amphetamines were being produced was discovered was not tainted by surveillance within the house based on warrantless use of device.—U. S. v. Clayborne, 584 F.2d 346.

Where agents, who lost contact with electronic tracking device that had been attached to container of ether after its movement from one defendant's house, had to use airplane to pick up beeper signal and locate clandestine laboratory, which was located in commercial building with windows covered to protect against viewing of materials inside, slight intrusion resulting from use of device was not per se in violation of the Fourth Amendment and its warrantless use by agents was therefore not invalid. U.S.C.A.Const. Amend. 4.—Id.

C.A.Colo. 1978. Utilization of electronic tracking device, without prior court approval, may be justified by probable cause and exigent circumstances. U.S.C.A.Const. Amend. 4.—U. S. v. Shovea, 580 F.2d 1382, certiorari denied Gaias v. U. S., 99 S.Ct. 581, 439 U.S. 986, 58 L.Ed.2d 659 and 99 S.Ct. 1216, 440 U.S. 908, 59 L.Ed.2d 456.

Federal agents had sufficient probable cause to attach electronic tracking device to defendant's car without first acquiring court order and did not violate defendant's Fourth Amendment rights in so doing, where agents knew that codefendant had purchased chemicals, a primary precursor of methamphetamine, and agents observed codefendant leave residence, carrying suitcase in careful manner, drive to airport in elusive manner, fly to another city where he was met by defendant and drive to defendant's residence. 18 U.S.C.A. § 2; Comprehensive Drug Abuse Prevention and Control Act of 1970, § 401(a)(1), 21 U.S.C.A. § 841(a)(1); U.S.C.A.Const. Amend. 4.—Id.

D.C.Colo. 1984. Summons issued by Internal Revenue Service to bank in connection with ongoing investigation into income tax liability of minister did not violate right of church and minister to be free from unreasonable searches and seizures, in that records requested were property of bank and minister and church had no proprietary interest in them and they had no valid expectation of privacy in bank's records. U.S.C.A. Const. Amend. 4.—Assembly of Yahveh Beth Israel v. U.S., 592 F.Supp. 1257.

D.C.Colo. 1980. Body cavity searches of prisoners are not necessarily unreasonable and thus do not violate the Fourth Amendment, but in determining the reasonableness of such searches, court must consider the manner in which they are conducted. U.S.C.A.Const. Amend. 4.—Massey v. Wilson, 484 F.Supp. 1332.

D.C.Colo. 1974. Stolen goods, and goods forfeited for breach of revenue laws, or concealed to avoid payment of duties, have always been seizable. U.S.C.A.Const. Amend. 4; 26 U.S.C.A. (I.R.C. 1954) §§ 7201, 7206(1).—Shaffer v. Wilson, 383 F.Supp. 554, affirmed 523 F.2d 175, certiorari denied 96 S.Ct. 3198, 427 U.S. 912, 49 L.Ed.2d 1203.

Government has always been permitted to search records required to be kept by the revenue laws and to search for and seize articles the possession of which is illegal. 26 U.S.C.A. (I.R.C. 1954) §§ 7201, 7206(1); U.S.C.A.Const. Amend. 4.—Id.

Colo. 1985. While administrative searches of private homes must ordinarily be conducted pursuant to a warrant, warrantless administrative searches of commercial property do not necessarily violate the Fourth Amendment. U.S.C.A. Const.Amend. 4.—Exotic Coins, Inc. v. Beacom, 699 P.2d 930.

Inspections of commercial property may be unreasonable if they are not authorized by law, are unnecessary for furtherance of government interest, or are so random, infrequent, or unpredictable that owner, for all practical purposes, has no real expectation that his property would be inspected from time to time by government officials. U.S.C.A. Const.Amend. 4.—Id.

Colo. 1985. Whether expectation of privacy is "legitimate" and thus is protected by Colorado Constitution is determined by a two part inquiry: whether one actually expects that area or activity subjected to governmental intrusion would remain free of such intrusion, and whether that expectation is one that society is prepared to recognize as reasonable. Const. Art. 2, § 7.—People v. Oates, 698 P.2d 811.

Broader definition of what constitutes legitimate expectation of privacy under Colorado Con-

stitution encompasses expectation that purchased commercial goods will be free of government surveillance devices such as beepers. Const. Art. 2, § 7; U.S.C.A. Const.Amend. 4.—Id.

Whether expectation of privacy is reasonable may be tested against customs, values and common understandings that confer sense of privacy upon many of our basic social activities. Const. Art. 2, § 7; U.S.C.A. Const.Amend. 4.—Id.

Government installation of a beeper in a drum of chemicals, a sealed container, violates the owner's expectation of privacy, and the violation continues through time that purchaser of the drum takes possession. Const. Art. 2, § 7.—Id.

Legitimate privacy expectation of one with proprietary or possessory interest in a commercially purchased item is violated under section of Colorado Constitution prohibiting unreasonable searches and seizures whenever the item contains a government installed beeper. Const. Art. 2, § 7.—Id.

Any determination that legitimate expectation of privacy has been violated must be based upon totality of circumstances surrounding the search and seizure. Const. Art. 2, § 7.—Id.

Colo. 1984. Minor did not have legitimate expectation of privacy in purse which was in possession of his companion and obtained by police in investigatory search of companion. U.S.C.A. Const.Amend. 4.—People in Interest of D.E.J., 686 P.2d 794.

Abandonment is determined by objective standards and turns on whether individual has retained any reasonable expectation of privacy in the property; individual forfeits his expectation of privacy in property when he voluntarily abandons the property. U.S.C.A. Const.Amend. 4.—Id.

Whether party retains expectation of privacy in object is question of intent which can be ascertained from the facts. U.S.C.A. Const.Amend. 4.—Id.

Colo. 1984. Reasonable expectation of privacy of a telephone subscriber is based on expectation that telephone company will not voluntarily disclose dialed numbers to the government, not on whether the calls are individually billed to a subscriber; thus, obtaining telephone toll records of individually billed calls of a telephone subscriber constitutes a search, within the meaning of the State Constitution, for which law enforcement officers generally must obtain a search warrant supported by probable cause. Const. Art. 2, § 7.—People v. Corr, 682 P.2d 20, certiorari denied Colorado v. Corr, 105 S.Ct. 181.

Colo. 1984. Driver of motor vehicle has no legitimate expectation of privacy in his physical traits and demeanor that are in plain sight of officer during valid traffic stop. U.S.C.A. Const. Amend. 4; Const. Art. 2, § 7.—People v. Carlson, 677 P.2d 310.

Colo. 1983. In determining legitimacy of defendant's privacy expectation in telephone numbers she dialed on home telephone, appropriate inquiry was whether she expected that numbers dialed by her on her home telephone would be free from governmental intrusion, and, if she did, whether that expectation was one that society was prepared to recognize as reasonable. Const. Art. 2, § 7; U.S.C.A. Const.Amend. 4.—People v. Sporleder, 666 P.2d 135.

Defendant's privacy expectation in telephone numbers dialed on home telephone qualified for constitutional protection under Colorado constitutional proscription of unreasonable searches and seizures. Const. Art. 2, § 7.—Id.

Fact that pen registers do not result in actual monitoring of telephone conversations does not render numbers themselves devoid of significant privacy interest on part of caller, for purpose of protection under state constitutional proscription of unreasonable searches and seizures. Const. Art. 2, § 7.—Id.

Any difference between bank customer's privacy interest in bank records and telephone subscriber's privacy interest in record of telephone numbers dialed from home telephone is too insubstantial to justify constitutional differentiation in treatment under state constitutional proscription of unreasonable searches and seizures. Const. Art. 2, § 7.—Id.

Inasmuch as telephone subscriber has legitimate expectation of privacy in telephone numbers dialed, installation of pen register and acquisition of information about telephone numbers dialed by subscriber is nothing less than full-scale "search and seizure" in constitutional sense. Const. Art. 2, § 7.—Id.

Colo. 1983. Fourth Amendment protections prevent governmental intrusions into or confiscations of bank records without use of appropriate legal processes. U.S.C.A. Const.Amend. 4.—Pignatiello v. District Court In and For Second Judicial Dist., State of Colo., 659 P.2d 683.

Colo. 1982. There is an enhanced privacy interest underlying attorney-client relationship which warrants heightened degree of judicial protection and supervision when law offices are the subject of a search for client files or documents.— Law Offices of Bernard D. Morley, P. C. v. MacFarlane, 647 P.2d 1215.

Judicial decisions regarding propriety of law office searches and protections accorded by attorney-client privilege must be made on an ad hoc basis, and it is within sound discretion of trial court to determine whether prosecution has established a proper foundation in fact for the applicability of the crime-fraud exception and whether the overall search and seizure was conducted in a reasonable manner in view of enhanced privacy interest.—Id.

Colo. 1982. Warrantless electronic transmission and monitoring of conversations taking place between suspect and police informant in informant's motel room, when informant has previously consented to electronic surveillance, does not violate Colorado Constitution's prohibition of unreasonable searches and seizures. Const.Art. 2, § 7.—People v. Velasquez, 641 P.2d 943, appeal dismissed, certiorari denied Velasquez v. Colorado, 103 S.Ct. 28, 459 U.S. 805, 74 L.Ed.2d 43, rehearing denied 103 S.Ct. 774, 459 U.S. 1138, 74 L.Ed.2d 986.

Colo. 1981. Defendant's mere occupancy of vehicle as passenger, without more, was insufficient to provide him a constitutionally cognizable expectation of privacy in area searched or objects seized.—People v. Henry, 631 P.2d 1122.

Colo. 1980. Possession of place searched or of items seized is but one factor bearing on issue of whether defendant had legitimate expectation of privacy in the invaded place; possession is not sole criterion to determine whether protected Fourth Amendment interest exists. U.S.C.A.Const. Amend. 4.—People v. Spies, 615 P.2d 710, 200 Colo. 434.

Issue of whether government officials violated any legitimate expectation of privacy held by defendant is appropriately based upon totality of the circumstances in each case. U.S.C.A.Const. Amend. 4.—Id.

Colo. 1980. Warrantless seizures of automobiles from public streets by tax enforcement authorities are not violative of Fourth Amendment. U.S.C.A.Const. Amend. 4.—Manka v. Martin, 614 P.2d 875, 200 Colo. 260, certiorari denied 101 S.Ct. 1354, 450 U.S. 913, 67 L.Ed.2d 338.

Colo. 1978. Rules permitting prison officials to make warrantless searches to preserve prison order or security apply with equal force to searches made in pretrial detention facilities.—Hudson v. People, 585 P.2d 580, 196 Colo. 211.

Colo. 1978. Defendant, who was detained in police custody in patrol car after police officer smelled marijuana and saw two "hash pipes" on dashboard of parked car in which defendant had been an occupant, had expectation of privacy with regard to his closed backpack in back seat of car sufficient to invoke constitutional protections against unreasonable police intrusion. U.S.C.A. Const. Amend. 4; Const. art. 2, § 7.—People v. Hines, 575 P.2d 414, 195 Colo. 71.

Evidence supported trial court's finding that police officer, who had detained defendant in police custody in patrol car after he had smelled marijuana and saw two "hash pipes" on dashboard on parked car in which defendant had been an occupant, unreasonably searched such car and that no special circumstances justified officer in searching defendant's closed backpack found in back of car without first obtaining a warrant, and thus marijuana found in backpack was suppressed on defendant's motion. U.S.C.A.Const. Amend. 4; Const. art. 2, § 7.—Id.

Colo. 1977. Defendant did not have reasonable expectation of privacy with respect to his leasehold interest in open pasture and with respect to his flatbed truck parked on private property but in general view of public, and therefore warrantless searches of pasture and truck and seizure of bee equipment were not searches and seizures of constitutional dimensions but involved actions which fell outside protections of Fourth Amendment. U.S.C.A.Const. Amend. 4.—People v. McClaugherty, 566 P.2d 361, 193 Colo. 360.

Colo. 1977. Legitimacy of privacy expectation which attaches to objects in sealed containers is recognized by courts although when container is sealed, but is nonetheless transparent so as to disclose its contents to world, both existence of subjective expectation of privacy and reasonableness of that expectation with regard to container may be questionable. U.S.C.A.Const. Amend. 4; Const. art. 2, § 7.—People v. Casias, 563 P.2d 926, 193 Colo. 66.

Pockets of person's clothing are recognized as areas to which justifiable expectation of privacy attaches. U.S.C.A.Const. Amend. 4; Const. art. 2, § 7.—Id.

Colo. 1976. A personal diary secreted under clothing in one's bedroom dresser drawer is an item of a kind intended to be protected by the Fourth Amendment's warrant requirements as such a diary is part of the "papers and effects" protected by the warrant requirements. Const. art. 2, § 7; U.S.C.A.Const. Amend. 4.—People v. Williams, 557 P.2d 399, 192 Colo. 249.

Where defendant had been removed from private residence along with decedent's body, pistol involved in shooting had been discovered in plain sight, house had been secured by the police, there was no indication of any risk that evidence might be lost or destroyed while a warrant was being obtained and there were otherwise no "exigent circumstances" justifying dispensing with warrant requirement, warrantless search of defendant's bedroom dresser drawer, which search first revealed diary, violated defendant's Fourth Amendment rights; seizure could not be justified on basis of subsequently obtained warrant. Const. art. 2, § 7; U.S.C.A.Const. Amend. 4.—Id.

Colo. 1976. When defendant's station wagon was taken into custody on his arrest, defendant had expectation of privacy with regard to his sealed knapsack in the vehicle sufficient to invoke constitutional protections against unreasonable police intrusion. Const. art. 2, § 7.—People v. Counterman, 556 P.2d 481, 192 Colo. 152.

Colo. 1975. Although the Fourth Amendment protects people, not places, what a person knowingly exposes to public, even in his own home, is not protected. U.S.C.A.Const. Amend. 4.—People v. Becker, 533 P.2d 494, 188 Colo. 160.

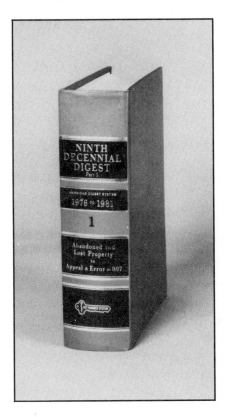

West's Ninth Decennial Digest from
West's American Digest System

American Digest Problem I

In your research, you have found a key number classified under the topic Negligence which is helpful to you. It deals with liability of business owners to visitors at the place of business. The key number is Negligence, ☞32(2.8). Trace it forward to date from the Ninth Decennial through the General Digest.

NINTH
DECENNIAL DIGEST

Part I

AMERICAN DIGEST SYSTEM

1976–1981

*A Complete Digest of All Decisions of the State and
Federal Courts as Reported in the National
Reporter System and the State Reports*

Volume 25

MINES AND MINERALS —
NEGLIGENCE ⊶120

ST. PAUL, MINN.
WEST PUBLISHING CO.

WEST'S
NINTH DECENNIAL DIGEST
PART I

This is Part I of the Ninth Unit of the American Digest System employing the unique KEY NUMBER classification, universally recognized as the standard classification of American case law.

The Ninth Unit, Part I is being published to provide a single source Digest for all American case law for the period 1976–1981. The rapid growth in the volume of reported cases digested and the introduction of new and expanded Digest topics is accommodated in a unit covering a five year rather than as previously in a ten year unit.

The following new and revised topics have been developed and are included in this Ninth Decennial Digest, Part I:

Abandoned and Lost Property
Abortion and Birth Control
Accountants
Administrative Law and Procedure
Bankruptcy
Chemical Dependents
Condominium
Consumer Credit
Consumer Protection
Copyrights and Intellectual
   Property
Credit Reporting Agencies
Debtor and Creditor

Deposits and Escrows
Dower and Curtesy
Employers' Liability
Extortion and Threats
Extradition and Detainers
Illegitimate Children
Implied and Constructive Contracts
Internal Revenue
Public Utilities
Social Security and Public Welfare
Urban Railroads
Zoning and Planning

Research is facilitated by references to **Corpus Juris Secundum**, America's great law encyclopedia, which appear under those Key Numbers for which the decade produced no case references, and which direct the researcher to a comprehensive discussion of the subject.

A **Descriptive-Word Index**, the "starting point of research," is included in West's Ninth Decennial Digest, Part I. It indexes the facts as well as the law of the cases covered by this digest, and is an indispensable guide to cases dealing with similar facts and legal principles.

The **Table of Cases** lists all decisions reported during the period, showing the title and citation, as well as the Digest topic and Key Number for each point of law drawn from the opinion. Additionally, the Table of Cases includes the case history of each decision, where such information was available at the time the Table was prepared, enabling the researcher to determine at a glance any action affecting the decision taken by the Courts subsequent to its rendition. Subsequent case history information will be set out in the Table of Cases Affirmed, Reversed or Modified, of the General Digest, Sixth Series.

THE PUBLISHER

March, 1983

25–9th Dec. Pt. 1

III *

circumstances.—Yalowizer v. Husky Oil Co., 629 P.2d 465.

🔑32(2.4). Implied invitation in general.

Ga.App. 1976. Where landowner knew that masonry man was helping him pour concrete, utilized his help, and by his actions accepted masonry man's implied offer of assistance, and benefit of masonry man's efforts was entirely for landowner, masonry man was landowner's invitee to whom landowner owed ordinary duty of care.—Speir v. Stephenson, 227 S.E.2d 469, 138 Ga.App. 690.

For purpose of establishing status of invitee, request by landowner that alleged invitee come to landowner's property for sole benefit of landowner may be either express or implied.—Id.

Ill.App. 1980. Person is invitee on land of another if he enters by invitation, express or implied, his entry is connected with owner's business or with activity that owner conducts or permits to be conducted on his land, and there is mutuality of benefit or a benefit to the owner.—Barmore v. Elmore, 38 Ill.Dec. 751, 403 N.E.2d 1355.

Ill.App. 1978. Generally an "invitee" is defined as one who enters upon premises of another in response to an express or implied invitation for the purpose of transacting business in which the parties are mutually interested.—Sepesy v. Archer Daniels Co., 16 Ill. Dec. 549, 375 N.E.2d 180, 59 Ill.App.3d 56, supplemented 24 Ill.Dec. 220, 384 N.E.2d 1378, 66 Ill.App.3d 1053, remanded 36 Ill. Dec. 957, 401 N.E.2d 1391, 71 Ill.2d 615, appeal after remand 53 Ill.Dec. 273, 423 N.E.2d 942, 97 Ill.App.3d 868.

Ind.App. 1980. Status of invitee is created by entering premises with occupant's express or implied invitation to transact business or to perform some act which is to commercial advantage of occupant.—Downham v. Wagner, 408 N.E.2d 606.

Md.App. 1977. Invitation by which one becomes an invitee may be express or implied.—Woodward v. Newstein, 377 A.2d 535.

Under implied invitation doctrine, before status of invitee may be established by implication there must be, in conduct or words of possessor of land, some inducement or encouragement to enter, and mere permission or acquiescence is not sufficient.—Id.

Fact that owners' newspaper advertisements stating that defendants' vacation home was for sale were published almost four years prior to accident, and realtors' advertisements one and one-half years prior, that neither advertisements gave address of vacation home, that owners posted no "For Sale" sign, and other facts compelled conclusion that no invitation could reasonably be construed under either theory applied in determination of implied invitee status as extending to plaintiffs who sustained injuries when deck of defendants' vacation home collapsed under them.—Id.

Mich.App. 1978. Permission to come upon land may be implied where the landowner acquiesces in the known, customary use of the property by the public.—Thone v. Nicholson, 269 N.W.2d 665, 84 Mich.App. 538.

Tex.Civ.App. 1978. "Invitee" is person who goes on the premises of another in answer to the express or implied invitation of the owner or occupant or the business of the owner or occupant or for their mutual advantage, and "implied invitation" is one which is extended by reason of owner or occupant doing something or permitting something to be done

which fairly indicates to the person entering that his entry and use of the property are consistent with the intentions and purposes of the owner or occupant and that the use is in accordance with the design for which the place is adapted and allowed to be used in mutuality of interests.—Atchison, T. & S. F. Ry. Co. v. Smith, 563 S.W.2d 660, ref. n.r.e.

🔑32(2.5). Automobile service stations and parking service.

D.C.D.C. 1981. Owner of parking lot could not be held liable for abduction and rape of patron as she left parking lot where assailant was not employee of owner, there had been no history of such criminals in area, and parking lot owner had no control over actions of assailant.—Gillot v. Washington Metropolitan Area Transit Authority, 507 F.Supp. 454.

🔑32(2.6). Bill collectors.

No cases for period of this Digest. See other Key Number Digests.

🔑32(2.7). Buildings in process of construction, alteration, or demolition.

Ala. 1981. Premises owner could not be deemed an independent contractor required to provide builders employees a safe place to work where owner had nothing to do with construction of scaffolding from which employees fell and builder provided its own materials for building scaffolding and directed manner of its construction.—Pate v. U. S. Steel Corp., 393 So.2d 992.

Premises owner could not be held liable, on theory of retained control over construction activity as a whole, for injuries which builder's employees sustained in fall from scaffolding notwithstanding that owner maintained team of engineers who daily visited the site with blueprints and specifications and pointed out deviations from contract and that owner itself oversaw activities of multiple contractors; none of such activities indicated owner control over manner of constructing furnace on which employees were working at time of injury and complexity and size of the project and elaborate means available to insure compliance did not create a master-servant relationship.—Id.

Premises owner could not be held liable, on theory of negligent inspection, for injuries which builder's employees sustained in fall from scaffold where owner made no safety inspections.—Id.

Fla.App. 1981. Metropolitan Dade County code did not adopt federal OSHA regulations by reference so as to place duty on landowners to provide safe place to work for employees of contractors engaged in construction on premises.—Goodman v. Kendall Gate-Investco., Inc., 395 So.2d 240.

Ind.App. 1980. Contractor and his employees are "invitees."—Downham v. Wagner, 408 N.E.2d 606.

🔑32(2.8). Business visitors, and store and restaurant patrons.

D.C.Neb. 1979. A "business visitor or invitee" is one who is expressly or impliedly invited or permitted to enter or remain on premises in possession of another for purpose directly or indirectly connected with business of possessor or with business dealings between them.—Strong v. Nebraska Natural Gas Co., 476 F.Supp. 1170.

D.C.Tex. 1978. Under Texas law, customer of grocery store at Air Force commissary was a "business invitee" for purposes of determining liability of storekeeper for slip and fall of customer.—Clayton v. U. S., 457 F.Supp. 173.

Ala. 1978. Duty owed by employers to baby-sitter as business invitee was exercise of ordinary and reasonable care to keep premises in reasonably safe condition.—Tice v. Tice, 361 So.2d 1051.

Ala. 1978. Log truck driver, who had been at defendants' wood yard for purpose of unloading logs that defendants had bought from driver's employer when log fell from truck and injured driver, had been a "business invitee" of defendants, and, thus, defendants had owed driver a duty not to injure him negligently, willfully or wantonly.—Elba Wood Products, Inc. v. Brackin, 356 So.2d 119.

Ala. 1977. Lady shopping in store was in store as invitee and store owed her duty of exercising ordinary or reasonable care to keep premises in reasonably safe condition.—Winn-Dixie v. Godwin, 349 So.2d 37.

Ala.Civ.App. 1981. Duty upon storekeeper is to exercise reasonable care in providing and maintaining reasonably safe premises for use of customer.—Winn-Dixie Store No. 1501 v. Brown, 394 So.2d 49.

Storekeeper is not insurer of customer's safety while on premises, but is liable for injury only in event he negligently fails to use reasonable care in maintaining his premises in reasonably safe condition.—Id.

Presence of vegetable matter on floor of store does not of itself show lack of reasonable care on part of storekeeper in maintenance of floors.—Id.

Ariz. 1979. Member of women's auxiliary of post of service club, who slipped on wet, slippery floor while assisting in kitchen of post, was neither a public invitee, since kitchen area of post was not open to public, nor a business visitor, since she volunteered her services, but was a simple licensee, to whom post was not liable in damages for open and obvious dangers.—Hicks v. Superstition Mountain Post No. 9399, Veterans of Foreign Wars of U. S., 601 P.2d 281, 123 Ariz. 518.

Ark.App. 1980. Store owner is not insurer of its customers' safety; where display is caused to fall, and customer is injured by independent act of negligence which merchant cannot reasonably be expected to foresee or guard against, merchant is not liable.—Fleming v. Wal-Mart, Inc., 595 S.W.2d 241, 268 Ark. 559.

Cal.App. 1976. Special relationship of landowner and invitee that may give rise to a duty of protection from a criminal attack by a third person involves principally two types of cases, to wit, where a person has been injured in a business establishment by criminal activity of a third person, or where a tenant or his employee has been injured by criminal conduct of a third person.—Totten v. More Oakland Residential Housing, Inc., 134 Cal.Rptr. 29.

An owner of land who holds the property open to members of the public for business purposes is subject to liability to those members when they are upon the property for such a purpose for physical harm caused by accidental, negligent, or intentionally harmful acts of third persons.—Id.

D.C.App. 1977. While grocery does not insure safety of its patrons, it must exercise reasonable care in keeping premises safe for them.—ITT Continental Baking Co. v. Ellison, 370 A.2d 1353.

Fla.App. 1980. Employee of an independent contractor of landowner had status of business visitor or invitee upon the premises of landowner.—Nurdin v. Anheuser-Busch, Inc., 392 So.2d 928.

Ga.App. 1976. In order for a person to be classified as an invitee, visitor must be on

NEGLIGENCE ☞32(2.10)

owner's premises in connection with owner's business and there must be some mutuality of interest in subject of visit between visitor and owner.—Epps v. Chattahoochee Brick Co., 231 S.E.2d 443, 140 Ga.App. 426.

Ill.App. 1980. In order for a person to be classified as an invitee it is sufficient that he go on land in furtherance of owner's business and it is not necessary that invited person gain an advantage by his entry on the land.—Barmore v. Elmore, 38 Ill.Dec. 751, 403 N.E.2d 1355.

Ill.App. 1980. Duty owed to business invitee is to exercise ordinary care in maintaining premises in a reasonably safe condition.—Hayes v. Bailey, 36 Ill.Dec. 124, 400 N.E.2d 544, 80 Ill.App.3d 1027.

Ill.App. 1979. Property owner has duty to business invitee to maintain its parking lot in reasonably safe condition.—Wolter v. Chicago Melrose Park Associates, 25 Ill.Dec. 224, 386 N.E.2d 495, 68 Ill.App.3d 1011.

Ill.App. 1979. In a business invitee situation, a landowner is required to maintain premises so as to be reasonably safe for invitee.—Sepesy v. Archer Daniels Co., 24 Ill.Dec. 220, 384 N.E.2d 1378, 66 Ill.App.3d 1053, appeal after remand 53 Ill.Dec. 273, 423 N.E.2d 942, 97 Ill.App.3d 868.

Ill.App. 1978. A person is a business invitee on premises of another if he enters by express or implied invitation, his entry is connected with possessor's business or with an activity possessor conducts or permits to be conducted on his premises and there is a mutuality of benefit or an advantage to possessor.—Longnecker v. Illinois Power Co., 21 Ill.Dec. 382, 381 N.E.2d 709, 64 Ill.App.3d 634.

Ill.App. 1978. Owners of campground containing small swimming lake in which a patron's son drowned had legal duty to make reasonable provisions and to take reasonable precautions to provide for safety of their patrons.—McClure v. Suter, 20 Ill.Dec. 308, 379 N.E.2d 1376, 63 Ill.App.3d 378.

Ind.App. 1978. When visitor has purpose that is related to occupant's pecuniary interest or advantage, invitation to use premises is inferred and visitor's status is changed with greater duty imposed.—Mullins v. Easton, 376 N.E.2d 1178, 176 Ind.App. 590.

First aspect of business invitee rule relates to economic benefit conferred upon possessor while second aspect focuses on specific invitation's implication that reasonable care has been taken; while invitation alone will not assure status of invitee, it nevertheless becomes critical to liability of private homeowner as means for distinguishing between duty he owes trespassing thief, soliciting salesman or requested repairman.—Id.

Voluntary helper of repairman, for whom landowner held rear door of her home open as he carried in one end of a heavy piece of equipment, was implicitly invited into house while carrying machine and performing function related to requested repair of clogged sewer and thus was a business invitee rather than a licensee.—Id.

La.App. 1977. Fact that female customer received free drinks at lounge on night of accident resulting in her injury did not preclude her from being considered as an invitee where it was readily inferable that lounge owner's giving of free drinks to unescorted ladies was motivated by business reasons.—Dillman v. Nobles, 351 So.2d 210.

Md.App. 1977. Application of mutual benefits theory, applied in determination of implied invitee status, generally involves conduct

of a business by possessor of land; when business is a retail store, open door is truly invitation during regular business hours.—Woodward v. Newstein, 377 A.2d 535.

Md.App. 1977. Customer of department store is classified as an "invitee."—Keene v. Arlan's Dept. Store of Baltimore, Inc., 370 A.2d 124, 35 Md.App. 250.

Mich.App. 1981. An individual can be an "invitee" if the visit may reasonably be said to confer or anticipate a business, commercial, monetary, or other tangible benefit to the occupant.—Socha v. Passino, 306 N.W.2d 316, 105 Mich.App. 445.

Mich.App. 1978. Owner of grocery store assumed duty of reasonable care as to business invitee.—McNeal v. Henry, 266 N.W.2d 469, 82 Mich.App. 88.

Minn. 1978. Construction company had continuing duty to keep premises upon which it was constructing home safe for business visitors.—Gaston v. Fazendin Const., Inc., 262 N.W.2d 434.

Mont. 1979. Where sawyer had been hired by property owner to fell trees growing on owner's ranch, cut limbs from them, and saw them into lengths capable of being hauled to an area sawmill, whether sawyer was an employee or an independent contractor, duty owed him by property owner was that of a business invitee.—Scott v. Robson, 597 P.2d 1150, 182 Mont. 528.

N.C. 1979. Owner of premises is liable for injuries resulting from his failure to exercise ordinary care to keep in a reasonably safe condition that part of premises where, during business hours, guests and other invitees may be expected.—Rappaport v. Days Inn of America, Inc., 250 S.E.2d 245, 296 N.C. 382.

N.C.App. 1980. While a store owes a customer, as an invitee, the duty of reasonable care in building its displays, the proprietor is not required to take extraordinary precautions for safety of invitees and is not an insurer of the safety of customer while on the premises.—Skinner v. Piggly Wiggly of LaGrange, Inc., 262 S.E.2d 709, 45 N.C.App. 301.

N.C.App. 1978. Grocery store customer, having entered store during business hours to purchase goods, was "invitee."—Lyvere v. Ingles Markets, Inc., 244 S.E.2d 437, 36 N.C. App. 560.

Ohio 1978. Business owner owes duty of ordinary and reasonable care for safety of his business invitees, and is required to keep his premises in reasonably safe condition; burden of producing sufficient proof that owner has failed to take safeguards that reasonable person would take under same or similar circumstances falls upon invitee.—Perry v. Eastgreen Realty Co., 372 N.E.2d 335, 53 Ohio St.2d 51, 7 O.O.3d 130.

Or. 1977. If visitor is invited to come on possessor's land to discuss business dealings between them after visitor has disclosed purpose of the visit, visitor is a "business visitor," and, thus, is entitled to expect that the portion of the house into which he has been invited has been made reasonably safe for him.—Taylor v. Baker, 566 P.2d 884, 279 Or. 139.

Or.App. 1981. Tavern owner owes to customer a duty to exercise reasonable care to protect him from injury while on tavern owner's premises; duty includes not requiring customer to leave the safety of the tavern when there is a reasonable risk of injury from patrons who have just left.—Jones v. Oberg, 628 P.2d 773, 52 Or.App. 601.

Owner of a tavern, restaurant, amusement place, or inn owes his business guests duty of

ordinary reasonable care to protect them from injury at the hands of other patrons.—Id.

Or.App. 1980. Grocery store operator had duty to provide and maintain reasonably safe place for patrons in reasonable pursuit of activities within scope of invitation, including duty to warn patrons of latent dangers of which operator was aware and also duty to ascertain condition of premises and exercise reasonable care to protect patrons from dangers foreseeable from arrangement or use of premises.—Yanzick v. Tawney, 605 P.2d 297, 44 Or.App. 59.

S.D. 1978. Landowner, was not liable for injuries sustained by utility employee on principle that landowner has nondelegable duty to keep premises safe for business invitees, where utility employees were on landowner's property to work on utility company equipment and in furtherance of utility company interests.—Moritz v. C & R Transfer Co., 266 N.W.2d 568.

Tenn.App. 1980. Where plaintiff was on shopping center parking lot owned by defendant for purpose of trading with business served by parking lot, plaintiff was an invitee and defendant owed duty of reasonable care for plaintiff's safety.—Mumford v. Thomas, 603 S.W.2d 154.

Tex.Civ.App. 1978. Servant or employee of another person who enters premises on the business of his master, in which business the master and the owner or occupant have a mutual interest, occupies the status of an invitee.—Atchison, T. & S. F. Ry. Co. v. Smith, 563 S.W.2d 660, ref. n.r.e.

Tex.Civ.App. 1977. Operators of dry cleaning establishment were not liable for injuries sustained by customer when she slipped on gravel located on driveway of premises in absence of proof that defendants placed the gravel on the driveway or knew or should have known in the exercise of reasonable care of the existence of the gravel before the accident and that it involved an unreasonable risk to customers.—Upton v. Town and Country Cleaners, 549 S.W.2d 778, ref. n.r.e.

Tex.Civ.App. 1977. Restaurant patrons were invitees of restaurant owner and therefore owner owed patrons duty of reasonable care to protect them from assaults of third persons while on the premises.—Eastep v. Jack-in-the-Box, Inc., 546 S.W.2d 116, ref. n.r.e.

Wash.App. 1976. Where customers were not prohibited from entering lubrication room of service station, customer entered lubrication room to discuss car maintenance with proprietor, customer waited his turn for service, and customer was injured when car fell from hoist, customer was not "licensee" at time of receiving injury.—Pagarigan v. Phillips Petroleum Co., 552 P.2d 1065, 16 Wash.App. 34.

☞32(2.9). Deliverymen and haulers.

No cases for period of this Digest. See other Key Number Digests.

☞32(2.10). Employees and contractors.

D.C.Ala. 1980. Under Alabama law, owner of premises owes same duty to employee of independent contractor that he owes to invitee and such duty is to maintain premises in reasonably safe condition.—Tatem v. U. S., 499 F.Supp. 1105.

D.C.Neb. 1979. Under Nebraska law, employees of gas company who were killed while inspecting hotel for gas leaks were "business invitees" of owner of hotel and she therefore

West's
GENERAL DIGEST

SIXTH SERIES

A Digest of all Current Decisions of the American
Courts as Reported in the National Reporter
System and other Standard Reports

Including
DESCRIPTIVE–WORD INDEX

Cumulative
TABLE OF KEY NUMBERS

TABLE OF CASES

Cumulative
TABLE OF CASES
Affirmed, Reversed or Modified

Continuing
The Ninth Decennial Digest Part I

Volume 44

ST. PAUL, MINN.
WEST PUBLISHING CO.
1986

relates to land or other immovables, it directly causes the injury, defendant was engaged directly in the injury-producing activity and the substandard conduct of a third party or the victim was not a necessary contributing cause of the injury.—Matthews v. Ashland Chemical, Inc., 770 F.2d 1303.

La.App. 4 Cir. 1985. Proper test of landowner's duty is whether, in management of his property, he acted as reasonable man in view of probability of injury to others.—Spurlock v. Schwegmann Bros. Giant Supermarket, 475 So.2d 20.

N.Y.A.D. 2 Dept. 1985. Standard of care applicable to occupiers of land is that of reasonable care under the circumstances, whereby foreseeability is the measure of liability.—Craft v. Mid Island Dept. Stores, Inc., 492 N.Y.S.2d 780.

⟜31. Requirements of statutes or ordinances.

Ariz.App. 1985. Regulations specifying the distance at which supports are to placed in the installation of mobile homes could not be used to impose duty on landowner to employee of independent contractor installing mobile home on landowner's land.—Cordova v. Parrett, 703 P.2d 1228.

Restatement (Second) of Torts § 424 (1965), imposing liability for failure to abide by statute or regulation imposing a duty to safeguard others, does not apply in the area of tort law governing the relationship of the employer of an independent contractor to an employee of that contractor.—Id.

Ill. 1985. Air-compressor equipment which rested on an elevated concrete platform was not a "structure" within meaning of the Structural Work Act [S.H.A. ch. 48, ¶ 60].—Innis v. Elmhurst Dodge, Inc., 89 Ill.Dec. 866, 481 N.E.2d 709, 107 Ill.2d 151.

Ill.App. 5 Dist. 1985. In order for plaintiff to recover in an action brought under Structural Work Act [S.H.A. ch. 48, ¶ 60 et seq.] plaintiff must establish that he was engaged in or was passing under or by a structural activity, that the activity was being performed with reference to a structure, that a scaffold or other mechanical device was being used, that a defect existed in construction or use of the device, that the defect proximately caused his injuries, that defendant had charge of the work, and that defendant wilfully violated the Act's safety standard.—McMahon v. Richard Gorazd, Inc., 89 Ill.Dec. 944, 481 N.E.2d 787, 135 Ill.App.3d 211.

A wilful violation of Structural Work Act [S.H.A. ch. 48, ¶ 60 et seq.] occurs when one having charge of the work knows that a dangerous condition exists or by exercise of reasonable care could have discovered existence of the dangerous condition.—Id.

Where only plaintiff's negligence causes the injuries, no liability arises under Structural Work Act [S.H.A. ch. 48, ¶ 60 et seq.].—Id.

N.Y. 1985. Absolute liability for injuries sustained by worker is imposed upon owner or contractor who has failed to provide any safety devices for workers at building work site where absence of such devices is proximate cause of injury to worker, and liability is mandated without regard to external considerations such as rules and regulations, contracts or custom and usage. McKinney's Labor Law §§ 240, subd. 1, 241, subds. 1–5.—Zimmer v. Chemung County Performing Arts, Inc., 493 N.Y.S.2d 102, 65 N.Y.2d 513, 482 N.E.2d 898.

Building owner and several contractors were liable to ironworker for injuries sustained when he fell while erecting steel skeleton for construction project, as no safety devices were provided to ironworker at the work site. McKinney's Labor Law §§ 240, subd. 1, 241, subd. 4.—Id.

Building owner and general contractor were liable to welder who fell from roof of building upon which he was working, as no safety devices were provided to welder at work site. McKinney's Labor Law § 240, subd. 1.—Id.

N.Y.A.D. 2 Dept. 1985. Where no work was being done in apartment subject to renovation at specific time minor plaintiffs sustained injury when dishwasher tipped over, causing hot water to fall upon them, plaintiffs had no cause of action against landlord under § 241 of Labor Law, requiring certain safety precautions at site of construction, excavation, or demolition work. McKinney's Labor Law §§ 241, 241, subds. 6–8.—Sharaby v. Gamel, 493 N.Y.S.2d 211.

⟜32. Care as to licensees or persons invited.

⟜32(1). In general.

Md.App. 1985. In negligence actions, standard of care required of owners and occupiers of land with respect to individual on their land is determined by individual's status on property, that is, whether he is invitee, licensee, or trespasser.—Mech v. Hearst Corp., 496 A.2d 1099, 64 Md.App. 422.

Common-law distinctions regarding standard of care to invitees, licensees, and trespassers would not be abolished.—Id.

⟜32(2). Who are licensees, and status of person going on land of another in general.

D.C.Me. 1985. A "licensee" differs from a trespasser in that he is lawfully on the premises by virtue of possessor's express or implied consent.—Bonney v. Canadian Nat. Ry. Co., 613 F.Supp. 997.

⟜32(2.2). Bare licensees.

D.C.Me. 1985. Under Maine law, a possessor of land owes same duty to a licensee as to an invitee, that is, a duty of ordinary care.—Bonney v. Canadian Nat. Ry. Co., 613 F.Supp. 997.

Md.App. 1985. Where person is "bare licensee," that is, one who enters property for his own purpose or convenience and with landowner's consent but not as social guest, or "trespasser," defined as those who enter without privilege or consent of landowner, law poses only minimal obligation on landowner to refrain from willfully or wantonly injuring or entrapping person once his presence is known.—Mech v. Hearst Corp., 496 A.2d 1099, 64 Md.App. 422.

⟜32(2.3). Invitees in general.

Ga.App. 1985. Two elements must exist in order for an invitee to recover for a proprietor's negligent failure to maintain safe premises: fault on part of proprietor; and ignorance of danger on part of invitee.—Bell v. Abercorn Toyota, Inc., 333 S.E.2d 880, 175 Ga.App. 668.

Ill.App. 5 Dist. 1985. Duty of reasonable care is owed to one on master's premises by express or implied invitation of master, and master is thus liable to such invitee for negligent acts of his servant.—Wilson v. Clark Oil & Refining Corp., 90 Ill.Dec. 40, 481 N.E.2d 840, 134 Ill.App.3d 1084.

Distinction between invitee of property owner and mere licensee, to whom owner is liable only for wilful and wanton conduct, rests upon whether injured person has entered premises to transact business in which parties are mutually interested, in which case he is invitee, or to satisfy his own purposes, in which case he is licensee.—Id.

Md.App. 1985. Generally, term "invitees," for purpose of determination of standard to be used in negligence action, are those who enter subject property in connection with owner's business.—Mech v. Hearst Corp., 496 A.2d 1099, 64 Md.App. 422.

Tex.App. 7 Dist. 1985. Occupier of land owes duty to invitee to exercise ordinary care to maintain premises in reasonably safe condition or to warn invitee of any dangerous conditions which occupier knows or should know about and which are not reasonably apparent to invitee.—Bryant v. Gulf Oil Corp., 694 S.W.2d 443.

⟜32(2.4). Implied invitation in general.

Ill.App. 5 Dist. 1985. Duty of reasonable care is owed to one on master's premises by express or implied invitation of master, and master is thus liable to such invitee for negligent acts of his servant.—Wilson v. Clark Oil & Refining Corp., 90 Ill.Dec. 40, 481 N.E.2d 840, 134 Ill.App.3d 1084.

Md.App. 1985. Invitation to enter upon land may be implied from circumstances such as custom, acquiescence of owner in habitual use, the apparent holding out of premises to particular use by public, or simply in general arrangement and design of premises.—Mech v. Hearst Corp., 496 A.2d 1099, 64 Md.App. 422.

In order for there to be implied invitation to enter upon land, there must be, in conduct or words of possessor, some inducement or encouragement to enter, and mere permission or acquiescence is not sufficient.—Id.

Neither open gateway to property, nor any of other characteristics of property described at trial suggested that property owner had acquiesced or consented, expressly or otherwise, to individual's entry on site, and absent such consent or acquiescence, individual could only have been trespasser.—Id.

⟜32(2.8). Business visitors, and store and restaurant patrons.

La.App. 2 Cir. 1985. High duty of a store owner toward a customer is twofold, first to discover unreasonably dangerous conditions, and second, to take reasonable steps to prevent injury resulting from unreasonably dangerous conditions.—Johnson v. Tayco Foods, 475 So.2d 65.

A store owner is not the insurer of the safety of its customer.—Id.

La.App. 4 Cir. 1985. A store owner, although having duty to take reasonable care for safety of patrons, is not the insurer of the patrons' safety.—Spurlock v. Schwegmann Bros. Giant Supermarket, 475 So.2d 20.

Owner of self-service gas station did not breach duty to customer pinned against rear of his automobile by another automobile left unattended in neutral gear with engine running, since incident was unforeseeable and too remote to come within scope of owner's duty to its customers.—Id.

N.C.App. 1985. Proprietor of place of business open to public patronage is obligated to keep approaches and entrances to his establishment in reasonably safe condition for use of customers entering or leaving premises and to give warning of hidden perils or unsafe conditions insofar as they are known or can be ascertained by reasonable inspection.—Pasour v. Pierce, 333 S.E.2d 314.

Tex.App. 1 Dist. 1985. Owner of business premises owes business invitee a duty to keep those premises in reasonably safe condition, to inspect premises to discover any latent defects, and to make safe any defects or else give adequate warnings.—K-Mart Apparel Fashions Corp. v. Ramsey, 695 S.W.2d 243.

⟜32(2.10). Employees and contractors.

Tex.App. 7 Dist. 1985. Owner/occupier of land is not insurer, where individual's injury arises out of performance of work for which independent contractor was employed and while

American Digest Problem II

Trace the same key number, Negligence, ☞32(2.8) back to the earliest cases in the Decennial digests.

NINTH
DECENNIAL DIGEST

Part I

AMERICAN DIGEST SYSTEM

1976–1981

*A Complete Digest of All Decisions of the State and
Federal Courts as Reported in the National
Reporter System and the State Reports*

Volume 25

MINES AND MINERALS —
NEGLIGENCE ⚷120

ST. PAUL, MINN.
WEST PUBLISHING CO.

circumstances.—Yalowizer v. Husky Oil Co., 629 P.2d 465.

32(2.4). Implied invitation in general.

Ga.App. 1976. Where landowner knew that masonry man was helping him pour concrete, utilized his help, and by his actions accepted masonry man's implied offer of assistance, and benefit of masonry man's efforts was entirely for landowner, masonry man was landowner's invitee to whom landowner owed ordinary duty of care.—Speir v. Stephenson, 227 S.E.2d 469, 138 Ga.App. 690.

For purpose of establishing status of invitee, request by landowner that alleged invitee come to landowner's property for sole benefit of landowner may be either express or implied.—Id.

Ill.App. 1980. Person is invitee on land of another if he enters by invitation, express or implied, his entry is connected with owner's business or with activity that owner conducts or permits to be conducted on his land, and there is mutuality of benefit or a benefit to the owner.—Barmore v. Elmore, 38 Ill.Dec. 751, 403 N.E.2d 1355.

Ill.App. 1978. Generally an "invitee" is defined as one who enters upon premises of another in response to an express or implied invitation for the purpose of transacting business in which the parties are mutually interested.—Sepesy v. Archer Daniels Co., 16 Ill. Dec. 549, 375 N.E.2d 180, 59 Ill.App.3d 56, supplemented 24 Ill.Dec. 220, 384 N.E.2d 1378, 66 Ill.App.3d 1053, remanded 36 Ill. Dec. 957, 401 N.E.2d 1391, 71 Ill.2d 615, appeal after remand 53 Ill.Dec. 273, 423 N.E.2d 942, 97 Ill.App.3d 868.

Ind.App. 1980. Status of invitee is created by entering premises with occupant's express or implied invitation to transact business or to perform some act which is to commercial advantage of occupant.—Downham v. Wagner, 408 N.E.2d 606.

Md.App. 1977. Invitation by which one becomes an invitee may be express or implied.—Woodward v. Newstein, 377 A.2d 535.

Under implied invitation doctrine, before status of invitee may be established by implication there must be, in conduct or words of possessor of land, some inducement or encouragement to enter, and mere permission or acquiescence is not sufficient.—Id.

Fact that owners' newspaper advertisements stating that defendants' vacation home was for sale were published almost four years prior to accident, and realtors' advertisements one and one-half years prior, that neither advertisements gave address of vacation home, that owners posted no "For Sale" sign, and other facts compelled conclusion that no invitation could reasonably be construed under either theory applied in determination of implied invitee status as extending to plaintiffs who sustained injuries when deck of defendants' vacation home collapsed under them.—Id.

Mich.App. 1978. Permission to come upon land may be implied where the landowner acquiesces in the known, customary use of the property by the public.—Thone v. Nicholson, 269 N.W.2d 665, 84 Mich.App. 538.

Tex.Civ.App. 1978. "Invitee" is person who goes on the premises of another in answer to the express or implied invitation of the owner or occupant or the business of the owner or occupant or for their mutual advantage, and "implied invitation" is one which is extended by reason of owner or occupant doing something or permitting something to be done

which fairly indicates to the person entering that his entry and use of the property are consistent with the intentions and purposes of the owner or occupant and that the use is in accordance with the design for which the place is adapted and allowed to be used in mutuality of interests.—Atchison, T. & S. F. Ry. Co. v. Smith, 563 S.W.2d 660, ref. n.r.e.

32(2.5). Automobile service stations and parking service.

D.C.D.C. 1981. Owner of parking lot could not be held liable for abduction and rape of patron as she left parking lot where assailant was not employee of owner, there had been no history of such criminals in area, and parking lot owner had no control over actions of assailant.—Gillot v. Washington Metropolitan Area Transit Authority, 507 F.Supp. 454.

32(2.6). Bill collectors.

No cases for period of this Digest. See other Key Number Digests.

32(2.7). Buildings in process of construction, alteration, or demolition.

Ala. 1981. Premises owner could not be deemed an independent contractor required to provide builders employees a safe place to work where owner had nothing to do with construction of scaffolding from which employees fell and builder provided its own materials for building scaffolding and directed manner of its construction.—Pate v. U. S. Steel Corp., 393 So.2d 992.

Premises owner could not be held liable, on theory of retained control over construction activity as a whole, for injuries which builder's employees sustained in fall from scaffolding notwithstanding that owner maintained team of engineers who daily visited the site with blueprints and specifications and pointed out deviations from contract and that owner itself oversaw activities of multiple contractors; none of such activities indicated owner control over manner of constructing furnace on which employees were working at time of injury and complexity and size of the project and elaborate means available to insure compliance did not create a master-servant relationship.—Id.

Premises owner could not be held liable, on theory of negligent inspection, for injuries which builder's employees sustained in fall from scaffold where owner made no safety inspections.—Id.

Fla.App. 1981. Metropolitan Dade County code did not adopt federal OSHA regulations by reference so as to place duty on landowners to provide safe place to work for employees of contractors engaged in construction on premises.—Goodman v. Kendall Gate-Investco, Inc., 395 So.2d 240.

Ind.App. 1980. Contractor and his employees are "invitees."—Downham v. Wagner, 408 N.E.2d 606.

32(2.8). Business visitors, and store and restaurant patrons.

D.C.Neb. 1979. A "business visitor or invitee" is one who is expressly or impliedly invited or permitted to enter or remain on premises in possession of another for purpose directly or indirectly connected with business of possessor or with business dealings between them.—Strong v. Nebraska Natural Gas Co., 476 F.Supp. 1170.

D.C.Tex. 1978. Under Texas law, customer of grocery store at Air Force commissary was a "business invitee" for purposes of determining liability of storekeeper for slip and fall of customer.—Clayton v. U. S., 457 F.Supp. 173.

Ala. 1978. Duty owed by employers to baby-sitter as business invitee was exercise of ordinary and reasonable care to keep premises in reasonably safe condition.—Tice v. Tice, 361 So.2d 1051.

Ala. 1978. Log truck driver, who had been at defendants' wood yard for purpose of unloading logs that defendants had bought from driver's employer when log fell from truck and injured driver, had been a "business invitee" of defendants, and, thus, defendants had owed driver a duty not to injure him negligently, willfully or wantonly.—Elba Wood Products, Inc. v. Brackin, 356 So.2d 119.

Ala. 1977. Lady shopping in store was in store as invitee and store owed her duty of exercising ordinary or reasonable care to keep premises in reasonably safe condition.—Winn-Dixie v. Godwin, 349 So.2d 37.

Ala.Civ.App. 1981. Duty upon storekeeper is to exercise reasonable care in providing and maintaining reasonably safe premises for use of customer.—Winn-Dixie Store No. 1501 v. Brown, 394 So.2d 49.

Storekeeper is not insurer of customer's safety while on premises, but is liable for injury only in event he negligently fails to use reasonable care in maintaining his premises in reasonably safe condition.—Id.

Presence of vegetable matter on floor of store does not of itself show lack of reasonable care on part of storekeeper in maintenance of floors.—Id.

Ariz. 1979. Member of women's auxiliary of post of service club, who slipped on wet, slippery floor while assisting in kitchen of post, was neither a public invitee, since kitchen area of post was not open to public, nor a business visitor, since she volunteered her services, but was a simple licensee, to whom post was not liable in damages for open and obvious dangers.—Hicks v. Superstition Mountain Post No. 9399, Veterans of Foreign Wars of U. S., 601 P.2d 281, 123 Ariz. 518.

Ark.App. 1980. Store owner is not insurer of its customers' safety; where display is caused to fall, and customer is injured by independent act of negligence which merchant cannot reasonably be expected to foresee or guard against, merchant is not liable.—Fleming v. Wal-Mart, Inc., 595 S.W.2d 241, 268 Ark. 559.

Cal.App. 1976. Special relationship of landowner and invitee that may give rise to a duty of protection from a criminal attack by a third person involves principally two types of cases, to wit, where a person has been injured in a business establishment by criminal activity of a third person, or where a tenant or his employee has been injured by criminal conduct of a third person.—Totten v. More Oakland Residential Housing, Inc., 134 Cal.Rptr. 29.

An owner of land who holds the property open to members of the public for business purposes is subject to liability to those members when they are upon the property for such a purpose for physical harm caused by accidental, negligent, or intentionally harmful acts of third persons.—Id.

D.C.App. 1977. While grocery does not insure safety of its patrons, it must exercise reasonable care in keeping premises safe for them.—ITT Continental Baking Co. v. Ellison, 370 A.2d 1353.

Fla.App. 1980. Employee of an independent contractor of landowner had status of business visitor or invitee upon the premises of landowner.—Nurdin v. Anheuser-Busch, Inc., 392 So.2d 928.

Ga.App. 1976. In order for a person to be classified as an invitee, visitor must be on wner's premises in connection with owner's ─usiness and there must be some mutuality of ─nterest in subject of visit between visitor and ─wner.—Epps v. Chattahoochee Brick Co., 231 ─.E.2d 443, 140 Ga.App. 426.

Ill.App. 1980. In order for a person to be ─lassified as an invitee it is sufficient that he ─o on land in furtherance of owner's business ─nd it is not necessary that invited person gain ─n advantage by his entry on the land.—Bar─more v. Elmore, 38 Ill.Dec. 751, 403 N.E.2d ─355.

Ill.App. 1980. Duty owed to business invi─ee is to exercise ordinary care in maintaining ─remises in a reasonably safe condition.— ─ayes v. Bailey, 36 Ill.Dec. 124, 400 N.E.2d ─44, 80 Ill.App.3d 1027.

Ill.App. 1979. Property owner has duty to ─usiness invitee to maintain its parking lot in ─easonably safe condition.—Wolter v. Chicago ─elrose Park Associates, 25 Ill.Dec. 224, 386 ─.E.2d 495, 68 Ill.App.3d 1011.

Ill.App. 1979. In a business invitee situa─ion, a landowner is required to maintain ─remises so as to be reasonably safe for invi─ee.—Sepesy v. Archer Daniels Co., 24 Ill.Dec. ─20, 384 N.E.2d 1378, 66 Ill.App.3d 1053, ─ppeal after remand 53 Ill.Dec. 273, 423 ─.E.2d 942, 97 Ill.App.3d 868.

Ill.App. 1978. A person is a business invi─ee on premises of another if he enters by ─xpress or implied invitation, his entry is con─ected with possessor's business or with an ─ctivity possessor conducts or permits to be ─onducted on his premises and there is a ─utuality of benefit or an advantage to pos─essor.—Longnecker v. Illinois Power Co., 21 ─ll.Dec. 382, 381 N.E.2d 709, 64 Ill.App.3d ─634.

Ill.App. 1978. Owners of campground con─aining small swimming lake in which a pa─ron's son drowned had legal duty to make ─easonable provisions and to take reasonable ─recautions to provide for safety of their pa─rons.—McClure v. Suter, 20 Ill.Dec. 308, 379 ─.E.2d 1376, 63 Ill.App.3d 378.

Ind.App. 1978. When visitor has purpose ─hat is related to occupant's pecuniary inter─est or advantage, invitation to use premises is ─nferred and visitor's status is changed with ─reater duty imposed.—Mullins v. Easton, 376 ─.E.2d 1178, 176 Ind.App. 590.

First aspect of business invitee rule relates ─o economic benefit conferred upon possessor ─while second aspect focuses on specific invita─tion's implication that reasonable care has ─been taken; while invitation alone will not ─assure status of invitee, it nevertheless be─comes critical to liability of private homeowner ─as means for distinguishing between duty he ─owes trespassing thief, soliciting salesman or ─requested repairman.—Id.

Voluntary helper of repairman, for whom ─landowner held rear door of her home open as ─he carried in one end of a heavy piece of ─equipment, was implicitly invited into house ─while carrying machine and performing func─tion related to requested repair of clogged ─sewer and thus was a business invitee rather ─than a licensee.—Id.

La.App. 1977. Fact that female customer ─received free drinks at lounge on night of ─accident resulting in her injury did not pre─clude her from being considered as an invitee ─where it was readily inferable that lounge ─owner's giving of free drinks to unescorted ─ladies was motivated by business reasons.— ─Dillman v. Nobles, 351 So.2d 210.

Md.App. 1977. Application of mutual ben─efits theory, applied in determination of im─plied invitee status, generally involves conduct

of a business by possessor of land; when business is a retail store, open door is truly invitation during regular business hours.— Woodward v. Newstein, 377 A.2d 535.

Md.App. 1977. Customer of department store is classified as an "invitee."—Keene v. Arlan's Dept. Store of Baltimore, Inc., 370 A.2d 124, 35 Md.App. 250.

Mich.App. 1981. An individual can be an "invitee" if the visit may reasonably be said to confer or anticipate a business, commercial, monetary, or other tangible benefit to the occupant.—Socha v. Passino, 306 N.W.2d 316, 105 Mich.App. 445.

Mich.App. 1978. Owner of grocery store assumed duty of reasonable care as to business invitee.—McNeal v. Henry, 266 N.W.2d 469, 82 Mich.App. 88.

Minn. 1978. Construction company had continuing duty to keep premises upon which it was constructing home safe for business visitors.—Gaston v. Fazendin Const., Inc., 262 N.W.2d 434.

Mont. 1979. Where sawyer had been hired by property owner to fell trees growing on owner's ranch, cut limbs from them, and saw them into lengths capable of being hauled to an area sawmill, whether sawyer was an employee or an independent contractor, duty owed him by property owner was that of a business invitee.—Scott v. Robson, 597 P.2d 1150, 182 Mont. 528.

N.C. 1979. Owner of premises is liable for injuries resulting from his failure to exercise ordinary care to keep in a reasonably safe condition that part of premises where, during business hours, guests and other invitees may be expected.—Rappaport v. Days Inn of America, Inc., 250 S.E.2d 245, 296 N.C. 382.

N.C.App. 1980. While a store owes a customer, as an invitee, the duty of reasonable care in building its displays, the proprietor is not required to take extraordinary precautions for safety of invitees and is not an insurer of the safety of customer while on the premises. —Skinner v. Piggly Wiggly of LaGrange, Inc., 262 S.E.2d 709, 45 N.C.App. 301.

N.C.App. 1978. Grocery store customer, having entered store during business hours to purchase goods, was "invitee."—Lyvere v. Ingles Markets, Inc., 244 S.E.2d 437, 36 N.C. App. 560.

Ohio 1978. Business owner owes duty of ordinary and reasonable care for safety of his business invitees, and is required to keep his premises in reasonably safe condition; burden of producing sufficient proof that owner has failed to take safeguards that reasonable person would take under same or similar circumstances falls upon invitee.—Perry v. Eastgreen Realty Co., 372 N.E.2d 335, 53 Ohio St.2d 51, 7 O.O.3d 130.

Or. 1977. If visitor is invited to come on possessor's land to discuss business dealings between them after visitor has disclosed purpose of the visit, visitor is a "business visitor," and, thus, is entitled to expect that the portion of the house into which he has been invited has been made reasonably safe for him.—Taylor v. Baker, 566 P.2d 884, 279 Or. 139.

Or.App. 1981. Tavern owner owes to customer a duty to exercise reasonable care to protect him from injury while on tavern owner's premises; duty includes not requiring customer to leave the safety of the tavern when there is a reasonable risk of injury from patrons who have just left.—Jones v. Oberg, 628 P.2d 773, 52 Or.App. 601.

Owner of a tavern, restaurant, amusement place, or inn owes his business guests duty of

ordinary reasonable care to protect them from injury at the hands of other patrons.—Id.

Or.App. 1980. Grocery store operator had duty to provide and maintain reasonably safe place for patrons in reasonable pursuit of activities within scope of invitation, including duty to warn patrons of latent dangers of which operator was aware and also duty to ascertain condition of premises and exercise reasonable care to protect patrons from dangers foreseeable from arrangement or use of premises.—Yanzick v. Tawney, 605 P.2d 297, 44 Or.App. 59.

S.D. 1978. Landowner, was not liable for injuries sustained by utility employee on principle that landowner has nondelegable duty to keep premises safe for business invitees, where utility employees were on landowner's property to work on utility company equipment and in furtherance of utility company interests.— Moritz v. C & R Transfer Co., 266 N.W.2d 568.

Tenn.App. 1980. Where plaintiff was on shopping center parking lot owned by defendant for purpose of trading with business served by parking lot, plaintiff was an invitee and defendant owed duty of reasonable care for plaintiff's safety.—Mumford v. Thomas, 603 S.W.2d 154.

Tex.Civ.App. 1978. Servant or employee of another person who enters premises on the business of his master, in which business the master and the owner or occupant have a mutual interest, occupies the status of an invitee.—Atchison, T. & S. F. Ry. Co. v. Smith, 563 S.W.2d 660, ref. n.r.e.

Tex.Civ.App. 1977. Operators of dry cleaning establishment were not liable for injuries sustained by customer when she slipped on gravel located on driveway of premises in absence of proof that defendants placed the gravel on the driveway or knew or should have known in the exercise of reasonable care of the existence of the gravel before the accident and that it involved an unreasonable risk to customers.—Upton v. Town and Country Cleaners, 549 S.W.2d 778, ref. n.r.e.

Tex.Civ.App. 1977. Restaurant patrons were invitees of restaurant owner and therefore owner owed patrons duty of reasonable care to protect them from assaults of third persons while on the premises.—Eastep v. Jack-in-the-Box, Inc., 546 S.W.2d 116, ref. n.r.e.

Wash.App. 1976. Where customers were not prohibited from entering lubrication room of service station, customer entered lubrication room to discuss car maintenance with proprietor, customer waited his turn for service, and customer was injured when car fell from hoist, customer was not "licensee" at time of receiving injury.—Pagarigan v. Phillips Petroleum Co., 552 P.2d 1065, 16 Wash.App. 34.

🗝32(2.9). Deliverymen and haulers.

No cases for period of this Digest. See other Key Number Digests.

🗝32(2.10). Employees and contractors.

D.C.Ala. 1980. Under Alabama law, owner of premises owes same duty to employee of independent contractor that he owes to invitee and such duty is to maintain premises in reasonably safe condition.—Tatem v. U. S., 499 F.Supp. 1105.

D.C.Neb. 1979. Under Nebraska law, employees of gas company who were killed while inspecting hotel for gas leaks were "business invitees" of owner of hotel and she therefore

EIGHTH
DECENNIAL DIGEST

AMERICAN DIGEST SYSTEM

1966-1976

A Complete Digest of All Decisions of the State and Federal Courts as Reported in the National Reporter System and the State Reports

Volume 31

MUNICIPAL CORPORATIONS 80

TO

NEGLIGENCE 55

ST. PAUL, MINN.
WEST PUBLISHING CO.

vice area in attempt to locate service manager was, in absence of signs prohibiting customers from going into service area and in light of testimony that customers did walk back into service area at times, an invitee and not a trespasser.—Geeck v. Garrard-Milner Chevrolet, Inc., 243 So.2d 294.

Md. 1972. Signs on parking lot which indicated that the pay lot was for nearby hotel would not lead reasonable pedestrian to assume that there was an express invitation to the public as well as to employees of the hotel to cross the premises in order to go to the hotel.—Gray v. Sentinel Auto Parks Co., 288 A.2d 121, 265 Md. 61.

Where lessees of parking lot for hotel were simply lessees of the parking area under commercial percentage lease and had no control over design of hotel complex, including the location of the employees' entrance, implied invitation, if any, from design of hotel complex for hotel employees to cross parking lot did not stem from the lessees and, in absence of any joint management or control of the parking lot by the lessees and the hotel management, hotel employee who fractured her left ankle when she slipped on thin sheet of ice while crossing the parking lot was not an invitee of the lessees.—Id.

Implied permission from lessees of parking lot for hotel employee to cross the lot in order to reach employees' entrance to hotel was not the same as implied invitation to cross the lot and there was no duty on part of the lessees to keep their premises safe for the employee who was a bare licensee.—Id.

Md. 1967. Woman injured in fall on stairway installed to provide access to road from parking area for defendant's department store was an invitee rather than a licensee, notwithstanding that she had not parked her automobile in defendant's parking area with intention of necessarily shopping in defendant's store, where general appearance of parking area as well as large number of parking spaces insured likelihood that place to park would be available and it appeared that public was invited to enter, make use of parking area and visit stores in shopping center.—Hutzler Bros. Co. v. Taylor, 230 A.2d 663, 247 Md. 228.

🗝 32(2.6). Bill collectors.

No cases for period of this Digest. See other Key Number Digests.

🗝 32(2.7). Buildings in process of construction, alteration, or demolition.

C.A.Md. 1967. Individual who, under separate contract with owner, was to install bedspreads, drapes and bed canopies in apartment house under construction and who was injured when, while working in the evening to finish certain work on time, he fell into hole in floor while he was walking in unfinished, unlighted work area in search of a stool, could not be deemed an invitee of the prime contractor which was not in any way concerned as to whether decoration of the apartment was completed in time to be suitable for showing on specified date, and the injured individual, with respect to the prime contractor, was at most a licensee or perhaps a trespasser.—Worz v. Abe Pollin, Inc., 384 F.2d 549.

Tex. 1968. A contractor's or subcontractor's employee using equipment of another subcontractor engaged on same general project is licensee of owner of equipment, at least in absence of showing that its use by others worked in some way to benefit of owner, and accordingly employee injured by defective condition of equipment is not enti-

tled to recover against its owner for ordinary negligence in construction or maintenance.—Olivier v. Snowden, 426 S.W.2d 545.

Where general contractor and plastering subcontractor followed the custom of using each other's scaffolds already in place and employee of general contractor used unsafe scaffold of plastering subcontractor and was injured when it broke, and where subcontractor received no benefit or advantage from the permitted use of the scaffold, relationship between subcontractor and general contractor's employee was that of licensor and licensee or that of lender and borrower of a chattel, and subcontractor was not liable for injuries sustained by employee.—Id.

🗝 32(2.8). Business visitors, and store and restaurant patrons.

C.A.Mass. 1968. Business invitee, under Massachusetts law, has right to expect reasonable care in maintenance of premises he visits.—Burns v. Turner Const. Co., 402 F.2d 332.

Licensee, under Massachusetts law, is entitled to complain of nothing short of wanton or reckless conduct.—Id.

Status of "business invitee" is created where there is a real or apparent intent on part of invitor to benefit in a business or commercial sense, under Massachusetts law.—Id.

Injured doctor who attended lecture at one hospital and subsequently visited lecturing doctor after lecture, for undisclosed reasons, at another hospital where he was injured, was not "business invitee" and could not recover for injuries sustained as result of contractor's failure to bolt railing into cradles of newly constructed outside platform that led to hospital stairway.—Id.

C.A.Tenn. 1966. Store customer was an invitee on store premises whose proprietor owed a duty to keep the premises in a reasonably safe condition for all persons who were lawfully on premises and in the exercise of due care for their own safety.—Sharp v. J. C. Penney Co., 361 F.2d 722.

D.C.Ohio 1967. Under Ohio law, person in possession and control of place of business, who invites people into premises, may be liable to patron who is injured because of dangerously slippery condition of floors.—Bardon v. U. S., 294 F.Supp. 797, affirmed 403 F.2d 713.

Party who came to premises to transact business with Social Security Office and who slipped on floor of premises was "business visitor".—Id.

D.C.Pa. 1972. A "business invitee" is one who is invited or permitted to enter or remain on premises of another for a purpose directly or indirectly connected with business dealings between them; a "licensee" is one who is privileged to enter or remain on premises only by virtue of possessor's consent.—Phillips v. Winters' Cleaners & Tailors, Inc., 344 F.Supp. 1040, affirmed 485 F.2d 681.

D.C.Pa. 1969. Under Pennsylvania law, government sub-subcontractor's employee was a business invitee on United States' property.—Fisher v. U. S., 299 F.Supp. 1, reversed 441 F.2d 1288.

D.C.Pa. 1966. Decedent, whose administrator brought wrongful death action, and who was employee for sub-subcontractor under general contract for construction of crane runway and supports, was a business visitor, and he was entitled to expect that general contractor, in possession and control of work premises, through its field superintendent and

its welding supervisor in actual charge [ ] welding work on day of accident would t[ ] reasonable care to ascertain actual conditi[ ] and give warning to decedent's foreman an[ ] decedent of presence of bronze plates in vic[ ] ty of rewelding project and risk involved i[ ] handhold was to be rigged so as to compl[ ] rewelding project.—Coyne v. Marquette [ ] ment Mfg. Co., 254 F.Supp. 380.

Ala. 1968. Grocery store customer was [ ] "invitee" of store operator.—Foodto[ ] Stores, Inc. v. Patterson, 213 So.2d 211, 2[ ] Ala. 477.

Ala.Civ.App. 1973. A person who g[ ] upon the premises of another for purpo[ ] connected with the business of the owner [ ] occupant of the premises is an "invitee.[ ] Winn-Dixie Montgomery, Inc. v. Rowell, 2[ ] So.2d 785, writ denied 288 So.2d 792.

Alaska 1968. Where homeowners' gra[ ] daughter was not trespasser when she sp[ ] night at their home without their knowle[ ] taxicab driver who was called to the prem[ ] by granddaughter and who, while upon prop[ ] ty, was injured in fall was a "licensee.[ ] McKean v. Hammond, 445 P.2d 679.

Cal. 1968. "Invitee" is business visitor [ ] vited or permitted to enter or remain on l[ ] for purpose directly or indirectly connec[ ] with business dealings between possessor a[ ] invitee.—Rowland v. Christian, 443 P.2d 5[ ] 70 Cal.Rptr. 97, 69 C.2d 108, 32 A.L.R[ ] 496.

Cal. 1966. An "invitee" is either pu[ ] invitee or business visitor; "public invitee[ ] person who is invited to enter or remain [ ] land as member of public for purpose for wh[ ] land is held open to public, while "busi[ ] visitor" is person who is invited to enter [ ] remain on land for purpose directly or indire[ ] ly connected with business dealings with p[ ] sessor.—O'Keefe v. South End Rowing C[ ] 414 P.2d 830, 51 Cal.Rptr. 534, 64 C.2d 7[ ] 16 A.L.R.3d 1.

Cal.App. 1967. Prospective patron w[ ] tripped over a drainage berm in a priv[ ] walkway that served as one of the approac[ ] to back door of defendants' restaurant [ ] quired status of invitee even though the p[ ] tion of drainage berm over which she trip[ ] was not located on defendants' property [ ] view of implied invitation to public to use b[ ] door of restaurant.—Ross v. Kirby, 59 C[ ] Rptr. 601, 251 C.A.2d 267.

Colo. 1966. "Invitee" is one who con[ ] upon premises of another to transact busin[ ] in which parties are mutually interested [ ] Husser v. School Dist. No. 11 in El P[ ] County, 413 P.2d 906, 159 Colo. 590.

Colo.App. 1971. Where grocery store op[ ] ator provided a check-cashing service for [ ] customers, customer was a business invitee [ ] whom operator had a duty to use reasona[ ] care to keep premises in a reasonably s[ ] condition whether customer was in store [ ] cash check or to buy groceries.—Millers Su[ ] Markets v. Hobart, 482 P.2d 413.

Del.Super. 1971. Under statute provid[ ] that no person who comes onto premises oc[ ] pied by another as his guest without paym[ ] shall have a cause of action for dama[ ] against the occupier unless such accident w[ ] intentional on occupier's part or was caused [ ] his willful and wanton disregard of the rig[ ] of others, "payment" is considered to h[ ] been made to the occupier if presence of [ ] guest, or business invitee as he may also [ ] called, confers a benefit on the occup[ ] whether in the form of a cash payment [ ] otherwise. 25 Del.C. § 1421.—Hoksch [ ] Stratford Apartments, Inc., 283 A.2d 6[ ]

For references to other topics, see Descriptive-Word Index

Del.Super. 1970. Person entering on land of occupier as business invitee or paying guest is not subject to rule of statute providing that no person who is guest on another's property without payment shall have cause of action for damages against host unless such accident was intentional on part of host or was caused by his wilful or wanton disregard of rights of others. 25 Del.C. § 1421.—Richmond v. Knowles, 265 A.2d 53.

D.C.App. 1974. With respect to duty of care owed by restaurant, customer is a business invitee.—Feldt v. Marriott Corp., 322 A.2d 913.

Fla. 1973. Class of invitees to whom landowner owes duty of reasonable care includes those who are licensees by invitation, either by express or reasonably implied invitation, and there is no distinction between commercial visitors and social guests; however, distinctions of standing and degrees of care owed exist with respect to uninvited licensees and trespassers on the one hand and invitees on the other; receding from contrary pronouncements in Hauben v. Melton, 267 So.2d 16; Goldberg v. Straus, 45 So.2d 883; Tomei v. Center, 116 So.2d 251; and Pinson v. Barlow, 209 So.2d 722.—Wood v. Camp, 284 So.2d 691.

Fla.App. 1974. Department store patron occupied legal position of business invitee, and thus department store owed him duty of keeping its premises in reasonably safe condition and of guarding against subjecting patron to dangers of which department store was cognizant or which it reasonably might have foreseen.—Rotbart v. Jordan Marsh Co., 305 So.2d 255.

Fla.App. 1970. Where business concerns advertise in order to induce regular and prospective customers to frequent their place of business and to examine their stocks and do not contemplate a sale to every invitee but hope to interest regular customers and cultivate prospective customers, guests that enter such concerns are "invitees" notwithstanding fact that they have not made a purchase.—Smith v. Montgomery Ward & Co., 232 So.2d 95.

Fla.App. 1969. Customer who came to store to make payment upon prior purchase on lay-away plan was "business invitee" to whom store owner owed duty to maintain premises in reasonably safe condition and further duty to warn of latent dangers of which owner knew or might reasonably have known but which were not apparent to invitee.—Partelow v. Edgar, 219 So.2d 72.

Fla.App. 1968. Department store owed patron duty of maintaining premises in reasonably safe condition but was not required to maintain premises in condition such that no injury could be sustained.—Maury v. City Stores Co., 214 So.2d 776.

Fla.App. 1966. Decedent, in tavern as customer, was business invitee and, although owner was not an insurer of his safety, owner was under duty to exercise due care to maintain premises in reasonably safe condition for customary and reasonable use to which they might be put, and to guard against subjecting decedent to dangers of which owner was cognizant or which he might have reasonably foreseen.—Sparks v. Ober, 192 So.2d 81.

Ga.App. 1976. Food store customer was invitee on food store premises; as such, retailer owed her duty to exercise ordinary care in keeping premises safe, to protect customer from hidden dangers and defects of which retailer was aware or of which he had constructive notice, and to warn customer of such defects.—Fender v. Colonial Stores, Inc., 225 S.E.2d 691, 138 Ga.App. 31.

Ga.App. 1975. Test of "mutuality of interest" within the statute pertaining to licensees is generally used in reference to a business in which occupant is engaged or which he permits to be carried on there; it has no application in regard to a mere social guest. Code, § 105-402.—Higginbotham v. Winborn, 218 S.E.2d 917, 135 Ga.App. 753.

Ga.App. 1970. Proprietor of beauty parlor did not owe or violate any duty toward patron who slipped in front of the beauty parlor on ice which had formed because of drizzle and cold weather.—Holtzclaw v. Lindsay, 178 S.E.2d 561, 122 Ga.App. 703.

Ga.App. 1968. Where plaintiff who tripped and fell on walkway from parking lot to entrance of building in which dentists had offices was patient of first dentist but had no professional relationship with second dentist who maintained separate suite of offices with separate entrance, plaintiff was not an invitee of second dentist and second dentist owed her no duty as an invitee and was not liable to plaintiff for injuries sustained by her.—McKnight v. Guffin, 162 S.E.2d 743, 118 Ga.App. 168.

Ga.App. 1967. One who enters premises for purpose connected with business conducted on premises is an "invitee."—Chambers v. Peacock Const. Co., 155 S.E.2d 704, 115 Ga.App. 670, affirmed 156 S.E.2d 348, 223 Ga. 515.

Idaho 1974. Customer in store occupied the status of an invitee, and store owner had the duty to maintain the premises in a reasonably safe condition and to warn of any hidden or concealed dangers of which it knew or should have known by the exercise of reasonable care.—Mann v. Safeway Stores, Inc., 518 P.2d 1194, 95 Idaho 732.

Idaho 1968. Operator of supermarket and operator's manager were not negligent in maintaining curbing to separate parking lot from sidewalk and were not liable for injuries sustained by customer when she tripped on curb and was injured. Rules of Civil Procedure, rules 41(b), 42(b).—Neer v. Safeway Stores, Inc., 442 P.2d 771, 92 Idaho 361.

Ill.App. 1974. Basically a landowner owes the duty of ordinary care to provide a safe place for the business invitee with respect to uses that are contemplated and to warn of dangers that are or should be known to the party in possession but which are not readily apparent to the invitee; however, a business invitee also has a responsibility for his own safety.—Genaust v. Illinois Power Co., 320 N.E.2d 412, 23 Ill.App.3d 1023, affirmed 343 N.E.2d 465, 62 Ill.2d 456.

Ill.App. 1973. Where prospective customer, upon entering defendant's store, saw fleeing shoplifter and store manager called "stop thief" and pointed in customer's direction, customer in attempting to stop shoplifter did not lose his status as a business invitee, and refusing to instruct on volunteer status in customer's personal injury suit action against store was not improper.—Jacobsma v. Goldberg's Fashion Forum, 303 N.E.2d 226, 14 Ill.App.3d 710.

Ill.App. 1972. To bank, savings and loan association or currency exchange, member of public who accepts invitation to do business is customer, to whom institution owes duty to use reasonable care for his protection.—Boyd v. Racine Currency Exchange, Inc., 289 N.E.2d 218, 8 Ill.App.3d 140.

Ill.App. 1968. Race track parking lot patron, who paid fee to park therein was "business invitee" and, as such, had right to rely on lot operator's use of ordinary care in operation of parking lot.—Coleman v. Chicago Thoroughbred Enterprises, Inc., 243 N.E.2d 333.

Same duty that applies to person of business invitee, by implication, applies to property of business invitee when lawfully on owner's premises.—Id.

Ill.App. 1967. Proprietor of a business establishment has the duty to exercise reasonable care to keep the property reasonably safe for the use of a customer, and such duty is violated when the proprietor negligently allows conditions to exist on the property which imperil safety of the business invitee upon the premises.—Koehler v. Great Atlantic & Pac. Tea Co., 232 N.E.2d 780, 90 Ill.App.2d 458.

Ill.App. 1967. Where plaintiff was invited into an area not customarily used by general public or by patrons of business and was injured in a fall, plaintiff was business invitee and defendant was therefore under duty to exercise ordinary care for plaintiff's safety.—Halpin v. Pekin Thrifty Drug Co., 223 N.E.2d 708, 79 Ill.App.2d 153.

Ind.App. 1976. One who enters land at owner's invitation, express or implied, to transact business of mutual benefit to both is an "invitee," while one who enters for his own "convenience, curiosity, or entertainment," is a "licensee" by permission or a mere licensee.—Swanson v. Shroat, 345 N.E.2d 872.

Ind.App. 1972. A person coming onto business premises for the purpose of doing business therein is an invitee or licensee by invitation.—Hammond v. Allegretti, 288 N.E.2d 197.

Iowa 1968. Defendant corporation and its truck driver, who was attempting to deliver lumber to plaintiff's land when accident occurred, were "invitees" on plaintiff's premises under rule that an "invitee" is either a public invitee or a business visitor, and a "business visitor" is a person who is invited to enter or remain on land for a purpose directly or indirectly connected with business dealings with the possessor of the land.—Bradt v. Grell Const., Inc., 161 N.W.2d 336.

Iowa 1967. Plaintiff who went to restaurant located in hotel basement to eat was a business invitee.—Chevraux v. Nahas, 150 N.W.2d 78, 260 Iowa 817.

Iowa 1966. Customer who entered supermarket for purpose of making purchase had status of invitee.—Meader v. Paetz Grocery Co., 147 N.W.2d 211, 259 Iowa 1101.

Iowa 1966. An "invitee" is either a public invitee or a business visitor; a "business visitor" is a person who is invited to enter or remain on land for a purpose directly or indirectly connected with business dealings with the possessor of the land.—Hanson v. Town & Country Shopping Center, Inc., 144 N.W.2d 870, 259 Iowa 542.

Plaintiff shopper on parking lot of shopping center had status of an invitee.—Id.

Kan. 1972. A "business invitee" or other invitee of equal status is one who goes on another's premises at express or implied invitation of owner or occupant for benefit of invitor or for mutual benefit and advantage of both invitor and invitee.—Campbell Sixty-Six Exp., Inc. v. Adventure Line Mfg. Co., 496 P.2d 1351, 209 Kan. 357.

Where owner of trailer which was destroyed by fire while parked at loading dock of manufacturer's plant could not fulfill its contract with government for transport of ordnance from plant unless it was permitted to place trailer in loading position at loading dock and manufacturer had called owner to furnish trailer for loading, owner of trailer was a "business invitee" and manufacturer would be liable for loss of trailer due to its negligence or negligence of its employees.—Id.

SEVENTH
DECENNIAL DIGEST

AMERICAN DIGEST SYSTEM

1956-1966

A Complete Digest of All Decisions of the State and Federal Courts as Reported in the National Reporter System and the State Reports

Volume 24

NEGLIGENCE ⟜ 28

TO

PARLIAMENTARY LAW

ST. PAUL, MINN.
WEST PUBLISHING CO.

old and that it had malfunctioned frequently and where, although the company had on hand the necessary equipment to replace the recorder and despite knowledge by company personnel that running a sulfuric acid plant without a reliable recorder was tantamount to "flying blind," the company failed to replace the recorder and thereafter failed to take appropriate actions that would have alleviated the dangers stemming from recorder malfunction.—Bangor & A. R. Co. v. Ship Fernview, 455 F.Supp. 1043.

⊂⇒**22. Dangerous instrumentalities and operations.**

D.C.Me. 1978. A manufacturer who negligently emits steam or other opaque gas that obstructs visibility on public highways, airways or waterways is liable for damages proximately caused by such negligent emissions.—Bangor & A. R. Co. v. Ship Fernview, 455 F.Supp. 1043.

⊂⇒**24. Knowledge of defect or danger.**

D.C.La. 1978. Where hose manufacturer supplied plaintiff's employer with defective hoses and, after defects were discovered in hoses, some of the hoses were returned to manufacturer, where manufacturer did not discover or warn plaintiff's employer against possibility of more defective hoses, where plaintiff's employer's purchasing manager thought that certain hoses were not made from same batch as defective hoses because of variation in shipping dates, where manufacturer's sa'esman assured purchasing agent that problems had been corrected, and where purchasing agent had no knowledge, actual or constructive, of defects in remaining hoses, purchasing agent had no duty to investigate hoses or to warn plaintiff of possible defects, and purchasing agent could not be held liable as joint tort-feasor with hose manufacturer.—Gates Rubber Co. v. Comeaux, 455 F.Supp. 531.

(C) CONDITION AND USE OF LAND, BUILDINGS, AND OTHER STRUCTURES.

⊂⇒**28. Care required in general.**

Mich.App. 1978. Common-law duty of a landowner to one who comes upon his land turns upon the status of the visitor.—Thone v. Nicholson, 269 N.W.2d 665.

Mont. 1978. Duties city owes to the public to keep streets and sidewalks in safe condition were not applicable to private landowner who, together with city, owned parking lot adjacent to creek in which 17-year-old girl drowned and private landowner owed no duty to the girl.—Folda v. City of Bozeman, 582 P.2d 767.

⊂⇒**31. Requirements of statutes or ordinances.**

Tex.Civ.App. 1978. Statutory provisions governing precautions to be taken to protect workmen on buildings were inapplicable to a building such as the Houston Astrodome which was not more than "three or more stories in height," but even if they were applicable, where there was evidence that it was more dangerous to install planking across base of gondola than it was for workmen to perform their work without planking, general contractor, seeking indemnification from subcontractor for its alleged negligence with respect to death of plaintiff's decedent when he fell from gondola while working inside dome of Astrodome, had burden to establish a jury finding not only of the statutory violation, but also a jury finding that such violation was unexcused. Vernon's Ann.Civ.St. arts. 5182, 5182–1.—Coastal Const. Co. v. Tex-Kote, Inc., 571 S.W.2d 400.

see Table of Cases Affirmed, Reversed or Modified

Wash. 1978. Failure to comply with an OSHA regulation is negligence per se.—Kelley v. Howard S. Wright Const. Co., 582 P.2d 500, 90 Wash.2d 323.

⊂⇒**32. Care as to licensees or persons invited.**

⊂⇒**32(1). In general.**

C.A.Pa. 1978. Under Pennsylvania law, proprietor of a business establishment is not responsible for injuries to patrons caused by criminal conduct of third party unless possibility or likelihood of criminal activity could reasonably have been foreseen or anticipated.—Kenny v. Southeastern Pennsylvania Transp. Authority, 581 F.2d 351.

Ala. 1978. Owner of premises is not insurer of safety of invitees, and principal of res ipsa loquitur is not applicable; there is no presumption of negligence which arises from mere fact of injury to invitee.—Tice v. Tice, 361 So.2d 1051.

Kan.App. 1978. Landowner owes invitee higher degree of care than he owes licensee; duty owed to invitee is active and positive, requires no showing of wilfulness or wantonness and is that of reasonable or ordinary care for invitee's safety, including duty to protect and warn invitee against any danger that may be reasonably anticipated.—Scales v. St. Louis-S. F. Ry. Co., 582 P.2d 300.

Ky.App. 1978. Although owner or operator of premises is under affirmative duty to make premises reasonably safe for use by guests and invitees, store operator is not insurer for safety of his patrons and is not required at his peril to keep premises absolutely safe.—Adkins v. Ashland Supermarkets, Inc., 569 S.W.2d 698.

Storeowner's basic duty of making his premises reasonably safe for invitees did not include additional duty not to increase risks of criminal activity by failing to comply with demands of armed robber; store owner's verbal resistance to demands of robber did not constitute violation of duty owed to patrons.—Id.

La. 1978. Where homeowner failed to take any steps to prevent guest from being injured as result of hazard presented by transparent, untempered, sliding glass doors, homeowner was negligent.—Dixon v. Allstate Ins. Co., 362 So.2d 1368.

N.C.App. 1978. While proprietor or owner of premises does not insure safety of invitees, proprietor or owner is under duty of exercising ordinary care to keep premises in such reasonably safe condition as not to expose invitees unnecessarily to danger.—Sibbett v. M. C. M. Livestock, Inc., 247 S.E.2d 2, 37 N.C.App. 704.

Operator of livestock auction house had duty to exercise reasonable care to maintain supervision and reasonably safe enclosure for protection of customers.—Id.

Wash.App. 1978. Owner or occupier of land has duty to maintain premises in reasonably safe condition for protection of invitee; further, owner or occupier must make any limitation on scope of invitation apparent to reasonable invitee.—Egede-Nissen v. Crystal Mountain, Inc., 584 P.2d 432.

Occupier of land is not insurer of safety of invitees.—Id.

Owner or occupier of land is generally responsible for maintaining land in reasonably safe condition for benefit of invitees; such duty extends only to those parts of property which are within scope of invitation.—Id.

Owner or occupier of land who fails to make reasonable effort to apprise invitee of limits of invitation becomes responsible for maintaining all apparently public sections of premises in nonnegligent manner.—Id.

Wis.App. 1978. Storekeeper is under duty to his customer to render aid to customer after he knows or has reason to know that customer is ill or injured and to care for customer until she can be cared for by others.—Lloyd v. S. S. Kresge Co., 270 N.W.2d 423.

Common carrier is under duty to his passengers to take reasonable action to protect them against unreasonable risk of physical harm and to give them first aid after it knows or has reason to know that they are ill or injured and to care for them until they can be cared for by others; possessor of lands who holds it open to public is under similar duty to members of public who enter in response to its invitation.—Id.

Landowners are under duty to exercise reasonable care to avoid creating unreasonable risk of harm to visitor through act of negligence and they owe this duty to all who are consensually upon their land whether they would have been classified as invitees or as licensees at common law.—Id.

Duty of landowner/entrepreneur to members of public to whom he holds out property is to be measured by standard of reasonableness and, in determining reasonability of landowner's actions, one must weigh likelihood of harm against inconvenience and discomfort of other customers and employees.—Id.

⊂⇒**32(2.2). Bare licensees.**

Kan.App. 1978. To support finding that party was either invitee or licensee, there must be implied consent by landowner.—Scales v. St. Louis-S. F. Ry. Co., 582 P.2d 300.

Distinguishing factor in determining whether one is invitee or licensee is whether landowner derived benefit from entrant's presence on his land.—Id.

⊂⇒**32(2.3). Invitees in general.**

Ala. 1978. "Invitee" is a visitor, a transient who enters property at express or implied invitation of owner or occupier for material or commercial benefit of occupier; tenant, on the other hand, does not merely visit, but acquires interest in property, including exclusive legal possession of leased premises.—Osborn v. Brown, 361 So.2d 82.

Kan.App. 1978. To support finding that party was either invitee or licensee, there must be implied consent by landowner.—Scales v. St. Louis-S. F. Ry. Co., 582 P.2d 300.

Distinguishing factor in determining whether one is invitee or licensee is whether landowner derived benefit from entrant's presence on his land.—Id.

⊂⇒**32(2.4). Implied invitation in general.**

Mich.App. 1978. Permission to come upon land may be implied where the landowner acquiesces in the known, customary use of the property by the public.—Thone v. Nicholson, 269 N.W.2d 665.

⊂⇒**32(2.8). Business visitors, and store and restaurant patrons**

Ala. 1978. Duty owed by employers to baby-sitter as business invitee was exercise of ordinary and reasonable care to keep premises in reasonably safe condition.—Tice v. Tice, 361 So.2d 1051.

Ill.App. 1978. Owners of campground containing small swimming lake in which a patron's son drowned had legal duty to make

La.App. 1963. Passenger in truck driven to automobile service station for refueling purposes was invitee and not licensee.—Wilson v. Cox Bros., Inc., 158 So.2d 326.

Mich. Where owner of parking lot directly or by lease operates a parking lot available to public, parking lessee is plainly an invitee as to the parking lot and its approaches, as are those whom parking lessee invites to accompany him in his automobile provided the invitation and use thereunder are such as to be within normal contemplation of parties.—Goldsmith v. Cody, 88 N.W.2d 268.

Where oral lessee of space in parking lot invited person to ride with him in automobile and such person was injured while using approach to parking lot, if jury found that lessee's invitation to injured party and injured party's use of approach to parking lot were within reasonable contemplation of parties to oral lease, injured party was invitee and owner of lot or persons found to be in control and operation of the premises owed him duty of reasonable care.—Id.

Mich. 1963. Members of the public in going across service station owner's premises with owner's knowledge and acquiescence were not trespassers but licensees, as regards owner's duty of care.—Draper v. Switous, 122 N.W. 2d 698.

Miss. Where automobile salesman went to gasoline filling station to see an employee there with reference to the sale of an automobile and was injured when he tripped and fell over handle of hydraulic jack, salesman was a mere "licensee", to whom filling station operator owed a duty only not to wilfully or wantonly injure him, and not an "invitee," and filling station operator was therefore not liable for salesman's injuries.—Graves v. Massey, 87 So. 2d 270.

A.D. 1962. Pedestrian who used gasoline station as short cut passageway was "licensee" and could not recover for injuries received as result of defect in condition of premises, where station owner did not in its business service other than motorized customers.—Rudolph v. Annunziata, 230 N.Y.S.2d 393.

Pa.Super. Where motorist took automobile to filling station in order to have certain adjustments made, motorist was a business invitee and filling station owner owed him duty of reasonable care.—Rodgers v. Sun Oil Co., 51 A.2d 673.

Where motorist took his automobile into filling station for certain repairs and adjustments which were to be made while engine was running and at direction of attendant owner moved vehicle to another place on lot and attendant told motorist to put automatic drive mechanism lever in neutral, there was no obligation on part of attendant to check motorist's action to determine whether he had followed instructions.—Id.

Pa.Com.Pl. 1965. It is incumbent upon the owner of premises upon which persons come by invitation, express or implied, to maintain such premises in a reasonably safe condition for the contemplated uses thereof and the purposes for which the invitation was extended.—Hall v. Great Atlantic & Pac. Tea Co., 47 West. 189.

S.C. 1965. Filling station operator who displays merchandise in automatic vending machines on exterior premises after regular business hours invites entry by prospective customers, and his relation to and duty toward one who enters with intent to buy is that of occupant to invitee.—Parker v. Stevenson Oil Co., 140 S.E.2d 177.

Tenn.App. 1965. Automobile passenger was an invitee at time she was walking back to automobile in parking lot, and lot owner owed duty

to exercise reasonable care to maintain lot's surface in a safe condition, including duty of removing or warning her against a dangerous condition which it knew, or in exercise of reasonable care, should have known to exist.—Interstate Life & Acc. Co. v. Cox, 396 S.W.2d 80.

Tex.Civ.App. 1964. By going into parking garage area not designed for use by public, plaintiff became licensee, and defendant only owed him duty to refrain from injuring him willfully, wantonly or through gross negligence.—Pogue v. Allright, Inc., 375 S.W.2d 533.

Tex.Civ.App. 1964. Generally, invitees of parking lot include not only those directly invited to use premises but those who might be reasonably expected to accompany primary invitee.—Parking, Inc. v. Dalrymple, 375 S. W.2d 758.

⟲32(2.6). Bill collectors
No cases for period of this Digest. See other Key Number Digests.

Library References
C.J.S. Negligence § 63(149).

⟲32(2.7). Buildings in process of construction, alteration, or demolition

D.C.App. 1964. Where plaintiff went to defendant's construction site for purpose of ascertaining defendant's correct address so plaintiff's employer could properly bill defendant for several items which it had purchased, and plaintiff was injured while on defendant's premises, court should have found, in absence of factual dispute, that plaintiff was at best no more than a licensee to whom defendant owed no duty except for wilful injuries.—Miller & Long Co. v. Shaw, 204 A.2d 697.

Kan. Wife, who went with employee-husband for mutual companionship and to assist him in his work performed in apartment building under agreement between employer and construction contractor, was a licensee and construction contractor was not liable for injuries sustained by wife when more than a half ton of siding fell upon her, in absence of showing that contractor willfully, intentionally or recklessly injured wife.—Hogan v. Hess Const. Co., 358 P.2d 755.

Ky. 1964. One who had gone to library building which was under construction upon college premises for purpose of employing a plumber who was working there, without knowledge or consent of college or contractor, was not an "invitee" but a "trespasser" to whom contractor owed only duty of ordinary care after discovery of his peril.—Bradford v. Clifton, 379 S.W.2d 249.

Mich. Presence of roofing subcontractor's ladder in building under construction was not an implied invitation to employee of another subcontractor to climb, and, in absence of express invitation, employee injured when he climbed ladder and fell through roof was not entitled to recover from roofing subcontractor as invitee.—Klovski v. Martin Fireproofing Corp., 108 N.W.2d 887.

Neb. 1964. Owner's sister who visited home under construction as owner's guest solely to accompany and assist owner and who had no contract with or authority over builder was "licensee" as to builder and was not entitled to recover from builder for injury received when wallboard fell on her foot, in absence of showing that builder or any of his employees were on premises on day of accident or had knowledge of placement of the wallboard.—Von Dollen v. Stulgies, 128 N.W.2d 115.

Homeowner who was invitee of builder could not extend scope or purpose of invitation granted to her by builder to include owner's

sister, who sought to recover from builder for injury received when stacked wallboard in home under construction fell on her foot.—Id.

A.D. Workmen coming onto premises to perform construction or repair work are, in effect, invitees, no matter whose employees they may be, and the duty owed them is generally analogous to that owed to any business invitee. Labor Law, § 200.—Employers Mut. Liability Ins. Co. of Wis. v. Di Cesare & Monaco Concrete Const. Corp., 194 N.Y.S.2d 103.

Pa.Com.Pl. 1961. The law applicable is stated in § 343 of the Restatement of Torts, which reads in part: "A possessor of land is subject to liability for bodily harm caused to business visitors by a natural or artificial condition thereon if, but only if, he (a) knows or by the exercise of reasonable care could discover, the condition which, if known to him, he should realize [it] as involving an unreasonable risk to them . . . (c) invites or permits them to enter or remain upon the land without exercising reasonable care (i) to make the condition reasonably safe, or (ii) to give a warning adequate to enable them to avoid the harm without relinquishing any of the services which they are entitled to receive, if the possessor is a public utility."—Ward v. Troyler Corp., 65 Lack.Jur. 17.

Held also, that the demolition company was not in possession and control of the roof, since its sole and separate assignment was to dismantle the cupolas and remove the smokestacks from a small portion of the roof, which remained in defendant's possession and under its control, and was not turned over to the demolition company.—Ward v. Troyler Corp., 65 Lack.Jur. 17.

⟲32(2.8). Business visitors, and store and restaurant patrons

C.A.Ill. 1962. Driver of truck which was serviced at garage of defendant was a business invitee of defendant to whom defendant owed a duty of reasonable inspection to ascertain that the conditions of the premises and chattels furnished for use by driver were free of danger.—Lentz v. Hayes Freight Lines, Inc., 302 F.2d 67.

C.A.Mo. A possessor of land may hold open or reasonably appear to be holding open a part of his premises to another as a business visitor in a particular situation, although it is not so held open by him to business visitors in general.—Bullock v. Safeway Stores, Inc., 236 F. 2d 29.

Under Kansas law, a business visitor may be more than a licensee in his entry to any part of premises to which customers reasonably may be expected to go or in his entry to any reserved part of premises which he has either expressly or impliedly been invited or induced to enter.—Id.

D.C.Alaska. Where plaintiff entered defendant's store for the purpose of making business inquiries, plaintiff was a business invitee to whom storekeeper owed a duty to exercise reasonable care in maintaining safe premises, although, in order for plaintiff to recover for injuries allegedly sustained when he fell in the store, it was incumbent upon him to prove that storekeeper breached such duty and that plaintiff suffered injury flowing from such breach.—Lucas v. City of Juneau, 168 F.Supp. 195.

D.C.Hawaii 1962. Restaurant patron who was business invitee as to dining room was mere "licensee" as to band platform on which was located piano which she was permitted to play and from which she fell when she attempted to descend after finishing playing.—West v. Shizuko Tan, 208 F.Supp. 708.

D.C.La. 1962. Generally, one who is on premises in the performance of his duty occupies the status of an invitee or a business visitor with respect to degree of care owed by him to owner or person in charge.—Hurst v. Point Landing, Inc., 212 F.Supp. 160, quoting 65 C.J.S. Negligence § 43(4).

D.C.S.C. 1964. Relationship between storekeeper and customer is that of invitor and invitee.—Rikard v. J. C. Penny Co., Columbia Division, 233 F.Supp. 133.

Cal.App. Customer in defendant's supermarket was a business invitee to whom defendant owed duty to exercise reasonable care in keeping the premises safe.—McKenney v. Quality Foods, Inc., 319 P.2d 448.

Cal.App. A patron of a tavern is a business invitee and proprietors thereof owe patron a duty of exercising ordinary care to keep premises in a safe condition.—Shaw v. Colonial Room, 1 Cal.Rptr. 28.

Cal.App. Adult accompanying friend into store where friend intended to make purchase was an invitee rather than a mere licensee.—Farrier v. Levin, 1 Cal.Rptr. 742.

Cal.App. Customer in a store was an invitee to whom the store owed the duty to exercise ordinary care to keep the premises in reasonably safe condition or to warn of danger, and duty was not limited to conditions actually known to be dangerous but extended also to conditions which might have been found dangerous by reasonable care.—Iloff v. Purity Stores, Limited, 2 Cal.Rptr. 735.

Cal.App. In order to be an invitee or business visitor, it is not necessary that visitor should himself be on land for purpose of possessor's business, but it is sufficient that he be on premises for convenience or necessity of one who is on land for such purpose.—Beeston v. Ow, 19 Cal.Rptr. 372.

Cal.App. 1962. Store patron was business invitee while walking on parking lot adjacent to store as well as while in store itself, and storekeeper owed invitee duty of exercising ordinary care to avoid injury to her.—Perez v. Ow, 19 Cal.Rptr. 372.

Cal.App. 1963. Generally, "invitee" or "business visitor" is person who is invited or permitted to enter or remain on land in possession of another for a purpose directly or indirectly connected with business dealings between them.—Clawson v. Stockton Golf and Country Club, 34 Cal.Rptr. 184.

Invitation to an invitee or business visitor may be implied from such circumstances as conduct of possessor, arrangement of premises, or local custom.—Id.

Colo. 1964. Plaintiff's driver while on shipper's premises in connection with plaintiff's business was an invitee.—Colorado-Wyoming Ry. Co. v. Wheelock Bros. Inc., 395 P.2d 1.

Del. A storekeeper is not an insurer of his patrons, and has only duty to exercise same standard of care reasonably prudent storekeepers would exercise under like circumstances to keep premises in reasonably safe condition for customers' use.—Robelen Piano Co. v. Di Fonzo, 169 A.2d 240.

D.C.Mun.App. An adult daughter who accompanied her mother who desired to purchase a rake needed in house where daughter lived with her mother was an "invitee" of store from the time she entered store because she was a potential customer.—Sears, Roebuck & Co. v. Donovan, 137 A.2d 716.

Under Maryland law an adult daughter who accompanied her mother for purpose of buying a rake was "invitee" of store notwithstanding fact that daughter at time of entering store had no intention of purchasing anything.—Id.

D.C.App. 1964. Under Maryland law, an "invitee" or business visitor is one invited or permitted to enter or remain for a purpose connected with or related to the business of the occupant.—Miller & Long Co. v. Shaw, 204 A.2d 697.

Fla. Where son dominated, operated, and controlled a "one man" corporation which had, for its place of business, a shop where shirts were made and store where the shirts were sold, mother, who had had run of the premises for many years before son took over business from father, and, who, after returning to shop shirts which father, who was corporation's employee, had forgotten to return to shop after having taken them home to work on them in evening, tripped and fell on worn carpet while attempting to go to rest room in shop, was, at time of her injury, a "licensee", not a "business invitee".—Eisen v. Sportogs, Inc., 87 So. 2d 14.

Fla.App. A customer who walked across service station premises for purpose of paying a bill for oil previously purchased was a "business invitee", and persons in control of premises had duty to exercise ordinary care for customer's safety and to warn customer of latent or concealed defects which should have been known to such persons; however, the persons in control had no duty to warn customer against patent or obvious conditions which were not dangerous per se.—Andrews v. Goetz, 104 So.2d 653.

Fla.App. Incidental motives of the visit of a social guest, other than purely social, or minor services performed by guest for host during visit will not be sufficient to change status of visitor from licensee to invitee or business visitor.—Cochran v. Abercrombie, 118 So.2d 636.

Fla.App. In absence of showing of reason why can fell from shelf and struck patron on leg and foot, patron could not recover for her injuries from store owners.—Food Fair Stores, Palm Beach, Inc. v. Spinelli, 122 So.2d 41.

Fla.App. 1962. An "invitee" is normally considered to be one who enters upon premises of another for purposes connected with business of owner or occupant of premises.—North Broward Hospital Dist. v. Adams, 143 So.2d 355.

Fla.App. 1964. Plaintiff who was injured when sacks of cow feed stacked in defendants' barn struck plaintiff on the back and head at a time when he was engaged, with permission of defendants, in removing bags of feed from their barn to plaintiff's truck for transportation to ranch on which he worked for another, was, while he was in the barn, a "licensee."—Jerrell v. Whitehurst, 164 So.2d 875.

Fla.App. 1966. Plaintiffs, as customers of defendants' cocktail lounge, were invitees of defendants' place of business.—Carter v. Parker, 183 So.2d 3.

Ga.App. While there must be at least some mutuality of interest in the subject matter to which the visitor's business relates, the particular subject of the visit need not be for the benefit or the profit of the occupant.—Knudsen v. Duffee-Freeman, Inc., 109 S.E.2d 339.

A mere permissive use of premises is sufficient to raise an implied invitation to those having business with the permittee to come upon the premises and the existence of the relation of landlord and tenant as between the owner and the person visited is not essential to the owner's liability.—Id.

Ga.App. Electrical fixture and accessor salesman who came to store and offered to re place burned out bulbs therein from owner' stock was invitee to whom owner owed duty o keeping premises safe.—Findley v. Lipsitz, 12 S.E.2d 299.

Ga.App. 1965. Where one enters premise of another for purposes connected with busines of owner on premises, one entering premises i an "invitee," and owner is liable to person en tering premises for injuries resulting from failure of owner to exercise ordinary care i keeping premises safe.—Higdon v. Georgi Winn-Dixie, Inc., 145 S.E.2d 808.

Ill.App. Customer of store was a busines invitee and storekeeper, although not an insur er of customer's safety, owed duty of keeping his premises in a reasonably safe condition s that customer would not be injured.—Olinge v. Great Atlantic & Pacific Tea Co., 167 N E.2d 595.

Ill.App. 1964. Railroad, through its agent and employees, was a business invitee at tim switchman was injured on railroad switc tracks owned by owner of land on whic switch tracks were located, where railroad through its employees, was at time of switch man's injury moving railroad cars over land owner's warehouses.—Chicago & I. M. Ry. Co v. Pillsbury Mills, Inc., 198 N.E.2d 126.

Ill.App. 1964. An "invitee" is one who en ters upon premises of another in response to an express or implied invitation for the pur pose of transacting business in which the parties are mutually interested.—Kapka v Urbaszewski, 198 N.E.2d 569.

Ind.App. "Business invitees" are those wh go upon lands of another with express or im plied invitation of owner or occupant, eithe to transact business with owner or occupant or to do some act which is of advantage t owner or occupant or of mutual advantage t both licensee and owner or occupant; and in vitation is implied from such a mutual in terest.—Standard Oil Co. of Ind., Inc. v. Sco ville, 175 N.E.2d 711.

Iowa. A customer who comes to a place of business for purpose of buying some goods offered for sale was impliedly invited to enter store.—Ather ton v. Hoenig's Grocery, 86 N.W.2d 252.

Iowa. Plaintiff entering a store to make a purchase was an invitee of the owner who owed her a duty to keep its premises in a reasonably safe condition, including ingress and egress.—Anderson v. Younker Bros., Inc. 89 N.W.2d 858.

Iowa. In view of present day custom, which now amounts to almost a requirement, that modern and up-to-date cafes maintain res rooms, a restaurant patron would be an in vitee while going to or coming from and while in a rest room.—Holmes v. Gross, 93 N.W 2d 714, citing 65 C.J.S. Negligence § 48(c).

Iowa. Patron of department store tea roor was invitee.—Corrigan v. Younker Bros., Inc. 110 N.W.2d 246.

Iowa 1962. Possessor of land who holds it out to public for entry for his business pur poses, is subject to liability to members of public while upon land for such purpose for bodily harm caused to them by accidental, neg ligent or intentionally harmful acts of third person if possessor by exercise of reasonable care could have discovered that such acts were being done or were about to be done and he could have protected members of public by controlling the conduct of third persons.—Foust v. Kinley, 117 N.W.2d 843.

Iowa 1963. Generally invitee is one wh goes to place of business either by expres

For subsequent case history information, see Table of Cases

SIXTH
DECENNIAL DIGEST

AMERICAN DIGEST SYSTEM

1946-1956

A Complete Digest of All Decisions of the State and Federal Courts as Reported in the National Reporter System and the State Reports

Volume 23

MUNICIPAL CORPORATIONS
⌐621—NEWSPAPERS

ST. PAUL, MINN.
WEST PUBLISHING CO.

ant owed the duty of using reasonable care in avoiding him injury through active negligence.—Naylor v. Elmhurst Country Club, 55 Lack.Jur. 121.

Utah. Where entrance upon land is connected with business dealings between person and occupier of land, law will imply an invitation to enter property.—Rogalski v. Phillips Petroleum Co., 282 P.2d 304, 3 Utah 2d 203.

Vt. The invitation required to qualify one as a business visitor on the premises of another may be either express or implied.—McAdams v. Raymond S. Roberts, Inc., 91 A.2d 706.

The invitation required to qualify one as a business visitor is implied whenever one makes such use of another's premises as the owner intends he shall, or such as he is reasonably justified in understanding the owner intended.—McAdams v. Raymond S. Roberts, Inc., 91 A.2d 706.

Vt. A "business visitor" is one invited or permitted to enter or remain on land in possession of another for purpose directly or indirectly connected with business dealings between them, and there is an implied invitation to a business visitor to make such use of another's premises as he is reasonably justified in understanding the owner intended.—Johnstone v. Bushnell, 102 A.2d 334, 118 Vt. 162.

W.Va. Where a person enters or uses another's premises for purpose beneficial to owner or occupant thereof or for mutual benefit of both such owner or occupant and entrant or user, an invitation to enter and use premises is implied.—Puffer v. Hub Cigar Store, 84 S.E.2d 145.

🔑**32(2.5).** *Automobile service stations and parking service*

D.C.D.C. Guest of motorist who parked automobile in gasoline filling station at time when station was closed for the night was a "trespasser" and not "licensee", as regards station owner's liability for injuries sustained when guest fell into grease pit on returning to parked automobile, notwithstanding that on prior occasions several other automobiles had been parked on station grounds and that owner had taken no steps to stop it.—Nimetz v. Shell Oil Co., 74 F.Supp. 1.

Conn. A motorist whose automobile was not operating properly and who drove into garage for repairs was as a matter of law an "invitee" to whom the garage keeper owed duty to use reasonable care to keep the premises reasonably safe so long as motorist did not exceed the limits of the invitation.—Smith v. L. & S. Corp., 48 A.2d 239, 133 Conn. 105.

Fla. Person on premises of service station for purpose of obtaining change for $10 bill was at most a mere licensee to which operator of service station owed no duty except not intentionally to expose her to danger.—Stewart v. Texas Co., 67 So.2d 653.

Fla. Plaintiff, who slipped and fell on grease spot on concrete areaway of defendant's gasoline filling station while walking across premises as short cut to public bus stop early in morning before defendant's premises were open for business, was licensee, and defendant owed him no duty except not to harm him wilfully or wantonly, or to set traps for him, or to expose him to danger recklessly or wantonly.—Bruno v. Seigel, 73 So.2d 674.

Mo. Where petitioner was injured by falling into unguarded grease pit adjacent to driveway of filling station while attempting to reach public restroom therein late at night, and it did not appear that petitioner was on premises as customer or during business hours, though driveway was used as walkway by public to enter upon

premises and those adjacent thereto, petitioner was deviating from driveway for his own purposes and could not recover for injuries.—Walters v. Markwardt, 237 S.W.2d 177.

N.C. Not every accident is in the category of actionable negligence, and keeper of a store or service station cannot be made insurer of safety of his customers.—Mills v. Waters, 70 S.E.2d 11, 235 N.C. 424.

Ohio App. One injured in fall from automobile parking floor to ground below while seeking shelter from rain after searching unsuccessfully for one who had offered to drive him home in prospective host's automobile was at most a gratuitous or bare licensee, to whom statutes requiring owners of places of employment to make them as free from danger for employees or frequenters as nature of employment reasonably permits were inapplicable, in absence of showing that prospective host had used parking facilities on such floor.—Gen. Code, §§ 871–13(5, 11), 871–15, 871–16.—Moran v. Wehrung, 103 N.E.2d 789.

Or. Where plaintiff went into defendant's garage at invitation of employee who did not have either express or implied authority to invite friends into garage for purpose of "showing them around", and she was injured while using escalator, plaintiff was at best a "bare licensee" to whom the defendant owed no duty to exercise due care.—Akerson v. D. C. Bates & Sons, 174 P.2d 953, 180 Or. 224.

Pa.Com.Pl. Where the evidence indicates that defendant's parking lot remained covered with snow and ice in mounds and ridges three to four inches in height three days later and that the defendant had made faulty or ineffectual efforts to clear the lot, a jury may reasonably and properly conclude that the defendant had failed to exercise reasonable care and to keep the lot in a reasonably safe condition thus breeching its duty to the plaintiff.—Morris v. Atlantic and Pacific Tea Co., 42 Del.Co. 366, affirmed 121 A.2d 135, 384 Pa. 464.

In such case where the testimony shows that many persons had been and were using defendant's lot on the day of the accident and prior thereto, it is not for the court, but for the jury, to determine whether the plaintiff performed the duty of reasonable care required of him under the circumstances.—Morris v. Atlantic and Pacific Tea Co., 42 Del.Co. 366, affirmed 121 A.2d 135, 384 Pa. 464.

Pa.Com.Pl. A person entering upon land occupied as a gasoline station for the purpose of patronizing the business of the operator is a business visitor.—Egan v. Bradican, 51 Lack.Jur. 173.

Tex.Civ.App. A person who stops at gasoline filling station to buy gasoline is an invitee, but he is not an invitee if he stops to obtain information about where he might find a trailer camp.—Dofner v. Branard, 236 S.W.2d 544, ref. n. r. e.

🔑**32(2.6).** *Bill collectors*

N.J.Super.A.D. Where collector was requested to call at residence and two weeks later called, and collector, who knew that defendants lived in second floor apartment, entered stairway to cellar without announcing her presence or requesting admittance, after she was informed that owner was in cellar, status of collector was not that of invitee, but rather that of "licensee."—Tomsky v. Kaczka, 85 A.2d 809, 17 N.J.Super. 211.

🔑**32(2.7).** *Buildings in process of construction, alteration, or demolition*

Ohio App. Where watchman entered leased portion of premises to lead

plumber to source of water leak, but watchman was not doing so to prevent waste and hence was a licensee, duty of company remodeling leased portion was not to wilfully cause watchman injury.—Helvich v. George A. Rutherford Co., 114 N.E.2d 514, 96 Ohio App. 367, appeal dismissed Helvich v. Eastman Kodak Stores, Inc., 117 N.E.2d 439, 160 Ohio St. 571.

🔑**32(2.8).** *Business visitors, and store and restaurant patrons*

C.A.2. One who is in possession of realty owes to a "business guest" or "invited person" no greater duty than to advise him of any dangers which reasonable prudence would foresee and correct.—Slattery v. Marra Bros., 186 F.2d 134, certiorari denied Marra Bros. v. Slattery, 71 S.Ct. 736, 341 U.S. 915, 95 L.Ed. 1351.

C.A.Ga. Purchaser of surplus goods stored in Government warehouse was an invitee upon the premises of the Government for purpose of loading the goods purchased, and Government was under a duty to exercise ordinary care in keeping the premises, approaches and instrumentalities to be used, for such purpose, in a safe condition.—U. S. v. Adams, 212 F.2d 912.

C.A.Ill. A storekeeper is not liable as an insurer to his customers, but may only be held liable for injuries caused by his negligence.—Ernst v. Jewel Tea Co., 197 F.2d 881, certiorari denied 73 S.Ct. 346, 344 U.S. 918, 97 L.Ed. —.

C.A.Kan. Under Kansas law, a merchant owes to his patrons and invitees the duty to maintain his premises in a reasonably safe condition, and his failure to do so constitutes negligence.—Parks v. Montgomery Ward & Co., 198 F.2d 772.

A merchant has the general duty to exercise the degree of care that an ordinarily cautious and prudent storekeeper would exercise under the same or similar circumstances to protect his customers and invitees from danger.—Parks v. Montgomery Ward & Co., 198 F.2d 772.

C.C.A.N.Y. Owner of automobile and his guests who went to garage to get automobile were "business visitors" to whom garage owner owed duty to maintain garage in a safe condition within the area of the business invitation.—Bollinger v. Gotham Garage Co., 155 F.2d 326, certiorari denied 67 S.Ct. 95, 329 U.S. 733, 91 L.Ed. 633.

C.A.N.Y. Owner owes duty to business visitor to exercise reasonable care to make the premises safe.—Stoffel v. New York, N. H. & H. R. Co., 205 F.2d 411, certiorari denied 74 S.Ct. 222, 346 U.S. 898, 98 L.Ed. 399.

C.A.Pa. A possessor of land is subject to liability to business visitors for personal injuries to them by artificial conditions on premises only if possessor knew, or by exercise of reasonable care could discover, condition which he should realize as involving unreasonable risk to invitees, and if possessor has no reason to believe that visitors will discover condition of realized risk involved, and he invites or permits them to enter or remain upon premises without exercising reasonable care to make conditions safe or give adequate warning to visitors.—Wild v. Atlantic Refining Co., 195 F.2d 151, certiorari denied 73 S.Ct. 92, 344 U.S. 857, 97 L.Ed. —.

C.A.Tenn. A person, to become a business invitee on another's premises, need not be expressly invited by owner to enter premises for purpose of doing business with him, but such invitation is implied from owner's acts leading visitor to believe that his use of premises is in accordance with design for which they are adapted and allowed and has no reason to believe that they will discover condition or realize risk involved therein.—Engle v. Reider, 77 A.2d 621, 366 Pa. 411.

Pa.Super. Employee of independent contractor had status of "business visitor" on defendant's property in doing work for defendant who had contracted with independent contractor to have painting work done on various structures on defendant's property and defendant owed visitor affirmative duty to keep premises in safe condition or to warn him of dangerous conditions which defendant knew or should have known to exist.—Debenjak v. Parkway Oil Co., 49 A.2d 521, 159 Pa.Super. 603.

Pa.Super. Shoe store operator was not insurer of safety of those who came to his store by implied invitation, but owed only affirmative duty of keeping premises reasonably safe for business visitors.—Kramer v. Meyer, 76 A. 2d 481, 168 Pa.Super. 13.

Pa.Super. Prospective tenant who fell down stairway of building while examining apartment building owner offered to rent, was a business invitee of building owner.—Hall v. Glick, 110 A.2d 836, 177 Pa.Super. 546.

Pa.Com.Pl. One who enters a store assumes all normal and ordinary risks and the owner is not liable for a danger which is obvious or should have been observed in the exercise of reasonable care.—DeCamillo v. Schwartz, 47 Berks 169.

The general rule is that one who holds his premises open for business visitors owes them a duty to have the premises in reasonably safe condition, but the owner is not an insurer of his invitees while on the premises.—DeCamillo v. Schwartz, 47 Berks 169.

Pa.Com.Pl. The owner of an automobile parked in a parking lot together with one accompanying the owner are regarded as being lawfully on the premises and hence may recover for personal injuries caused by the ordinary negligence of the parking lot owner.—Little v. Wallace, 17 Cambria 169, 17 Som. 299.

Pa.Com.Pl. Where one enters a saloon or tavern, open for the entertainment of the public, the proprietor is bound to see that he is properly protected from the assaults or insults, as well of those who are in his employ, as of the drunken and vicious men whom he may choose to harbor.—Hertzler v. Molly Pitcher Hotel Co., 5 Cumb. 105.

Pa.Com.Pl. Since plaintiff was lawfully on defendant's premises for a purpose directly connected with business dealings between them, plaintiff was a business visitor, and while not an insurer, defendant owed plaintiff the duty of reasonable care for his protection and safety. This duty was to keep and maintain the scaffolding in a reasonably safe condition and if there were therein any defects known or discoverable by the exercise of reasonable care and diligence, to warn plaintiff of these defects and dangers. However, defendant was not liable for defects in the scaffolding of which he was ignorant and which could not be discovered in the exercise of reasonable care and diligence.—Bentz v. Parmer, 65 Dauph. 288.

Pa.Com.Pl. It was defendant's duty to all business visitors, including the decedent, to take reasonable steps to make the condition reasonably safe or to give adequate warning to enable business visitors to avoid harm.—Schon v. Scranton-Spring Brook Water Service Co., 55 Lack.Jur. 245, affirmed 112 A.2d 89, 381 Pa. 148.

Pa.Com.Pl. Owner or occupant of premises who induces others to come

upon it by invitation, expressed or implied, owes them the duties of responsible care to keep premises in a safe condition. The liability of the defendant rests upon notice whether actual or constructive. The owner must keep the premises and the sidewalks free from ice and snow and remove the same after notice of the dangerous condition. There can be no recovery where the injury is sustained due to general condition of the sidewalk, although there may be liability where ridges of ice have formed and are allowed to remain there for a reasonable length of time. The defendants were not insurers of the safety of their customers, but liable only for breach of duty, and it must be shown that the condition existed and that defendants knew it, actually or constructively.—Dunsavage v. Zelonis, 45 Mun. 84.

Pa.Com.Pl. The proprietor of a place of business which is kept open to public patronage is obliged to keep the approaches and entrances to his place of business in reasonably safe condition for the use of customers entering or leaving the premises. The proprietor, however, is not under an insurer's liability in this respect.—Dunsavage v. Zelonis, 48 Sch.L.R. 8.

It is a well established principle of law that notice, either actual or constructive, is an essential element of claims of this character. No liability can be placed upon the owner or proprietor of the business, unless he had actual or constructive notice of the condition complained of, or constructive notice by reason of the unreasonable length of time the defect existed.—Dunsavage v. Zelonis, 48 Sch.L.R. 8.

R.I. Owner and operator of a diner was not an insurer of safety of business invitees.—Bryce v. Jackson Diners Corp., 96 A.2d 637.

S.C. One who operates mercantile establishment is not an insurer of safety of those who enter his store but he does owe them duty of exercising ordinary care to keep aisles, passageways, and such other parts of premises as are ordinarily used by customers in transacting business, in reasonably safe condition.—Mullinax v. Great Atlantic & Pac. Tea Co., 70 S.E.2d 911.

S.D. The possessor of land owes invitee or business visitor only the duty of exercising reasonable or ordinary care for his safety, and is not an insurer.—Norris v. Chicago, M., St. P. & P. R. Co., 51 N.W.2d 792.

Tenn. A retail store owner is not insurer of customer's safety, but customer is invitee and owner is obligated to exercise ordinary care to maintain store premises in reasonably safe condition for store patrons.—Phillips v. Harvey Co., 264 S.W.2d 810.

Tenn.App. The proprietor, owner, or manager of a retail store is under an obligation to exercise ordinary care and diligence to maintain the premises in a reasonably safe condition for patrons or customers of the store who enter and remain there as invitees.—O'Brien v. Southern Bell Tel. & Tel. Co., 259 S.W.2d 554.

Tex. If, in attempting to pass through doorway leading from parking garage into drug store where he was injured, plaintiff, as to drug store proprietor, was no more than a mere licensee, drug store proprietor owed him no duty of care except to not injure him willfully, wantonly, or through gross negligence, but if plaintiff was an invitee of drug store proprietor, express or implied, drug store proprietor owed him a duty to use ordinary care to keep premises in a reasonably safe condition so that he would not be injured.—Renfro Drug Co. v. Lewis, 235 S.W.2d 609.

One who maintains a merchandise establishment, or other public place, to which by reason of the business so conducted thereon, the public is impliedly invited to enter, knows that strangers may enter his premises and therefor owes those who may so enter the duty to exercise ordinary care to see that premises are in a reasonably safe condition for their protection.—Renfro Drug Co. v. Lewis, 235 S.W.2d 609.

In determining whether a particular person is a business visitor of a possessor of land, the important thing is the desire or willingness to receive that person which a reasonable man would understand as expressed by words or conduct of the possessor.—Renfro Drug Co. v. Lewis, 235 S.W.2d 609.

Fact that a building is used as a shop gives the public reason to believe that the shopkeeper desires them to enter or is willing to permit their entrance not only for purpose of buying but also for purpose of passing through the shop, as regards issue whether persons entering the shop are business visitors of shopkeeper.—Renfro Drug Co. v. Lewis, 235 S.W.2d 609.

Where shopkeeper permits shop to be used as a shortcut between two streets, those so using it are "business visitors" of the shopkeeper.—Renfro Drug Co. v. Lewis, 235 S.W.2d 609.

Tex. Where owner of dry goods store had invited public to opening sale and had advertised that free merchandise would be given to each of the first 300 persons entering the store, persons entering the store were there by invitation, and it was store owner's duty to exercise ordinary care and to take proper precautions to prevent injury to such persons.—Lane v. Fair Stores, 243 S.W.2d 683.

Tex. Where plumber was on defendant's premises as a business invitee to perform services, defendant owed him duty to use reasonable care to make and keep premises reasonably safe for his use, including duty to warn him of dangers which were not obvious, reasonably apparent, or as well known to plumber as they were to defendant.—Triangle Motors of Dallas v. Richmond, 258 S.W.2d 914.

Tex. Where plaintiff had taken her children to physician and was sitting in physician's reception room awaiting an interview with him, she was a business invitee on physician's premises which status imposed upon physician the duty to use reasonable care to keep the premises in a reasonably safe condition.—McElhenny v. Thielepape, 285 S.W.2d 940.

Tex.Civ.App. Where plaintiff, after parking automobile in public garage, while attempting to pass through adjoining drug store to office building, fell when he opened door leading from garage which was unsafe because door opened abruptly upon two steep steps leading into drug store, owner of drug store was liable to plaintiff, at least as implied invitee of drug store.—Renfro Drug Co. v. Lewis, 228 S.W.2d 221, reversed 235 S.W.2d 609, 149 Tex. 507, 23 A.L.R.2d 1114.

Tex.Civ.App. Owner of premises owed business invitee duty to take reasonable care for his safety on premises, including opening and closing of gate, which was permanent fixture upon premises and used daily in owner's business.—Texas Livestock Marketing Ass'n v. Rogers, 244 S.W.2d 859, error ref. n. r. e.

Tex.Civ.App. Merchant did not insure customer, who was in merchant's store for purpose of trading, but did undertake to protect customer against merchant's negligence.—G. I. Surplus v. Renfro, 246 S.W.2d 293, error refused n. r. e.

Tex.Civ.App. A fraternal association's building, which was open to public, except on special occasions or for special events, and in which food and drinks were served to public daily, was a public building, and woman entering it to be served a drink was association's invitee, to whom it owed duty to use reasonable care to keep premises in reasonably safe condition except as to dangerous conditions which were obvious, reasonably apparent, or as well known to her as to association.—San Antonio Hermann Sons Home Ass'n v. Harvey, 256 S.W.2d 906, ref. n. r. e.

Utah. A "business visitor" is a person who is invited or permitted to enter or remain on land in the possession of another for a purpose directly or indirectly connected with dealings between them.—In re Wimmer's Estate, 182 P.2d 119, 111 Utah 444.

A workman who goes upon land of another to make alterations or repairs is a "business visitor."—In re Wimmer's Estate, 182 P.2d 119, 111 Utah 444.

Vt. A "business visitor" is one who is invited or permitted to enter or remain on land in the possession of another, for a purpose directly or indirectly connected with business dealings between them.—McAdams v. Raymond S. Roberts, Inc., 91 A.2d 706.

Vt. A "business visitor" is one invited or permitted to enter or remain on land in possession of another for purpose directly or indirectly connected with business dealings between them, and there is an implied invitation to a business visitor to make such use of another's premises as he is reasonably justified in understanding the owner intended.—Johnstone v. Bushnell, 102 A.2d 334, 118 Vt. 162.

Vt. A "business visitor" is one who is invited or permitted to enter or remain on land in possession of another for purpose directly or indirectly connected with business dealings between them and term "invitee" is used to denote same concept.—Robillard v. Tillotson, 108 A.2d 524, 118 Vt. 295.

Invitation required to qualify one as "business visitor" on premises of another may be either express or implied and invitation is implied whenever one makes use of another's premises as the owner intended he should or such as he is reasonably justified in understanding that the owner intended and to give person standing of business visitor it must appear that his purpose for entering the premises is one of interest or advantage to the occupant.—Robillard v. Tillotson, 108 A.2d 524, 118 Vt. 295.

Where plaintiff's husband had driven into gasoline station as business visitor and after concluding business at station had parked on premises to wait for plaintiff to join him, husband had ceased to be a business visitor and was at most licensee and station owner owed him no duty to provide place for plaintiff to join husband and would not be liable to plaintiff for injuries suffered when she fell into grease pit while en route to join husband.—Robillard v. Tillotson, 108 A.2d 524, 118 Vt. 295.

Principle that in some instances it is not necessary that visitor should himself be upon land for purposes of possessor's business to be entitled to status of business visitor would not apply to situation where plaintiff had come to gasoline station premises through invitation of her husband whose status on premises had ceased to be that of business visitor.—Robillard v. Tillotson, 108 A.2d 524, 118 Vt. 295.

Where there was no evidence that gasoline station owner expected customers to park on premises after concluding their business in order to have their friends meet them there, woman who went upon premises to meet her husband, who had concluded his business there and had ceased to have status of business visitor, did not herself have status of business visitor when she fell in grease pit.—Robillard v. Tillotson, 108 A.2d 524, 118 Vt. 295.

Vt. Where plaintiff entered defendant's store for purpose connected with defendant's business there carried on, and where parties had mutual interest in subject matter of plaintiff's visit, plaintiff was invitee.—Wakefield v. Levin, 110 A.2d 712, followed in 110 A.2d 716.

Va. Operator of tearoom was not an insurer of safety of a patron but did owe patron duty to exercise ordinary care to see that premises and equipment were in reasonably safe condition for patron's use in manner and to extent operator invited use of premises and equipment by patron.—Thalhimer Bros. v. Buckner, 76 S.E.2d 215, 194 Va. 1011.

Wash. An "invitee" is one who is either expressly or impliedly invited onto premises of another for some purpose connected with business in which owner or occupant is then engaged.—Grove v. D'Allessandro, 235 P.2d 826.

W.Va. A customer who enters a store to purchase merchandise is an "invitee", and owner of store owes to customer duty of ordinary care to keep the store in a reasonably safe condition.—Wendell v. G. C. Murphy Co., 70 S.E.2d 252.

The owner of a store is not an insurer of the safety of customers and does not contract against unknown defects not discoverable by ordinary care but implied warrants that premises are safe for customers and is required to exercise the care which an ordinary careful or prudent man would exercise, under like circumstances.—Wendell v. G. C. Murphy Co., 70 S.E.2d 252.

W.Va. One entering and present in restaurant for purpose of purchasing his lunch when accidentally injured by intoxicated man therein was restaurant owner's "invitee" or "business visitor," as his visit was for purpose connected with business conducted by owner on premises.—Puffer v. Hub Cigar Store, 84 S.E.2d 145.

Wyo. The legal relationship between storekeeper and customer shopping in store is that of invitor and invitee, as between whom law demands exercise of ordinary care in view of attendant facts and circumstances.—Dudley v. Montgomery Ward & Co., 192 P.2d 617, 64 Wyo. 357.

⚷32(2.9). *Deliverymen and haulers*

Ark. A truck driver, loading sand, which he was engaged to obtain and haul for another, at corporation's sand and gravel plant, was "invitee" of corporation, which owed him duty to use ordinary care to keep its premises in reasonably safe condition to prevent injury to him.—Glidewell v. Arkhola Sand & Gravel Co., 208 S.W.2d 4, 212 Ark. 838.

Conn. Truck driver who entered building to make delivery of goods was an invitee, and building owner could be held liable only if it failed to exercise reasonable care to have its premises safely constructed and maintained and to guard against subjecting truck driver to dangers of which it was cognizant or which it might reasonably have anticipated.—Rickey v. E. H. Jacobs Mfg. Co., 115 A.2d 336, 142 Conn. 495.

Ga.App. Service company's employee was an "invitee" while delivering ice to hotel and was entitled to protection of the Code requiring owner or occupier of land to exercise ordinary care in keeping premises and approaches safe for persons thereby express or implied invitation. Code, § 105-401.—Nabors v. Atlanta Biltmore Corp., 49 S.E.2d 688, 77 Ga.App. 730.

Iowa. Truck driver delivering freight to warehouse of another trucking company for further transportation under reciprocal arrangement with driver's employer was an "invitee" as affecting degree of care to be exercised for his safety.—McGrean v. Bos Freight Lines, 36 N.W.2d 374.

Ky. Truck driver employed by railway express agency was business invitee of owner at whose warehouse driver stopped to pick up freight, and owner, though not an insurer of driver's safety, owed to him the duty of exercising ordinary care to see that its premises were in reasonably safe condition so as not unnecessarily to expose driver to danger.—Standard Oil Co. v. Hagan, 218 S.W.2d 969, 309 Ky. 767.

Minn. One who was at a place of business at the express invitation of the owner for the purpose of delivering merchandise was an "invitee" to whom the owner owed the duty of exercising reasonable care to keep premises in a safe condition.—Folsom v. Hojny, 26 N.W.2d 219, 223 Minn. 223.

Miss. Truck driver, delivering lumber for his employer to lumber yard of buyers, was a "business invitee" of lumber yard operators.—Nowell v. Harris, 68 So.2d 464.

When truck driver, delivering lumber for his employer to lumber yard of buyer, was directed by lumber yard foreman to remove chain binder from nearby stack of lumber to be used in unloading truck and he undertook to do so, truck driver was an "express invitee" of lumber yard operators.—Nowell v. Harris, 68 So.2d 464.

N.J.Sup. Under contract between company and independent contractor for delivery of large pump to loading platform of company, one employed by independent contractor to make delivery was an invitee of company, and company had duty to exercise ordinary care to render premises reasonably safe for prospective use.—Gaglione v. J. S. Coffin, Jr., Co., 59 A.2d 806, 137 N.J.L. 303.

N.C. Plaintiff who, when injured, was on defendant's premises for purpose of delivering truck load of bagged feed for his employer, was an invitee.—Blake v. Great Atlantic & Pac. Tea Co., 75 S.E.2d 921, 237 N.C. 730.

Or. Implied invitation to truck driver to go upon logging company's premises for purpose of hauling logs did not authorize driver to enter danger zone of loading operations while another driver's truck was being loaded and when driver thus entered an area not within terms of his implied invitation, he became at most a mere "licensee" not entitled to invoke res ipsa loquitur doctrine to raise an inference of negligence of logging company in conduct of loading operations.—Short v. D. R. B. Logging Co., 235 P.2d 340.

R.I. Deliveryman for department store was not a mere "licensee" but a "business invitee" on premises to which he was making a delivery to whom, as such invitee, owners and occupants of premises owed the duty to use reasonable care to maintain in a condition that was reasonably safe for the purposes of the invitation, that portion of premises to be used by him.—Nottie v. Picchione, 59 A.2d 177, 74 R.I. 93.

Tex.Civ.App. In action for injuries sustained by plaintiff employed by another to haul ash from defendant's premises when he fell into a bed of hot ashes while walking down a side of a

FIFTH
DECENNIAL DIGEST

AMERICAN DIGEST SYSTEM

1936 - 1946

Volume 34
Municipal Corporations ☛ 827 — Newspapers

A Complete Digest Of All Decisions
Of The
State And Federal Courts As Reported In
The National Reporter System
And The State Reports

By the Publisher's Editorial Staff

ST. PAUL, MINN.
WEST PUBLISHING CO.

Tex.Civ.App. 1937. One injured by fall into unguarded hole, dug by owner of filling station in pathway leading therefrom to store owned by one operating filling station as tenant, *held* not mere licensee or trespasser, but implied invitee of station owner.—Beane v. Gulf Refining Co., 105 S.W.2d 334, affirmed Gulf Refining Co. v. Beane, 127 S.W.2d 169, 133 Tex. 157.

W.Va. 1938. A member of the family, or an invited guest of a motorist who goes to gasoline filling station as a customer, is an "invitee" of the operator of the station, and may recover for injuries sustained at station because of unsafe condition of premises.—Wingrove v. Home Land Co., 196 S.E. 563, 120 W.Va. 100, 116 A.L.R. 1197.

⟬32(2.6). Bill collectors.

Kan. 1939. A collector who was on partnership premises for purpose of making collections from partner on account with partner's son was at least a "licensee" as respects right of licensee to recover against partnership for injuries received on premises.—Montague v. Burgerhoff, 92 P.2d 98, 150 Kan. 217.

⟬32(2.7). Buildings in process of construction, alteration, or demolition.

C.C.A.N.Y. 1939. A woman, reasonably believing from condition of post office building being demolished that post office business was still being conducted therein when she mounted steps to enter building for purpose of mailing letter, was not a "trespasser," but gratuitous "licensee" or "business visitor."—Lewis-Kures v. Edward R. Walsh & Co., 102 F.2d 42, certiorari denied 60 S.Ct. 132, 308 U.S. 596, 84 L.Ed. 499.

C.C.A.Va. 1940. Where plaintiff who was member of building committee of board of trustees of town library and who had undertaken active supervision of building of library was injured by falling of defective scaffold while plaintiff was upon town property while contractors were constructing library thereon, formal or written authority from town or board of trustees was not necessary to clothe plaintiff with status of an "invitee," in determining contractors' liability for injuries, irrespective of whether plaintiff was authorized representative of town or board.—Robey v. Keller, 114 F.2d 790.

Cal.App. 1939. Corporation for which building was being constructed was "invitor" of employee of a subcontractor, and by exercising ordinary care in its conduct, discharged obligation, as an invitor, to the employee.—Hayden v. Paramount Productions, 91 P.2d 231, 33 Cal.App.2d 287.

Contractor and subcontractor were "invitees" of corporation for which they were constructing building, but as between each other contractor and subcontractor were strangers, owing to employees of each other the same duty of exercising ordinary care for their safety during progress of work as contactor and subcontractor owed to the public generally.—Hayden v. Paramount Productions, 91 P.2d 231, 33 Cal.App.2d 287.

⟬32(2.8). Business visitors, and store and restaurant patrons.

C.C.A. Idaho 1944. A patron who entered a store for purpose of purchasing merchandise was an "invitee" to whom store owner owed duty of maintaining its premises in reasonably safe condition and exercising reasonable care to protect patrons from injury and store owner was negligent if it violated that duty.—Montgomery Ward & Co. v. Lamberson, 144 F.2d 97.

A store owner's duty to patron was not that of an insurer but was merely that of maintaining his premises in a reasonably safe condition and of exercising reasonable care to protect patron from injury.—Montgomery Ward & Co. v. Lamberson, 144 F.2d 97.

C.C.A. Minn. 1939. A department store patron was on steps in store at implied invitation of owner, and was entitled to protection afforded by ordinance requiring handrails on both sides of department store "stairways."—Montgomery Ward & Co. v. Snuggins, 103 F.2d 458.

C.C.A.N.Y. 1938. The "business visitor" relation with its resulting duty arises only when person who enters premises does so in the interest of the owner, or upon some business of his own, of which the owner has notice and to an entry in pursuit of which he consents, directly or indirectly.—Gunnarson v. Robert Jacob, Inc., 94 F.2d 170, certiorari denied Robert Jacob, Inc., v. Gunnarson, 58 S.Ct. 764, 303 U.S. 660, 82 L.Ed. 1119, rehearing denied 58 S.Ct. 948, 304 U.S. 588, 82 L.Ed. 1548.

C.C.A.N.C. 1938. A customer who after having made purchases and left store, returned merely to recover pocketbook which she had left by mistake was nevertheless an invitee to whom store owed ordinary care, rather than a mere licensee, especially in view of store rule requiring customers to go to the office to recover lost articles.—H. L. Green Co. v. Bobbitt, 99 F.2d 281.

C.C.A.N.C. 1939. While a storekeeper is not an insurer of safety of customers, customers are "invitees" and he owes them the duty of keeping his premises in a reasonably safe condition and must use ordinary care to avoid accidents or injuries.—Baskin v. Montgomery Ward & Co., 104 F.2d 531.

C.C.A. Va. 1940. A "business visitor" is a person who is invited or permitted to enter or remain on land in possession of another for a purpose directly or indirectly connected with business dealings between them.—Robey v. Keller, 114 F.2d 790.

D.C.W.Va. 1945. A customer entering retail store at actual or implied request of storekeeper, to make purchases therein, is an invitee to whom storekeeper owes duty of exercising ordinary care to look out for customer's safety, including duty to use ordinary care to see that aisles and entrances are maintained in reasonably safe condition for ordinary use of customers.—Rankin v. S. S. Kresge Co., 59 F.Supp. 613, affirmed 149 F.2d 934.

Cal. 1942. One lawfully entering store during business hours to purchase goods does so at implied invitation of owner, on whom law imposes duty to exercise ordinary care and prudence to keep aisles and passageways, in and through which, by their location and arrangement, customer is induced to go in making purchases, in reasonably safe condition, so as not to expose him to danger or accident unnecessarily.—Neel v. Mannings, Inc., 122 P.2d 576, 19 Cal.2d 647.

Cal. 1944. It is sufficient to constitute one an "invitee" or "business visitor", to whom proprietor of premises must exercise ordinary care, that he be on premises for the convenience or necessity of one who is upon the premises for the purpose of the possessor's business, and it is not necessary that the visitor should himself be upon the premises for such purpose.—Crane v. Smith, 144 P.2d 356, 23 Cal.2d 288.

Cal. 1944. A prospective tenant calling at apartment building to look for apartment was a "business visitor" to whom building owners and operators owed ordinary care.—Oettinger v. Stewart, 148 P.2d 19, 24 Cal. 2d 133, 156 A.L.R. 1221.

Cal.App. 1936. Customer in restaurant who was injured when she fell on stairway which was being mopped, while customer was ascending stairs while returning from ladies rest room, *held* "invitee," to whom restaurant owner owed duty to exercise ordinary care to keep passageway in reasonably safe condition.—De Verdi v. Weiss, 60 P.2d 879, 16 Cal.App.2d 439.

Cal.App. 1939. One who patronizes a bank or shop in a hotel which has accommodations for a large patronage, with a theater, assembly rooms, shops, etc., abutting upon the corridors, has the same right in a corridor as one who comes to buy his luncheon or to occupy a room.—Koppelman v. Ambassador Hotel Co. of Los Angeles, 96 P.2d 196, 35 Cal.App.2d 537.

Cal.App. 1940. A customer conducted into a room in a store by the store manager for purpose of selling customer a pair of slippers was an "invitee," as respects liability of store for injuries received when customer fell into an opening in floor when a trapdoor gave way.—John v. B. B. McGinnis Co., 99 P.2d 323, 37 Cal.App.2d 176.

Cal.App. 1942. Generally, one who during business hours lawfully enters a store to purchase goods does so at implied invitation of owner, upon whom the law imposes the duty of exercising ordinary care to keep aisles and passageways, in and through which by their location and arrangement a customer in making his purchases is induced to go, in a reasonably safe condition so as not to unnecessarily expose customer to danger or accident.—Thompson v. B. F. Goodrich Co., 120 P.2d 693, 48 Cal.App.2d 723.

Cal.App. 1943. Where defendants were engaged in business of renting apartments and displayed sign visible to public indicating that business, there was "invitation" to persons looking for apartments to rent to enter and make inquiry, so that person making inquiry was an "invitee" and the invitation included an invitation for departure from building.—Oettinger v. Stewart, 137 P.2d 852, subsequent opinion 148 P.2d 19, 24 Cal.2d 133, 156 A.L.R. 1221.

Cal.App. 1944. One who enters premises pursuant to a general invitation to discuss employment is an "invitee" and entitled to protection as such.—Delay v. Braun, 146 P.2d 32, 63 Cal.App.2d 8.

Cal.App. 1944. One who went to defendant's vegetable market to buy greens to garnish meats in meat market where he worked and who was told to go into back room and get them and who fell while in such back room was an "invitee", and defendant owed him duty of exercising ordinary care.—Walker v. Greenberger, 147 P. 2d 105, 63 Cal.App.2d 457.

Cal.App. 1944. Where defendant acting through booking agents invited plaintiff to appear and demonstrate her act, plaintiff was a business "invitee" and defendants owed her all duties attendant thereon.—Gastine v. Ewing, 150 P.2d 266, 65 Cal.App.2d 131.

Cal.App. 1944. Customer who entered store for purpose of purchasing a dress and who remained until closing time for purpose of procuring dress after it had been altered and who was injured while leaving building when she stepped into a hole in an aisle was not a "licensee" but was an "invitee" toward whom proprietor was bound to exercise ordinary care to keep aisles in reasonably safe condition and to warn her of existing dangers.—Locke v. Red River Lumber Co., 150 P.2d 506, 65 Cal.App.2d 322.

Cal.App. 1944. Where decedent had contracted to deliver ore to mining company's tramway for transportation to its mill and it had been the regular custom for decedent and his employees to ride in tramway buckets as a means of transportation to and from the mines, deceased was a "business invitee" and not a "trespasser" in going to mines by means of the tramway.—Bee v. Tungstar Corp., 151 P.2d 537, 65 Cal. App.2d 729.

Colo. 1939. An invitation to a customer or patron to go to certain parts of business premises may arise by implication from a known customary use, as respects liability for injuries sustained by customer or patron.—Rudolph v. Elder, 95 P.2d 827, 105 Colo. 105.

A "business invitation" includes an invitation to use such part of the premises as the visitor reasonably believes is held open to him as a means of access to or egress from the place where his business is to be transacted, as respects liability for injuries sustained on the premises.—Rudolph v. Elder, 95 P.2d 827, 105 Colo. 105.

Conn. 1937. In action for injuries sustained in fall on icy steps of undertaking parlor, finding that plaintiff at request of another called at undertaking parlor to have undertaker call at home of plaintiff's neighbor on certain street to arrange funeral and was lawfully on defendant's premises, when record of Bureau of Vital Statistics showed no death to have occurred on that particular street on day in question, was not error, since plaintiff's purpose being what court found it was, though founded on misapprehension of fact, significance of purpose was not affected.—Chatkin v. Talarski, 193 A. 611, 123 Conn. 157.

Where plaintiff was injured on steps of undertaking parlor, when calling on undertaker at request of another to arrange funeral, plaintiff was an "invitee".—Chatkin v. Talarski, 193 A. 611, 123 Conn. 157.

Fla. 1942. Where salesman who had been invited to enter customer's machine shop on former visits entered when calling at customer's request to discuss an order, salesman was an "invitee" to whom customer owed a duty to have its place of business in a reasonably safe condition.—National Brands v. Norton Tire Co., for Use of Ocean Acc. & Guarantee Corp., 7 So.2d 456, 150 Fla. 349.

Ga.App. 1939. A petition alleging that plaintiff by implied invitation had visited defendant's store to make a purchase and by defendant's permission had ascended stairway in rear of store to visit a relative of plaintiff's husband employed in alteration department, and that because of alleged defects in stairway plaintiff was injured while descending stairway, showed as a matter of law that while on stairway plaintiff was not an "invitee" but was a "licensee," and petition was demurrable in absence of an allegation that plaintiff occupied stairway incidental to or connected with the purchase and sale of merchandise or a charge of violation of any duty towards her as licensee.

Code 1933, § 105-401.—Freeman v. Levy, 5 S.E.2d 61, 60 Ga.App. 861.

Ga.App. 1943. One entering another's premises for purposes connected with his business conducted on the premises is an "invitee" and the other is liable to him for failure to exercise ordinary care in keeping the premises safe. Code, § 105-401.—United Theatre Enterprises v. Carpenter, 23 S.E.2d 189, 68 Ga.App. 438.

Ill.App. 1940. The law raises on the part of a proprietor of a store an implied invitation to the public to come into his building or upon his premises should they seek to do business with him, and he is under a legal obligation to exercise ordinary and reasonable care to make his premises safe for the protection of his customers.—Todd v. S. S. Kresge Co., 24 N.E.2d 899, 303 Ill.App. 89.

Ill.App. 1940. As respects liability of owner of building for injuries sustained by plaintiff in falling on steps when leaving building, sign in window announcing that a rummage sale would be held on the following day amounted to an invitation to persons interested to enter upon the premises either for purpose of purchasing or ascertaining with certainty the goods which would be on sale.—Rasmussen v. National Tea Co., 26 N. E.2d 523, 304 Ill.App. 353.

Ill.App. 1942. If a person enters a store, not for purpose of business, but on some personal errand, or if a person goes into a part of store where customers are not supposed to be in ordinary course of their business, then the person becomes merely a "licensee", and only duty that storekeeper has to such licensee is to not wilfully or wantonly injure him.—Wesbrock v. Colby, Inc., 43 N.E.2d 405, 315 Ill.App. 494.

Where plaintiff, after making some purchases in defendant's store, was injured when she fell down basement steps as she attempted to make use of telephone located in stairway of store which was not intended for public use, and there was no evidence that clerk who showed plaintiff where telephone was had authority to give plaintiff permission to use it, plaintiff at time she received her injuries was a "licensee", and not an "invitee", and hence could not recover for her injuries, in absence of any willful or wanton misconduct by defendant.—Wesbrock v. Colby, Inc., 43 N.E.2d 405, 315 Ill.App. 494.

Ind. 1943. While corporation operating store was not "insurer" of its customers' safety, they were "invitees", to whom it owed duty to keep premises, including stairway leading to its restaurant on second floor, in reasonably safe condition for their use.—F. W. Woolworth Co. v. Moore, 48 N.E.2d 644, 221 Ind. 490.

Iowa 1939. Store customer was "invitee" of owners of the store, who therefore had duty to be reasonably sure that they

FOURTH
DECENNIAL DIGEST

AMERICAN DIGEST SYSTEM

A COMPLETE DIGEST OF ALL DECISIONS
OF THE
STATE AND FEDERAL COURTS AS REPORTED IN
THE NATIONAL REPORTER SYSTEM
AND THE STATE REPORTS

1926 TO 1936

Volume 24
Names—Party Walls

BY THE PUBLISHER'S EDITORIAL STAFF

ST. PAUL, MINN.
WEST PUBLISHING CO.

Wis. 1934. Employer must make premises safe for performance by frequenters of acts which he knows or reasonably should know are going to be performed there. St.1929, § 101.-06.—Neitzke v. Kraft-Phenix Dairies, 253 N.W. 579, 214 Wis. 441.

Where employees or frequenters are injured as result of unsafe condition of place to work against which employer could reasonably have protected them, employer is liable where injured persons had exercised ordinary care. St.1929, § 101.06.—Neitzke v. Kraft-Phenix Dairies, 253 N.W. 579, 214 Wis. 441.

Wyo. 1927. Garage proprietor *held* required to exercise reasonable care to protect customer's agent from danger; "invitee."—Loney v. Laramie Auto Co., 255 P. 350, 36 Wyo. 339, 53 A.L.R. 73.

Garage keeper's duty to protect invitee is coextensive with invitation limited by character and purpose of visit.—Loney v. Laramie Auto Co., 255 P. 350, 36 Wyo. 339, 53 A.L.R. 73.

☞32 (2). Who are licensees, and status of persons going on land of another.

C.C.A.Cal. 1928. Owner has duty to refrain from subjecting to unnecessary peril employee of contractor working on unfinished building.—McCready v. Southern Pac. Co., 26 F.2d 569.

C.C.A.Ill. 1926. Person injured considered invitee rather than licensee, when on premises for mutual benefit of parties.—Fleischmann Malting Co. v. Mrkacek, 14 F.2d 602.

Person injured *held* invitee in going on premises with permission of foreman in immediate control.—Fleischmann Malting Co. v. Mrkacek, 14 F.2d 602.

C.C.A.Md. 1931. One who, considering nature of shop and use made of it by public, feels reasonably free to enter by implied invitation, is invitee.—Elkton Auto Sales Corporation v. State of Maryland, to Use of Ferry, 53 F.2d 8.

C.C.A.Mass. 1932. One entering restaurant and falling on floor was "invitee" to whom proprietor owed duty to maintain premises in reasonably safe condition.—Holmes v. Ginter Restaurant Co., 54 F.2d 876.

C.C.A.N.Y. 1932. Applicants for work in construction gang, while in temporary building of contractor, were invitees, entitled to reasonably safe place for their entertainment.—Mideastern Contracting Corporation v. O'Toole, 55 F.2d 909.

C.C.A.N.Y. 1934. "Invited person" is one entering another's premises not only for his own purposes, but in interest of owner aware that mutual interest of both may lead to such entry.—Radoslovich v. Navigazione Libera Triestina, S. A., 72 F.2d 367.

C.C.A.Tenn. 1931. One entering storage building in search of work, who was told to see man in rear thereof, was not invitee when injured.—American Ry. Express Co. v. Gilbreath, 48 F.2d 809.

D.C.N.Y. 1928. Repair company permitting ship's employees to use its gangway, must use ordinary care to keep gangway in proper condition; owner's employees being invitees.—Standard Oil Co., N.J., v. Robbins Dry Dock & Repair Co., 25 F.2d 339, affirmed, C.C.A., Standard Oil Co. v. Robins Dry Dock & Repair Co., 32 F.2d 182.

D.C.Pa. 1933. Customer, in using pay telephone maintained by storekeeper for customers' use, *held* invitee, not mere licensee, as respects storekeeper's liability for negligence.—Randolph v. Great Atlantic & Pacific Tea Co., 2 F.Supp. 462, affirmed, C.C.A., Great Atlantic & Pacific Tea Co. v. Randolph, 64 F.2d 247.

Ala. 1927. Customer using toilet *held* "invitee," to whom storekeeper owed duty to use ordinary care.—McClusky v. Duncan, 113 So. 250, 216 Ala. 388.

Ala. 1928. Boy on employer's premises at invitation of employee for whom he was working for purpose of receiving pay *held* an "invitee."—Stephens v. Walker, 117 So. 22, 217 Ala. 466.

Ala. 1928. Plaintiff carrying cotton into public warehouse must have been in warehouse on business on which invitation was extended to be "invitee."—Farmers' & Merchants' Warehouse Co. v. Perry, 118 So. 406, 218 Ala. 223.

Ark. 1931. Customer in habit of going to defendant's place of business on Sunday for seven or eight years *held* "invitee," not "licensee."—Armour & Co. v. Rose, 36 S.W.2d 70, 183 Ark. 413.

Volunteer or person on premises with permission of owner from motives of curiosity or private convenience is mere "licensee."—Armour & Co. v. Rose, 36 S.W.2d 70, 183 Ark. 413.

Licensee going on premises for owner's purpose on invitation becomes "invitee" to whom owner owes duty of taking ordinary care to prevent injury.—Armour & Co. v. Rose, 36 S.W.2d 70, 183 Ark. 413.

Ark. 1933. Invitation to come upon premises will not be implied ordinarily from fact that owner or occupant has acquiesced in or tolerated trespasses thereon.—Missouri Pac. R. Co. v. English, 61 S.W.2d 445, 187 Ark. 557.

Owner or occupant who has permitted persons generally to use or establish way under such circumstances as to induce belief that it is public in character, owes to persons availing themselves thereof duty due to those who come upon premises by invitation.—Missouri Pac. R. Co. v. English, 61 S.W.2d 445, 187 Ark. 557.

Cal. 1931. One having business in office building and, while searching for washroom, stepping through open door into totally dark space and falling down air shaft, *held* not then invitee.—Medcraft v. Merchants' Exchange, 295 P. 822, 211 Cal. 404.

Person may be invitee in one portion of building and not in others.—Medcraft v. Merchants' Exchange, 295 P. 822, 211 Cal. 404.

Cal. 1933. One taking possession of stall in newly completed produce building occupied status of tenant, though rent payments had not started, and subcontractor constructing doors owed such occupant duty of due care.—Hall v. Barber Door Co., 23 P.2d 279, 218 Cal. 412.

Cal. 1935. Where defendant did not expressly consent to plaintiff being in place where plaintiff was at time of injury and plaintiff was there for personal reasons having no connection with defendant's business, there could be no implied consent to plaintiff's presence within area occupied by defendant.—Hamakawa v. Crescent Wharf & Warehouse Co., 50 P.2d 803, 4 Cal.2d 499.

Cal.App. 1927. Persons entering store during business hours to purchase goods are invitees.—Oles v. Kahn Bros., 253 P. 158, 81 Cal.App. 76.

Cal.App. 1928. Salesman slipping on runway entering receiving room of defendant's store *held* an "invitee" and not a trespasser or mere naked "licensee."—Madigan v. O. A. Hale & Co., 265 P. 574, 90 Cal.App. 151.

Cal.App. 1930. To be "invitee," one must have entered premises at invitation of owner or occupant thereof.—Aguilar v. Riverdale Co-op. Creamery Ass'n, 285 P. 889, 104 Cal.App. 263.

Invitation is implied when one enters premises for mutual benefit of owner and himself, or in connection with owner's business.—Aguilar v. Riverdale Co-op. Creamery Ass'n, 285 P. 889, 104 Cal.App. 263.

One entering premises merely for purposes of his own or of third party, having no relation to business of owner, is bare "licensee."—Aguilar v. Riverdale Co-op. Creamery Ass'n, 285 P. 889, 104 Cal.App. 263.

Employee of prune grower using drier with permission of drier owner but without charge *held* licensee, and could not recover from owner for loss of hand severed by revolving fan in drier.—Aguilar v. Riverdale Co-op. Creamery Ass'n, 285 P. 889, 104 Cal.App. 263.

Cal.App. 1930. One invited upon premises for special purpose may be mere licensee with respect to certain parts of premises, approaches, or appliances.—State Compensation Ins. Fund v. Allen, 285 P. 1053, 104 Cal.App. 400.

That subcontractor's employee used runway several times during morning of accident, without knowledge of contractor, did not establish invitation.—State Compensation Ins. Fund v. Allen, 285 P. 1053, 104 Cal.App. 400.

Cal.App. 1931. One in loading room and also in stage at express invitation of driver and for purpose of aiding in looking for passenger's purse was "invitee."—Smith v. Pickwick Stages System, 297 P. 940, 113 Cal.App. 118.

Cal.App. 1931. As regards liability of contractor constructing bridge, state engineer inspecting work under construction was invitee, not licensee, though injured while voluntarily carrying tool to workman.—Christy v. Ulrich, 298 P. 135, 113 Cal.App. 338.

Cal.App. 1933. Person may become invitee for specific purpose, and, at same time, become mere licensee with respect to parts of premises.—Buckingham v. San Joaquin Cotton Oil Co., 16 P.2d 807, 128 Cal.App. 94.

Invitation to use premises is inferred where there is common interest or mutual advantage. —Buckingham v. San Joaquin Cotton Oil Co., 16 P.2d 807, 128 Cal.App. 94.

License is inferred where object is mere pleasure or benefit of person using premises.— Buckingham v. San Joaquin Cotton Oil Co., 16 P.2d 807, 128 Cal.App. 94.

Truck driver who delivered cotton seed to mill, and sustained injuries when feet slipped into screw conveyor through bars while on top to dislodge seed clogging conveyor, *held* implied invitee.—Buckingham v. San Joaquin Cotton Oil Co., 16 P.2d 807, 128 Cal.App. 94.

Cal.App. 1933. While landowner owes no duty to trespasser or licensee, except to refrain from willful injury, invitation to go on land may be implied.—Lambert v. Western Pac. R. Co., 26 P.2d 824, 135 Cal.App. 81.

Cal.App. 1934. Property owners failing to discover that electric company's pole supporting power lines on owners' premises was decayed beneath ground *held* not negligent, so as to be liable for injuries to electrician when pole he climbed on to cut wires broke and fell, though electrician was invitee, in absence of showing property owners knew pole was unsafe.—Hall v. Southern California Edison Co., 30 P.2d 1013, 137 Cal.App. 449.

Cal.App. 1935. In determining status of person upon property as respects duty of care of property owner toward such person,"invitation" to use premises is inferred when there is a common interest or mutual advantage whereas "license" is inferred when object is mere pleasure or benefit of person using property.— McStay v. Citizens' Nat. Trust & Savings Bank of Los Angeles, 43 P.2d 560, 5 Cal.App.2d 595.

Cal.App. 1935. Invitation to use premises of another is inferred where there is common interest or mutual advantage, while license is inferred where object is mere pleasure or benefit of person using premises.—Lawand v. California Products Co., 48 P.2d 979, 9 Cal.App.2d 147.

Colo. 1932. Request that one delivering coal, and subsequently injured, move away from fence so cattle would go into chute did not amount to revocation of license to be upon premises.—Averch v. Johnston, 9 P.2d 291, 90 Colo. 321.

Conn. 1926. One entering door leading from cloak room of public assembly hall *held* to be invitee, to whom defendant owed duty of reasonable care.—Bunnell v. Waterbury Hospital, 131 A. 501, 103 Conn. 520.

Conn. 1928. Customer helping himself to gasoline from pump, thereby following practice which owner's conduct of business had sanctioned *held* licensee and not trespasser.— Hanlon v. City of Waterbury, 142 A. 681, 108 Conn. 197.

Conn. 1928. One returning to building as directed, to get pay for removing wood, *held* invitee, whom owner and lessee owed duty of reasonable care to protect from injury because of defects therein.—Werebeychick v. Morris Land & Development Co., 142 A. 739, 108 Conn. 226.

Conn. 1931. One invited to enter store and use telephone was an "invitee."—Ward v. Avery, 155 A. 502, 113 Conn. 394.

Conn. 1933. Customer entering store is invitee to whom storekeeper owes duty of exercising reasonable care to keep premises in reasonably safe condition.—Lunny v. Pepe, 165 A. 552, 116 Conn. 684.

Ga. 1935. Person injured on another's property is not "licensee" unless he has permission, express or implied, to go upon other's property.—Atlantic Coast Line R. Co. v. O'Neal, 178 S.E. 451, 180 Ga. 153, reversing 172 S.E. 740, 48 Ga.App. 706, and conformed to 179 S.E. 655, 51 Ga.App. 100.

Ga.App. 1931. Independent contractor was at most mere licensee in entering on another portion of premises than necessary for performing work.—West v. Smith & Kelly Co., 157 S.E. 261, 42 Ga.App. 653.

Independent contractor *held* mere licensee in going to lavatory on premises, and could not recover for injuries caused by defective step leading from lavatory.—West v. Smith & Kelly Co., 157 S.E. 261, 42 Ga.App. 653.

Ga.App. 1932. Member of city fire department enters premises as licensee when entering in exercise of his duty.—Todd v. Armour & Co., 162 S.E. 394, 44 Ga.App. 609.

Ga.App. 1934. Customary permissive use of pond on defendants' premises for swimming *held* not to constitute users "invitees."—McCall v. McCallie, 171 S.E. 843, 48 Ga.App. 99.

"Invitee" under implied invitation, as distinguished from mere "licensee," must come upon premises for benefit, real or supposed, of owner or occupant, or in matter of mutual interest, or in usual course of business, or for performance of some duty, but invitation may be implied from any state of facts upon which it naturally and necessarily arises.—McCall v. McCallie, 171 S.E. 843, 48 Ga.App. 99.

"Licensee" is person who is neither customer, servant, nor trespasser and stands in no contractual relation with owner of premises, but is permitted, expressly or impliedly, to go thereon merely for his own interest, convenience, or gratification.—McCall v. McCallie, 171 S.E. 843, 48 Ga.App. 99.

Idaho 1927. One entering place of business to make purchase is "invitee."—Williamson v. Neitzel, 260 P. 689, 45 Idaho, 39.

Idaho 1929. One on premises merely by permission or toleration is licensee.—Pincock v. McCoy, 281 P. 371, 48 Idaho, 227.

Police officer entering premises in emergency in discharge of duty is "licensee."—Pincock v. McCoy, 281 P. 371, 48 Idaho, 227.

Ill.App. 1926. Letter carrier, going to second floor rooms leased as offices *held* invitee.—Sutton v. Penn, 238 Ill.App. 182.

Ill.App. 1929. Person entering store to telephone from booth is invitee.—Dowling v. MacLean Drug Co., 248 Ill.App. 270.

Ind.App. 1929. Neither silence, acquiescence, nor permission alone etablishes "invitation" to go on premises, as regards liability for negligence.—Indianapolis Motor Speedway Co. v. Shoup, 165 N.E. 246, 88 Ind.App. 572.

One invited to place by employee without authority becomes trespasser or licensee, to whom master owes no duty to exercise care.—Indianapolis Motor Speedway Co. v. Shoup, 165 N.E. 246, 88 Ind.App. 572.

Ind.App. 1930. Customer of company whose employee led him across elevator was invitee and entitled to suppose that course was reasonably safe.—Clark Fruit Co. v. Stephan, 170 N.E. 558, 91 Ind.App. 152.

Iowa 1930. Customer in store, injured by falling down open stairway behind counter, was invitee at least while in aisles provided for customers.—Nelson v. F. W. Woolworth & Co., 231 N.W. 665, 211 Iowa, 592.

Iowa 1932. One going on defendant's premises to prepare junk bought for removal was invitee.—Pomerantz v. Pennsylvania-Dixie Cement Corporation, 243 N.W. 283, 214 Iowa, 1002.

Iowa 1934. Doctor who called at office of patient's employer to get insurance report blanks was "invitee," and, when he left office and started through plant to see patient, he became a mere "licensee" to whom plant owner owed no duty other than not to wantonly or willfully cause him injury.—Wilson v. Goodrich, 252 N.W. 142, 218 Iowa, 462.

Iowa 1934. Repeated trespasses alone, or trespasses by many, do not ripen into license unless attended by circumstances showing knowledge and acquiescence, or of such character as to charge owner with knowledge.—Battin v. Cornwall, 253 N.W. 842, 218 Iowa, 42.

Kan. 1934. One who without business goes into oil company's storage room to loaf, knowing that such conduct is forbidden by company's rules, is not "invitee," as regards company's liability for employee's alleged negligence causing fatal injury to loafer.—Dye v. Rule, 28 P.2d 758, 138 Kan. 808.

Ky. 1926. "Invitee" and "licensee" distinguished.—L. E. Meyers' Co. v. Logue's Adm'r, 280 S.W. 107, 212 Ky. 802.

Ky. 1930. "Invitation," as regards duty of owner of premises, is inferred where there is common or mutual advantage, whereas "license" is inferred where object is mere pleasure or benefit of person using it.—Louisville & N. R. Co. v. Snow's Adm'r, 30 S.W.2d 885, 235 Ky. 211.

Ky. 1935. Merchant and customer stand in relation of "invitor" and "invitee."—F. W. Woolworth Co. v. Brown, 79 S.W.2d 362, 258 Ky. 29.

La.App. 1927. Carpenter, applying for work and told by foreman to wait, becomes invitee while waiting for foreman to investigate.—Noble v. Southland Lumber Co., 4 La.App. 281.

La.App. 1930. Bottling machine salesman, observing operation of competitor's machine by purchaser's permission, *held* licensee when injured by explosion of bottle.—Vargas v. Blue Seal Bottling Works, 126 So. 707, 12 La.App. 652.

Mutuality of interest is necessary to create status of invitee.—Vargas v. Blue Seal Bottling Works, 126 So. 707, 12 La.App. 652.

La.App. 1935. Wife of man for whom house was being constructed upon lot belonging to legal community of wife and husband, while perhaps having right of owner to go into house while in course of construction for purpose of examining work as it progressed, was not an "invitee."—Perbos v. Barrelli, 159 So. 631, followed in 159 So. 633.

Me. 1929. One who paused on sidewalk in front of shooting gallery to watch shooting was neither invitee nor licensee as to owner of gallery.—Silverman v. Usen, 147 A. 421, 128 Me. 349.

AMERICAN DIGEST SYSTEM

1926

THIRD

DECENNIAL EDITION

OF THE

AMERICAN DIGEST

A COMPLETE DIGEST OF ALL
REPORTED CASES FROM 1916 TO 1926

VOLUME 21

NAMES—PATENTS

ST. PAUL
WEST PUBLISHING CO.
1929

(Pa.1924) Where defendant company permitted persons to use its passageway, it was defendant's duty to use reasonable care either to keep the way free from obstruction, or to give reasonable notice to persons using the way of existing danger.—John v. Reick-McJunkin Dairy Co., 127 A. 143, 281 Pa. 543.

(Pa.1925) One inviting another to his place of business assumes toward him certain duties, and is liable if he negligently permits a danger of any kind to exist which results in injury to person invited without negligence on his part.—Fredericks v. Atlantic Refining Co., 127 A. 615, 282 Pa. 8, 38 A. L. R. 666.

(S.C.1921) Where defendant's own requested charge conceded that plaintiff was a licensee, it was proper to modify that portion of the charge which stated that defendant's only duty was not to willfully or wantonly injure him, and impose on defendant the duty of reasonable care.—McAlister v. Thomas & Howard Co., 108 S. E. 94, 116 S. C. 319.

(Tex.Com.App.1919) The duty of an owner or occupant of real property to keep it reasonably safe and give warning of concealed perils applies only to invitees, and not to trespassers or mere licensees.—Bustillos v. Southwestern Portland Cement Co., 211 S. W. 929, reversing judgment (Civ. App. 1914) Southwestern Portland Cement Co. v. Bustillos, 169 S. W. 638, and opinion of Supreme Court conformed to by (Civ. App.) 216 S. W. 268, dismissed for want of jurisdiction.

(Vt.1916) An owner does not owe to a person employed on his premises in the service of an independent contractor any duty to furnish a safe working place, yet as such employé is on the premises by invitation, the owner if retaining control must exercise reasonable care to see that the premises are safe.—Richards v. Consolidated Lighting Co., 99 A. 241, 90 Vt. 552.

(Va.1919) An occupant of land is charged with knowledge of the use of his premises by a licensee, and while not chargeable with the duty of provision or preparation for the safety of the licensee, he is chargeable with the duty of lookout.—John P. Pettyjohn & Sons v. Basham, 100 S. E. 813, 126 Va. 72.

An occupant of land owes to an invitee, to the extent of the invitation, the duty of prevision, preparation, and lookout, and must use ordinary care to see that his premises are in a reasonably safe condition.—Id.

(Va.1924) Employer of independent contractor engaged to paint skylight *held* not liable for injuries to contractor's employés who fell when light collapsed with his and a helper's weight, though such employé be deemed while on skylight to have been an invitee, in absence of showing of employer's negligence.—Davis Bakery v. Dozier, 124 S. E. 411, 139 Va. 628.

(Wash.1919) The duty of care which the owner of a building owes to invitees differs from the duty of care he owes to a mere licensee, the duty to an invitee being to keep the ways reasonably safe for him and open to entry at all reasonable hours, and the duty to a licensee being only the negative one of not wantonly injuring him.—Konick v. Champneys, 183 P. 75, 108 Wash. 35, 6 A. L. R. 459.

(Wash.1921) All persons having occasion to enter an office building on legitimate business have an implied invitation from the owner of the building for that purpose, and such owner owes a duty to all such persons to exercise reasonable care to provide a reasonably safe entrance, and such entrance, or the approach thereto, must be so constructed and maintained that visitors will not be liable to step into dangerous pitfalls by reason of misleading doors or deceptive landings.—Johnson v. Smith, 194 P. 997, 114 Wash. 311.

v.21,3D DEC.DIG.—9

(Wash.1925) An owner or occupier of realty is not obliged to make it safe, or to keep it in any particular condition for benefit of trespassers, intruders, mere volunteers or bare licensees.—Bolden v. Independent Order of Odd Fellows, 233 P. 273, 133 Wash. 293.

(W.Va.1918) One using premises of another by owner's invitation has right to assume that such premises are reasonably safe for purpose for which he is invited thereon.—Starcher v. South Penn Oil Co., 95 S. E. 28, 81 W. Va. 587.

(Wis.1921) In cases of invitor and invitee, where the invitor is sought to be made liable for failure to exercise ordinary care to keep and maintain the premises in a safe condition, there must be some mutuality of interest or benefit in order to render the invitor liable.—Greenfield v. Miller, 180 N. W. 834, 173 Wis. 184, 12 A. L. R. 982.

Ordinarily there is no liability on the part of a licensor for injuries sustained by those coming on the premises as mere licensees, unless there is something on the premises in the nature of a trap or the licensor was guilty of active negligence.—Id.

The owner of a house is not liable to a guest for injuries sustained when the guest slipped on an unfastened oriental rug on a polished hardwood floor; the guest being a mere licensee, and it not appearing that the floor and rug constituted any trap.—Id.

32 (2). Who are licensees, and status of persons going on land of another.

See Automobiles, 155; Electricity, 15 (1).
Burden of proof, see post, 121(1).
Employé of contractor to repair, see Municipal Corporations, 848.
Licensees on master's premises, see Master and Servant, 302(1).
Wharf, see Wharves, 21.

To come under an implied invitation, as distinguished from a mere license, the visitor must come for a purpose connected with the occupant's business, and there must be some mutuality of interest to which the visitor's business relates.

—**(Cal.App.1923)** Bush v. Weed Lumber Co., 218 P. 618, 63 Cal. App. 426;

(Me.1918) Kidder v. Sadler, 103 A. 159, 117 Me. 194;

(N.Y.App.Div.1922) Brister v. Flatbush Leasing Corporation, 195 N. Y. S. 424, 202 App. Div. 294;

(Vt.1921) Coburn v. Village of Swanton, 115 A. 153, 95 Vt. 320;

(Wash.1916) Gasch v. Rounds, 160 P. 962, 93 Wash. 317.

One who during business hours lawfully enters a store to purchase goods does so at the implied invitation of the owner upon whom the law imposes the duty of exercising ordinary care.

—**(Cal.App.1921)** Brinkworth v. Sam Seelig Co., 197 P. 427, 51 Cal. App. 668;

(Iowa,1922) Keeran v. Spurgeon Mercantile Co., 191 N. W. 99, 194 Iowa, 1240, 27 A. L. R. 579;

(N.Y.App.Div.1923) Tryon v. Chalmers, 200 N. Y. S. 362, 205 App. Div. 816, appeal dismissed (1925) 148 N. E. 713, 240 N. Y. 580.

If purpose of persons going on premises of another is common interest or mutual advantage of parties, implied invitation may be inferred, making it duty of owner or occupier to maintain premises in a reasonably safe condition.

—**(Iowa,1925)** Printy v. Reimbold, 202 N. W. 122, 200 Iowa, 541, 41 A. L. R. 1423, petition for rehearing overruled (1925) 205 N. W. 211, 200 Iowa, 541, 41 A. L. R. 1423;

(Okl.1918) City of Shawnee v. Drake, 171 P. 727, 69 Okl. 209, L. R. A. 1918D, 810.

(U.S.C.C.A.Ga.1917) Landowner, who leaves on his premises, which are frequented by children, an unguarded dangerous agency, is liable to a third person who, without negligence on his part, is injured in an attempt to rescue child or children in peril.—Atlanta & W. P. R. Co. v. Green, 246 F. 676, 158 C. C. A. 632.

(Ala.1918) Where a roadway under a shed was so situated that it was a convenient passageway from one street to another, and was so used by people generally, such use of the roadway was at the implied invitation of the railroad owning it.—Nashville, C. & St. L. Ry. v. Blackwell, 79 So. 129, 201 Ala. 657.

(Ala.1922) A trainman on a freight train serving defendant's industry *held* invitee to whom defendant was obliged to keep the premises in a reasonably safe condition for the trainman's presence thereon, and his use thereof within contemplation of the invitation.—Montevallo Mining Co. v. Little, 93 So. 873, 208 Ala. 131.

(Ala.1923) Where plaintiff was working for an independent contractor who was engaged in doing work for defendant upon defendant's premises, defendant owed him a duty of reasonable care to avoid injuring him.—Shelby Iron Co. v. Cole, 95 So. 47, 208 Ala. 657.

(Ark.1919) Where defendant's agent, who had exclusive charge of selling its wood, sold plaintiff, who was an employé of defendant, a load of wood, and promised to make arrangements with the night watchman to allow hauling at night, plaintiff, when he entered on defendant's premises for the purpose of getting the wood, was not a mere licensee, but was an invitee, going on the premises for the mutual advantage of himself and defendant.—Alfrey Heading Co. v. Nichols, 215 S. W. 712, 139 Ark. 462.

(Ark.1923) Where one visiting a cotton gin plant had been invited to the plant on his own inquiry for the purpose of looking it over as one of the stockholders interested in its operation, the corporation had no such interest in the visit as would make him an invitee, but he was a mere licensee, and the corporation was not liable for his injuries caused by the breaking of a belt.—Knight v. Farmers' & Merchants' Gin Co., 252 S. W. 30, 159 Ark. 423.

(Cal.1917) Cleaning of defendant's private stable being duty easily performed by stableman, stableman's request of boy 14 years old to clean stable was unauthorized, and could impose no additional duty upon defendant.—Giannini v. Campodonico, 169 P. 80, 176 Cal. 548.

Cleaning of defendant's private stable being duty easily performed by stableman, stableman's promise to pay boy to clean stable could not make boy invitee.—Id.

(Cal.1925) One extended accommodations of hotel pending commencement of her employment therein being mere licensee until such time, it was not duty of hotel owner to keep dark pathway through grounds, parallel to well-lighted roadway, in repair for her accommodation and safety.—Powers v. Raymond, 239 P. 1069, 197 Cal. 126.

(Cal.App.1917) Where plaintiff entered defendants' saloon to use toilet, and then ordered a drink, and then walked into an open and unguarded trapdoor, he had become a customer, and defendants owed him duty of ordinary care.—Braun v. Vallade, 164 P. 904, 33 Cal. App. 279.

(Cal.App.1917) Where a merchant invites a customer to follow him to his workshop to look at goods, such customer is not a mere licensee, but the merchant must use all reasonable means to make that part of the store safe for one visiting it.—Foley v. Hornung, 169 P. 705, 35 Cal. App. 304.

(Cal.App.1918) A customer in a store who asked for the toilet and was shown by a clerk to a toilet in the rear of the premises supplied for employés only was a mere licensee.—Corbett v. Spanos, 173 P. 769, 37 Cal. App. 200.

(Cal.App.1922) Where a lumber company employing plaintiff to bore a well offered a reward to any one finding a spring of water, and plaintiff, while waiting for repairs on his outfit, went in search of a spring, the offer was an invitation to go on the company's premises for the purpose of the search, and while so engaged he was entitled to the protection of ordinary care by the company.—Bush v. Weed Lumber Co., 204 P. 24, 55 Cal. App. 588.

(Cal.App.1923) Where lumber company posted an advertisement offering a reward to any one who found a spring that would furnish the company's camp with water, and the company's foreman encouraged a well driller to search for a spring and invited him to use the company's train in going to and returning from the place of his search, the well driller, while on the company's premises, was an invitee to whom the company owed the duty to exercise ordinary care to render the premises reasonably safe.—Bush v. Weed Lumber Co., 218 P. 618, 63 Cal. App. 426.

(App.D.C.1924) Permission to enter premises, whether expressed or implied, is not an invitation to enter, and establishes no higher relation than that of mere licensor and licensee.—Branan v. Wimsatt, 298 F. 833, 54 App. D. C. 374, certiorari denied 44 S. Ct. 639, 265 U. S. 591, 68 L. Ed. 1195.

Persons engaged in business invite the public to enter their place of business for that purpose, but the invitation is not broad enough to include those who have no business to transact and enter for other purposes.—Id.

An owner, who tolerates a trespasser and takes no steps to interfere with his practice of trespassing, does not impliedly extend an invitation to use the premises.—Id.

(Ga.1923) The duty of a proprietor of premises towards a contractor's servant coming lawfully upon the premises to repair machinery or instrumentalities for such proprietor under a contract between the proprietor and the contractor is controlled by Civ. Code 1910, § 4420, relative to invitees.—(App.) Fulton Ice & Coal Co. v. Pece, 116 S. E. 57, 29 Ga. App. 507, judgment affirmed 120 S. E. 636, 157 Ga. 105.

(Ga.App.1919) Where the operation of an elevator results in injury to an expressman, entering premises to remove goods for shipment, the owner is liable in damages under Civ. Code 1910, § 4420, for failure to exercise ordinary care.—Southern Paramount Pictures Co. v. Gaulding, 101 S. E. 311, 24 Ga. App. 478.

(Ga.App.1923) An invitation, within Civ. Code 1910, § 4420, may be implied by dedication or arise from known customary use, or it may be inferred from conduct, if notorious or actually known to the owner or his authorized representative, or from any state of facts upon which it naturally and necessarily arises. —Smith v. Jewell Cotton Mill Co., 116 S. E. 17, 29 Ga. App. 461.

(Ga.App.1923) To constitute one an invitee, there must be some mutuality of interest.—Crossgrove v. Atlantic Coast Line R. Co., 118 S. E. 694, 30 Ga. App. 462.

Mere permission by railroad company to member of section foreman's family to go on premises furnished him as dwelling house without contractual relationship, or for any purpose of mutual interest, or for the railroad's benefit, created only relation of licensee.—Id.

A "licensee" is one who is neither customer, servant, nor trespasser, and does not stand in any contractual relation with owner of premises, but who is permitted expressly or impliedly to go thereon for his own interest, convenience, or gratification.—Id.

(Ga.App.1923) Invitation by owner or occupant of premises is implied where one goes on the premises for benefit, real or supposed, of the owner or occupant, or in matter of mutual interest or in usual course of business, or for performance of some duty.—Petree v. Davison-Paxon-Stokes Co., 118 S. E. 697, 30 Ga. App. 490.

To constitute one person an invitee of another, there must be some mutuality of interest.—Id.

A "licensee" is one who is neither customer, servant, nor trespasser, and does not stand in any contractual relation to owner of premises, but who is permitted, expressly or impliedly, to go thereon for his own interest, convenience, or gratification.—Id.

A member of the general public of the class usually allowed to enter a store, who enters lawfully and peaceably, though not a customer, actual or anticipatory, at the time, does not, unless admission has been forbidden him, become a trespasser, but is a licensee.—Id.

(Idaho,1918) As between the proprietor of premises and employé of an independent contractor doing work thereon, the employé is an invitee.—Carr v. Wallace Laundry Co., 170 P. 107, 31 Idaho, 266.

(Ill.1919) The distinction between mere licensee and invitee turns largely on the nature of the business that brings him upon premises, rather than on the words or acts of the owner which precede his coming.—Milauskis v. Terminal R. Ass'n of St. Louis, 122 N. E. 78, 286 Ill. 547.

Though permission or license is a justification for licensee's entry upon premises, and though licensee is not technically a trespasser, owner's duty toward licensee is governed by rules applicable to trespassers; "permission" involving leave and license, but giving no right.—Id.

To come under an "implied invitation," as distinguished from a mere "license," visitor must come for a purpose connected with the business in which the occupant is engaged, or which he permits to be carried on there; mutuality of interest in the subject to which the visitor's business relates being necessary, although the particular thing which is the object of the visit may not be for the benefit of the occupant.—Id.

(Ill.1919) One need not be specifically engaged in the work of the owner of premises before he can lawfully enter on the premises, and it is sufficient if he is engaged in work the prosecution of which implies that he should enter on such premises, or if there is an expressed invitation to enter on the premises.—(1918) Milauskis v. Terminal R. Ass'n of St. Louis, 211 Ill. App. 120, judgment affirmed 122 N. E. 78.

(Ill.App.1915) One entering premises by permission only, without enticement, allurement, or inducement held out by the owner or occupant, cannot recover for injuries caused by obstructions or pitfalls existing in the premises.—De Wolfe v. Pierce, 196 Ill. App. 360.

In an action for injuries sustained by falling through a hole in the floor of an entrance to a building where defendants conducted a tin and hardware business, it appearing that the entrance in question through which plaintiff sought to enter such store was not the entrance provided for the purpose, *held*, that plaintiff was not a mere licensee without invitation.—Id.

(Ill.App.1917) A city building inspector who is inspecting a building is a mere licensee.—Ross v. Becklenberg, 209 Ill. App. 144.

(Ill.App.1918) A city fireman who enters, as authorized by law upon the leased premises of an electric light company for the purpose of ascertaining if there is a fire in the transformer building is a mere licensee, and the lessee owes him no duty except not to willfully injure him.—Volluz v. East St. Louis Light & Power Co., 210 Ill. App. 565.

(Ind.App.1920) Where decedent's employer had paid for privilege of using private way of other parties, decedent, as a user for hire, was on the way as an invitee of the owners, to whom they owed the duty of having such way in reasonably safe condition and to give warning of concealed perils.—Clark v. City of Huntington, 127 N. E. 301, 74 Ind. App. 437, rehearing denied 128 N. E. 453, 74 Ind. App. 437.

(Iowa,1921) Where plaintiff was injured in falling down a stairway near the entrance to defendant's bank, and it appeared that he went to the bank to transact business with the bank regarding the settlement of a sale, and to see one of the officers in regard to a township matter, such officer being also a township officer, plaintiff was more than a mere licensee.—Downing v. Merchants' Nat. Bank of Greene, Iowa, 184 N. W. 722, 192 Iowa, 1250, 20 A. L. R. 1138.

(Iowa,1922) One going to a store to procure his overcoat which he had left there earlier in the day, who went behind a counter to a small room, where the coat was hung, and fell down a dark stairway, after opening a door not used by the public, *held* a mere licensee, being at the store for his own accommodation, and hence could not recover for his injuries.—Keerman v. Spurgeon Mercantile Co., 191 N. W. 99, 194 Iowa, 1240, 27 A. L. R. 579.

One who comes to a store to procure his overcoat and falls down a dark stairway after opening a door in a small room behind a counter, where the coat was hung by a clerk, *held* a licensee and not an invitee, though he had an undisclosed intention of purchasing a suit before leaving the store after securing his coat.—Id.

A conversation between one who entered a store to secure his overcoat and a clerk relative to the whereabouts of the coat, which had been left with her earlier in the day and hung in a room behind a counter, a place not used by customers, *held* a mere license and not an invitation.—Id.

(Iowa,1923) Where plaintiff with others had entered defendant's garage for a social visit with one of the proprietors, but had left the garage and was waiting outside for her husband, she was merely a licensee in thereafter entering the garage in pursuit of her child and cannot recover for injuries resulting from catching her foot in a guard rail located at the garage entrance, even though she could have been considered an invitee when she first entered the garage.—Flatley v. Acme Garage, 194 N. W. 180, 196 Iowa, 82.

(Kan.1921) One in search of employment, who is injured through negligence while seeking a factory foreman, to whom he is directed by the superintendent of the establishment, is entitled to recover damages from the owner.—Zeigler v. Oil Country Specialties Mfg. Co., 196 P. 603, 108 Kan. 589.

(Ky.1918) Where steel company without charge and for accommodation of family and relatives of deceased employé had its engine and flat car, used exclusively in its business, carry remains, members of family, and relatives to and from cemetery, plaintiff, who without invitation or request, got on car and made return trip, *held* not entitled to recover for injuries sustained while getting off car.—Laxton v. Wisconsin Steel Co., 201 S. W. 15, 179 Ky. 652, L. R. A. 1918D, 249.

1916

SECOND

DECENNIAL EDITION

OF THE

AMERICAN DIGEST

A COMPLETE DIGEST OF ALL REPORTED
CASES FROM 1906 TO 1916

VOL. 17

NEGLIGENCE — PLEA

ST. PAUL
WEST PUBLISHING CO.
1921

I. Acts or Omissions Constituting Negligence. (C) Condition and Use of Land, Buildings, and Other Structures.

Care as to licensees or persons invited (Cont'd).

to unreasonable risk.—Bloomer v. Snellenburg, 69 A. 1124, 221 Pa. 25, 21 L. R. A. (N. S.) 464.

(Pa.1909) Where an owner permits the public to use his land as a playground, he must protect it from dangerous machinery located thereon.—Millum v. Lehigh & Wilkes-Barre Coal Co., 73 A. 1106, 225 Pa. 214.

(Pa.1911) Newingham v. J. C. Blair Co., 81 A. 556. See Master and Servant, 322 in this Digest.

(Pa.Super.Ct.1914) Defendant occupied for its telegraph offices a front room in a small building, access to which room from the street was by a hall running along the side of the room. The hall could be lighted by opening a shutter. The public transacted its business with the company through a window in the partition between the hall and the front room. Between this window and the door to the back room there was a trap in the floor of the hall leading to the cellar. Defendant had no control over the cellar nor the door to the trap. Plaintiff went to the defendant's office about 10 o'clock in the morning to deliver a telegraph message. She entered the hall, found the window closed, and, not receiving any answer to her knock, she started along the hall to enter the back room in order to secure attention. As she did so she fell into the trap, the door of which had been left open by a plumber employed by the owner of the house, a few minutes before. *Held*, that there was no negligence of defendant, except that it had failed to open the shutter by which the hall could have been adequately lighted.—Donohue v. Western Union Telegraph Co., 57 Pa. Super. Ct. 251.

A telegraph company is not bound to supply its patrons a safe place to do business, but only a reasonably safe place.—Id.

(Tex.1910) Invitation, license, or allurement of others to come on premises may give rise to responsibility on the part of the owner which, without it, would not exist, for injuries sustained by them from dangerous things thereon against which he has not exercised ordinary care to guard them.—Stamford Oil Mill Co. v. Barnes, 128 S. W. 375, 103 Tex. 409, 31 L. R. A. (N. S.) 1218, Ann. Cas. 1913A, 111, reversing judgment (Civ. App. 1909) 119 S. W. 871.

(Tex.Civ.App.1907) Where a railway track is constructed and used through a smelter company's premises by its permission and for its benefit, it is the duty of the smelter company to exercise ordinary care to avoid injury to the employés of the railway company rightfully upon its premises in the discharge of their duties.—Consolidated Kansas City Smelting & Refining Co. v. Binkley, 99 S. W. 181, 45 Tex. Civ. App. 100.

(Tex.Civ.App.1907) Defendant owed a customer's employé on its premises the legal duty to exercise at least ordinary care to protect him from injury.—Waters-Pierce Oil Co. v. Snell, 106 S. W. 170, 47 Tex. Civ. App. 413.

(Utah,1912) A gas company maintaining an office for the payment of gas bills *held* only bound to exercise ordinary care to provide a reasonably safe place for customers.—Quinn v. Utah Gas & Coke Co., 129 P. 362, 42 Utah, 113, 43 L. R. A. (N. S.) 328.

(Wash.1911) Defendant engaged in removing a rock bluff, incident to the construction of its railroad, contracted with plaintiff to drive a tunnel in the face of the bluff in which to explode powder. A heavy blast in another tunnel, for the purpose of loosening part of the face of the bluff, brought down a quantity of rock immediately in front of plaintiff's tunnel, blocking the entrance to it. Plaintiff, at the direction of defendant's foreman, commenced to remove the débris, but being alarmed by the fall of a rock, ceased work, and reported such fall to defendant's foreman who said he would make the bluff safe. Plaintiff did not return to work till the next morning, after the foreman had assured him that he had caused the wall and slope to be made safe. *Held* that, even if plaintiff was an independent contractor, and not an employé, defendant having told him the wall would be made safe, and assured him that this had been done, owed him the duty of making it safe, in so far as this could be done by inspection and barring down of loose rock; so that, plaintiff having a right to rely on the assurance that it had been made safe, defendant was liable for injury to him through the falling of a rock, caused by negligence in not making the place safe.—Gibson v. Chicago, M. & P. S. Ry. Co., 112 P. 919, 61 Wash. 639.

(Wash.1914) Where defendant's servant, dropped the skip of a derrick on deceased, who was on defendant's premises after refusal of employment, *held* that defendant was not liable.—Kroeger v. Grays Harbor Const. Co., 145 P. 63, 83 Wash. 68.

(W.Va.1914) A property owner owes a higher degree of care in keeping the premises reasonably safe, to persons entering by his inducement or by his invitation, than to persons who are mere licensees.—Smith v. Sunday Creek Co., 82 S. E. 608, 74 W. Va. 606.

(Wis.1911) Maintenance of an open stairway in part of a store not intended for use by customers, but merely for storage, is not negligence, so as to create a liability to a customer falling down the stairway, unless he was expressly or impliedly invited there.—Lehman v. Amsterdam Coffee Co., 131 N. W. 362, 146 Wis. 213.

(Wis.1913) A manufacturing company maintaining in its yard a switch track owes the duty to the members of a railroad switching crew, switching on the track, of removing obstructions on the track.—Landry v. Great Northern Ry. Co., 140 N. W. 75, 152 Wis. 379.

32(2). *Who are licensees, and status of persons going on land of another.*

See 37 Cent. Dig. Negllg. § 43.

(U.S.C.C.A.Ga.1914) One who goes on the premises of another for the benefit, real or supposed, of the owner or occupant, or in a matter of mutual interest, or in the ordinary course of their business, or for the performance of some duty, is an invitee.—Middleton v. P. Sanford Ross, 213 F. 6, 129 C. C. A. 622, reversing order (D. C. 1913) 202 F. 799.

The rule that an owner or occupant of premises is required to use ordinary care to keep them in safe condition for invitees' use is applicable to a servant of an independent contractor.—Id.

(U.S.C.C.A.Neb.1913) Plaintiff accompanying a friend owning an automobile to defendant's garage, where he was injured by falling down a cellar stairway, *held* a mere licensee for whose injury defendant was not liable, where the place was lighted, with a door at the head of the stairway.—Rhode v. Duff, 208 F. 115, 125 C. C. A. 343.

(U.S.C.C.A.N.Y.1914) Employé of seller of oil, who went upon buyer's tank to measure the oil therein before and after delivery, *held* an invitee, and it was the buyer's duty to exercise ordinary care to keep the premises in a safe condition.—New York Lubricating Oil Co. v. Pusey, 211 F. 622, 129 C. C. A. 88.

(U.S.C.C.A.Pa.1908) Where defendant had consented to the use of a crane runway in defendant's mill by plaintiff, a servant of an independent contractor, in moving scaffolding from one truss in an addition to the mill to another, plaintiff in so using the runway was not a trespasser, but was within the class of persons present in dangerous premises by the owner's express permission, as to whom defendant was chargeable with an affirmative duty to take special precautions against injury that might happen to plaintiff by reason of the operation of the crane on that part of the runway on which he was standing.—Standard Steel Car Co. v. McGuire, 161 F. 527, 88 C. C. A. 469.

(U.S.C.C.A.Wash.1913) Where an elevated roadway leading to a dock was constructed by the landowner for general use, and the public had been permitted to use it since its construction without let or hindrance, plaintiff, in using the roadway at the time he was injured by the load of an auto truck, was not a trespasser, but an invitee, as to whom the chauffeur was bound to exercise reasonable care.—Pacific Hardware & Steel Co. v. Monical, 205 F. 116, 123 C. C. A. 348.

(Ala.1908) The word "invitation," within the rule that an owner of land who holds out any invitation for others to go thereon must keep his premises in a safe condition, imports that the person entering on the premises did not act merely for his own convenience and pleasure, and from motives to which no act of the owner contributed, but that he entered the premises because he was led to believe that they were intended to be used by visitors, and that such use was not only acquiesced in by the owner, but that it was in accordance with the intention and design with which the place was adapted and prepared or allowed to be so used.—Alabama Great Southern R. Co. v. Godfrey, 47 So. 185, 156 Ala. 202, 130 Am. St. Rep. 76.

(Ala.1912) One who invites another to come on his premises on business must take care that his premises are safe, or give warning of any danger; but as to a guest or bare licensee he need only warn him of anything in the nature of a trap.—Scoggins v. Atlantic & Gulf Portland Cement Co., 60 So. 175, 179 Ala. 213.

One who goes on the premises of another on business of his own is a licensee, to whom the owner owes no further duty than to refrain from putting traps in his way.—Id.

(Ark.1912) An industrial company such as a railroad company impliedly invites persons seeking employment to go upon its land.—St. Louis, I. M. & S. Ry. Co. v. Wirbel, 149 S. W. 92, 104 Ark. 236, Ann. Cas. 1914C, 277.

(Cal.1910) In absence of ordinance or statute, a fireman entering a building is only a licensee, who assumes the risks, and to whom the owner of the premises owes no special duty to maintain them in a safe condition.—Pennebaker v. San Joaquin Light & Power Co., 112 P. 459, 158 Cal. 579, 31 L. R. A. (N. S.) 1099, 139 Am. St. Rep. 202.

(Cal.App.1907) Deceased entered defendants' tamale stand with another, by the license and permission of defendants, and volunteered to show his companion the way to the urinal, often used by customers, and always pointed out by defendants, when requested, and permission to use which was always granted by them. The route thereto lay through an adjoining room to a stair landing, with two flights of stairs; the one to the left going above, and that to the right going down to the urinal in the basement. The landing was not lighted, and because of that deceased fell into a hole to the left of the lefthand stairway, and received the injuries from which he died. The urinal was not designed for the use of patrons of the stand, nor was it designed for use or used as a part of the business conducted on the premises. Held, that deceased was a mere licensee, so that defendants assumed no duty to him except not to inflict any wanton or willful injury.—Herzog v. Hemphill, 93 P. 899, 7 Cal. App. 116.

The owner or occupier of lands or buildings must exercise ordinary care to render the premises reasonably safe to persons whom he induces to come thereon by invitation, express or implied, which invitation may be manifested by the arrangement of the premises or the conduct of the owner; but mere permission, or a habit of an owner in allowing people to enter and use a certain portion of his premises, is not indicative of an invitation, but a license.—Id.

(Cal.App.1913) One who is upon premises as an employé of a subcontractor under defendant, the principal contractor, is an invitee rather than a licensee, and is entitled to the observance of ordinary care toward him upon the part of defendant.—Lucas v. Walker, 134 P. 374. 22 Cal. App. 296. rehearing denied (Sup.) 134 P. 379. 22 Cal. App. 296.

(Colo.1907) Defendant operated a railroad to the summit of Pikes Peak and leased certain buildings to H. for a hotel for 25 per cent. of H.'s gross receipts. The hotel was higher than the station platform, and a retaining wall protected the platform from loose stones which might roll down on the side of the mountain. The wall was ascended by a flight of steps, and the buildings were located 16 feet from the top thereof. Plaintiff arrived at the hotel at about 10 o'clock p. m., and after being informed that the beds were all full, he obtained an employé's bed. Later in the night he went out of doors for a private purpose, and, not keeping within the light reflection from the house, stepped off the retaining wall and was injured. Held, that plaintiff was not an invited guest of the railroad company, but was at most a mere licensee thereof, as to whom it owed no active duty to light or rail the wall.—Watson v. Manitou & Pikes Peak Ry. Co.. 92 P. 17, 41 Colo. 138, 17 L. R. A. (N. S.) 916.

(Colo.1910) Defendant, a publishing company, on seeing nitric acid fumes resembling smoke emitted from the etching room of its establishment, turned in a fire alarm, and plaintiff's husband, a fireman, went into the room and there breathed the fumes of the acid, causing his ultimate death from traumatic pneumonia. Held, that defendant by turning in the alarm did not thereby invite deceased on its premises, but that deceased came there in the performance of his public duty as a fireman, under the rule that firemen who enter a building in response to a fire alarm are licensees merely, and the owner or occupant is not liable for their injury by reason of any defects in the premises.—Lunt v. Post Printing & Publishing Co., 110 P. 203, 48 Colo. 316, 30 L. R. A. (N. S.) 60, 21 Ann. Cas. 492.

(Colo.App.1912) A railroad company operating cars on a spur track leading from its main line into the yard of a manufacturing plant held not a mere licensee, but the owner of the plant was required to use reasonable care to see that the premises were reasonably safe for switching crews.—Great Western Sugar Co. v. Parker, 123 P. 670, 22 Colo. App. 18.

(D.C.1910) Where an insurance company has the right under its policy to inspect the premises of the insured and one of its inspectors, under the guidance of an employé of the insured, is engaged in inspecting them, he is on them by invitation, and not as a mere licensee; and the insured is liable to him in damages, if he is using due care, for injuries occasioned by the unsafe condition of the premises, unknown to him, but known to the insured.—Dashields v. W. B. Moses & Sons, 35 App. D. C. 583, 31 L. R. A. (N. S.) 380.

(Fla.1912) One who conducts a store for the sale of goods invites the public to come into his place of business, and owes a duty for their safety which may be varied with the circumstances of each case.—J. G. Christopher Co. v. Russell, 58 So. 45, 63 Fla. 191, Ann. Cas. 1913C, 564.

For earlier cases in First Decennial or cases in later Digests, see same topic and Key-Number.

☞32(2)　　　　　　　NEGLIGENCE　　　　[17—2d Dec.Dig.,Page 53]

I. Acts or Omissions Constituting Negligence.　(C) Condition and Use of Land, Buildings, and
Other Structures.

(**Ga.App.**1907) A member of the general public who enters a saloon, though not a customer actual or anticipatory, unless admission is forbidden him, is not a trespasser, but a licensee.—Rollestone v. T. Cassirer & Co., 59 S. E. 442, 3 Ga. App. 161.

(**Idaho,**1914) Gagnon v. St. Maries Light & Power Co., 141 P. 88. See Master and Servant, ☞321 in this Digest.

(**Ill.**1907) Plaintiff went to defendants' warehouse to obtain goods stored there by his employer. After the goods had been pointed out to him, he left them, and for purposes of his own walked through a passageway through which one would necessarily have to pass to get to part of the stored goods, and fell down an elevator shaft. *Held*, that plaintiff was on the premises on the implied invitation of defendants, and they owed him the duty to exercise reasonable care for his safety, while thereon.—Pauckner v. Wakem, 83 N. E. 202, 231 Ill. 276, 14 L. R. A. (N. S.) 1118.

The invitation extended to the place of injury, since it was broad enough to include all the space occupied by the goods, together with necessary passageways in and out of the warehouse.—Id.

Defendants' liability is not affected by the fact that plaintiff at the exact moment of his injury was not engaged in his employer's business.—Id.

(**Ill.**1908) Defendant maintained an unguarded elevator shaft opening into an alley, and operated in the shaft an elevator for the use of tenants of his building. One of the tenants sent for an express wagon to convey certain goods from the building on which wagon decedent, during a strike, had been detailed as a policeman to protect the express company's employés and property from strikers. On the wagon being backed against the door opening into the elevator shaft, decedent stepped into the shaft while the elevator was at an upper floor, and fell to the bottom, receiving injuries from which he died. *Held*, that deceased, in entering the building, was either a trespasser or a mere licensee, as to whom defendant owed no duty except to refrain from inflicting a willful or wanton injury on him, and therefore defendant was not liable.—Casey v. Adams, 84 N. E. 933, 234 Ill. 350, 17 L. R. A. (N. S.) 776, 123 Am. St. Rep. 105, affirming judgment (1907) 137 Ill. App. 404.

(**Ill.**1908) A person using a highway which the owner, for a great number of years, has permitted the public to use as a public highway, is not a mere licensee to which the owner of such highway owes no other duty than to refrain from purposely or willfully injuring him.—Chicago Junction Ry. Co. v. Reinhardt, 139 Ill. App. 53, judgment affirmed Reinhardt v. Chicago Junction Ry. Co., 85 N. E. 605, 235 Ill. 576.

(**Ill.**1908) Defendant owned pens and furnished them to shippers of stock, receiving compensation therefor. It furnished both feed and water, but it was the business of the shipper or his agent to supply the same to the stock. *Held*, that a shipper while on the premises for such purpose was not a trespasser or licensee, but was there by virtue of an implied invitation, and that it was defendant's duty to exercise reasonable care to guard him against injury. Judgment (1907) Union Stockyards Transit Co. v. Franey, 138 Ill. App. 215, affirmed.—Franey v. Union Stockyard & Transit Co. of Chicago, 85 N. E. 750, 235 Ill. 522.

(**Ill.**1909) A person in the employ of another to whom a portion of premises has been demised in going upon such premises in connection with the performance of his duties as such an employé is not a mere licensee to whom the person in control of such premises owes no duty.—(1908) Devine v. National Safe Deposit Co., 145 Ill. App. 322, judgment affirmed 88 N. E. 804, 240 Ill. 369.

(**Ill.**1909) Where a public sale of horses was being conducted in an auction ring at the time plaintiff was injured by being run against by a blind horse, plaintiff was not a mere licensee, but was present by the implied invitation of the seller.—Craney v. Union Stockyard & Transit Co., 88 N. E. 1046, 240 Ill. 602, affirming judgment Craney v. Schloeman, 145 Ill. App. 313.

(**Ill.**1912) A person is on the premises of another by implied invitation of the owner, where he is there for a purpose connected with the business in which the owner is engaged or which he permits to be carried on.—Purtell v. Philadelphia & Reading Coal & Iron Co., 99 N. E. 899, 256 Ill. 110, 43 L. R. A. (N. S.) 193, Ann. Cas. 1913E, 335, affirming judgment 167 Ill. App. 125.

A boy, hired and paid by the employés of a coal company engaged in unloading coal from vessels at a yard to carry water for them, was on the premises by the employer's implied invitation, and it must exercise reasonable care for his safety while at work.—Id.

(**Ill.App.**1907) A person lawfully upon premises by the permission of the law, but without the invitation of the owner, is a mere naked licensee, to whom the owner owes no duty other than to refrain from willful or affirmative acts injurious to him.—Eckels v. Maher, 137 Ill. App. 45.

(**Ill.App.**1908) One on premises "not with a view of transacting any business with the owner is a mere licensee and the owner owes him no higher duty to protect him from injury than he would if he were a trespasser," but, on the other hand, "the duty of the owner to one who comes there by the owner's invitation to transact business in which the parties are mutually interested is to exercise reasonable care for his safety while upon that portion of the premises required for the purpose of his visit," and "under such circumstances the party is said to be on the premises by implied invitation of the owner."—Huff v. Wells, Fargo & Co., 141 Ill. App. 434.

(**Ill.App.**1908) Where a police officer or a fireman enters upon premises in order that he may better perform his duties as such, but without any express or implied invitation of the owner of the premises, he is a mere licensee, and such owner owes him no duty except to refrain from inflicting willful or wanton injury upon him.—Thrift v. Vandalia R. Co., 145 Ill. App. 414.

(**Ill.App.**1911) A car inspector employed by a railroad company engaged in the regular course of business in inspecting cars of his employer in the yards of the defendant, is not a mere licensee, but is in such yards by defendant's invitation.—Arens v. Chicago Junction Ry. Co., 159 Ill. App. 427.

(**Ill.App.**1911) A person who enters a store to make purchases is not a mere licensee or a trespasser, but is there by the implied invitation of the owner, and, if injured while properly using such premises in an effort to inspect merchandise, such owner is liable if he has failed to exercise ordinary care.—Petty v. Stebbins, 164 Ill. App. 439.

(**Ill.App.**1913) Where a person, operating a traction engine, enters a private road with the permission of the tenant of the land, but without permission of the owner or a lessee of the gas and oil rights, he is a licensee.—Rousch v. Oblong Gas Co., 179 Ill. App. 600.

(**Ill.App.**1913) An owner of a building, who leases a part thereof, giving lessee the right to install a separate water meter, impliedly invites a city water inspector to enter his premises for the purpose of inspection, and is liable for injury to the inspector, resulting from the unsafe condition of the premises.—Kennedy v. Heisen, 182 Ill. App. 200.

Invitation is to be inferred where there is

1906

DECENNIAL EDITION

OF THE

AMERICAN DIGEST

A COMPLETE DIGEST OF ALL REPORTED
CASES FROM 1897 TO 1906

VOL. 15

NAMES—PENAL STATUTES

TABLE OF PATENTS ENUMERATED

ST. PAUL
WEST PUBLISHING CO.
1910

I. Acts or Omissions Constituting Negligence.   (C) Condition and Use of Land, Buildings, and Other Structures.

and thereafter in getting them falls through a trapdoor, shut at the time when the packages were placed there, but left open by the negligence of the merchant, he is liable for resulting injuries.—League v. Stradley, 47 S. E. 975, 68 S. C. 515.

[z]   (Vt. 1899)

Where decedent, while at work for a third party repairing a digester in defendant's paper mill, was killed by steam and acid gas entering the digester, owing to the negligence of a servant of defendant in leaving open a valve in a pipe, through which the steam and gas entered, it was not error to charge that it was the duty of defendant to use reasonable care, and see that nothing took place which would render the situation of the decedent while at work more hazardous than ordinary, and that such care was the care of a prudent man under like circumstances.—Hoadley v. International Paper Co., 47 A. 169, 72 Vt. 79.

[zz]   (W. Va. 1902)

The owner of property owes to an independent contractor going upon the premises to do work under a contract with the owner the duty of reasonable care to have the premises in safe condition for the work, unless the defects be known to the contractor.—Sesler v. Rolfe Coal & Coke Co., 41 S. E. 216, 51 W. Va. 318.

§ 32 (2).   Who are licensees, and status of persons going on land of another.

Burden of proof, see post, § 121.(1).

[a]   (U.S. C.C.A., Colo., 1902)

A mining corporation which erects dwelling houses on a tract of land owned by it, and operated for mining purposes, extends an implied invitation to the public to treat the tract as a residence tract, and to enter and depart therefrom for all proper purposes incident to its use as such, and must therefore exercise reasonable care to have the premises in safe condition; and where it omits to open streets or highways, but requires persons desiring to visit the residences to cross the tract "at any point most convenient," and leaves unguarded a deep and abandoned shaft alongside one of the paths leading thereto, into which a person returning from one of the residences falls and is injured, it is guilty of negligence; the injured party not being, in such case, a mere trespasser or licensee.—Foster v. Portland Gold Min. Co., 114 F. 613, 52 C. C. A. 393.

[b]   (Ill. 1899)

Defendant's lumber was being unloaded from a vessel into defendant's dock. Defendant's yard men were piling up the lumber after it was passed out of the boat by another set of men, who were employed by H., who had a contract with defendant to unload the lumber. Plaintiff, belonging to the latter set, was injured, by the falling of a pile of lumber, while he was passing from the vessel to a water-closet maintained by defendant on its docks for the men then engaged. *Held*, that defendant was bound to exercise reasonable care for plaintiff's safety, as plaintiff was not a mere licensee. Judgment (1899) 80 Ill. App. 394, affirmed.—John Spry Lumber Co. v. Duggan, 54 N. E. 1002, 182 Ill. 218.

[c]   (Ill. App. 1903)

An invitation to come on the premises of an owner exists, where some benefit accrues or is supposed to accrue to the one who extends the invitation.—Northwestern Elevated R. Co. v. O'Malley, 107 Ill. App. 599.

[d]   (Ind. 1893)

The owner of a building in a populous city does not owe it as a duty at common law, independent of any statute or ordinance, to keep such building safe for firemen or other officers, who in a contingency may enter the same without a license. It seems to be settled, however, that such duty may be imposed by statute or by an ordinance adopted for that purpose.—Woodruff v. Bowen, 34 N. E. 1113, 136 Ind. 431, 22 L. R. A. 198.

[e]   (Ind. App. 1893)

It is not necessary that the invitation to enter premises should be special or even direct, as it may be implied from the circumstances and facts of the particular case.—Howe v. Ohmart, 33 N. E. 466, 7 Ind. App. 32.

[f]   (Ind. App. 1900)

Where the jury found that defendants owned and operated the factory in which decedent received his injuries, and that M., one of the owners, had authority to manage and look after its business, and that at the time of the accident M. was showing decedent through the factory, with the intention of hiring him as watchman, it cannot be contended that decedent was a mere licensee, since he was viewing the premises on invitation of M.—Warner v. Mier Carriage & Buggy Co., 58 N. E. 554, 59 N. E. 873, 26 Ind. App. 350.

[g]   (Ind. App. 1906)

Where the contract between a telephone company and the proprietor of a building in which a telephone was located required the company to keep it in order, and on receipt of a request from the building for the repair of the telephone, plaintiff, a servant of the company, was sent to repair it, and while in the elevator shaft making the repairs he was injured through the negligence of defendant's servant in operating the elevator, the facts warranted a finding that the servant was injured in repairing the telephone upon the invitation of defendant, who owed the servant protection. —Rink v. Lowry, 77 N. E. 967, 38 Ind. App. 132.

[h]   (Ky. 1898)

A United States revenue storekeeper on duty at a private distillery, and required to daily inspect all parts of it, is present at the implied invitation of the distiller, and is not a mere licensee.—Anderson & Nelson Distilling Co. v. Hair, 44 S. W. 658, 19 Ky. Law Rep. 1822, 103 Ky. 196.

[i]   (Ky. 1904)

Where the acting superintendent on defendant's premises saw plaintiff come up on the elevator, and allowed him to get on to go down again, it could not be said that plaintiff was using the elevator without defendant's consent.— Kentucky Distilleries & Warehouse Co. v. Leonard, 79 S. W. 281, 25 Ky. Law Rep. 2046.

[j]   (Me. 1902)

The owners of a steamer, desiring to make repairs on her, contracted with the owners of the marine railway to take the steamer out of the water for the purpose of repairs; the owners of the steamer to have the use of the railway, and to employ their own men on the repairs and furnish their own material, paying a certain sum per day for the use of the railway. *Held*, that the relation of the parties was that of licensor and licensee.—Moore v. Stetson, 52 A. 767, 96 Me. 197.

[k]   (Me. 1903)

Persons going on the property on the business of the owner are deemed to do so by the implied invitation of the property owner, who owes him the duty of keeping the premises reasonably safe, and giving warning of their dangerous condition.—Dixon v. Swift, 56 A. 761, 98 Me. 207.

[l]   (Me. 1903)

Where plaintiff's intestate, who lost his life by falling into a tank on defendants' premises left open by the negligence of servants, went upon the premises not on any business connected with defendants, but had a gratuitous message to deliver to an employé there, having no relation to the business conducted there, and was indulging his curiosity to look over the place, he was a mere licensee, and defendants owed him no duty except that they should not wantonly injure him.—Dixon v. Swift, 56 A. 761, 98 Me. 207.

Care as to licensees or persons invited (Cont'd).

[m] (Me. 1905)

A bank had partially constructed a walk on its own premises adjoining a public street. In this walk, about 17 feet from its end, was a rollway to the cellar of the bank building, which was unprotected. There were various obstructions on the walk, such as material for the construction of the walk, practically preventing entrance on the walk from either end. Plaintiff in the nighttime fell into the rollway. *Held*, that the obstructions and unfinished condition of the walk were a plain indication that it was not open for travel, and plaintiff in going upon it was a mere licensee, to whom the bank owed no duty except not to wantonly injure her.—McClain v. Caribou Nat. Bank, 62 A. 144, 100 Me. 437.

[mm] (Mass. 1865)

If, an owner directly or by implication induces persons to enter on and pass over his premises, he thereby assumes an obligation that they are in a safe condition, suitable for such use; and for a breach of this obligation he is liable in damages to a person injured thereby. Sweeny v. Old Colony & N. R. Co., 92 Mass. (10 Allen) 368, 87 Am. Dec. 644; Elliott v. Pray, 92 Mass. (10 Allen) 378, 87 Am. Dec. 653.

[n] (Mass. 1865)

A mere passive acquiescence by an owner or occupier in a certain use of his land by others, involves no liability.—Zoebisch v. Tarbell, 92 Mass. (10 Allen) 385, 87 Am. Dec. 660.

[nn] (Mass.)

The owner or occupant of land is liable in damages to those coming to it, using due care, at his invitation or inducement, express or implied, on any business to be transacted with or permitted by him, for an injury occasioned by the unsafe condition of the land or of the access to it, which is known to him and not to them, and which he has negligently suffered to exist, and has given them no notice of.—(1868) Carleton v. Franconia Iron & Steel Co., 99 Mass. 216; (1879) Nickerson v. Tirrell, 127 Mass. 236.

[o] (Mass.)

Where the defendants opened a paved private way into a public street without putting up any sign to notify travellers that the passageway was not a public way, and the plaintiff, who was not shown to have any right in the passageway unless as one of the public, while on his way to premises beyond those of the defendants, was injured by driving over a curbstone in the passageway hidden by snow, no active force being used against him, it was *held* that the plaintiff was at most but a licensee, and went upon the defendants' land at his own risk.—(1892) Stevens v. Nichols, 155 Mass. 472, 29 N. E. 1150, 15 L. R. A. 459. See also (1889) Reardon v. Thompson, 149 Mass. 267, 21 N. E. 361; (1892) Walker v. Winstanley, 155 Mass. 301, 29 N. E. 518.

[oo] (Mass. 1898)

A fireman employed at the building where defendants, through subcontractors, were erecting a stairway, finding his usual route to the engine house blocked, started to go over the stairway. One of the steps was without a tread, and he stepped through the opening, and was injured. The accident happened in the nighttime, and the fireman had a lantern. The opening was plainly visible in the daytime. *Held* that, the fireman being a mere licensee, defendants were not liable.—Blackstone v. Chelmsford Foundry Co., 170 Mass. 321, 49 N. E. 635.

[p] (Mass. 1899)

One inquiring at a building to ascertain if a certain person lived there, on being informed by a tenant that she might go in and see, does not thereby become a guest, so as to impose on the owner of the building any greater degree of care than he owed to any person not a trespasser.—McCarvel v. Sawyer, 54 N. E. 259, 173 Mass. 540, 73 Am. St. Rep. 318.

[pp] (Mass. 1899)

Where plaintiff was injured from defects in a way which had been dedicated to a city, but never accepted, at the entrance to which the city posted a sign that the street was a private way, and was dangerous, plaintiff was a mere licensee, and hence was not entitled to recover against an abutting owner.—Moffatt v. Kenny, 54 N. E. 850, 174 Mass. 311.

[r] (Mass. 1902)

One who, after putting his team in a livery stable, and receiving a check therefor, returned, and in attempting to put packages into the wagon is injured, is, at best, in the absence of custom of business, or a special invitation to do as he did, a licensee, to whom the owner owes no duty to keep the premises safe.—Cowen v. Kirby, 62 N. E. 968, 180 Mass. 504.

[qq] (Mass. 1903)

Where a construction company is engaged in altering a building of a manufacturing company, which at the same time continues its business, so that the construction company is not in the exclusive occupation of the grounds, but the employés of the manufacturing company are expected to use them so far as necessary, such an employé is not a mere licensee, as against the construction company, and the latter is bound to use reasonable care to prevent his injury.—Gile v. J. W. Bishop Co., 68 N. E. 837, 184 Mass. 413.

[r] (Mass. 1906)

Where all the owners of property abutting on a private way had a right in common to use the way, a person using it in order to see one of the abutting owners on business was not a mere licensee, but stood in the place of an abutter.—Cavanagh v. Block, 77 N. E. 1027, 192 Mass. 63, 6 L. R. A. (N. S.) 310, 116 Am. St. Rep. 220.

[rr] (Mo.)

Plaintiff, having come to defendant's office at his invitation on business, while waiting for him to be at leisure, requested and obtained permission to go to the toilet, in the basement, and was given the key thereto, it being locked. The way was blocked with boxes, of which defendant did not know, and, in going round them, in the poorly lighted basement, plaintiff fell into an elevator pit. *Held*, that plaintiff was a licensee, so that defendant was not liable for negligence at common law.—(1904) Glaser v. Rothschild, 80 S. W. 332, 106 Mo. App. 418, affirmed (1909) 120 S. W. 1.

[s] (Mo. App. 1904)

Plaintiff, owning a lot in and having a card of admission to defendant's cemetery, instead of following the road leading to the lot, started across the grounds, and stepped into a hole concealed by the grass. Though visitors were expected to keep to the walks and roadways, they were not required to, and were in the habit of traveling over the grounds at will. *Held*, that she was merely a licensee, and therefore could not recover for her injury.—Barry v. Calvary Cemetery Ass'n, 106 Mo. App. 358, 80 S. W. 709.

[ss] (Neb.)

Where a water bucket had been placed near an elevator in a building in process of construction to supply the masons with water, and a carpenter in a gang which was otherwise supplied with water, who was neither going nor returning from his place of business at the time of the accident, while using water from such bucket, was injured by a wheelbarrow which fell from the elevator, he was a bare licensee, and his only right of action against the defendant would be for wanton injury inflicted upon him by defendant or his employés.—(1903) Chesley v. Rocheford & Gould, 96 N. W. 241, 4 Neb. (Unof.) 768, affirmed on rehearing (1904) 98 N. W. 429, 4 Neb. (Unof.) 777.

Main titles, divisions, and section NUMBERS in this Digest and in later Am. Digests agree exactly.

77

I. Acts or Omissions Constituting Negligence.   (C) Condition and Use of Land, Buildings, and Other Structures.

[t]   (Neb.)

Where one enters on the premises of another with his consent, but without his invitation, and not in the discharge of any public or private duty, he is a bare licensee, and the occupier of the premises owes no duty to him as long as no wanton or willful injury is inflicted upon him by the licensor or his servants. —(1903) Chesley v. Rocheford & Gould, 96 N. W. 241, 4 Neb. (Unof.) 768, affirmed on rehearing (1904) 98 N. W. 429, 4 Neb. (Unof.) 777.

[tt]   (Neb. 1905)

In the absence of any municipal ordinance or statute, a fireman who enters on property without special authority or invitation of the owner is a bare licensee, taking the risk of the premises as he finds them.—New Omaha Thomson-Houston Electric Light Co. v. Anderson, 102 N. W. 89, 73 Neb. 84; Same v. Bendson, 102 N. W. 96, 73 Neb. 49.

[u]   (N. Y. Sup. 1898)

Defendant, the proprietor of a storage warehouse, was engaged in delivering to the employés of a truckman, of whom plaintiff was one, goods which had been on storage, and in the course of their work directed them to carry back into the building, and place temporarily in a designated room, a picture for which there was no room on the load. In complying, plaintiff fell through an open doorway in the floor and was injured. *Held*, that plaintiff was not a mere licensee upon the premises.—Wilson v. Olano, 51 N. Y. S. 109, 28 App. Div. 448.

[uu]   (N. Y. Sup. 1898)

A seller was delivering goods to purchasers at a leased building, and by request of one of their employés he entered an elevator exclusively controlled by them, and ascended to one of the upper floors, to aid in delivering the goods, and took the same elevator to return. *Held*, that the seller was in the elevator by the purchasers' invitation, imposing on them the duty to use care while he was therein.—Miller v. Brewster, 53 N. Y. S. 1, 32 App. Div. 559.

[v]   (N. Y. Sup. 1898)

The wife of a prospective purchaser of lumber, while in the lumber yard, at her husband's instance, to ascertain the fitness of a board selected by him for her use, was injured by the falling of a pile of lumber through the proprietor's negligence. *Held*, that she was properly in the yard, and hence might recover. —Davis v. Ferris, 53 N. Y. S. 571, 29 App. Div. 623.

[vv]   (N. Y. Sup. 1899)

In the absence of direction to apply elsewhere, a notice, in the window of an apartment house, "Flat to Let," constituted an implied invitation to persons desiring such apartments to apply there for information concerning the flat offered.—Fogarty v. Bogert, 60 N. Y. S. 81, 43 App. Div. 430.

[w]   (N. Y. Sup. 1901)

A person using a pathway across a vacant city lot, without the permission of the owner, but also without any objection from him, is a mere licensee, and is entitled to be protected only from wanton and willful injury. Judgment (City Ct. N. Y.) 72 N. Y. S. 1117, 35 Misc. Rep. 855, reversed.—McCann v. Thilemann, 72 N. Y. S. 1076, 36 Misc. Rep. 145.

[ww]   (N. Y. Sup. 1904)

Defendant, a contractor of a portion of a subway tunnel, opened a ditch, the walls of which were braced by beams, and provided bridges to cross the same at close intervals. Plaintiff, an inspector of sewers, having occasion to make certain check marks in the excavation, walked on one of such beams, and when in that position was struck by a slack cable attached to a traveling bucket, and was injured. *Held* that, though plaintiff was a licensee, defendant was not bound to anticipate that plaintiff or others would walk on the beams, and was not liable.—Dooley v. Degnon-

McLean Contracting Co., 91 N. Y. S. 30, 45 Misc. Rep. 593.

[x]   (N. Y. Sup. 1904)

An invitation to plaintiff to so use the beam could not be implied from its occasional use by defendant's employés in disregard of defendant's apparent intention, as indicated by the construction of the bridges.—Dooley v. Degnon-McLean Contracting Co., 91 N. Y. S. 30, 45 Misc. Rep. 593.

[xx]   (N. Y. Sup. 1904)

Where plaintiff, by permission of defendant's janitor, went into defendant's cellar to use its grindstone, and was injured by the breaking of a defective floor, plaintiff was not there by invitation, so that defendant owed him no duty except to refrain from intentional injury, and was not liable for his injuries.— Forbrick v. General Electric Co., 92 N. Y. S. 36, 45 Misc. Rep. 452.

[y]   (Vt. 1898)

An owner of a building gave permission to certain parties to use certain rooms in the building until such time as repairs should be begun in the building. After the repairs were commenced, such persons continued to use the rooms. *Held*, that a third party, attempting to use the rooms after the repairs were begun, on the invitation of the licensee, and injured because of the dangerous condition of the passageway because of the repairs, could not recover from the owner of the building.—Brehmer v. Lyman, 42 A. 613, 71 Vt. 98.

[yy]   (Va. 1897)

The street railroad company is liable for injuries to one visiting its park to witness a baloon ascension promoted by it, whether deceased went to the park on its cars or not.— Richmond & M. Ry. Co. v. Moore's Adm'r, 27 S. E. 70, 94 Va. 493, 37 L. R. A. 258.

[z]   (Wis. 1902)

Defendant, a distilling company, sold its slop to parties who drove their wagons under the slop vat and filled them therefrom. Defendant had an employé to stir the slop, but customers who wished to do so were allowed to stir it for themselves. Plaintiff's intestate was repeatedly allowed to go upon the platform around the vat and stir the slop, and once, while doing so, the vat burst, and he was scalded to death. *Held*, that deceased, being where he was with defendant's permission, and on business for their mutual benefit, was not a mere licensee, and defendant owed him the duty of ordinary care to see that the vat was kept in safe condition.—Hupfer v. National Distilling Co., 90 N. W. 191, 114 Wis. 279.

[zz]   (Wis. 1903)

Where plaintiff went on defendant's premises to transact private business with the defendant's employés, in which defendant had no interest, he was a mere licensee, though defendant directed him to use the elevator in which he was injured; and, no active negligence being shown, he was not entitled to recover for injuries sustained in using the elevator.—Muench v. Heinemann, 96 N. W. 800, 119 Wis. 441.

§ 32 (3).   *Exceeding or abusing license or invitation.*

[a]   (U.S. C.C.A., N.H., 1902)

A declaration in an action against a college corporation for injuries alleged that plaintiff contracted with the college to furnish him a collegiate education and a suitable lodging place, and safe and suitable grounds, buildings, and appliances for obtaining healthful recreation, in consideration of certain payments by plaintiff. Plaintiff was injured by the falling of a chimney on the college grounds, which was being torn down by its owners. Plaintiff was not present at the place in the course of his collegiate duties, nor by defendant's invitation, but he was there with others on a holiday as a volun-

---

For later cases in Am. Digest 1907A and continuations, see same topic and section NUMBER.

AMERICAN DIGEST SYSTEM

1906

DECENNIAL EDITION

OF THE

AMERICAN DIGEST

A COMPLETE TABLE OF AMERICAN CASES
FROM 1658 TO 1906

VOL. 21

TABLE OF KEY-NUMBER SECTIONS FOR CENTURY DIGEST

TABLE OF CASES DIGESTED IN CENTURY AND
DECENNIAL DIGESTS

A—B

ST. PAUL
WEST PUBLISHING CO.
1911

NAVIGABLE WATERS—Cont'd

Cent. Sec.	Dec. & Key No. Sec.	Cent. Sec.	Dec. & Key No. Sec.	Cent. Sec.	Dec. & Key No. Sec.	Cent. Sec.	Dec. & Key No. Sec.	Cent. Sec.	Dec. & Key No. Sec.	Cent. Sec.	Dec. & Key No. Sec.	Cent. Sec.	Dec. & Key No. Sec.
185	36(2)	202	37(1)	219	37(4)	233	38	248	41(1)	264	43(6)	281	44(1-5)
186	36(3)	203	37(2)	220	37(4)	234	38	249	41(1)	265	43(1-6)	282	44(6)
187	36(2)	204	37(1)	221	37(4)	235	38	250	41(1)	266	44(1)	283	46(1)
188	36(4)	205	37(3)	222	37(4)	236	38	251	41(1)	267	44(2)	284	46(1)
189	36(4)	206	37(1)	223	37(5)	237	38	252	41(1)	268	44(2)	285	37(1)
190	36(4)	207	37(1)	224	37(6)	238	38	253	42(1)	269	44(2)		46(1)
191	36(4)	208	37(1)	225	37(1)	239	39(2)	254	42(1)	270	44(3)	286	46(2)
192	36(4)	209	37(1)	226	37(1)	240	39(1)	255	42(1)	271	44(1)	287	46(3)
193	36(4)	210	37(1)	227	Em. Dom.		Bound. 20(1-5)	256	43(1)	272	44(4)	288	46(3)
194	36(5)	211	37(4)		45, 46	241	39(2)	257	43(2)	273	44(5)	289	46(3)
195	36(5)	212	37(7)			242	39(2)	258	43(3)	274	44(5)	290	46(4)
196	36(2)	213	37(7)	228	38	243	39(3)	259	43(4)	275	44(5)	291	46(1)
197	36(6)	214	37(7)	228½	38	244	39(3)	260	22(3)	276	44(5)	292	Em. Dom. 317(1)
198	36(6)	215	37(7)	229	38	245	40	261	43(1)	277	44(3)	293	46(1)
199	36(7)	216	37(1)	230	38	246	41(1)	262	43(5)	278	44(1)		
290	36(1)	217	37(1)	231	38	247	41(1)	263	43(1)	279	45		
201	37(1)	218	37(4)	232	38					280	45		

NE EXEAT

Cent. Sec.	Dec. & Key No. Sec.	Cent. Sec.	Dec. & Key No. Sec.	Cent. Sec.	Dec. & Key No. Sec.	Cent. Sec.	Dec. & Key No. Sec.	Cent. Sec.	Dec. & Key No. Sec.	Cent. Sec.	Dec. & Key No. Sec.	Cent. Sec.	Dec. & Key No. Sec.
1	1	4	3	7	4	10	8	12	10	14	12	16	14
2	2	5	3	8	6	11	9	13	11	15	13	17	15
3	3	6	3	9	7								

NEGLIGENCE

Cent. Sec.	Dec. & Key No. Sec.	Cent. Sec.	Dec. & Key No. Sec.	Cent. Sec.	Dec. & Key No. Sec.	Cent. Sec.	Dec. & Key No. Sec.	Cent. Sec.	Dec. & Key No. Sec.	Cent. Sec.	Dec. & Key No. Sec.	Cent. Sec.	Dec. & Key No. Sec.
1	1	64	51	128	85(7)	184	111(1)	244	125	305	136(14)	358	138(1)
2		65	52	129	23(1)	185	112	245	126(1)	306	136(14)		Trial 188
3	2	66	54	130	89(1)	186	113(1)	246	126(2)	307	136(18)		191(6,7)
4	2	67	54	131	89(1)	187	113(2)	247	126(2)	308	136(18)		194(15)
5	3	68	55	132	89(2)	188	113(3)	248	127	309	136(16)	359	138(1)
6	4	69	56(1, 2)	133	89(3)	189	113(4)	249	128	310	136(18)		Trial
7	5	70	56(3)	134	89(4)		Bridges 46(3)	250	130(1)	311	136(17)		188
8	6	71	58	135	89(1)	190	113(5)	251	130(1)	312	136(18)		191(6,7)
9	7	72	59	136	89(1)	191	113(6)	252	130(1)	313	136(19)		194(15)
10	8	73	60	137	89(1)	192	113(7)	253	130(1)	314	136(24)	360	138(1)
11	9	74	61(1)	138	90	193	113(8)	254	130(1)	315	136(24)		Trial
12	10	75	61(2)	139	90	194	116	255	131	316	136(14)		188
13	11	76	62(1)	140	90	195	117	256	131	317	136(16)		191(6,7)
14	12	77	62(2)	141	91	196	117	257	132(1)	318	136(14)		194(15)
15	13	78	62(1)	142	92	197	117	257½	132(1)	319	136(15)	361	138(3)
16	14	79	62(3)	143	92	198	118	258	132(2)	320	136(14)	362	138(3)
17	14	80	63	144	92	199	118	259	132(3)	321	136(20)	363	138(3)
18	15	81	63	145	92	200	119(2)	260	132(3)	322	136(19)	364	138(3)
19	16	82	64	146	92	201	119(3)	261	132(1)	323	136(21)	365	138(4)
20	16	83	65	147	93(1)	202	119(6)	262	132(1)	324	136(22)	366	138(4)
21	16	84	80	148	93(1)	203	119(1)	263	132(4)	325	136(23)	367	138(4)
22	17	85	80, 100 101	149	93(2)	204	119(1)	264	132(1)	326	136(25)	368	138(4)
23	18	86	66(1)	150	93(3)	205	119(1)	265	132(1)	327	136(25)	369	138(4)
24	24	87	66(1)	151	95(1)	206	119(2)	266	132(5)	328	136(25)	370	138(2)
25	27	88	66(2)	152	95(2)	207	119(3)	267	134(1)	329	136(25)	371	139(1)
26	19	89	66(2)	153	95(1)	208	119(4)	268	134(8)	330	136(25)	372	139(2)
27	20	90	67	154	95(3)	209	119(5)	269	134(9)	331	136(25)	373	139(3)
28	21	91	67	155	95(1)	210	119(6)	270	134(10)	332	136(25)	374	139(4)
29	21	92	68	156	95(4)	211	119(2)	271	121(2)	333	136(26)	375	139(5)
30	21	93	97, 98	157	96	212	119(7)	272	134(2)	334	136(26)	376	139(6)
31	22	94	65, 68	158	96	213	119(7)	273	134(11)	335	136(26)	377	139(7)
32	22	95	68	159	96	214	119(7)	274	135	336	136(27)	378	140
33	23(1)	96	69	160	96	215	119(7)	275	135	337	136(27)	379	140
34	23(2)	97	70	161	96	216	119(7)	276	135	338	136(26)	380	140
35	25	98	71	162	97	217	121(1)	277	136(1)		Anim. 74(8)	381	140
36	25	99	72	163	101	218	121(2, 3)	278	136(1)	339	136(26)	382	141(1)
37	25	100	72	164	101	219	121(4)	279	136(2)	340	136(28)	383	141(2)
38	25	101	73	165	98	220	121(1)	280	136(3)	341	136(28)	384	141(3)
39	26	102	74	166	99	221	122(2)	281	136(2)	342	136(26)	385	141(4)
40	26	103	75	167	101	222	122(5)	282	136(5)	343	136(26)	386	141(5)
41	28, 29	104	76	168	102	223	122(6)	283	136(5)	344	136(26)	387	141(6)
42	32(1)	105	76	169	103	224	121(1)	284	136(5)	345	136(26)	388	141(7)
43	32(2)	106	76	170		225	121(2)	285	136(6)	346	136(32)	389	141(1)
44	32(4)	107	76	171	105	226	121(4)	286	136(26)	347	136(29)	390	141(1)
45	33(1)	108	77	172	105	227	121(1)	287	136(7)	347½	136(29)	391	141(8)
46	33(2)	109	78	173	106	228	121(5)	288	136(7)	348	136(29)	392	141(9)
47	33(3)	110	79	174	108(1)	229	122(1)	289	136(14)	349	136(29)	393	141(10)
48	34	111	81	175	108(2)	230	122(2)	290	136(8)	350	136(30)	394	141(1)
49	30	112	82	176	109	231	122(3)	291	136(8)	351	136(30)	395	141(11)
50	31	113	82	177	110	232	122(4)	292	136(8)	352	136(30)	396	141(11)
51	48	114	82	178	110	233	122(1)	293	136(9)	353	136(26)	397	141(12)
52	37	115	83	179	108(3)	234	122(1)	294	136(9)	354	138(1)	398	141(12)
53	37	116	84	180	108(1)	235	124(1)	295	136(9)	355	138(2)	399	141(12)
54	35, 38	117	86	181	114	236	124(1)	296	136(9)	356	138(1)	400	142
55	39	118	87	182	111(1)	237	124(2)	297	136(9)		Trial	401	142
56	41	119	88		Bridges 46(3)	238	124(3)	298	136(10)		188	402	142
57	42	120	88		Carr. 314(2)	239	125	299	136(10)		191(6,7)	403	142
58	43	121	85(1)		Plead. 8(17)	240	125	300	136(10)		194(1, 8, 15)	404	143
59	44	122	85(1)	183	111(2)		Mast. & S 330(1-3)	301	136(11)	357	138(1)	405	143
60	45	123	85(2)	183½	111(3)	241	125		Carr. 320(2)		Trial	406	143
61	47	124	85(3)		Bridges 46(3)	242	125	302	136(12)		188	407	143
62	50	125	85(4)			243	125	303	136(14)		191(6,7)	408	144
63	50	126	85(5)					304	136(14)		194(15)	409	144
		127	85(6)										

NEUTRALITY LAWS

Cent. Sec.	Dec. & Key No. Sec.	Cent. Sec.	Dec. & Key No. Sec.	Cent. Sec.	Dec. & Key No. Sec.	Cent. Sec.	Dec. & Key No. Sec.	Cent. Sec.	Dec. & Key No. Sec.
1	1	6	3	10½	4	15	5	16	5
2	1	7	3	11	4		Ind. & Inf. 110(1-23)	17	5
3	2, 3	8	3	12	4				
4	3	9	4	13	4				
5	3	10	4	14	5				

CENTURY EDITION

OF THE

AMERICAN DIGEST

A COMPLETE DIGEST OF ALL REPORTED AMERICAN CASES FROM THE EAR-LIEST TIMES TO 1896

VOL. 37
Navigable Waters—Parties

ST. PAUL
WEST PUBLISHING CO.
1902

property, as to a similar use of such property. —McCafferty v. Spuyten Duyvil & P. M. R. Co., 61 N. Y. 178, 19 Am. Rep. 267.

[d] (N. Y. 1876) So long as the owner of property violates no duty which he owes to others or to the state, he cannot be called in question for the manner in which he uses or manages it; and if, in the lawful exercise of his right to use it, another is injured, he is not liable.— Victory v. Baker, 67 N. Y. 366.

[e] (N. Y. 1885) Reasonable care is all that the law requires of the occupant of a building, and what is reasonable care depends on the nature of the property, and the dangers in its use ordinarily to be apprehended.—Odell v. Solomon, 99 N. Y. 635, 1 N. E. 408, reversing (1884) 50 N. Y. Super. Ct. (18 Jones & S.) 119.

§ 42. Care required and liability as to licensees or persons invited.

See post, § 60.

Knowledge by owner of defect or danger, see post, § 51 [h].

Machinery and other instrumentalities, see ante, § 20.

Notices and warnings, see post, § 65 [f].

Places open to public, see post, § 52.

Pleading, see post, § 177 [c, e].

[a] (U. S. 1880) The owner or occupant of land, who induces or leads others to come upon it for a lawful purpose, is liable in damages to them, they using due care, for injuries occasioned by the unsafe condition of the land or its approaches, if such condition was known to him and not to them, and he negligently suffered it to exist without giving timely notice thereof to them or the public.—Bennett v. Louisville & N. R. Co., 102 U. S. 577, 26 L. Ed. 235.

[b] (Ill. 1872) M., upon whose land was an unguarded "slough well," and C., an adjoining owner, in order to save expense of fencing, mutually agreed that the stock of each, in the fall of the year, might pasture upon the land of the other. There was no special stipulation to protect from injury the stock of one while on the land of the other. Held, that M. was not liable for the loss of C.'s horse in the slough well.—McGill v. Compton, 66 Ill. 327.

[c] (Ill. 1873) If private warehousemen, merchants, blacksmiths, millers, or other persons engaged in business, construct approaches to their places of business, knowing the same to be defective, or have trapdoors known to be unsafe, where their customers must necessarily pass, and such defects are concealed, or not apparent, they will be liable for any injury resulting therefrom; but unless a person is under some public duty to repair a way, even though to his place of business, he will not be liable, on failing to do so, for injury thereby caused to others.—Buckingham v. Fisher, 70 Ill. 121.

[d] (Ill. 1874) Persons who hold a fair, and erect structures for the use of their patrons, are liable for any injury such patrons may receive by the breaking down or falling of such structures, if caused by the negligent or unskillful manner of their construction.—Latham v. Roach, 72 Ill. 179.

[e] (Ill. 1891) Plaintiff's intestate, having a son in defendant's employ, in taking to him his dinner entered a passageway in defendant's building in which was an unguarded elevator shaft, and, falling therein, was killed. There was no express invitation to enter upon the premises. Held, that defendant was not liable. —Gibson v. Sziepienski, 37 Ill. App. 601.

[ee] (Ill. 1895) Plaintiff was loading coal at a mine while his team was not tied or unhitched from the wagon. The whistle on the engine sounded as a usual and customary signal to the engineer, and the team became frightened, and tried to run away. In trying to stop them he was run down and injured. Held that, in the absence of proof that the sounding of the whistle was a willful or wanton act, plaintiff could not recover.—Grogan v. Big Muddy Coal & Coke Co., 58 Ill. App. 154.

[f] (Ind. 1883) A trader is bound to make reasonably safe all the approaches to his premises which are intended for use by his customers, and a breach of such duty gives one who goes on the premises by the express or implied invitation of the dealer, and is injured without his negligence, a cause of action.—Nave v. Flack, 90 Ind. 205, 46 Am. Rep. 205.

[g] (Ind. 1883) Where a warehouseman who maintains a driveway for the use of customers permits a defect to exist, and keeps the driveway so dark that the defect is not discernible, he is liable for an injury caused by such defect to a customer while delivering to him at his request a load of grain.—Nave v. Flack, 90 Ind. 205, 46 Am. Rep. 205.

[h] (Ind. 1894) A person injured by falling down a warehouse elevator shaft, which was negligently left unguarded, in order to recover of the warehouseman, must show that the latter was under obligation to protect him from the danger.—South Bend Iron Works v. Larger, 11 Ind. App. 367, 39 N. E. 209.

[i] (Mass. 1888) A house belonging to defendant's wife was let to a tenant. Defendant, while personally supervising repairs, directed a plank to be removed from the floor of a passageway, causing a dangerous hole, which was left unguarded. The passageway afforded a back entrance to the house, and was, as defendant knew, constantly used by the employés of the city to remove ashes and offal from the house; and plaintiff, as such employé, while rightfully using the passageway, and in the exercise of due care, fell into the hole. Held, that the court properly refused to rule that he was not entitled to recover.—Toomey v. Sanborn, 146 Mass. 28, 14 N. E. 921.

[j] (Mass. 1889) Even if plaintiff were a licensee, the danger of falling into a hole, which is not concealed except by the darkness of night, is one which she must avoid at her peril. —Reardon v. Thompson, 149 Mass. 267, 21 N. E. 369.

[k] (Mass. 1892) A licensee enters land at his own risk, and cannot recover for injuries caused by existing defects in the premises.—Stevens v. Nichols, 155 Mass. 472, 29 N. E. 1150, 15 L. R. A. 459.

[l] (Mich. 1895) Leaving open an unguarded trap door in the back part of a store, where goods are stored, is negligence rendering the storekeeper liable for injuries caused thereby to persons coming into that part of the store at the owner's invitation.—Pelton v. Schmidt, 104 Mich. 345, 62 N. W. 552, 53 Am. St. Rep. 462.

[m] (Minn. 1878) The owner or occupant of real property is bound to use ordinary care and diligence to keep the premises in a safe condition for the access of persons coming thereon by his invitation, express or implied, for the transaction of business, or any other purpose beneficial as to him.—Nash v. Minneapolis Mill Co., 24 Minn. 501, 31 Am. Rep. 349.

[n] (Minn. 1894) When a person enters upon the premises of another by invitation, either express or implied, or simply by permission, the owner must exercise ordinary care.—Emery v. Minneapolis Industrial Exposition, 56 Minn. 460, 57 N. W. 1132.

[o] (Mo. 1888) Mere licensees, using a road leading over a lot, assumed the risk of injury from all obvious and patent defects in the road. —Eisenberg v. Missouri Pac. Ry. Co., 33 Mo. App. 85.

377 (§ 42)   NEGLIGENCE.   (§ 43) 378

Cent. Ed.] I. Acts or Omissions Constituting Negligence. (C) Condition and Use of Land, Buildings, and Other Structures. 1. In General.

[p] (N. J. 1871) It is well settled that the mere permission to pass over lands which are dangerous, either naturally or by reason of the use which is made of them, imposes no duty or obligation upon the owner of such lands, except to refrain from acts which are willfully injurious or knowingly in the nature of a trap, and except, also, where there are hidden dangers, the concealment of which would be in the nature of a fraud. He who enjoys the permission or passive license is only relieved from the responsibility of being a trespasser, and must assume all the ordinary risk attached to the nature of the place or the business carried on there.—Vanderbeck v. Hendry, 34 N. J. Law (5 Vroom) 467.

[q] (N. Y. 1874) One owning a sawmill, and carrying on the business of sawing logs for others, is bound to keep the mill and its appliances reasonably safe for those having a right or license to come into it for business purposes, and is liable for any damages arising from a neglect of this duty.—Ackert v. Lansing, 59 N. Y. 646.

[r] (N. Y. 1890) Placing a truck in the rear of a store, in plain sight of every one, where it is frequently used to move heavy goods, is not negligence on the part of the merchant, so as to render him liable for an injury to a customer who unnecessarily follows a clerk to that part of the store, and in so doing stumbles over the truck.—Hart v. Grennell, 122 N. Y. 371, 25 N. E. 354.

[s] (N. Y. 1892) While plaintiff was on premises adjoining her own, seeking her children, who were accustomed to play there, she was injured by the breaking of a decayed stairway. Held, that she could not recover from the owner of such premises on the ground that he negligently permitted the stairs to remain in an unsafe condition, because, she being on the premises without invitation and as a mere licensee, the owner owed her no duty of protection.—Sterger v. Vansiclen, 132 N. Y. 499, 30 N. E. 987, 28 Am. St. Rep. 594, 16 L. R. A. 640, affirming (1890) 55 Hun, 605, 7 N. Y. Supp. 805.

[t] (Ohio, 1884) Where a lot is left unfenced, a person who goes upon it by bare permission, because there is no obstruction to keep him off, goes at his own risk; and the owner is not liable for injuries resulting to him from the unsafe or dangerous condition of the lot.—Kelley v. City of Columbus, 41 Ohio St. 263.

[u] (S. C. 1873) The plaintiff was in the store of the defendant as a customer. A clerk invited her to walk into a dark part of the store, in which there was an open trapdoor, through which she, without negligence on her part, fell and broke her arm. Held, that the defendant was liable.—Freer v. Cameron, 4 Rich. Law, 228, 55 Am. Dec. 663.

[v] (Vt. 1875) Plaintiff went to defendant late in the evening to buy oats. Defendant had no oats to sell, but, yielding to plaintiff's importunity, he consented to sell him the oats, to accommodate him. Defendant always kept his granary locked, but he obtained the key by sending some distance for it, and went with plaintiff to the upper floor of the granary, where the oats were, and, while defendant stepped back to get a measure, plaintiff walked about the floor in the dark, and fell through an aperture therein, and was injured. Held, defendant was not liable for the injury.—Pierce v. Whitcomb, 48 Vt. 127, 21 Am. Rep. 120.

[w] (Wis. 1895) Plaintiff alleged that his intestate was invited by defendant into an uncompleted building, to make certain estimates. At the head of the stairs there was a hallway, in which there was a partially open window. Deceased followed defendant up the stairs, thrust his head through the window, without knowledge that the window was part of the elevator shaft, and was struck by the descending elevator. Held, that defendant was not guilty of any breach of duty to the deceased, and therefore the facts alleged did not constitute a cause of action.—Peake v. Buell, 90 Wis. 508, 63 N. W. 1053, 48 Am. St. Rep. 946.

§ 43. —— Who are licensees.

Places open to public, see post, § 53 [b].

[a] (Ill. 1892) A person who breaks into a building to protect property from fire is a mere licensee, to whom the owner owes no duty to keep the premises in safe repair.—Gibson v. Leonard, 143 Ill. 182, 32 N. E. 182, 36 Am. St. Rep. 376, 17 L. R. A. 588, affirming (1890) 37 Ill. App. 344.

[b] (Ind. 1893) In an action for personal injuries caused by falling through an open cellarway in a college building, there was evidence that plaintiff was a visitor, but had previously been a student; that he was in attendance at a literary society at the invitation of a student; that circulars had been prepared, advertising the society as a feature of the college; that the students were authorized to send out the circulars; that plaintiff received one by mail; and that he was personally asked by the superintendent to visit the building. Held, that plaintiff was in the building at the invitation of the college authorities.—Howe v. Ohmart, 7 Ind. App. 32, 33 N. E. 466.

[c] (Ind. 1893) Where plaintiff came into defendant's store without invitation on part of defendant, and solely on plaintiff's own business, and fell into an elevator shaft in a part of the store unfrequented by visitors, whereby he sustained injuries, defendant cannot be held liable for negligence, as plaintiff can only be regarded as a licensee.—Faris v. Hoberg, 134 Ind. 269, 33 N. E. 1028, 39 Am. St. Rep. 261.

[d] (Ind. 1893) A fireman in the course of his duty goes on the roof of a building on fire as a mere licensee, and not as of right or by invitation of the owner.—Woodruff v. Bowen, 136 Ind. 431, 34 N. E. 1113, 22 L. R. A. 198.

[e] (Mass. 1880) If a religious society gives notice of a meeting to be held at its house of worship, and invites the members of other societies to attend, a member of a church so invited, while on the land of the society, is not a mere licensee, and may maintain an action against the society for a personal injury sustained, while in the exercise of due care, from the dangerous condition of the defendant's premises.—Davis v. Central Congregational Soc., 129 Mass. 367, 37 Am. Rep. 368.

[f] (Mass. 1892) A person who enters a building containing offices, to inquire about a servant of the occupier of one of the offices, who keeps no servant's registry and who has no connection with such business, the building not being used or designed in any part for such purpose, is a mere licensee therein; and the owner is not liable for injuries received by her through the unsafe condition of the building.—Plummer v. Dill, 156 Mass. 426, 31 N. E. 128, 32 Am. St. Rep. 463.

[g] (Mich. 1893) A teamster, after delivering merchandise at the back door of a store, started towards the desk for a receipt, and fell through an open trapdoor. Held, that the proprietor was not liable for the injuries; it not appearing that there had been any express or implied invitation to the teamster to pass to the desk, but that it was the custom of truckmen to make their presence known by calling, when no one was at the door.—Pelton v. Schmidt, 97 Mich. 231, 56 N. W. 689.

[h] (N. Y. 1890) Plaintiff having gone, in the course of his business, to defendant's factory, to find an employé of defendant who usually attended to the business, went through a passageway not generally used for that purpose,

into a portion of the factory from which all persons but defendant's employés were excluded, and while going toward the stairs to which he had been directed by S., an employé of defendant, the place being dark, fell into an elevator hole, and was injured. *Held,* that defendant was not liable for the injury, being under no duty to plaintiff to guard the elevator hole, and that the direction given by S. did not add to defendant's obligation.—Flannigan v. American Glucose Co. (Super. Buff.) 11 N. Y. Supp. 688.

[i] (N. Y. 1895) Plaintiff, who went to defendant's brewery to get "brewery slops," entered a tunnel, without defendant's permission, to answer a call of nature, and was injured by stepping into a hole. The tunnel contained no closet or urinal, and its use was unnecessary for any purpose connected with plaintiff's visit to the brewery. *Held,* that plaintiff was at most a mere licensee, and could not recover.—Castoriano v. Millers (Super. Buff.) 15 Misc. Rep. 254, 36 N. Y. Supp. 419.

[j] (Pa. 1854) Where an area had been used by the public for over 30 years, though the defendant had erected hitching posts and made a hatchway in it, and the defendant had left the hatchway open, so that the plaintiff, on a dark and stormy night, fell into it, it was *held,* that the public had gained a right to use the area, and that the defendant was bound to prove ordinary care on his part.—Bush v. Johnston, 23 Pa. (11 Harris) 209.

[k] (R. I. 1894) In the absence of statute as to guards, or of invitation upon the premises, the owner is not liable to a fireman, who has entered in the course of his duty at a fire, for leaving his elevator well open, and so stacking his merchandise as to guide one into it.—Beehler v. Daniels, 18 R. I. 563. 29 Atl. 6, 49 Am. St. Rep. 790, 27 L. R. A. 512.

§ 44. —— Children.

[a] (Ill. 1891) An employé of defendant brought his son, a boy 5½ years old, to defendant's store, and the boy was injured through an unguarded elevator shaft in the back of the store, with which it was connected by a passageway. The elevator was seldom used, except by employés. Defendant saw the boy playing about the store. *Held,* that a verdict for the boy could not stand, defendant owing him no duty in the circumstances.—Jansen v. Siddal, 41 Ill. App. 279, reversed on another point Siddal v. Jansen (1892) 30 N. E. 357.

[b] (Md. 1893) Where the president of a corporation grants a request of a teacher for permission for a class of 30 or more pupils to visit the company's power house, and one of such pupils, while inspecting the machinery, stepped into an unprotected vat of hot water which he was unable to see, the company was not liable for damages for failure either to warn him of the danger, or to protect the vat by a railing, or to sufficiently light the building to enable him to see it.—Benson v. Baltimore Traction Co., 77 Md. 535, 26 Atl. 973, 39 Am. St. Rep. 436, 20 L. R. A. 714.

[c] (N. Y. 1876) Plaintiff's intestate, P., a lad 18 years old, lost his life by falling into a vat of boiling liquid in defendants' saltpeter factory, where he had gone, by direction of his employer, to pay a bill due one of the defendants. In the factory were a large number of vats and tanks. The vat into which the deceased fell was at one side, and under a passageway nine feet wide at the angle of its intersection with another leading to defendants' office. There was an opening to the vat in the floor, closed by a cover, which was removed at the time of the accident. A skylight was directly over the passageway at this point, making it very light in the daytime. The deceased did not enter the factory at the usual en-trance, but crossed an adjoining lot and canal, climbed a fence, and entered by a back door, and, in passing along the passage to the office, fell into the vat. Defendants' workmen were in the habit of entering the factory in the same way P. did, and occasionally others did so also. On each of the doors in front was a sign, "No admittance," save one, where the sign was, "No admittance except on business," at which a person was usually in attendance to admit persons to the factory. In an action to recover damages, *held,* that defendants were not liable; that P., if not a trespasser, was, at most, in the factory by defendants' sufferance, and took the risks attendant upon being there in the condition in which the factory was; that no duty rested upon defendants to guard the vat for the protection of the deceased.—Victory v. Baker, 67 N. Y. 366.

§ 45. Care required and liability as to trespassers.

Machinery and other instrumentalities, see ante, § 21.

Pleading, see post, § 192.

Trespassing as contributory negligence, see post, § 106.

Unintended consequences, see ante, § 12 [f].

[a] (Ga. 1871) The occupant of a store fronting on a street had an excavation in the rear of the store, about 100 feet from the street, for the purpose of admitting light into the cellar. An alarm of fire was given in the night, and the plaintiff, who lived near, went to the store and through it, and fell into the excavation, receiving severe injuries. *Held,* that the occupant was not liable. A man may dig upon his own soil away from the highway, and his right is not subject to abridgment by parties happening to go out of their way and receiving injuries.—Kohn v. Lovett, 44 Ga. 251.

[b] (Ga. 1895) Where a stranger in a city stepped, at night, into the doorway of a dilapidated building, without any invitation, and fell into a cellar opening at the doorway, and received injuries, the owner was not liable.—Hutson v. King, '95 Ga. 271, 22 S. E. 615.

[c] (Ill. 1882) Plaintiff's intestate, an adult, while on defendant's land without any invitation from defendant, either express or implied, and without legal right, fell into a pool of water, over which a crust had so formed that it resembled dry land, and was drowned. *Held* that plaintiff's intestate being a trespasser, defendant was not liable.—Union Stockyards & Transit Co. v. Rourke, 10 Ill. App. (10 Bradw.) 474.

[d] (Ill. 1893) Where stock escapes to the premises of another, it is a trespasser, and the owner of such premises is under no obligation to secure its safety.—McNeer v. Boone, 52 Ill. App. 181.

[e] (Ill. 1894) A person going on the premises of another for his own purpose cannot recover for injuries received, due to the unsafe condition of a stairway, on account of the absence of guard rails.—Elliott v. Carlson, 54 Ill. App. 470.

[f] (Ind. 1881) The plaintiff, while a trespasser, entered an abandoned and decaying freight house, and was injured by a piece of the building being blown against him in a sudden storm. *Held,* that he could not recover of the company.—Lary v. Cleveland, C. C. & I. R. Co., 78 Ind. 323, 41 Am. Rep. 572.

[g] (Iowa, 1873) A trespasser, who was injured by a spring gun set by the owner of the premises without giving notice of its presence, is entitled to recover from such owner for injuries thereby received.—Hooker v. Miller, 37 Iowa, 613, 18 Am. Rep. 18.

WESTLAW Terminal

WESTLAW®

This chapter shows WESTLAW screens you see when you sign on to the system, choose a database and run a WESTLAW search. The screens include an example of a WESTLAW research problem and typical Shepard's and INSTA-CITE displays.

```
WALT                           WESTLAW           ONLINE
===================================================================
   **          ** ******      **** ******** **          *  **        **
  **    *   **  **              **        **  **           ***  **  *   **
  ** *** **    *****            **        **  **           ** **  ** *** **
  *** ***      **           _  **         **  **           **  **  ** *** ***
   *   *    ****** *****         **     ****** **          **  *  *
```

        A COMPUTER-ASSISTED LEGAL RESEARCH SERVICE OF WEST PUBLISHING COMPANY

        COPYRIGHT © 1986 BY WEST PUBLISHING COMPANY.   COPYRIGHT IS NOT CLAIMED
        AS TO ANY PART OF THE ORIGINAL WORK PREPARED BY A U. S. GOVERNMENT OFFICER
        OR EMPLOYEE AS PART OF THAT PERSON'S OFFICIAL DUTIES.   ALL RIGHTS
        RESERVED.   NO PART OF A WESTLAW TRANSMISSION MAY BE COPIED, DOWNLOADED,
        STORED IN A RETRIEVAL SYSTEM, FURTHER TRANSMITTED OR OTHERWISE REPRODUCED,
        STORED, DISSEMINATED, TRANSFERRED OR USED, IN ANY FORM OR BY ANY MEANS,
        WITHOUT WEST'S PRIOR WRITTEN AGREEMENT.   EACH REPRODUCTION OF ANY PART OF
        A WESTLAW TRANSMISSION MUST CONTAIN NOTICE OF WEST'S COPYRIGHT AS FOLLOWS:
        "COPR. © WEST 1986 NO CLAIM TO ORIG. U.S. GOVT. WORKS".   WESTLAW IS A
        REGISTERED SERVICE MARK OF WEST PUBLISHING CO. REG. U.S. PAT. AND TM. OFF.

             AVAILABLE 3 AM TO THE FOLLOWING 1 AM, CDT, MONDAY THROUGH FRIDAY
                   7 AM TO 8 PM, CDT, SATURDAY AND SUNDAY
        PLEASE TYPE YOUR PASSWORD AND PRESS ENTER: (PASSWORD MAY NOT BE DISPLAYED)

This screen gives copyright information and asks the user for her password.

```
WALT                           WESTLAW           ONLINE
                         WELCOME TO WESTLAW
        Decisions of the New Jersey courts have been extended back to 1899.

        To read the opinions authored by U.S. Supreme Court Justice nominee
        Antonin Scalia in the CTA database, enter the query:  JUDGE(SCALIA).

        Decisions of the Federal Power Commission, FEN-FERC, have been extended back
        to volume 1.  See page 216 of the Directory for details.

        Decisions of the Colorado Supreme Court have been extended back to 1883.

        New Jersey Attorney General Opinions are now available in NJ-AG and in
        Multistate Attorney General, AG.

        ***PROMOTION*** Through June 30, 1986, you can receive one FREE HOUR on
        VU/TEXT'S database -- Wall Street Transcript.

                  (For more information, please see the Directory.)
        PLEASE IDENTIFY THIS RESEARCH SESSION BY ENTERING YOUR CLIENT OR FILE
        INFORMATION OR YOUR INITIALS.
```

This screen gives new database information and asks the user to enter client
identification.

```
:   WESTLAW DIRECTORY                                              P1
:
: DATABASES                              SERVICES
:  FEDERAL                                CUSTOMER SERVICE ..............P33
:    GENERAL- statutes, cases ....P2      TRAINING COURSES ..............P34
:      -administrative materials,         PRACTICE DATABASES ............P35
:        additional databases .....P3     WESTLAW CASE HIGHLIGHTS ........P36
:    TOPICAL (tax, securities,            OTHER PUBLISHERS' DATABASES ....P37
:       labor, etc.) ............P4      CITATORS
:  STATE - MULTISTATE                       INSTA-CITE ..................P42
:    GENERAL (includes Regional            SHEPARD'S ...................P44
:      Reporter databases) ......P5      REFERENCE MANUAL PAGE LIST .....P45
:    TOPICAL (tax, insurance,            NEW BOOKS FROM WEST ...........P55
:       family law, etc.) ........P6     BLACK'S LAW DICTIONARY ........P1184
:  STATE - INDIVIDUAL STATES .....P8     LIST OF WEST DIGEST TOPICS .....P1186
:  NATIONAL                              LIST OF DATABASE IDENTIFIERS ...P1200
:    GENERAL (includes texts
:       and periodicals) ........P9
:    TOPICAL ...................P32
:
:
:
:For information about Databases or Services, enter page number, e.g., P2 ____
```

```
:___WESTLAW DIRECTORY_____P1_____:
:: FEDERAL GENERAL DATABASES                                       P2
::        STATUTES                          CASES, cont'd
:: USC   U.S. Code ............P77     CTA11  Eleventh Circuit ......P121
::                                     CTADC  D.C. Circuit .........P124
::        CASES                        CTAF   Federal Circuit
:: ALLFEDS  Federal Cases .....P81            (includes former
:: SCT    U.S. Supreme Court ....P84          Court of Claims) .....P127
:: CTA    U.S. Courts of Appeals.P87   MJ   Military Justice
::   CTA1   First Circuit ......P91           (includes Court of
::   CTA2   Second Circuit .....P94           Military Appeals) ....P294
::   CTA3   Third Circuit ......P97
::   CTA4   Fourth Circuit .....P100   DCT   U.S. District Courts
::   CTA5   Fifth Circuit ......P103         (includes Court of
::   CTA6   Sixth Circuit ......P106         International Trade) ..P130
::   CTA7   Seventh Circuit ....P109   DCTR   Reported .............P137
::   CTA8   Eighth Circuit .....P112   DCTU   Unreported ...........P141
::   CTA9   Ninth Circuit ......P115
::   CTA10  Tenth Circuit ......P118   CLCT  U.S. Claims Court........P145
::
:: For Administrative materials and additional databases, see next page.
:: To access a database, enter its identifier, e.g., USC
:__For information about a database enter its page number, e.g., P77 _____
```

Both screens on this page illustrate listings from the WESTLAW Directory of Databases.

Illustrated Problem

The research question (WESTLAW QUERY) is illustrated below. The fact situation involves a pet owner suing for mental anguish or emotional distress caused to the owner by an act harming the pet.

The query asks WESTLAW to search in its' Pacific Reporter database for cases that have words in a specific proximity to each other. In this example, we are looking for the word MENTAL or EMOTIONAL within 3 words of the word ANGUISH, DISTRESS or SUFFERING to appear in the same sentence as the word DOG, CAT or PET.

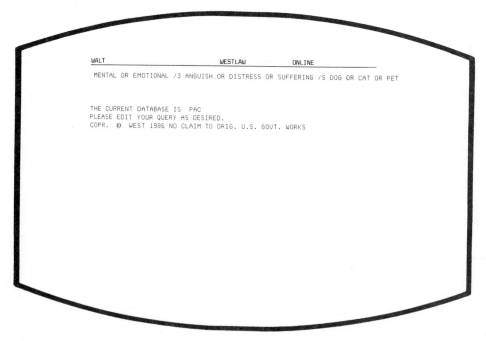

```
WALT                          WESTLAW          ONLINE
MENTAL OR EMOTIONAL /3 ANGUISH OR DISTRESS OR SUFFERING /S DOG OR CAT OR PET


THE CURRENT DATABASE IS  PAC
PLEASE EDIT YOUR QUERY AS DESIRED.
COPR.  ©  WEST 1986 NO CLAIM TO ORIG. U.S. GOVT. WORKS
```

This figure shows the query as it looks when typed on the WESTLAW screen.

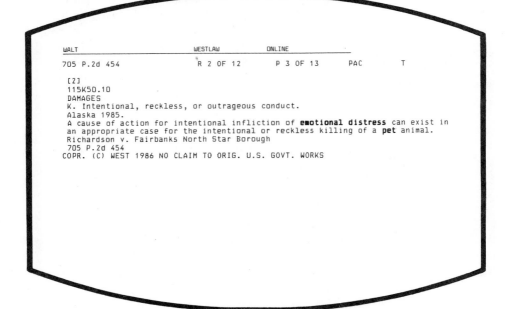

```
WALT                   WESTLAW        ONLINE

Citation               Rank(R)        Page(P)        Database   Mode
705 P.2d 454           R 2 OF 12      P 1 OF 13      PAC        T
               Fred RICHARDSON and Jill Richardson, Appellants,
                                    v.
                 FAIRBANKS NORTH STAR BOROUGH, Appellee.
                              No. S-391.
                        Supreme Court of Alaska.
                           Aug. 30, 1985.
    Owners of pet dog sought to recover against borough for damages allegedly
  sustained by them when dog was mistakenly killed by an employee of borough
  animal shelter.  The Superior Court, Fourth Judicial District, Fairbanks, Jay
  Hodges, J., limited damage award to dog's market value or replacement costs,
  and owners appealed.  The Supreme Court, Moore, J., held that:  (1) proper
  measure of damages for death of pet dog caused by negligence of borough when an
  employee of animal shelter maintained by borough mistakenly killed dog was that
  figure which represented animal's market value at time of death rather than
  owners' subjective estimation of animal's value as a pet, and (2) severity of
  owners' alleged mental and emotional suffering did not warrant a claim of
  intentional infliction of emotional distress for the intentional or reckless
  killing of a pet animal.
    Affirmed.
  COPR. (C) WEST 1986 NO CLAIM TO ORIG. U.S. GOVT. WORKS
```

The WESTLAW screen above shows the first page of the second case retrieved by the WESTLAW search. Note that search terms are highlighted.

```
WALT                   WESTLAW        ONLINE

705 P.2d 454           R 2 OF 12      P 3 OF 13      PAC        T

  [2]
  115K50.10
  DAMAGES
  K. Intentional, reckless, or outrageous conduct.
  Alaska 1985.
  A cause of action for intentional infliction of emotional distress can exist in
  an appropriate case for the intentional or reckless killing of a pet animal.
  Richardson v. Fairbanks North Star Borough
   705 P.2d 454
  COPR. (C) WEST 1986 NO CLAIM TO ORIG. U.S. GOVT. WORKS
```

This screen shows a West key number digest paragraph from the same case.

```
WALT                      WESTLAW         ONLINE

705 P.2d 454              R 2 OF 12      P 8 OF 13      PAC       P

   Thomas R. Wickwire, Fairbanks, for appellants.
   Chris Bataille, Asst. Borough Atty., Michael B. Markham, Acting Borough Atty.,
 for appellee.

   Before RABINOWITZ, C.J., and BURKE, MATTHEWS, COMPTON and MOORE, JJ.
                              OPINION

   MOORE, Justice.

   This case concerns the proper measure of damages for the death of a pet dog
 caused by a municipality's negligence.  The Fairbanks North Star Borough Animal
 Shelter (hereafter Borough or pound) violated a Borough ordinance and
 mistakenly killed the Richardsons' pet dog, Wizzard.  The Richardsons had owned
 the dog for about two months.  At trial the superior court limited the damage
 award to the dog's market value or replacement cost.  The Richardsons appeal
 the measure of damages applied by the court.  We affirm.
 I. FACTS AND PROCEEDINGS
  After an unsuccessful search for their missing dog, the Richardsons called the
 pound.  A pound employee confirmed that the pound had the dog and informed the
 Richardsons that they could redeem their dog between 8:00 a.m. and 5:00 p.m.
 The Richardsons went to the pound after work that day, arriving at 4:50 p.m.
 COPR. (C) WEST 1986 NO CLAIM TO ORIG. U.S. GOVT. WORKS
```

The display above is in the same case where the judge's opinion begins.

```
WALT                      WESTLAW         ONLINE

CITATIONS LIST (Page 1)    Database: PAC            Total Documents: 12

   1.   Or.App. 1986.   Saechao v. Matsakoun   717 P.2d 165, 78 Or.App. 340

   2.   Alaska 1985.   Richardson v. Fairbanks North Star Borough
 705 P.2d 454

   3.   Cal. 1985.   Ochoa v. Superior Court (Santa Clara County)
 703 P.2d 1, 216 Cal.Rptr. 661, 39 Cal.3d 159, 54 U.S.L.W. 2107

   4.   Or.App. 1985.   Sease v. Taylor's Pets, Inc.
 700 P.2d 1054, 74 Or.App. 110

   5.   Idaho App. 1985.   Gill v. Brown   695 P.2d 1276, 107 Idaho 1137

   6.   Or. 1982.
 Norwest, By and Through Crain v. Presbyterian Intercom. Hosp.
 652 P.2d 318, 293 Or. 543

   7.   Hawaii 1981.
 Campbell v. Animal Quarantine Station, Division of Animal Industry, Dept. of
 Agriculture, State of Hawaii, Bd. of Agriculture   632 P.2d 1066, 63 Hawaii 557
 COPR. (C) WEST 1986 NO CLAIM TO ORIG. U.S. GOVT. WORKS
```

This is the citation and title list of cases retrieved by the WESTLAW query.

Shepard's® Illustration

A separate service on WESTLAW is Shepard's. You can find legal decisions citing the case you are researching as legal precedent. Below is a Shepard's display from WESTLAW showing legal decisions citing to Savage v. U.S. (322 Federal Supplement 33).

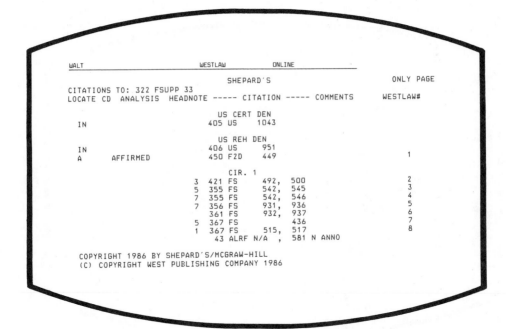

```
WALT                         WESTLAW         ONLINE                        

                                  SHEPARD'S                        ONLY PAGE
CITATIONS TO: 322 FSUPP 33
LOCATE CD   ANALYSIS  HEADNOTE ----- CITATION ----- COMMENTS      WESTLAW#

                                US CERT DEN
      IN                        405 US    1043

                                US REH DEN
      IN                        406 US     951
      A     AFFIRMED            450 F2D    449                        1

                                   CIR. 1
                        3   421 FS     492,  500                      2
                        5   355 FS     542,  545                      3
                        7   355 FS     542,  546                      4
                        7   356 FS     931,  936                      5
                            361 FS     932,  937                      6
                        5   367 FS           436                      7
                        1   367 FS     515,  517                      8
                           43 ALRF N/A  ,  581 N ANNO

      COPYRIGHT 1986 BY SHEPARD'S/MCGRAW-HILL
      (C) COPYRIGHT WEST PUBLISHING COMPANY 1986
```

INSTA-CITE™ Illustration

INSTA-CITE is another service available on WESTLAW. Its main uses are to provide case history, citation verification and parallel citations. The illustration below is the INSTA-CITE display for National Freight v. Larson (760 Federal Reporter 2nd 499).

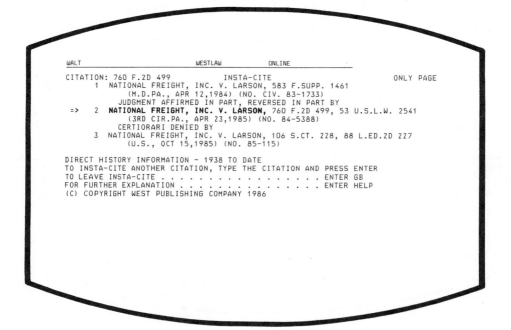

```
WALT                      WESTLAW        ONLINE

CITATION: 760 F.2D 499            INSTA-CITE                    ONLY PAGE
      1  NATIONAL FREIGHT, INC. V. LARSON, 583 F.SUPP. 1461
            (M.D.PA., APR 12,1984) (NO. CIV. 83-1733)
         JUDGMENT AFFIRMED IN PART, REVERSED IN PART BY
   =>  2  NATIONAL FREIGHT, INC. V. LARSON, 760 F.2D 499, 53 U.S.L.W. 2541
            (3RD CIR.PA., APR 23,1985) (NO. 84-5388)
         CERTIORARI DENIED BY
      3  NATIONAL FREIGHT, INC. V. LARSON, 106 S.CT. 228, 88 L.ED.2D 227
            (U.S., OCT 15,1985) (NO. 85-115)

DIRECT HISTORY INFORMATION - 1938 TO DATE
TO INSTA-CITE ANOTHER CITATION, TYPE THE CITATION AND PRESS ENTER
TO LEAVE INSTA-CITE . . . . . . . . . . . . . . . . . ENTER GB
FOR FURTHER EXPLANATION . . . . . . . . . . . . . . ENTER HELP
(C) COPYRIGHT WEST PUBLISHING COMPANY 1986
```

Corpus Juris Secundum

C.J.S.

Corpus Juris Secundum is West's comprehensive legal encyclopedia. The example which follows uses words much the same way as the digest problem. You list the important words or concepts, consult the indexes and are led to sections in CJS where the law regarding your problem is discussed.

C.J.S. Problem

A young, blind woman walks into an open elevator shaft at her hotel. She falls one story breaking her hip. She sues for damages claiming the hotel was negligent in leaving the elevator doors open. In defense, the attorney for the hotel claims that the woman was contributorily negligent because she didn't have a cane to check for obstacles or dangers in her path. Is she contributorily negligent for not having a cane to help compensate for her blindness? Find cases discussing the issue.

Worksheet

Parties:

Places and Things:

Basis of Action or Issue:

Defense:

Relief Sought:

GENERAL INDEX

TO

CORPUS JURIS SECUNDUM

A

A
Defined, **Vol. 1**

A MENSA ET THORO
Alimony, **Divorce §§ 229, 238**
Condonation, **Divorce § 61**
Defined, **Vol. 3A**
Evidence, **Divorce § 135**
Grounds, **Divorce §§ 15, 42, 86, 160**
Intestate inheritance, **Des & Dist § 59**
Recrimination, **Divorce § 67**
Rights as husband, **Hus & W § 611**
Setting aside, etc., **Divorce § 168(1)**
Support, continuing duty, **Hus & W § 15**
Venue, **Divorce § 83**
Witnesses, competency, **Witn § 81**

A POSTERIORI
Defined, **Vol. 3**

A PRENDRE
Defined, **Vol. 6**
Profits a prendre,
    Deeds and conveyances, passing of by deed, **Deeds § 15**
    Easements, **Ease §§ 3, 65**
    Fish and game, right to hunt, **Game § 4**
    Frauds, statute of, **Frauds S §§ 71, 116**
    License distinguished, **Ease § 3**
    Oil and gas lease, **Mines §§ 195, 201**
        Subsurface ownership of oil and gas, **Mines § 134**
    Partition, allotment of property, **Partit § 155**
    Perpetuities, applicability, **Perp § 11**
    Vendor and purchaser, encumbrances, **Ven & Pur § 203**

A PRIORI
Defined, **Vol. 6**

A A A
United States Agricultural Adjustment Act, generally, this index

AB
Defined, **Vol. 1**

AB ACTIS
Defined, **Vol. 1**

AB INITIO
Aliens,
    Denaturalization, citizenship, hearing, **Aliens § 336**
    Devises, acquisition of property, **Aliens § 32**
Armed services,
    Courts-martial, proceedings, incompetency of one member, **Armed S § 168**
    Discharge, correction, **Armed S § 89**
Attachment, see **Title Index to Attachment**
Contracts, confederate money, consideration, **Contracts § 270**
Criminal law,
    Coram nobis, validity of proceedings, **Crim Law § 1606(33)**
    Preliminary complaints, void for lack of oath, **Crim Law § 308**
    Preliminary proceedings, void for want of sufficient affidavit, **Crim Law § 303**
    Trespasser ab initio, officer failing to make return on warrant of arrest, **Crim Law § 329**
Defined, **Vol. 1**
Divorce,
    Annulment of, void marriage, **Divorce § 1**
    Collateral attack on judgment, **Divorce § 173(3)**
    Void marriage, consanguinity or affinity, **Divorce § 1**
Equity, decree void ab initio, **Equity § 632**
    Fraud, **Equity § 682**

BLEED
Defined, **Vol. 11**

BLEES
Defined, **Vol. 11**

BLEND
Defined, **Vol. 11**

BLEPHARITIS
Defined, **Vol. 11**

BLIGHT ELIMINATION
Eminent domain, **Em Dom § 64(1)**
  Particular property, necessity for taking, **Em Dom § 90**
  Site location, **Em Dom § 91**

BLIGHTED AREAS
Housing, generally, this index

BLIMP
Defined, **Vol. 11**

BLIND
Defined, **Vol. 11**

BLIND ALLEY
Cul de Sac, generally, this index

BLIND AMENDMENTS
Statutes, constitutional prohibition, **Stat § 260**

BLIND BILLED
Carriers, defined, **Carr § 122**

BLIND CAR
Railroads, defined, **R R § 1**

BLIND CROSSING
Evidence, conclusion of witness, **Evid § 453**

BLIND FLUE
Railroads, defined, **R R § 1**

BLIND HORSES
Highways and roads, driving on contributory negligence, **High § 274**
Streets or other public ways, negligence in driving on, **Mun Corp §§ 854, 855**

BLIND INTERSECTIONS
Generally, see **Title Index to Motor Vehicles**

BLIND PERSONS
  Generally, see **Title Index to Social Security and Public Welfare**
Abatement and revival, blindness caused by wood alcohol, **Abate & R § 144**
Aliens, exclusion, **Aliens § 106**
Appeal and review, blind pension, decisions reviewable, **App & E §§ 47, 50**
Armed services, insurance, risks and causes of loss, **Armed S § 211**
Asylums and institutional care facilities,
  Exemption from taxation, **Tax §§ 285, 296**
  Scalding water, liabilities, **Asyl § 14**
Attorney, admission to practice, examination, **Atty & C § 18**

BLIND PERSONS—Continued
Bills and notes, fraud, defense, **Bills & N § 498**
Carriers,
  Duty of transporting, **Carr § 538**
  Moving trains, partial blindness as requiring carrier to prevent leaving, **Carr § 725**
  Wrongful ejection, defense, **Carr § 832**
  Highways, injuries from defects or obstructions, **High § 269**
Civil rights, complaint charging discrimination against teacher, **Civil R § 153**
Contracts, capacity to contract, **Contracts § 133(1)**
Contributory negligence, **Neglig § 142**
  Question of law or fact, **Neglig § 260**
  Streets or other public ways, injuries from defects or obstructions, **Mun Corp § 849**
County liabilities, equal protection of law, **Const Law § 553**
Criminal law, new trial, blindness of accused, **Crim Law § 1462**
Damages, **Damag § 238**
  Jury questions, proximate cause, **Damag § 176(4)**
  Medical expenses, **Damag § 91(3)**
Deeds and conveyances, validity, **Deeds § 54**
Elections,
  Assistance to voters on ground of blindness, **Elections § 208**
  Manner of voting, observance of statutory regulations, **Elections § 208**
  Secret ballots, exception, **Elections § 201(2)**
  Writing in names of candidates, **Elections § 208**
Equal protection of law, county liabilities, **Const Law § 553**
Fraud,
  Bills and notes, defense, **Bills & N § 498**
  Signing instrument misread by defendant, recovery for fraud, **Fraud § 34**
Highways and roads, injuries from defects or obstructions, contributory negligence, **High § 269**
Indigent persons, participation in general distribution of poor relief funds,
  Paupers § 1
  Pension, § 82
Inns, hotels, and eating places,
  Personal injuries, contributory negligence, **Inn § 28**
  Safety of premises, **Inn § 25**
Institutions, exemption from taxation, **Tax §§ 285, 296**
Landlord and tenant, contributory negligence descending stairway with assistance, **Land & Ten § 417(19)**
Motor vehicles,
  Care required to avoid injury, **Motor V § 394**
  Competency of driver, **Motor V § 264**
  Pedestrians, contributory negligence, jury question, **Motor V § 527(28)**
Negligence, sufficiency of care exercised as to, **Neglig § 12**
Pensions,
  Decisions reviewable, **App & E §§ 47, 50**
  Paupers, **Paupers § 82**

555

NEGLIGENCE

Beds,
>Dealer's liability for injury from faulty design, § 100(3), p. 1113, n. 50
>
>Failure of dealer representing himself as manufacturer to test, § 100(3), p. 1114, n. 58
>
>Products liability, weight of evidence, § 243(10), p. 699
>
>Purchaser's duty to inspect, § 100(3), p. 1110, n. 33

Beer containers, explosion,
>Evidence of defective regulator, § 222, n. 30
>
>Proximate cause, fermentation pressure, § 265, p. 933, n. 42
>
>Weight of evidence, § 243(10), p. 701

Beer distributor, duty to inspect cases, § 100(3), p. 1112, n. 48

Bees, poisonous insecticides, weight and sufficiency of evidence, § 243(1), p. 671, n. 28

Belief of person charged as to existence or nonexistence of danger, § 5(3), p. 512

Beneficiaries of estate, notice of injury and claim, § 180, p. 316

Beverages,
>Bottles and bottling, generally, post
>
>Products liability, § 100(2), p. 1092

Bicycles,
>Imputation of contributory negligence of operator to guest, § 168(10), p. 236
>
>Tripping over bicycle in hallway, weight of evidence, § 243(11), p. 704, n. 48

Bill collector, negligence toward, jury question, § 272, p. 960, n. 31

Billboards, construction, weight of evidence, § 243(10), p. 697

Bills, persons entering premises to pay, § 63(149)
>Service station invitee, § 63(128), n. 20

Bills of particulars,
>Complaint alleging acts in violation of statutes and ordinances, § 187(4), n. 42
>
>General averment of negligence as ground for bill by plaintiff, § 187(9)
>
>Res ipsa loquitur where plaintiff furnishes bill of defendant's negligence, § 220.23, p. 607, n. 62

Bingo,
>Injuries on premises, evidence, § 243(11), p. 705
>
>Liability for injury to invitee, § 63(45), p. 730, n. 95
>
>Persons entering halls, rules governing, § 63(133)

Blameworthy conduct, culpable negligence distinguished, § 1(13), p. 456

Blank form, status of person entering bank to obtain note form, licensee, § 63(133), n. 94

Blind persons,
>Contributory negligence, § 142
>>Question of law or fact, § 260, p. 894
>
>Sufficiency of care exercised as to, § 12, p. 587

Blocks, concrete blocks, attractive nuisance, § 63(96)

Blood donors, reasonable care in testing and examining by donee, § 66, p. 943, n. 30

Blood poisoning, Boncilla treatment, weight and sufficiency of evidence, § 243(8), n. 84

Blood tests, intoxication, evidence of contributory negligence, § 242, n. 91

Blowtorch,
>Evidence of negligence and fire caused by, § 243(9), n. 90
>
>Infant trespasser, burns, § 63(61), n. 50

Blowtorch—Continued
>Pleading willfulness or wantonness, injuries to child, § 190, n. 40

Blueberries, burning blueberry lands, weight of evidence, § 243(9), n. 92

Boarding and lodging houses, transmission of contagious diseases by placing of afflicted children, § 71

Boards and commissions, violation of rules and regulations, contributory negligence, § 127

Boats,
>Contributory negligence of operator, imputation to passenger or guest, § 168(10), p. 236
>
>Duty to invitees, § 63(46), p. 747
>
>Engines, purchaser's liability for injury from condition of boat after removal, § 95, p. 1061, n. 5
>
>Sinking, questions of law and fact, § 252, p. 813, n. 12.40

Boilers,
>Contributory negligence, failure to observe or take precaution against danger, § 257(2), p. 890
>
>Evidence of negligence in erection, maintenance, etc., § 243(10), p. 697
>
>Explosions, weight of evidence, § 243(10), p. 701
>
>Increase of water pressure in boiler as proximate cause, § 112, n. 9
>
>Lifting of section, physical possibility, § 251(1), p. 777, n. 70
>
>Partial defense of contributory negligence of employee injured by violation of boiler inspection act, § 172, p. 280
>
>Products liability, weight of evidence, § 243(10), p. 699
>
>Res ipsa loquitur doctrine, bursting or exploding, § 220.24, p. 615
>
>State inspection as affecting manufacturer's liability for negligent construction, § 100(3), p. 1098, n. 94

Boncilla treatment, evidence of negligence, § 243(8), n. 84

Bond, criminal proceeding, forfeiture, evidence, § 239, n. 69.5

Bonfires,
>Nuisance per se, § 72, p. 952, n. 1
>
>Safeguarding children from injury, § 72, p. 955

Booking agent, business invitee by invitation, § 63(137), n. 92

Bottles and bottling,
>Contributory negligence, breaking or explosion, § 257(2), p. 890
>
>Denatured alcohol, attractive nuisance, § 63(102)
>
>Evidence,
>>Cause of injury, § 244(6)
>>
>>Contributory negligence of person injured by explosion, § 247(3), p. 760, n. 95
>>
>>Custom or usage in handling, § 232, p. 640, n. 2
>>
>>Defendant's precaution against injury from explosion, § 243(14), n. 13
>>
>>Expert testimony, injury by explosion, § 244(4), n. 72
>>
>>Medical testimony, dead mouse in bottle, § 244(4), n. 74
>
>Negligence,
>>Injury by exploding bottle to one watching bottling machine, § 243(10), p. 697, n. 95

NEGLIGENCE

jury, but is merely of dull mind, is chargeable with the same degree of care for his personal safety as one of brighter intellect.[5]

§ 142. Persons under Physical Disability

A person under any physical disability is required to exercise ordinary care to avoid injury, and if he fails to do so, and such failure contributes proximately to the injury, he is guilty of contributory negligence.

Library References

Negligence ☞86.

A person laboring under any physical disability increasing his liability to injury must nevertheless exercise ordinary care to avoid injury;[6] and if he fails to exercise that degree of care, and such failure contributes proximately to cause his injury, he is guilty of contributory negligence.[7] Such a person is not required to exercise a higher degree of care to that end than is required of a person under no disability;[8] ordinary care is all that is required.[9]

However, in determining whether such a person exercised ordinary care for his own safety, his disability is a circumstance to be considered.[10] Thus, while it has been said that ordinary care is such care as an ordinarily prudent person with the same disability would exercise under the same or similar circumstances,[11] it has also been held that it may be incumbent on one with a physical disability to put forth a greater degree of effort than would otherwise be necessary in order to attain that standard of care which is required of everyone.[12]

Blind persons and persons with defective vision. The fact that a person is wholly or partially blind does not relieve him of the duty to exercise ordinary care for his own safety;[13] and if he fails to exercise such care, and his failure to do so contributes proximately to cause his injury, he is guilty of contributory negligence.[14] It is not negligence as a matter of law for a blind person to be present in a public place[15] or to walk unattended on a public street.[16] In the absence of knowledge to the contrary, actual or imputed, such a person may assume that he is not exposed to, or threatened by, injury which can come to him only from a breach of the duty which others owe to avoid injury to him.[17]

---

5. Ala.—Worthington v. Mencer, 11 So. 72, 96 Ala. 310, 17 L.R.A. 407.
45 C.J. p 995 note 54.

6. Iowa.—**Corpus Juris Secundum cited in** Tisserat v. Peters, 99 N.W. 2d 924, 926, 251 Iowa 250.
Mass.—Keith v. Worcester, etc., R. Co., 82 N.E. 680, 196 Mass. 478, 14 L.R.A.,N.S., 648.
N.J.—Berger v. Shapiro, 152 A.2d 20, 30 N.J 89.
Karmazin v. Pennsylvania R. Co., 196 A.2d 803, 82 N.J.Super. 123, rehearing denied 198 A.2d 97, 82 N.J. Super. 435.
45 C.J. p 995 note 56.
Care required to avoid injury to person under physical disability see supra § 12.

Knowledge of danger
(1) Old woman of frail and slight physique suing for injuries resulting from fall sustained when salesman in provision, fruit, and vegetable market slightly brushed woman's elbow or arm must be charged with knowledge of her physical condition and of the risk she incurred in stationing herself so near to salesman that an ordinary movement on his part might jeopardize her safety.
Cal.—Ury v. Fredkin's Markets, 79 P.2d 749, 26 C.A.2d 501.

(2) Person whose faculties of observation are temporarily suspended as regards a dangerous condition is virtually in the same mental position as one who has never acquired knowledge of such condition.
Kan.—Cox v. City of Coffeyville, 110 P.2d 772, 153 Kan. 392.

7. Tenn.—Felton v. Horner, 37 S.W. 696, 97 Tenn. 579.
45 C.J. p 995 note 57.
Failure of passengers on trains to have an attendant as contributory negligence see Carriers § 776 a.

8. Cal.—Jones v. Bayley, 122 P.2d 293, 49 C.A.2d 647.
Me.—McCullough v. Lalumiere, 166 A.2d 702, 156 Me. 479.
S.C.—**Corpus Juris Secundum cited in** Conner v. Farmers and Merchants Bank, 132 S.E.2d 385, 392, 243 S.C. 132.
45 C.J. p 996 note 58.

9. Cal.—Jones v. Bayley, 122 P.2d 293, 49 C.A.2d 647.
S.C.—Conner v. Farmers and Merchants Bank, 132 S.E.2d 385, 243 S.C. 132.
45 C.J. p 996 note 59.

10. Conn.—Goodman v. Norwalk Jewish Center, Inc., 139 A.2d 812, 145 Conn. 146.
Mass.—Keith v. Worcester, etc., R. Co., 82 N.E. 680, 196 Mass. 478, 14 L.R.A.,N.S., 648.
45 C.J. p 996 note 60.

11. Cal.—Conjorsky v. Murray, 287 P.2d 505, 135 C.A.2d 478—Jones v. Bayley, 122 P.2d 293, 49 C.A.2d 647.
Conn.—Goodman v. Norwalk Jewish Center, Inc., 139 A.2d 812, 145 Conn. 146.
Me.—Ham v. Lewiston, 47 A. 548, 94 Me. 265.
S.C.—**Corpus Juris Secundum cited in** Conner v. Farmers and Merchants Bank, 132 S.E.2d 385, 392, 243 S.C. 132.

12. U.S.—Darter v. Greenville Community Hotel Corp., C.A.S.C., 301 F.2d 70.
Cal.—Jones v. Bayley, 122 P.2d 293, 49 C.A.2d 647—Armstrong v. Day, 284 P. 1083, 103 C.A. 465.
Me.—McCullough v. Lalumiere, 166 A.2d 702, 156 Me. 479.
Neb.—Trumbley v. Moore, 39 N.W.2d 613, 151 Neb. 780.
45 C.J. p 996 note 62.

Requirement stated in terms of degree of care
In some cases the text requirement has been stated in terms of a commensurately greater degree of care.
U.S.—Darter v. Greenville Community Hotel Corporation, C.A.S.C., 301 F.2d 70.

13. Cal.—**Corpus Juris Secundum cited in** Krause v. Apodaca, 186 C. A.2d 413, 9 Cal.Rptr. 10, 12.
Iowa.—Balcom v. Independence, 160 N.W. 305, 178 Iowa 685, L.R.A.1917C 120.
Pa.—Davis v. Feinstein, 88 A.2d 695, 370 Pa. 449.
45 C.J. p 996 note 64.
Care required to avoid injury to blind person see supra § 12.

14. Pa.—Karl v. Juniata County, 56 A. 78, 206 Pa. 633.
45 C.J. p 996 note 65.

15. N.Y.—Harris v. Uebelhoer, 75 N. Y. 169.

16. Or.—Weinstein v. Wheeler, 271 P. 733, 127 Or. 406, 62 A.L.R. 574.

17. Tenn.—**Corpus Juris cited in** East Tennessee Light & Power Co.

172

In determining what constitutes ordinary care on his part, his blindness, and all other circumstances affecting the question as to what care was reasonably necessary to avoid injury, should be considered.[18] Thus, the fact that he is blind, or has defective vision, may make it incumbent on him to make greater use of his other senses to prevent injury than if in full possession of his faculty of sight.[19] Ordinary care to protect himself from injury, however, is all that is required of him.[20] Ordinary care in the case of such a person is such care as an ordinarily prudent person with a like infirmity would have exercised under the same or similar circumstances.[21]

Deaf persons. It is the duty of a person who is deaf, or whose hearing is defective, to use ordinary care for his own safety;[22] and if he fails to use such care, and such failure contributes proximately to cause his injury, he is guilty of contributory negligence.[23] The fact that he is deaf, or has defec-

tive hearing, may impose on him a duty to make greater use of his other senses to protect himself from injury than if in full possession of his faculty of hearing;[24] but ordinary care, such as an ordinarily prudent person laboring under a like infirmity would exercise under the same or similar circumstances, is all that is required of him.[25]

§ 143. Intoxicated Persons

The voluntary intoxication of a person does not excuse him from exercising the due care required of a sober person, and where such intoxication prevents him from using the necessary care, and his negligent conduct contributes directly to the injury, he cannot recover.

Library References

Negligence ⊜88.

The care required of a person who has become intoxicated voluntarily is the same as that required of one who is sober.[26] Accordingly, the voluntary

---

v. Gose, 130 S.W.2d 984, 987, 23 Tenn.App. 280.
45 C.J. p 996 note 66.

Intrusting safety to others
Blind persons may, within reasonable limits, intrust their safety to those who are younger and stronger mentally and physically than themselves without being guilty of negligence.
Minn.—Anderson v. Winkle, 5 N.W. 2d 355, 213 Minn. 77.

18. Iowa.—Hill v. Glenwood, 100 N. W. 522, 124 Iowa 479.
45 C.J. p 996 note 67.

19. Cal.—**Corpus Juris Secundum cited in** Pennington v. Southern Pac. Co., 304 P.2d 22, 29, 146 C.A.2d 605, 65 A.L.R.2d 690—**Corpus Juris cited in** Jones v. Bayley, 122 P.2d 293, 297, 49 C.A.2d 647—**Corpus Juris cited in** Armstrong v. Day, 284 P. 1083, 1086, 103 C.A. 465.
N.J.—Berger v. Shapiro, 144 A.2d 900, 52 N.J.Super. 94, affirmed 152 A.2d 20, 30 N.J. 89.
Pa.—Taylor v. Rollins, Com.Pl., 9 Chest.Co. 65.
Tenn.—Riddell v. Great Atlantic & Pac. Tea Co., 241 S.W.2d 406, 192 Tenn. 304.
45 C.J. p 996 note 68.

Care required of sighted person compared
(1) As a rule in determination of liability in a tort action, a person with defective vision will be held to a greater degree of care than a person of normal vision when confronted with unfamiliar, dark surroundings.
La.—Mahfouz v. United Broth. of Carpenters and Joiners of America —Local Union No. 403, App., 117 So. 2d 295.

(2) Where persons have defective vision, they should use greater care in proportion to the dangers to which men are constantly exposed than is required of those in full possession of the faculty of sight.
Tenn.—Riddell v. Great Atlantic & Pac. Tea Co., 241 S.W.2d 406, 192 Tenn. 304.

Use of artificial aids required
Due care for a blind person includes a reasonable effort to compensate for his unfortunate affliction by the use of artificial aids for discerning obstacles in his path.
Pa.—Davis v. Feinstein, 88 A.2d 695, 370 Pa. 449.

20. Cal.—**Corpus Juris Secundum cited in** Pennington v. Southern Pac. Co., 304 P.2d 22, 29, 146 C.A.2d 605, 65 A.L.R.2d 690—**Corpus Juris cited in** Jones v. Bayley, 122 P.2d 293, 297, 49 C.A.2d 647.
45 C.J. p 996 note 69.

21. Cal.—**Corpus Juris cited in** Jones v. Bayley, 122 P.2d 293, 297, 49 C.A. 2d 647.
Conn.—**Corpus Juris cited in** Muse v. Page, 4 A.2d 329, 331, 125 Conn. 219.
Iowa.—**Corpus Juris Secundum quoted in** Tisserat v. Peters, 99 N.W.2d 924, 926, 251 Iowa 250.
Ky.—Gill v. Sable Hide & Fur Co., 4 S.W.2d 676, 223 Ky. 679.
N.C.—**Corpus Juris Secundum cited in** Cook v. City of Winston-Salem, 85 S.E.2d 696, 701, 241 N.C. 422.
45 C.J. p 996 note 70.

Care commensurate with risk
Where defendant's mother-in-law was over seventy years old, had suffered a stroke, walked with a shuffling gait and was afflicted with "barrel" or "tunnel" vision, mother-in-law had a duty to exercise a degree

of care for her own safety which would be commensurate with risk involved.
Wis.—Cordula v. Dietrich, 101 N.W. 2d 126, 9 Wis.2d 211.

22. Me.—McCullough v. Lalumiere, 166 A.2d 702, 156 Me. 479.
Md.—Fenneman v. Holden, 22 A. 1049, 75 Md. 1.
45 C.J. p 996 note 72.
Care required to avoid injury to deaf person see supra § 12.

23. Wash.—Hamlin v. Columbia, etc., R. Co., 79 P. 991, 37 Wash. 448.
45 C.J. p 996 note 73.

24. Cal.—**Corpus Juris cited in** Jones v. Bayley, 122 P.2d 293, 297, 49 C.A.2d 647—**Corpus Juris cited in** Armstrong v. Day, 284 P. 1083, 1086, 103 C.A. 465.
Me.—McCullough v. Lalumiere, 166 A. 2d 702, 156 Me. 479.
45 C.J. p 997 note 74.

25. Cal.—**Corpus Juris cited in** Jones v. Bayley, 122 P.2d 293, 297, 49 C. A.2d 647.
Conn.—Kerr v. Connecticut Co., 140 A. 751, 107 Conn. 304.
45 C.J. p 997 note 75.

26. Cal.—**Corpus Juris cited in** Cloud v. Market St. Ry. Co., 168 P.2d 191, 194, 74 C.A.2d 92—**Corpus Juris cited in** Emery v. Los Angeles R. Corporation, 143 P.2d 112, 115, 61 C. A.2d 455.
Ga.—Southland Butane Gas Co. v. Blackwell, 88 S.E.2d 6, 211 Ga. 665, conformed to 88 S.E.2d 424, 92 Ga. App. 288.
Idaho.—**Corpus Juris cited in** Geist v. Moore, 70 P.2d 403, 409, 58 Idaho 149.
Kan.—Townsend v. Jones, 331 P.2d 890, 183 Kan. 543.

173

CORPUS JURIS SECUNDUM

1985
Cumulative
Annual Pocket Part

Volume 65A

Insert this Pocket Part in back of volume
It replaces prior pocket part

NOTICE

**Consult General Index pocket parts
for references to new matter.**

ST. PAUL, MINN.

WEST PUBLISHING CO.

CITE BY TITLE AND SECTION

Thus

65A C.J.S. Negligence § 203

This Cumulative Annual Pocket Part contains supplementary material as well as new principles and decisions, closing with cases reported in:

Supreme Court Reporter	104 S.Ct. 3497
United States Reports	463 U.S. (part)
Lawyers' Edition, Second Series	83 L.Ed.2d (part)
Federal Reporter, Second Series	740 F.2d 979
Federal Supplement	588 F.Supp. 1450
Federal Rules Decisions	102 F.R.D. 327
Bankruptcy Reporter	40 B.R. 1022
Atlantic Reporter, Second Series	479 A.2d 1190
California Reporter	205 Cal.Rptr. 774
Illinois Decisions	81 Ill.Dec. 708
Military Justice Reporter	18 M.J. 805
New York Supplement, Second Series	478 N.Y.S.2d 1022
North Eastern Reporter, Second Series	467 N.E.2d 579
North Western Reporter, Second Series	353 N.W.2d 373
Pacific Reporter, Second Series	685 P.2d 1125
South Eastern Reporter, Second Series	318 S.E.2d 926
Southern Reporter, Second Series	453 So.2d 1304
South Western Reporter, Second Series	673 S.W.2d 958
United States Claims Court Reporter	5 Cl.Ct. 760
American Law Reports, Fourth Series	34 A.L.R.4th

COPYRIGHT © 1967 through 1984 WEST PUBLISHING CO.

COPYRIGHT © 1985
By
WEST PUBLISHING CO.

Minn.—Koval v. Thompson, 136 N.W.2d 789, 272 Minn. 53.

page 163

3. Ga.—Hunter v. Batton, 288 S.E.2d 244, 160 Ga. App. 849.

Reasonable effort

U.S.—Sawyer v. U.S., D.C.N.Y., 297 F.Supp. 324, affd., C.A., 436 F.2d 640.

Ky.—Bolus v. Martin L. Adams and Son, 438 S.W.2d 79.

54. U.S.—Whaley v. U.S., D.C.Tenn., 432 F.Supp. 37, affd. C.A., 598 F.2d 1038.

Ga.—Mercer v. Braswell, 231 S.E.2d 431, 140 Ga.App. 624.

Ky.—General Tel. Co. of Ky. v. Yount, 482 S.W.2d 567.

N.C.—Presnell v. Payne, 157 S.E.2d 601, 272 N.C. 11.

Ohio—Peters v. B. & F. Transfer Co., 219 N.E.2d 27, 7 Ohio St.2d 143.

Proper care

Mo.—Hood v. Heppler, App., 503 S.W.2d 452.

page 164

55.5. Continuing duty

N.J.—Latta v. Caulfield, 385 A.2d 910, 158 N.J.Super. 151, affd. 398 A.2d 91, 79 N.J. 128.

57. Continuing duty

N.J.—Latta v. Caulfield, 385 A.2d 910, 158 N.J.Super. 151, affd. 398 A.2d 91, 79 N.J. 128.

58. Iowa—Pieper v. Harmeyer, 235 N.W.2d 122.

Ky.—Bolus v. Martin L. Adams and Son, 438 S.W.2d 79.

59. La.—Nelson v. Hirschbach Motor Line, App., 239 So.2d 438, writ ref. 241 So.2d 256, 256 La. 1158, cert. den. 91 S.Ct. 1382, 402 U.S. 909, 28 L.Ed.2d 650.

page 165

72.25. Mo.—Kinealy v. Goldstein, App., 400 S.W.2d 438.

page 166

It has been held that the doctrine of last clear chance does not apply to a case involving an intentional tort.[75.15]

75.15. D.C.—Wager v. Pro, C.A., 603 F.2d 1005, 195 U.S.App.D.C. 423.

§ 139. —— Concurrent Negligence of Plaintiff

76. U.S.—Lones v. Detroit, T. & I.R. Co., C.A.Ohio, 398 F.2d 914, cert. den. 89 S.Ct. 714, 393 U.S. 1063, 21 L.Ed.2d 705—Spellacy v. Southern Pac. Co., C.A.Or., 428 F.2d 619—Peterman v. Chicago, R.I. & P.R. Co., C.A.Iowa, 516 F.2d 328, cert. den. 96 S.Ct. 133, 423 U.S. 869, 46 L.Ed.2d 99. Moses v. Scott Paper Co., D.C.Me., 280 F.Supp. 37—Grisanti v. U.S., D.C.N.C., 284 F.Supp. 308.

Ga.—Shuman v. Mashburn, 223 S.E.2d 268, 137 Ga. App. 231, 85 A.L.R.3d 741.

Kan.—McElhaney v. Rouse, 415 P.2d 241, 197 Kan. 136—Rohr v. Henderson, 483 P.2d 1089, 207 Kan. 123.

Ky.—General Tel. Co. of Ky. v. Yount, 482 S.W.2d 567.

La.—Glatt v. Hinton, App., 205 So.2d 91, writ ref. 206 So.2d 712, 251 La. 861.

Md.—Johnson v. Dortch, 342 A.2d 326, 27 Md.App. 605—Pitts v. Mahan, 382 A.2d 1092, 39 Md.App. 95.

Mich.—**C.J.S. cited in** Zeni v. Anderson, 224 N.W.2d 310, 320, 56 Mich.App. 283.

Neb.—Muirhead v. Gunst, 281 N.W.2d 207, 204 Neb. 1.

N.M.—Lewis v. English, App., 588 P.2d 563, 92 N.M. 362.

N.Y.—Hayes v. State, 362 N.Y.S.2d 994, 80 Misc.2d 385.

S.D.—Rumbolz v. Wipf, 145 N.W.2d 520, 82 S.D. 327.

page 167

76.5. N.Y.—Poli v. Castleberry, 353 N.Y.S.2d 239, 44 A.D.2d 591.

77. Kan.—Summers v. Alliance Mut. Cas. Co., 499 P.2d 1067, 210 Kan. 57.

La.—Kraft v. U. Koen & Co., App., 188 So.2d 203.

page 168

79. Mich.—Jackson v. Rauch, 171 N.W.2d 551, 18 Mich.App. 533.

page 169

87. Sequential

Md.—Pitts v. Mahan, 382 A.2d 1092, 39 Md.App. 95.

88. Kan.—Sander v. Union Pac. R. Co., 470 P.2d 748, 205 Kan. 592.

N.C.—Vernon v. Crist, 231 S.E.2d 591, 291 N.C. 646.

Wash.—Chapman v. State, 492 P.2d 607, 6 Wash.App. 316.

89. Ind.—Elgin, J. & E. Ry. Co. v. Hood, 336 N.E.2d 417, 166 Ind.App. 336.

Tenn.—Gardner's Masonry Contractors, Inc. v. St. Louis–San Francisco Ry. Co., 470 S.W.2d 945, 63 Tenn.App. 288.

page 170

90. Fla.—Connolly v. Steakley, App., 165 So.2d 784, cert. discharged, Sup., 197 So.2d 524.

§ 140. In General

93.50. La.—King v. Investment Equities, Inc., App., 264 So.2d 297.

94. Kan.—Avey v. St. Francis Hospital and School of Nursing, Inc., 442 P.2d 1013, 201 Kan. 687.

page 171

95. Ill.—Borus v. Yellow Cab Co., 367 N.E.2d 277, 9 Ill.Dec. 843, 52 Ill.App.3d 194.

N.Y.—**C.J.S. cited in** Mochen v. State, 352 N.Y.S. 290, 294, 43 A.D.2d 484.

§ 141. Persons Under Mental Disability

96. U.S.—Howland v. Sears, Roebuck & Co., C.A. Ohio, 438 F.2d 725.

99. Cal.—Fox v. City and County of San Francisco, 120 Cal.Rptr. 779, 47 C.A.3d 164.

2. N.Y.—Young v. State Dept. of Social Services, Dept. of Mental Hygiene, 401 N.Y.S.2d 955, 92 Misc.2d 795.

2.5. U.S.—Snider v. Callahan, D.C.Mo., 250 F.Supp. 1022.

3. N.Y.—Young v. State Dept. of Social Services, Dept. of Mental Hygiene, 401 N.Y.S.2d 955, 92 Misc.2d 795.

Okl.—Warner v. Kiowa County Hospital Authority, App., 551 P.2d 1179.

§ 142. Persons Under Physical Disability

page 172

6. Ind.—**C.J.S. quoted at length in** Memorial Hospital of South Bend, Inc. v. Scott, 300 N.E.2d 50, 58, 261 Ind. 27.

Iowa—Chevraux v. Nahas, 150 N.W.2d 78, 260 Iowa 817.

7. La.—King v. Investment Equities, Inc., App., 264 So.2d 297.

N.Y.—Schreiber v. Philip & Morris Restaurant Corp., 268 N.Y.S.2d 510, 25 A.D.2d 262, affd. 226 N.E.2d 537, 19 N.Y.2d 786, 279 N.Y.S.2d 730.

8. Ill.—Borus v. Yellow Cab Co., 367 N.E.2d 277, 9 Ill.Dec. 843, 52 Ill.App.3d 194.

10. N.H.—Perry v. Fredette, 261 A.2d 431, 110 N.H. 114.

Infirmities of old age

La.—Garner v. Crawford, App., 288 So.2d 886.

11. U.S.—Sterling v. New England Fish Co., D.C. Wash., 410 F.Supp. 164.

Ala.—Shepherd v. Gardner Wholesale, Inc., 256 So.2d 877, 288 Ala. 43.

N.H.—Mutterperl v. Lake Spofford Hotel, Inc., 216 A.2d 35, 106 N.H. 538.

Wis.—Merkley v. Schramm, 142 N.W.2d 173, 31 Wis.2d 134.

12. Ill.—**C.J.S. quoted in** Atchley v. Berlen, 408 N.E.2d 1177, 1179, 42 Ill.Dec. 468, 87 Ill.App.3d 61.

page 173

19. Pa.—Argo v. Good Co., 53 Del.Co. 275.

20. Ala.—Shepherd v. Gardner Wholesale, Inc., 256 So.2d 877, 288 Ala. 43.

§ 143. Intoxicated Persons

26. Ga.—Shuman v. Mashburn, 223 S.E.2d 268, 137 Ga.App. 231, 85 A.L.R.3d 741.

Ill.—Dursch v. Fair, 209 N.E.2d 509, 61 Ill.App.2d 273.

Ky.—Harlow v. Connelly, App., 548 S.W.2d 143.

La.—Vaughn v. Cortez, App., 180 So.2d 796.

Neb.—Webber v. City of Omaha, 211 N.W.2d 911, 190 Neb. 678.

page 174

26.5. Alaska—Wilson v. City of Kotzebue, 627 P.2d 623.

Ga.—Shuman v. Mashburn, 223 S.E.2d 268, 137 Ga. App. 231, 85 A.L.R.3d 741.

Ill.—Dezort v. Village of Hinsdale, 342 N.E.2d 468, 35 Ill.App.3d 703, 79 A.L.R.3d 1199, app. after remand 396 N.E.2d 855, 33 Ill.Dec. 328, 77 Ill. App.3d 775 and 441 N.E.2d 367, 65 Ill.Dec. 454, 109 Ill.App.3d 976.

Mont.—Folda v. City of Bozeman, 582 P.2d 767, 177 Mont. 537.

N.J.—Tiger v. American Legion Post No. 43, 311 A.2d 179, 125 N.J.Super. 361.

Rule not applicable where evidence insufficient

La.—Barlow v. City of New Orleans, App., 228 So.2d 47, affd. 241 So.2d 501, 257 La. 91—**C.J.S. cited in** Barlow v. City of New Orleans, 241 So.2d 501, 505, 257 La. 91.

27. U.S.—Guss v. Jack Tar Management Co., C.A. La., 407 F.2d 859.

La.—**C.J.S. cited in** Lee v. Peerless Ins. Co., 183 So.2d 328, 330, 248 La. 982.

N.Y.—Rodak v. Fury, 298 N.Y.S.2d 50, 31 A.D.2d 816.

28. U.S.—Lambert v. Ford Motor Co., D.C.Ga., 46 F.R.D. 46.

Ill.—Dezort v. Village of Hinsdale, 342 N.E.2d 468, 35 Ill.App.3d 703, 79 A.L.R.3d 1199, app. after remand 396 N.E.2d 855, 33 Ill.Dec. 328, 77 Ill. App.3d 775 and 441 N.E.2d 367, 65 Ill.Dec. 454, 109 Ill.App.3d 976.

Md.—Quinn Freight Lines, Inc. v. Woods, 292 A.2d 669, 266 Md. 381.

Neb.—Webber v. City of Omaha, 211 N.W.2d 911, 190 Neb. 678.

N.Y.—Coleman v. New York City Transit Authority, 332 N.E.2d 850, 37 N.Y.2d 137, 371 N.Y.S.2d 663.

Voluntary drunkenness ordinarily constitutes contributory negligence

N.J.—Anslinger v. Martinsville Inn, Inc., 298 A.2d 84, 121 N.J.Super. 525.

29. Ill.—French v. City of Springfield, 283 N.E.2d 18, 5 Ill.App.3d 209.

Tex.—Hemmenway v. Skibo, Civ.App., 498 S.W.2d 9, err. ref. no rev. err.

4   United States Code Annotated

United States Code Annotated

U.S.C.A.

The United States Code Annotated (U.S.C.A.) is a helpful resource to find case law which interprets or defines federal law. The problem again assumes you will isolate descriptive words, consult the U.S.C.A. indexing system and locate a statute. The statute you locate has annotations to cases citing it which deal with your legal problem.

U.S.C.A. Problem

A man was observed by government agents in his parked car talking on his car phone. Later other cars were seen to drive up and stop. The drivers received brown bags in exchange for money. The man was questioned and his car was searched. Cocaine, a controlled substance, was found in the car.

   a) Is there any authority in the U.S. Code for forfeiture of the vehicle?

   b) Find a case discussing forfeiture of a car phone.

Worksheet

Parties:

Places and Things:

Basis of Action or Issue:

Defense:

Relief Sought:

UNITED STATES CODE ANNOTATED

1985
GENERAL INDEX
Di to F

ST. PAUL, MINN.
WEST PUBLISHING CO.

DROUGHTS

Community emergency drought relief, **42 § 5184 note**

Cotton, acreage not planted because of,
Effect upon rates of payments to producers, **7 § 1444**
Price support payments, **7 § 1444**

Croplands, designated areas, grazing, etc., adjustments, certification, **7 § 1838**

"Emergency" as meaning this type of disaster requiring Federal emergency assistance, disaster relief, **42 § 5122**

Emergency Conservation Program, this index

Feed for assistance in preservation and maintenance of foundation herds of cattle, sheep, and goats, sale by CCC in areas stricken by, **7 § 1427**

Feed grain, termination or modification, agreements concerning diversion of acreage, emergencies created by, **16 § 590p**

Flood control, construction of wells in drought areas, **33 § 701n**

Grazing lands, reduction or refund, **43 § 315b**

Income tax,
Orchards and vineyards, exception where damage caused by, capital expenditure to replant items not deductible, **26 § 278**
Special rule for proceeds from livestock sold on account of, taxable year of inclusion, **26 § 451**

Indian lands, emergency livestock feed, distressed areas, Federal aid, delegation of Presidential authority, **7 § 1427 note, Ex. Ord. No. 11336**

Livestock feed program, duties of Secretary of Agriculture in emergency, **7 § 2267**

"Major disaster" as meaning, disaster relief, **42 § 5122**

Poultry feed program, duties of Agriculture Secretary in emergency, **7 § 2267**

Public Works Employment, generally, this index

Relief assistance for disasters, **42 § 5121 et seq.**

Schools,
Construction assistance, disasters, **20 § 646**
Expenditures, assistance for, **20 § 241–1**

Tobacco, emergency allotment leases and transfers, disaster areas of Georgia and South Carolina, **7 § 1314b**

Weather, generally, this index

Wheat marketing allocation, marketing certificates, issuance of, conditions, etc., **26 § 1379c**

DRUG ABUSE CONTROL AMENDMENTS OF 1965

Text of Act, **18 § 1114; 21 §§ 321, 321 note, 331, 333, 334, 352 note, 360, 372**

Drugs, generally, this index

Effect on State laws, **21 § 301 note**

Short title, **21 § 301 note**

DRUG ABUSE FUNCTIONS

See Drug Abuse Prevention, Control and Treatment, this index

DRUG ABUSE OFFICE AND TREATMENT ACT OF 1972

Text of Act. See Popular Name Table

Drug Abuse Prevention, Control and Treatment, generally, this index

References made in Federal law, regulation, ruling, or order considered references to Drug Abuse Prevention, Treatment, and Rehabilitation Act, **21 § 1101 note**

DRUG ABUSE POLICY, OFFICE OF

See Drug Abuse Prevention, Control and Treatment, this index

DRUG ABUSE PREVENTION, CONTROL AND TREATMENT

Text of,
Amendments of 1978. See Popular Name Table
Preservation, Treatment, and Rehabilitation Amendments of 1979. See Popular Name Table

Abandonment or forfeiture of property to U.S., exclusion of narcotic drugs from allocation, **40 § 304m**

Access to pertinent information for audit and examination, grants and contracts, recipients of, **21 § 1178**

Accountants, appointment by court upon entry of order of forfeiture, criminal forfeitures, **21 § 853**

Acetorphine, schedule I drug, designation, **21 § 812**

Acetyldihydrocodeine, schedule I drug, designation, **21 § 812**

Acetylmethadol, schedule I drug, designation, **21 § 812**

Action against U.S. concerning interest in property subject to forfeiture prohibited subsequent to filing indictment or information, **21 § 853**

Activities and training, etc., materials, National Drug Abuse Training Center, **21 § 1179**

Addict, defined, **21 § 802**

Administer, defined, **21 §§ 802, 951**

Administration and enforcement, **21 § 871 et seq.**
Applicability of provisions to import and export violations, **21 § 965**
Contracts, education and research activities, **21 § 872**
Delegation of functions, Attorney General, **21 § 871**
Education and research programs of Attorney General, **21 § 872**
Laws respecting, enforcement of, **21 § 801 note, Ex. Ord. No. 11727**
Studies in special projects, education and research programs of Attorney General, **21 § 872**

Administrative hearings, powers of Attorney General, **21 § 875**

DRUG ABUSE PREVENTION, CONTROL AND TREATMENT—Cont'd

Fines, penalties and forfeitures—Cont'd

Disclosure of patient's records, first and subsequent offenses—Cont'd

Veterans' Administration patients, **38 § 4134**

Dispensing controlled substances, **21 §§ 841, 842**

Distributing controlled substances, **21 §§ 841, 842, 843, 845**

To persons under age 21, **21 § 845**

Imports and exports,

Marihuana, hashish or hashish oil, certain amounts, penalties, **21 § 960**

Violations, **21 §§ 960, 961**

Additional penalties, **21 § 964**

Attempt and conspiracy, **21 § 963**

Imposed upon conviction, limitations, **21 § 853**

Investment of illicit drug profits, prohibition, penalties, **21 § 854**

Manufacturing, distributing or possessing with intent to manufacture, etc., controlled substances, on board vessels,

Attempt or conspiracy to commit offenses, **21 § 955c**

Offenses committed, **21 § 955a**

Seizure or forfeiture, **21 § 955d**

Manufacturing controlled substances, **21 § 841**

Piperidine,

Possession with intent to manufacture phencyclidine, etc., criminal penalties, **21 § 841**

Prohibited acts which are unlawful respecting identification requirements in reports, **21 §§ 842, 843**

Possession, extended probation, conditional discharge, expunging of record, **21 § 844**

Property subject to forfeiture to U.S., **21 § 853**

Enumeration, **21 § 881**

Registrants,

Offenses involving, **21 § 843**

Unlawful acts by, **21 § 842**

Revocation of registration, forfeiture of controlled substances, **21 § 824**

Robberies and burglaries involving controlled substances, **18 § 2118**

Schools, elementary or secondary, distribution of controlled substances in or near, **21 § 845a**

Fiscal year availability, appropriations for National Drug Abuse Training Center, **21 § 1179**

Food Stamps, generally, this index

Foreign countries,

Interrogation of U.S. person involved in narcotics control enforcement activities abroad, **22 § 2291**

Presidential report to Congress, list, narcotic drugs and other controlled substances produced, etc., for unlawful entry into U.S., **19 § 2484**

DRUG ABUSE PREVENTION, CONTROL AND TREATMENT—Cont'd

Forfeitures. Fines, penalties and forfeitures, generally, ante, this heading

Formal or informal diplomatic, etc., negotiations with foreign governments relating to traffic in drugs subject to abuse, etc., "drug traffic prevention function" as meaning, **21 § 1103**

Health systems agency, review and approval or disapproval of use of Federal funds for, **42 § 300/-2**

Fraud or forgery, acquisition of controlled substances by, prohibited acts, **21 § 843**

Furethidine, schedule I drug, designation, **21 § 812**

General policies, National Drug Abuse Training Center, **21 § 1179**

General provisions, **21 § 1101 et seq.**

General Services Administration, disposal of forfeited property, **21 § 881**

Gifts, bequests, devices, etc., power of Attorney General to accept, **21 § 871**

Glutethimide, schedule III drug, designation, **21 § 812**

Government and other employees, drug abuse among, responsibility, development and maintaining prevention, treatment, etc., programs and services for, **42 § 290ee-1**

Grand jury, witnesses before, immunity, **21 § 884**

Grants and contracts,

Access to pertinent information of recipients of assistance, audit and examination, **21 § 1178**

Assistance records, contents, **21 § 1178**

Authority to enter into contracts, **21 § 1181**

Authorization by chief executive officer of State required, **21 § 1177**

Block grants, generally, ante, this heading

Demonstration and evaluation projects, **21 § 1177**

Demonstration projects, authority of Secretary to enter, **42 § 290cc-1**

Diversion of controlled substances from,

Legitimate channels, applications for assistance in preventing, controlling, etc., **21 § 873**

Medical, scientific, etc., channels, preventing, control of, **21 § 873**

Duration, **21 § 1177**

Improved drug maintenance and detoxification techniques and programs, research respecting, **42 § 290cc**

Individuals and public and nonprofit entities, determination of causes of drug abuse in particular area, **42 § 290cc**

Maximum amount, **21 § 1177**

Policies and priorities, recommendations, etc., of National Advisory Council on Drug Abuse, **42 § 218**

Prevention and early intervention projects, **21 § 1177**

DRUG ABUSE PREVENTION, CONTROL AND TREATMENT—Cont'd

Possession—Cont'd

Prohibited acts, extended probation conditional discharge, expunging of record, **21 § 844**

Vessels, possession on board vessels. Controlled substances, etc., generally, ante, this heading

Possessions of U.S.,

Courts, injunctions, jurisdiction, **21 § 882**

Inclusion in term "State", **21 § 802**

Practitioners,

Administering controlled substance, records and reports, applicability, **21 § 827**

Administration of controlled substances by, **21 §§ 802, 951**

Defined, **21 §§ 802, 951**

Dispensing narcotic drugs for maintenance or detoxification treatment,

Attorney General,

Compliance, standards respecting security of stocks and maintenance of records, determination, **21 § 823**

Suspension or revocation of registration, **21 § 824**

Compliance, standards, security of stocks of drugs and maintenance of records, qualifications for registration, **21 § 823**

Detoxification treatment, defined, **21 § 802**

Maintenance treatment, defined, **21 § 802**

Registration,

Annual, qualifications, **21 § 823**

Period of suspension, **21 § 824**

Revocation or suspension, failure to comply with standards, grounds for, **21 § 824**

Secretary of HHS, determination, compliance, standards, **21 § 823**

Separate registration, **21 § 823**

Special project grants and contracts, **21 § 1177**

Prescribing controlled substances, records and reports of registrants, requirements, applicability, **21 § 827**

Prescription requirement, exception, **21 § 829**

Requirements as to records, reports and inventories, applicability, **21 § 827**

Precedence restriction, special project grants and contracts, **21 § 1177**

President of U.S.,

Dangerous drugs, notice relating to control of, drug abuse policy coordination, **21 § 1115**

Drug representative, designation, drug abuse policy coordination, **21 § 1112**

Establishment, Office of Drug Abuse Policy, in Executive Office of, **21 § 1111**

Office of Policy Development assigned to assist in performance of drug abuse policy functions, **21 § 1112 note, Ex. Ord. No. 12368**

Records and reports, post, this heading

DRUG ABUSE PREVENTION, CONTROL AND TREATMENT—Cont'd

President or delegate, Administrator of Veterans' Affairs, consultation with, regulations, coordination, **38 § 4134**

Prevention, programs designed to reach general population and members of high risk populations such as youth, women and elderly, **21 § 1101**

Preventive efforts directed to individuals not users of drugs or marginal users thereof, "drug abuse prevention function" as meaning programs, etc., concerning, **21 § 1103**

Primary prevention programs,

Appropriations, limitations, **21 § 1177**

Defined, applications for grants or contracts for, **21 § 1177**

Priorities, applications for grants or contracts for primary prevention and early intervention projects, **21 § 1177**

Private hospitals. Hospitals, etc., generally, ante, this heading

Probable cause, defined, administrative inspection warrants, issuance, **21 § 880**

Probation,

Continuing criminal enterprise, denial, **21 § 848**

Extended, offense of simple possession, **21 § 844**

Proceeds, property, derived from violation, property subject to forfeiture, **21 § 853**

Process,

Forfeiture, property subject to, issuance, **21 § 881**

Right to, presentence hearing of dangerous special drug offender, **21 § 849**

Procurement, weapons or ammunition, use of appropriated funds for, prohibition, international narcotics control, **22 § 2291a**

Production,

Defined, **21 §§ 802, 951**

Evidence and documents,

Administrative inspection warrant not required, controlled premises, **21 § 880**

Powers of Attorney General, **21 § 876**

Smuggling of controlled substances into U.S., investigations, **21 § 967**

Programs,

Congressional findings, **21 § 1101**

Contract authority of Secretary, **21 § 1181**

Drug abuse prevention, treatment, and rehabilitation, grants and contracts to establish, conduct and evaluate, **21 § 1177**

Education. Drug Abuse Educational Programs and Activities, generally, this index

National Institute on Drug Abuse, participation of certain related disciplines in, **42 § 290aa–2**

Other Federal programs, **21 § 1171 et seq.**

Public Health Service, availability of appropriations to for grants to Federal institutions, **42 § 300aa–6**

DRUG ABUSE PREVENTION, CONTROL AND TREATMENT—Cont'd

Treatment, "drug abuse prevention function" as meaning treatment programs, etc., **21 § 1103**

Trial,

Appeal of criminal case involving forfeiture of property, intervention, bar on, **21 § 853**

Burden of proof, **21 § 885**

Injunctions, violation, jury, **21 § 882**

Trimeperidine, schedule I drug, designation, **21 § 812**

Trust Territory of Pacific Islands, inclusion in term "State", **21 § 802**

Trustees, appointment by court upon entry of order of forfeiture, criminal forfeitures, **21 § 853**

Ultimate user,

Applicability of registration requirement, **21 § 822**

Defined, **21 §§ 802, 951**

Exemption from import and export registration requirement, **21 § 957**

Underserved populations, consideration to applications for programs and projects aimed at, **21 § 1177**

Uniform forms for, procedures for submission, etc., applications of State, etc., governments for grants and contracts, **42 § 290ee**

Uniform methodology and technology for determining extent and kind of drug abuse and effects, investigation and publication of information, **42 § 290aa–2**

United Nations, generally, this index

United States, defined, **21 §§ 802, 951**

United States attorneys,

Dangerous special drug offender, filing notice with court, **21 § 849**

Prior convictions, filing of information with court and defendant, **21 § 851**

Import and export violations, **21 § 962**

Request for order compelling testimony of witnesses, **21 § 884**

United States magistrates,

Administrative inspection warrants, issuance, **21 § 880**

Search warrants, issuance, **21 § 879**

Unlawful acts. Prohibited acts, generally, ante, this heading

Use of existing governmental facilities, responsibility of Office, **42 § 290ee–1**

Vehicle,

Import and export, transshipment and in-transit shipment of controlled substances, **21 § 954**

Possession on, arriving or departing from U.S., **21 § 955**

Used for illegal conveyance of controlled substances, **21 § 881**

Venue, property subject to criminal forfeiture, **21 § 881**

Vessel,

Burden of proof, lawful use of, **21 § 885**

DRUG ABUSE PREVENTION, CONTROL AND TREATMENT—Cont'd

Vessel—Cont'd

Import and export, transshipment and in-transit shipment of controlled substances, **21 § 954**

Manufacture, etc., on board. Controlled substances, generally, ante, this heading

Possession on, arriving or departing from U.S., **21 § 955**

Used for illegal conveyance of controlled substances, forfeiture, **21 § 881**

Veterans, treatment and rehabilitation for drug dependence or abuse disabilities, pilot program, **38 § 620A**

Veterans' Administration,

Administrator of Veterans' Affairs, generally, ante, this heading

Confidentiality of certain medical records, **38 § 4131**

Department of Medicine and Surgery, Chief Medical Director, National Advisory Council on Drug Abuse, ex officio member of, **42 § 218**

Nondiscrimination in admission of alcohol abusers to health care facilities, **38 § 4133**

Violations punishable by imprisonment for more than one year, applicability of criminal forfeiture provisions, **21 § 967**

Virgin Islands, inclusion in term "State", **21 § 802**

Voluntary and uncompensated services in carrying out drug abuse policy coordination, **21 § 1114**

Warehousemen,

Delivery of piperidine to or by for storage, lawful business, etc., exception, piperidine reporting requirements, **21 § 830**

Import and export registration requirement, exemption, **21 § 957**

Order forms requirement, applicability, **21 § 828**

Registration requirement, applicability, **21 § 822**

Warrant issued authorizing seizure of property subject to criminal forfeiture, requirements, **21 § 853**

Warrants. Administrative inspection warrants, generally, ante, this heading

Witnesses,

Compelling attendance and testimony of, **21 § 876**

Examination, powers of Attorney General, **21 § 875**

Immunity, compelling testimony, **21 § 884**

Smuggling of controlled substances into U.S., generally, ante, this index

Women,

Consideration to applications for programs and projects aimed at, **21 § 1177**

Programs and projects for, special project grants and contracts, **21 § 1177**

INDEX

TO

TITLE 21—FOOD AND DRUGS

References are to Sections

ABUSE BY DRUGS
Drug Abuse Prevention, Control and Treatment, generally, this index.

ACETANILID
Drugs, labeling requirements, § 352(e).

ACETORPHINE
For general provisions, relating to prevention, control and treatment of abuses. See Drug Abuse Prevention, Control and Treatment, generally, this index.

ACETPHENETIDIN
Drugs, labeling requirements, § 352(e).

ACETYLDIHYDROCODEINE
For general provisions relating to prevention, control and treatment of abuses. See Drug Abuse Prevention, Control and Treatment, generally, this index.

ACETYLMETHADOL
For general provisions, relating to prevention, control and treatment of abuses. See Drug Abuse Prevention, Control and Treatment, generally, this index.

ACTIONS AND PROCEEDINGS
See specific index headings.

ADDICTS
Drug Abuse Prevention, Control and Treatment, generally, this index.

ADDITIVES
Color Additives, generally, this index.
Food Additives, generally, this index.

ADMINISTER
Defined, imports and exports, drug abuse prevention, control and treatment, §§ 802, 951.

ADMINISTRATIVE PROCEDURE ACT
Color additives, proceedings for issuance, amendment, or repeal of regulation, applicability, § 376.

ADMINISTRATORS
See specific index headings.

ADMIRALTY
Eggs and egg products, seizure and condemnation, proceedings to conform to supplemental rules of, § 1049.

ADULTERATION
Absence, substitution or addition of constituents, food, § 342.

T. 21 U.S.C.A. §§ 951 to End   **265**

DRUG ABUSE PREVENTION, CONTROL AND TREATMENT—Continued

Fines, penalties and forfeitures—Continued
    Property subject to forfeiture to U. S.,
        Custody under seal, § 881.
            Removing seal, prohibited acts, § 842.
        Enumeration, § 881.
    Registrants,
        Offenses involving, § 843.
        Unlawful acts by, § 842.
    Revocation of registration, forfeiture, controlled substances, § 824.
Fiscal year availability,
    Appropriations for National Drug Abuse Training Center, § 1179.
    State allotments and reallotment of unobligated amounts, formula grants, § 1176.
Forfeitures. Fines, penalties and forfeitures, generally, ante, this heading.
Formal or informal diplomatic, etc., negotiations with foreign governments, traffic in drugs subject to abuse, etc., "drug traffic prevention function" as meaning, rehabilitation, etc., § 1103.
Formula grants, shifts in demographic and drug abuse patients, § 1176.
Fraud or forgery, acquisition, controlled substances by, prohibited acts, § 843.
Furethidine, schedule I drug, designation, § 812.
General policies, National Drug Abuse Training Center, § 1179.
General provisions, rehabilitation, etc., § 1101 et seq.
General Services Administration, removal, forfeited property, § 881.
Gifts, bequests, devises, etc., power of Attorney General to accept, § 871.
Glutethimide, schedule III drug, designation, § 812.
Government and other employees, drug abuse among, responsibility, development and maintaining prevention, treatment, etc., programs and services for, § 1180.
Grand jury,
    Impanelment of, law enforcement activities, etc., respecting, "drug traffic prevention function" as meaning, rehabilitation, etc., § 1103.
    Witnesses before, immunity, § 884.
Grants and contracts,
    Access to pertinent information of recipients of assistance, audit and examination purposes, § 1178.
    Assistance records, contents, § 1178.
    Authority to enter into contracts, § 1181.
    Community mental health centers, construction, state plans, drug abuse prevention functions, review, provisions respecting, § 1173.
    Contract carrier, registration requirement, applicability, § 822.
    Formula grants, § 1176.
    Records, recipients of assistance under, § 1178.
    Reports to Congressional committees on number grants and contracts entered into, § 1193 note.
    Special project grants and contracts, generally, post, this heading.
    Task forces to provide technical assistance, etc., to state, etc., governments, contracts to serve on or work with, § 1192.
    Uniform procedures for submission, etc., of application of state, etc., governments for, § 1192.
Groups representing medical, scientific, etc., disciplines to determine drug abuse causes, special project grants and contracts, § 1177.
Guam, formula grants, § 1176.
Hallucinogenic substances. See Schedule I drugs, generally, post, this heading

334

FOOD AND DRUGS

DRUG ABUSE PREVENTION, CONTROL AND TREATMENT—Continued

United States, defined, § 802.
    Imports and exports, § 951.
United States attorneys,
    Dangerous special drug offender, filing notice with court, § 849.
    Prior convictions, filing information with court and defendant, § 851.
        Import and export violations, § 962.
    Request for order compelling testimony of witnesses, § 884.
United States magistrates, issuance,
    Administrative inspection warrants, § 880.
    Search warrants, § 879.
Unobligated amounts, fiscal year availability, formula grants, § 1176.
Ultimate user,
    Applicability of registration, requirement, § 822.
    Defined, § 802.
        Imports and exports, § 951.
    Exemption from import and export registration requirement, § 957.
Unlawful acts. Prohibited acts, generally, ante, this heading.
Use for certain purposes, formula grants, § 1176.

Vehicle,
    Burden of proof, unlawful use of, § 885.
    Import and export, transshipment and in-transit shipment, controlled substances, § 954.
    Possession on, arriving or departing from U. S., § 955.
    Used for illegal conveyance of controlled substances, § 881.
Vessel,
    Burden of proof, lawful use of, § 885.
    Import and export, transshipment and in-transit shipment, controlled substances, § 954.
    Manufacture, etc., on board. Controlled substances, ante, this heading.
    Possession on, arriving or departing from U. S., § 955.
    Used for illegal conveyance of controlled substances, forfeiture, § 881.
Veterans' Administration,
    Administrator of Veterans' Affairs, generally, ante, this heading.
    Inventory of public and private resources in state plan, § 1176.
Virgin Islands,
    Formula grants, § 1176.
    Inclusion in term "State", § 802.
        Formula grants, § 1176.
Vocational rehabilitation, state plans, review and evaluation, provisions relating to drug abuse prevention functions, § 1173.
Voluntary and noncompensated services in carrying out drug abuse policy coordination, § 1114.

Wages. Compensation and wages, generally, ante, this heading.
Warehousemen,
    Administrative inspections and warrants, § 880.
    Delivery of piperidine to or by for storage, lawful business, etc., exception, piperidine reporting requirements, § 830.
    Import and export registration, requirement exemption, § 957.
    Order forms requirement, applicability, § 828.
    Registration requirement, applicability, § 822.
Warrants. Administrative inspection warrants, generally, ante, this heading.
Witnesses,
    Compelling attendance and testimony of, § 876.

357

117

10. Suppression of evidence

Where inspection of defendant's premises was conducted following issuance of inspection warrant under this section, inspection was limited to administrative inspection and was conducted in accordance with this section, any matters revealed by such inspection were not subject to suppression in criminal proceeding. U. S. v. Prendergast, D.C.Pa.1977, 436 F.Supp. 931, affirmed 585 F.2d 69.

Where subsequent statements made by defendant were directly related to information gathered by Drug Enforcement Agency compliance officers as result of illegal search of defendant's pharmacy, defendant was entitled to suppression of such statements. U. S. v. Enserro, D.C. N.Y.1975, 401 F.Supp. 460.

§ 881. Forfeitures

Property subject

(a) The following shall be subject to forfeiture to the United States and no property right shall exist in them:

(1) All controlled substances which have been manufactured, distributed, dispensed, or acquired in violation of this subchapter.

(2) All raw materials, products, and equipment of any kind which are used, or intended for use, in manufacturing, compounding, processing, delivering, importing, or exporting any controlled substance in violation of this subchapter.

(3) All property which is used, or intended for use, as a container for property described in paragraph (1) or (2).

(4) All conveyances, including aircraft, vehicles, or vessels, which are used, or are intended for use, to transport, or in any manner to facilitate the transportation, sale, receipt, possession, or concealment of property described in paragraph (1) or (2), except that—

(A) no conveyance used by any person as a common carrier in the transaction of business as a common carrier shall be forfeited under the provisions of this section unless it shall appear that the owner or other person in charge of such conveyance was a consenting party or privy to a violation of this subchapter or subchapter II of this chapter; and

(B) no conveyance shall be forfeited under the provisions of this section by reason of any act or omission established by the owner thereof to have been committed or omitted by any person other than such owner while such conveyance was unlawfully in the possession of a person other than the owner in violation of the criminal laws of the United States, or of any State.

(5) All books, records, and research, including formulas, microfilm, tapes, and data which are used, or intended for use, in violation of this subchapter.

(6) All moneys, negotiable instruments, securities, or other things of value furnished or intended to be furnished by any

624

person in exchange for a controlled substance in violation of this subchapter, all proceeds traceable to such an exchange, and all moneys, negotiable instruments, and securities used or intended to be used to facilitate any violation of this subchapter, except that no property shall be forfeited under this paragraph, to the extent of the interest of an owner, by reason of any act or omission established by that owner to have been committed or omitted without the knowledge or consent of that owner.

Seizure pursuant to Supplemental Rules for Certain Admiralty and Maritime Claims

(b) Any property subject to forfeiture to the United States under this subchapter may be seized by the Attorney General upon process issued pursuant to the Supplemental Rules for Certain Admiralty and Maritime Claims by any district court of the United States having jurisdiction over the property, except that seizure without such process may be made when—

(1) the seizure is incident to an arrest or a search under a search warrant or an inspection under an administrative inspection warrant;

(2) the property subject to seizure has been the subject of a prior judgment in favor of the United States in a criminal injunction or forfeiture proceeding under this subchapter;

(3) the Attorney General has probable cause to believe that the property is directly or indirectly dangerous to health or safety; or

(4) the Attorney General has probable cause to believe that the property has been used or is intended to be used in violation of this subchapter.

In the event of seizure pursuant to paragraph (3) or (4) of this subsection, proceedings under subsection (d) of this section shall be instituted promptly.

Custody of Attorney General

(c) Property taken or detained under this section shall not be repleviable, but shall be deemed to be in the custody of the Attorney General, subject only to the orders and decrees of the court or the official having jurisdiction thereof. Whenever property is seized under the provisions of this subchapter, the Attorney General may—

(1) place the property under seal;

(2) remove the property to a place designated by him; or

(3) require that the General Services Administration take custody of the property and remove it to an appropriate location for disposition in accordance with law.

Other laws and proceedings applicable

(d) The provisions of law relating to the seizure, summary and judicial forfeiture, and condemnation of property for violation of

625

the customs laws; the disposition of such property or the proceeds from the sale thereof; the remission or mitigation of such forfeitures; and the compromise of claims shall apply to seizures and forfeitures incurred, or alleged to have been incurred, under the provisions of this subchapter, insofar as applicable and not inconsistent with the provisions hereof; except that such duties as are imposed upon the customs officer or any other person with respect to the seizure and forfeiture of property under the customs laws shall be performed with respect to seizures and forfeitures of property under this subchapter by such officers, agents, or other persons as may be authorized or designated for that purpose by the Attorney General, except to the extent that such duties arise from seizures and forfeitures effected by any customs officer.

Disposition of forfeited property

(e) Whenever property is forfeited under this subchapter the Attorney General may—

(1) retain the property for official use;

(2) sell any forfeited property which is not required to be destroyed by law and which is not harmful to the public;

(3) require that the General Services Administration take custody of the property and remove it for disposition in accordance with law; or

(4) forward it to the Drug Enforcement Administration for disposition (including delivery for medical or scientific use to any Federal or State agency under regulations of the Attorney General).

The proceeds from any sale under paragraph (2) and any moneys forfeited under this subchapter shall be used to pay all proper expenses of the proceedings for forfeiture and sale including expenses of seizure, maintenance of custody, advertising, and court costs. The Attorney General shall forward to the Treasurer of the United States for deposit in the general fund of the United States Treasury any amounts of such moneys and proceeds remaining after payment of such expenses.

Forfeiture of schedule I substances

(f) All controlled substances in schedule I that are possessed, transferred, sold, or offered for sale in violation of the provisions of this subchapter shall be deemed contraband and seized and summarily forfeited to the United States. Similarly, all substances in schedule I, which are seized or come into the possession of the United States, the owners of which are unknown, shall be deemed contraband and summarily forfeited to the United States.

Plants

(g)(1) All species of plants from which controlled substances in schedules I and II may be derived which have been planted or cultivated in violation of this subchapter, or of which the owners or cul-

626

tivators are unknown, or which are wild growths, may be seized and summarily forfeited to the United States.

(2) The failure, upon demand by the Attorney General or his duly authorized agent, of the person in occupancy or in control of land or premises upon which such species of plants are growing or being stored, to produce an appropriate registration, or proof that he is the holder thereof, shall constitute authority for the seizure and forfeiture.

(3) The Attorney General, or his duly authorized agent, shall have authority to enter upon any lands, or into any dwelling pursuant to a search warrant, to cut, harvest, carry off, or destroy such plants.

Pub.L. 91–513, Title II, § 511, Oct. 27, 1970, 84 Stat. 1276; Pub.L. 95–633, Title III, § 301(a), Nov. 10, 1978, 92 Stat. 3777; Pub.L. 96–132, § 14, Nov. 30, 1979, 93 Stat. 1048.

Historical Note

References in Text. "This subchapter", referred to in text, was in the original "this title" which is Title II of Pub.L. 91–513, Oct. 27, 1970, 84 Stat. 1242, and is popularly known as the "Controlled Substances Act". For complete classification of Title II to the Code, see Short Title note set out under section 801 of this title and Tables volume.

"Subchapter II of this chapter", referred to in subsec. (a)(4)(A), was in the original "title III", meaning Title III of Pub.L. 91–513, Oct. 27, 1970, 84 Stat. 1285. Part A of Title III comprises subchapter II of this chapter. For classification of Part B, consisting of sections 1101 to 1105 of Title III, see Tables volume.

The criminal laws of the United States, referred to in subsec. (a)(4)(B), are classified generally to Title 18, Crimes and Criminal Procedure.

The Supplemental Rules for Certain Admiralty and Maritime Claims, referred to in subsec. (b), are set out in Title 28, Judiciary and Judicial Procedure.

The customs laws, referred to in subsec. (d), are classified generally to Title 19, Customs Duties.

Schedules I and II, referred to in subsecs. (f) and (g)(1), are set out in section 812(c) of this title.

Codification. "Drug Enforcement Administration" was substituted for "Bureau of Narcotics and Dangerous Drugs"

in subsec. (e)(4) to conform to congressional intent manifest in amendment of section 802(4) of this title by Pub.L. 96–132, § 16(a), Nov. 30, 1979, 93 Stat. 1049, now defining term "Drug Enforcement Administration" as used in this subchapter.

1979 Amendment. Subsec. (d). Pub.L. 96–132 substituted "The provisions" for "All provisions", and struck out "and the award of compensation to informers in respect of such forfeitures" following "compromise of claims".

1978 Amendment. Subsec. (a)(6). Pub.L. 95–633, § 301(1), added par. (6).

Subsec. (e). Pub.L. 95–633, § 301(a)(2), (3), struck out of cl. (2) provisions relating to use of proceeds of sale and added provision relating to the forwarding by the Attorney General of money and proceeds remaining after payment of expenses.

Effective Date. Section effective Oct. 27, 1970, see section 704(b) of Pub.L. 91–513, set out as an Effective Date note under section 801 of this title.

Legislative History. For legislative history and purpose of Pub.L. 91–513, see 1970 U.S.Code Cong. and Adm. News, p. 4566. See, also, Pub.L. 95–633, 1978 U.S. Code Cong. and Adm.News, p. 9496; Pub. L. 96–132, 1979 U.S.Code Cong and Adm. News, p. 2003.

Cross References

Contraband articles, including narcotic drugs, seizure and forfeiture of carriers transporting, see section 781 et seq. of Title 49, Transportation.
Narcotic drug defined, see section 787 of Title 49.

627

Library References

Drugs and Narcotics ☞191.   C.J.S. Drugs and Narcotics § 141.

West's Federal Forms

Forfeiture proceedings, see § 5891 et seq.
Judgment of condemnation, forfeiture and destruction, see § 4543.
Process in admiralty, see § 11271 et seq.

Code of Federal Regulations

Administrative policies, practices, and procedures, see 21 CFR 1316.01 et seq.
Inspection, search, and seizure, see 19 CFR 162.0 et seq.

Notes of Decisions

Acquittal or dismissal of charges, effect of 18
Admissibility of evidence 40
Authority of enforcement agents 14
Burden of proof
    Generally 38
    Shifting of burden 39
Civil nature of proceedings 25
Common carriers 8
Completed transactions 21
Concealment as grounds for forfeiture 6
Conditional sales 22
Constitutionality 1
Construction
    Generally 2
    With other laws 3
Custody of Attorney General 9
Defenses
    Generally 32
    Double jeopardy 33
    Innocent ownership 34
    Laches 35
Delay in institution of proceedings 27
Destruction of seized articles 12
Discretion of court 30
Disfavoring of forfeitures 13
Dismissal 36
Disposition or sale of forfeited property 11
Double jeopardy, defenses 33
Effect of acquittal or dismissal of charges 18
Evidence, admissibility 40
Facilitation of prohibited activities 7
Innocent ownership, defenses 34
In rem nature of proceedings 26
Intent 17
Inventory search 23
Issues in proceedings 31
Jurisdiction 29
Knowledge or intent 17
Jury trial 37
Laches, defenses 35
Mitigation of forfeitures 10
Objections to forfeiture 19
Probable cause
    Generally 15
    Particular cases 16
Property subject to forfeiture 5
Purpose 4
Remission or mitigation of forfeitures 10

Sale of forfeited property 11
Scope of review 41
Shifting of burden of proof 39
Standing to challenge forfeiture 28
Tax liens 24
Time of forfeiture 20
Transportation, concealment, etc. as grounds for forfeiture 6
Trial by jury 37

----

1. Constitutionality

This section, section 1595a of Title 19, and section 781 of Title 49 are not unconstitutional in failing to provide a prior hearing before seizure of the property. U. S. v. One 1973 Volvo, D.C.Tex.1974, 377 F.Supp. 810.

2. Construction

Provisions of subsec. (d) of this section relating to remission of forfeited vehicles should be liberally construed to effectuate remission. U. S. v. One 1976 Buick Skylark, 2-Door Coupe, Vehicle Identification No. 4W27C6K148647, D.C.Colo.1978, 453 F.Supp. 639.

This section authorizing seizure of derivative contraband articles, which are not intrinsically illegal in character, but derive their contraband status only from their association with criminal activity, must be strictly construed. U. S. v. One 1972 Datsun, Vehicle Identification No. LB1100355950, D.C.N.H.1974, 378 F.Supp. 1200.

3. Construction with other laws

Warrant requirement of this section would not be read into section 1595a of Title 19. U. S. v. One 1972 Chevrolet Nova, C.A.Mass.1977, 560 F.2d 464.

Forfeiture proceedings arising out of drug offenses are governed by same provisions as apply to customs forfeitures under section 1595 et seq. of Title 19. U. S. v. One Motor Yacht Named Mercury, C.A.R.I.1975, 527 F.2d 1112.

628

4. Purpose

A primary purpose of this section providing for forfeiture of conveyances used, or intended for use, to transport, or in any manner to facilitate transportation, sale, receipt, possession or concealment of contraband is to cripple illegal drug trafficking and narcotic activity by depriving narcotics peddlers of the operating tools of their trade. U. S. v. One 1972 Datsun, Vehicle Identification No. LB1100355950, D.C.N.H.1974, 378 F.Supp. 1200.

5. Property subject to forfeiture

Evidence which was received to support charge of unlawful acquisition of marihuana in violation of narcotics laws was "contraband" and not repleviable. Rea v. U. S., N.M.1956, 76 S.Ct. 292, 350 U.S. 214, 100 L.Ed. 233.

"Traditional or per se contraband" are objects the possession of which, without more, constitutes a crime, and claimant has no right to have per se contraband returned to him. U. S. v. Farrell, 1979, 606 F.2d 1341, 196 U.S.App.D.C. 434.

In absence of statutory authority, there is no basis for confiscation of derivative contraband merely because it is derivative contraband. Id.

Money used by defendant in attempt to purchase narcotics from undercover agent was used in unlawful manner as an instrumentality of crime, and thus it fell within category of derivative contraband for purposes of deciding defendant's claim for return of money following conviction for attempt to distribute heroin. Id.

Derivative contraband must be substantially and instrumentally connected with illegal behavior before such contraband is subject of forfeiture. U. S. v. One 1972 Datsun, Vehicle Identification No. LB1100355950, D.C.N.H.1974, 378 F.Supp. 1200.

There must be a substantially significant connection with criminal activity before an ordinary automobile may be seized and forfeited to government. Id.

6. Transportation, concealment, etc. as grounds for forfeiture

Forfeiture of vehicle used by party to illegal drug transaction did not depend upon accident of whether dope was physically present in vehicle, but vehicle's use to transport peddler or his confederates to scene of sale or to meeting where sale was proposed was sufficient. U. S. v. One 1974 Cadillac Eldorado Sedan, Serial No. 6L47S4Q407966, C.A.N.Y.1977, 548 F.2d 421.

Plain meaning of "to transport" as used in this section is simply to carry or convey from one place to another, and, this section being silent as to purpose for which the transportation is undertaken, no limitations such as limitation to commercial trafficking will be read into words used. U. S. v. One Clipper Bow Ketch Nisku, C.A.Mass.1977, 548 F.2d 8.

Forfeiture provisions are not limited to commercial trafficking, and it is not role of the courts to mitigate harshness of the statutes. Id.

This section does not limit forfeiture of vehicles to transportation situations, and where automobile was used to help sale of contraband, in that government informant paid another person for heroin while both were in the automobile, automobile was subject to forfeiture. U. S. v. One 1970 Pontiac GTO, 2-Door Hardtop, C.A.Cal.1976, 529 F.2d 65.

Intentional transportation or concealment of marijuana in a vehicle, no matter how small the amount, will subject the conveyance to forfeiture. U. S. v. One 1975 Chevrolet K–5 Blazer Vehicle No. CKY185F135794, D.C.Mich.1980, 495 F. Supp. 737.

Even the presence within vehicle of small amount of marijuana, strictly for personal consumption, will justify forfeiture of the vehicle. Id.

Uncontradicted testimony of three government witnesses established that truck was used to transport methamphetamine, justifying its forfeiture. U. S. v. One 1975 Ford Ranger XLT Serial No. F26YCV47607, D.C.Pa.1979, 463 F.Supp. 1389.

Aircraft which was found to be intended to be used to transport controlled substances in the future was subject to forfeiture and application of this section to such aircraft was constitutionally permissible. U. S. v. One 1945 Douglas (C–54–DC–4) Aircraft, D.C.Mo.1978, 461 F. Supp. 324 remanded on other grounds 604 F.2d 27.

Automobile which claimant was driving while carrying cocaine on his person and in which a suitcase containing traces of marijuana was found was subject to forfeiture as it has been used to "transport" controlled substances, even though only small amounts were found. U. S. v. One 1975 Mercury Monarch Serial No. 5E35L539729, D.C.N.Y.1976, 423 F.Supp. 1026.

Mere fact that there was an empty green suitcase, with a residue of marijuana, in trunk of vehicle in question was insufficient to support forfeiture of the vehicle on theory that it was intended to be used to transport marijuana away from a particular address to which four

629

UNITED STATES CODE ANNOTATED

ANNOTATED

Title 21

Food and Drugs

§§ 801 to 950

1986

Cumulative Annual Pocket Part

Replacing prior pocket part in back of volume

Includes the Laws of the
99th CONGRESS, FIRST SESSION (1985)

For close of Notes of Decisions
See page III

CURRENT LAWS AND LEGISLATIVE HISTORY
Consult
United States Code
Congressional and Administrative News

ST. PAUL, MINN.

WEST PUBLISHING CO.

EXPLANATION

This Cumulative Annual Pocket Part contains the laws of a general and permanent nature enacted by the Congress through Public Law 99–240, the final law of the First Session of the 99th Congress which adjourned on December 20, 1985. This Pocket Part also includes Executive Orders, Proclamations and Reorganization Plans affecting such general and permanent laws.

The laws are classified to the United States Code. Under the same classification will be found the annotations from the decisions of the State and Federal courts, the Comptroller General, and the United States Merit Systems Protection Board, and the opinions of the Attorney General construing the statutes.

The annotations close with the following:

Supreme Court Reporter	106 S.Ct. 285
United States Reports	467 U.S. (part)
Lawyers' Edition, Second Series	87 L.Ed.2d (part)
Federal Reporter, Second Series	774 F.2d 489
U.S. Court of Appeals,	
Dist. of Columbia	249 U.S.App.D.C.
Federal Supplement	617 F.Supp. 100
Federal Rules Decisions	107 F.R.D. 138
Atlantic Reporter, Second Series	498 A.2d 1043
California Reporter	218 Cal.Rptr. 912
New York Supplement, Second Series	493 N.Y.S.2d 987
North Eastern Reporter, Second Series	483 N.E.2d 875
North Western Reporter, Second Series	374 N.W.2d 648
Pacific Reporter, Second Series	706 P.2d 1134
South Eastern Reporter, Second Series	335 S.E.2d 283
Southern Reporter, Second Series	476 So.2d 35
South Western Reporter, Second Series	697 S.W.2d 84
Opinions Attorney General	43 Op.Atty.Gen. (part)
Decisions Comptroller General	64 Op.Comp.Gen. (part)
United States Merit Systems Protection	
Board Reporter	29 M.S.P.R. 186
Claims Court Reporter	8 Cl.Ct. 756
Court of Claims	228 Ct.Cl.
Court of International Trade	10 C.I.T.
Customs Court	85 Cust.Ct.
United States Tax Court	84 Tax Ct. (part)
Military Justice Reporter	21 M.J.
	#1 Mil.App. p. 10
	#1 Mil.Rev. p. 523
Bankruptcy Reporter	53 B.R. 125
Other Standard Reports	

For subsequent judicial constructions, pending the publication of the next supplementary service, see Table of Statutes Construed in the later permanent volumes and weekly Advance Sheets of the Reporters listed above.

under this section shall, upon motion of the United States and for good cause shown, stay the civil forfeiture proceeding.

(j) Venue

In addition to the venue provided for in section 1395 of Title 28 or any other provision of law, in the case of property of a defendant charged with a violation that is the basis for forfeiture of the property under this section, a proceeding for forfeiture under this section may be brought in the judicial district in which the defendant owning such property is found or in the judicial district in which the criminal prosecution is brought.

(As amended Pub.L. 98–473, Title II, §§ 306, 309, 518, Oct. 12, 1984, 98 Stat. 2050, 2051, 2075.)

1984 Amendment. Subsec. (a)(7). Pub.L. 98–473, § 306(a), added subsec. (a)(7).

1984 Amendment. Subsec. (a)(8). Pub.L. 98–473, § 518, added subsec. (a)(8).

Subsec. (b). Pub.L. 98–473, § 306(b)(1), added "civil or criminal" following "property subject to".

Subsec. (b)(4). Pub.L. 98–473, § 306(b)(2), substituted "is subject to civil or criminal forfeiture under" for "has been used or is intended to be used in violation of".

Subsec. (c). Pub.L. 98–473, § 306(c)(1), added "any of" following "seized under".

Subsec. (c)(3). Pub.L. 98–473, § 306(c)(2), added ", if practicable," following "remove it".

Subsec. (d). Pub.L. 98–473, § 306(d), added "any of" following "incurred, under".

Subsec. (e). Pub.L. 98–473, § 306(e)(1), added "civilly or criminally" following "Whenever property is".

Pub.L. 98–473, § 309(b), added provisions relating to authority of Attorney General to insure equitable transfer of any forfeited property.

Pub.L. 98–473, § 309(c), substituted provisions relating to section 524(c) of Title 28, for provisions relating to the general fund of the United States Treasury.

Subsec. (e)(1). Pub.L. 98–473, § 309(a), added provisions relating to transfer of custody or ownership of forfeited property.

Subsec. (e)(3). Pub.L. 98–473, § 306(e)(2), struck out provisions relating to removal of property.

Subsecs. (h) to (j). Pub.L. 98–473, § 306(f), added subsecs. (h) to (j).

Legislative History. For legislative history and purpose of Pub.L. 98–473, see 1984 U.S. Code Cong. and Adm. News, p. 3182.

Notes of Decisions

Connection with offense 5b
Default judgments 48
Estoppel 36a
Habeas corpus 47
Interest 46
Mandatory forfeiture 43
Notice 27a
Priority in disbursement 45
Probable cause
    Exigence, additional requirement of 15a
Proceeds traceable to exchange 11a
Quantity as factor determining forfeiture 6a
Seizure incident to arrest 5a
Stay of proceedings 27b
Tracing proceeds 44
Unlawful arrest 42

1. Constitutionality

In view of protections provided in sections 1602–04 of Title 19, owner of vehicle seized on the ground that it had been used to facilitate sale of controlled substance was not entitled under due process clause of U.S.C.A. Const. Amend. 5 to additional probable cause hearing within 72 hours of government's seizure of his automobile. U.S. v. One 1971 BMW 4-Door Sedan, Model 2800, Gray in Color VIN 2320587, AZ. LIC. RNM–898, C.A.Ariz.1981, 652 F.2d 817.

Provision of this section for a warrantless seizure when the Attorney General has probable cause to believe that the property has been or is intended to be used in violation of the subchapter does not require exigent circumstances, and the application of that provision does not violate U.S. C.A. Const. Amend. 4. U.S. v. One 1977 Lincoln Mark V Coupe, C.A.Pa.1981, 643 F.2d 154, certiorari denied 102 S.Ct. 97, 454 U.S. 818, 70 L.Ed.2d 88.

Eventual forfeiture of money paid to attorneys which has been determined to be derived from drug crimes does not deprive attorneys of their property without due process and does not constitute unwarranted government interference with attorneys' practice of law. U.S. v. One Parcel of Land ... Commonly Known as 4204 Cedarwood, Matteson, Il, D.C.Ill.1985, 614 F.Supp. 183.

Forfeiture of car under drug forfeiture statute did not deprive owner of his property without due process where, although owner was innocent with respect to drug transaction with which user of the car was involved, owner left the car for long period of time in care of person he knew was parolee and who frequented social clubs where consumption of illegal narcotics was part of the life style, and failed to instruct the caretaker not to let others use the car, and where caretaker loaned the car to third person who used it in drug transaction. U.S. v. One Mercedes-Benz 380 SEL VIN. No. WDBCA 33A1BB10331, D.C.N.Y. 1984, 604 F.Supp. 1307, affirmed 762 F.2d 991.

Constitutional prohibition against enactment of ex post facto laws was applicable to government's forfeiture claim brought under this section which provides for forfeiture to the United States of all proceeds traceable to an exchange for a controlled substance, since this section requires a close relationship to criminal activity and in effect does punish persons who own property subject to its provisions. U.S. v. Lot No. 50, as Shown on Map of Kingsbury Village, Unit 5, Filed in Office of

County Recorder of Douglas County, State of Nev., on Sept. 7, 1966, in Book 1 of Maps, as File No. 33786, D.C.Nev.1982, 557 F.Supp. 72.

2. Construction

With respect to forfeiture, "derivative contraband" consists of automobiles, boats, planes and currency which may be lawfully possessed, but which become forfeitable because of unlawful use. U.S. v. Eighty-Eight, Five Hundred Dollars, C.A.Mo.1982, 671 F.2d 293.

3. Construction with other laws

In action for forfeiture of currency furnished in exchange for controlled substance, Government's burden of showing probable cause that currency was furnished in exchange for controlled substance is same as that applicable to forfeiture under customs laws. U.S. v. Fifty Thousand Dollars ($50,000) U.S. Currency, C.A.6 (Mich.) 1985, 757 F.2d 103.

To be justifiable under section 782 of Title 49 governing seizure and forfeiture of automobile used to carry or conceal contraband, seizure of automobile used for that purpose must comport with the generally accepted standards of warrantless seizures under U.S.C.A. Const. Amend. 4; however, to be justifiable under this section, seizure must not only be reasonable under U.S.C.A. Const. Amend. 4, but Attorney General must have had probable cause to believe at time of seizure that vehicle had been used in violation of drug laws. U.S. v. Kemp, C.A.Md.1982, 690 F.2d 397.

This section applies to importation of marijuana in violation of section 951 et seq. of this title. U.S. v. Gordon, C.A.Fla.1981, 638 F.2d 886, certiorari denied 101 S.Ct. 3038, 452 U.S. 909, 69 L.Ed.2d 411.

Fifth Amendment minimally requires that no warrant for arrest in rem of real property under drug forfeiture statute [21 U.S.C.A. § 881(b)] should issue unless and until judicial officer has reviewed complaint in ex parte proceeding and has concluded that complaint sets forth reasonable basis for believing that property is subject to forfeiture. U.S. v. Certain Real Estate Property Located at 4880 S.E. Dixie Highway, D.C.Fla. 1985, 612 F.Supp. 1492.

4. Purpose

Legislative history suggests that Congress in providing for forfeiture of vehicles used for transportation of contraband was concerned with drug trafficking, but other conduct was not excluded from this section. U.S. v. One 1976 Porsche 911S, Vin 911–6200323, California License 090 NXC, C.A.Cal.1979, 670 F.2d 810.

Seizure and forfeiture of vehicles for violation of narcotics laws foster public interest. U.S. v. One 1971 BMW 4-Door Sedan, Model 2800, Gray in Color VIN 2320587, AZ. LIC. RNM-898, C.A. Ariz.1981, 652 F.2d 817.

5. Property subject to forfeiture

Government produced sufficient evidence other than currency and other items suppressed to link currency to illegal drug trafficking; therefore, the currency was subject to forfeiture, notwithstanding that it was illegally seized and was inadmissible in forfeiture proceeding. U.S. v. U.S. Currency $31,828, C.A.8 (Iowa) 1985, 760 F.2d 228.

Currency paid to federal undercover agents for purchase of large amount of marijuana by defendant, whose criminal conviction was reversed and remanded for new trial, was subject to forfeiture, in absence of dispute as to use of currency to attempt to purchase marijuana or as to defendant's ownership of it. U.S. v. Fifty Thousand Dollars ($50,000) U.S. Currency, C.A.6 (Mich.) 1985, 757 F.2d 103.

Under plain-view doctrine, police who were conducting surveillance of house at which state agent was negotiating marijuana sale and inadvertently discovered automobile on premises in plain view while they were lawfully on premises to make arrest, who had probable cause to believe that automobile was being used to transport marijuana, and who thus were authorized by this section to seize car without process, did not violate U.S.C.A. Const. Amend. 4 when they searched trunk of automobile and seized $29,000 in cash lying under large amount of marijuana. U.S. v. $29,000-U.S. Currency, C.A.N.C.1984, 745 F.2d 853.

Where ex-wife allowed ex-husband to drive her automobile to sister state to show it to prospective buyer and while in latter state ex-husband was arrested for possession of cocaine with intent to distribute and for conspiring to distribute cocaine and marijuana, the remedial goals of this section would not be directly promoted by forfeiture of the vehicle. U.S. v. One 1979 Datsun 280 ZX, VIN HS130–143161, C.A.Iowa 1983, 720 F.2d 543.

Although automobile was properly forfeited to government on basis of its use in violation of drug control laws, automobile telephone attached to automobile, which was easily removable, had identity and use separate from automobile, and was separately insured, was not subject to forfeiture with automobile itself, especially where there was no evidence that telephone was used in furtherance of underlying crime. U.S. v. One 1978 Mercedes Benz, Four-Door Sedan, VIN: 116–036–12–004084, C.A.Tex.1983, 711 F.2d 1297.

A vehicle may be seized if there is probable cause to believe that it was used or was intended for use to facilitate transportation of contraband. U.S. v. Ogden, C.A.Me.1983, 703 F.2d 629.

Where automobile of defendant charged with possession with intent to distribute and distribution of marijuana had been used in connection with distribution of drugs, automobile, under this section, was already property of United States and it only remained for government to assert its right to immediate possession. U.S. v. Kemp, C.A.Md. 1982, 690 F.2d 397.

It could not be determined whether defendant whose residence had been searched was entitled to return of $7,500 seized during that search where government had not yet been given opportunity to establish that money was connected to conspiracy to distribute methamphetamine which was subject of prosecution. U.S. v. Sweeney, C.A.Ill.1982, 688 F.2d 1131.

Where government showed that codefendant arrived at defendant's house in automobile carrying $10,000 in cash and participated with defendant in drug transaction, but codefendant offered nothing but speculation to establish that currency was not furnished or intended to be furnished in exchange for controlled substance and that automobile was not used or intended for use to transport controlled substance, currency and automobile were subject to forfeiture. U.S. v. Fleming, C.A.Ill.1982, 677 F.2d 602.

Attorney fees and costs of litigation incurred by criminal defendant involved in drug activities could not be excluded from forfeiture under Comprehensive Drug Abuse Prevention and Control Act of 1970, § 511, 21 U.S.C.A. § 881 if "tainted funds" were used to pay attorneys. U.S. v. One Parcel of Land ... Commonly Known as 4204 Cedarwood, Matteson, Il, D.C.Ill.1985, 614 F.Supp. 183.

Banks accounts seized pursuant to complaint in forfeiture against moneys suspected to have been involved in money laundering scheme contained forfeitable res if account owner was knowing participant in laundering of narcotics proceeds; however, warrants' attempted attachment of after-acquired property was invalid. U.S. v. Banco Cafetero Intern., D.C.N.Y.1985, 608 F.Supp. 1394.

Although lessor of aircraft was uninvolved in and unaware of illegal activity in transportation of drugs on the aircraft, it failed to prove that it had done all it reasonably could to prevent illegal transportation of drugs, and thus the aircraft was subject to forfeiture since the lessee was not a common carrier, where the aircraft was based at an airport in an area well known for drug-related activities, lessor had no plan or procedures for detecting smuggling and did not require any of the aircraft operator and, though lessor had talked to lessee's president about making sure that regulations necessary to common carrier status were complied with and had provided him with the necessary paperwork, lessor did not check certificates. U.S. v. One Rockwell Intern. Commander 690 C/840, Serial Number 11627, D.C.N.D.1984, 594 F.Supp. 133.

Government agent's testimony that forfeiture claimant told agent that briefcase contained money which he intended to use to purchase drugs and showed agent entire contents and that money was seized from claimant directly afterward, establishing probable cause for belief that claimant intended to furnish cash in return for large quantity of marijuana, was not overcome by claimant's testimony that he did not intend to use entire contents to purchase marijuana, in view of implausibility of claimant's other testimony, and thus, entire sum was subject to forfeiture as money intended to be furnished in exchange for controlled substance. U.S. v. $23,530 in U.S. Currency, D.C.Md.1985, 601 F.Supp. 179.

Warrantless seizure and impoundment of vehicles from motel parking lots were authorized on basis of officers' adequate grounds for belief that vehicles were being used in furtherance of marijuana smuggling venture. U.S. v. Cresta, D.C. Me.1984, 592 F.Supp. 889.

Where vessel owners, who chartered vessel to third party subsequently killed while engaged in marijuana transaction with vessel, never requested that third party produce identification, never inquired of local law enforcement agencies about him, and inquiries of community members as to third party's reputation in community were superficial and cursory at best, vessel owners did not do all that reasonably could be expected to prevent proscribed use of their property, and therefore

vessel, which was used in, inter alia, transportation of marijuana, a controlled substance, was subject to forfeiture. U.S. v. One (1) 1980 Stapelton Pleasure Vessel Named THREESOME, Registration No. FL4180EA, D.C.Fla.1983, 575 F.Supp. 473.

Since government met its burden of establishing probable cause to believe that truck was purchased with proceeds of drug transaction and since defendant's wife, even if she were found to have standing, had not demonstrated that truck was purchased with legally obtained funds, truck was subject to forfeiture. U.S. v. One 1980 Chevrolet Blazer Auto., VIN No. CKL18AF111432, D.C.N.Y.1983, 572 F.Supp. 994.

Evidence that claimant had not been employed since 1976, that he had no known source of income other than drug dealings, that he appeared to have been extensively engaged in drug transactions, evidence of his large cash purchases, evidence of his evasive or unsubstantiated answers to question concerning ownership of property and evidence of the presence of illegal drugs in his house demonstrated that the house, the land on which it sat, a boat, and jewelry, furniture, and cash constituted proceeds traceable to drug transactions and were thus subject to forfeiture. U.S. v. Certain Real Property Situated at Route 3, Box 247E, Mountain Home, AR., D.C.Ark.1983, 568 F.Supp. 434.

Claimants established that jewelry owned by the defendants was obtained by inheritance and, therefore, claimants established that that jewelry was not subject to forfeiture as being traceable to narcotics transaction. U.S. v. $131,602.00 in U.S. Currency, D.C.N.Y.1982, 563 F.Supp. 921.

In a civil forfeiture action pursuant to this section relating to forfeiture of money traceable to an illegal drug transaction, a direct or substantial connection between property subject to forfeiture and the underlying criminal activity which this section seeks to prevent may not be required if facts and circumstances would lead a reasonable fact finder to believe that a crime was committed and that the res subject to forfeiture was connected with that commission. U. S. v. Four Million Two Hundred and Fifty-Five Thousand, Six Hundred and Twenty-Five Dollars and Thirty-Nine Cents, D.C.Fla.1982, 551 F.Supp. 314, affirmed 762 F.2d 895.

January 1981 cocaine transactions did not justify December 1981 warrantless seizure of automobile and forfeiture of vehicle was required to be based on a transaction occurring at or about time of seizure. U.S. v. 1979 Mercury Cougar Vin. 9H93H669155 Its Tools and Appurtenances, D.C. Colo.1982, 545 F.Supp. 1087.

Owner of vehicle involved in illegal transaction may forfeit vehicle despite owner's lack of direct, personal involvement in illegal transaction. U.S. v. One 1978 Chrysler LeBaron Station Wagon VIN No. FH 45D8G278912, D.C.N.Y.1981, 531 F.Supp. 32.

Under this section providing for forfeiture of automobiles used to facilitate narcotics transactions, warrantless seizure of vehicle used by defendant in transporting quinine given in exchange for heroin was proper where seizure occurred immediately after defendant's arrest, even though defendant's arrest occurred in apartment outside which vehicle was parked. U.S. v. Jackson, D.C. Md.1981, 529 F.Supp. 1047.

Since, consistent with decision in prior criminal case, defendant's $10,000 in currency was intended to be furnished by defendant in exchange for controlled substance in violation of law, this section mandated forfeiture of currency to the United States. U.S. v. $10,000 U.S. Currency, D.C.Ill. 1981, 521 F.Supp. 1253.

Although there was no direct evidence to indicate that impounded automobile was intended for use to transport cocaine, since defendant did not demonstrate that any of the other range of possibilities that he outlined supported a denial of forfeiture and use of Cadillac to drive to contact point to make exchange of money for cocaine facilitated the drug transaction, Cadillac was subject to forfeiture. Id.

United States was entitled to forfeiture of pickup, which was used by owner's roommate to transport a crate containing one ounce of cocaine from the airport to the owner's residence, where the owner's roommate at all pertinent times had lawful possession of the pickup with the owner's consent. U.S. v. One 1977 Chevrolet Pickup No. CKL147J107642, Its Tools and Appurtenances, D.C.Colo.1980, 503 F.Supp. 1027.

5a. Seizure incident to arrest

Right to search automobile subject to forfeiture exists even though police do not actually seize it. U.S. v. $29,000-U.S. Currency, C.A.N.C.1984, 745 F.2d 853.

Subsec. (b)(1) of this section permitting seizure of vehicle subject to forfeiture for being used to facilitate sale of cocaine if seizure is incident to arrest did not apply to seizure of automobile 15 hours after arrest even though keys to automobile had been seized incident to arrest. U.S. v. McMichael, D.C.Md.1982, 541 F.Supp. 956.

5b. Connection with offense

Forfeiture of truck observed on one occasion being used to visit and inspect marijuana crop was unwarranted since there was no evidence that truck was regularly used to visit and inspect marijuana crop, and no marijuana was found in truck. U.S. v. One 1976 Ford F–150 Pick-Up VIN F14YUB03797, C.A.8 (Mo.) 1985, 769 F.2d 525.

6. Transportation, concealment, etc. as grounds for forfeiture

Forfeiture is proper if vehicle is used "in any manner" to facilitate the sale or transportation of a controlled substance or raw material used in the manufacture of a controlled substance; the stricter "substantial connection" test applicable to forfeiture actions under subsec. (a)(6) of this section against money or other things of value negotiated in exchange for drugs does not apply to the vehicle forfeiture provision of subsec. (a)(4) of this section. U. S. v. 1964 Beechcraft Baron Aircraft, TC–740, FAA Reg., No. N444CP, Actual No. N914C, C.A.Tex.1982, 691 F.2d 725, rehearing denied 696 F.2d 996, certiorari denied 103 S.Ct. 1893, 461 U.S. 914, 77 L.Ed.2d 283.

Evidence that owner of automobile and codefendant drove automobile from McAllen to Midland to find an airstrip upon which airplane bringing in marijuana could land, that they drove it to find a storage building for the marijuana and to

rent a motor home in which to live while selling the marijuana, that two of the conspirators drove the automobile to Midland to rent a truck, and that one of the conspirators planned to take marijuana samples to Dallas in the automobile established a sufficient nexus between the automobile and the drug transaction to warrant forfeiture. U.S. v. One 1979 Mercury Cougar XR–7 VIN: 9H93F720727, C.A.Tex.1982, 666 F.2d 228.

Forfeiture is proper if automobile is used in any manner to facilitate the sale or transportation of a controlled substance. Id.

This section authorizing forfeiture of a vehicle used "in any manner" to facilitate transportation or sale of drugs encompasses an automobile used to transport the drug dealer and the accomplice to the scene of transaction; hence, although one individual negotiated preliminary arrangements and furnished his apartment for the meeting and although another individual, who had driven automobile owner to the apartment for the meeting, acted as courier to subsequently transfer drugs from another site in a different vehicle, owner's vehicle was subject to forfeiture as owner was introduced as supplier and approved the price and the buyers and signalled for the delivery. U.S. v. One 1977 Cadillac Coupe DeVille VIN: 6D47S7Q234771, C.A.Fla.1981, 644 F.2d 500.

Evidence that vehicle transported person carrying heroin from Ottawa to Windsor, Canada, that the occupant was arrested after entering the United States, and that the plan called for the occupant to be transported in the vehicle after the drug transaction had been completed in the United States provided sufficient basis for forfeiture of the vehicle. U.S. v. One 1983 Pontiac Gran Prix Vin: 2G2AJ37H802244633, D.C.Mich.1985, 604 F.Supp. 893.

Evidence in forfeiture proceeding that a "runner" for one claiming to be a professional money exchanger brought large sums of cash to an office in which undercover Federal Bureau of Investigation agents had set up a money laundering operation dealing exclusively with narcotics proceeds and that "runner" was driving particular vehicle, supported conclusion that vehicle was used to facilitate sale or transportation of controlled substances, and thus was subject to forfeiture. U.S. v. One (1) 1980 Silver Volvo, Model 264–VIN VC 26445A1086596, D.C.Fla.1984, 582 F.Supp. 1166.

There is no requirement that contraband be actually found within the vehicle in order to warrant its forfeiture. U.S. v. One 1980 BMW 3201, V.I. No. 7154989, D.C.N.Y.1983, 559 F.Supp. 382.

If automobile was used by supplier for surveillance during drug transaction, order of forfeiture would be required. Id.

Fact that owner of pickup was acquitted of narcotic charges arising out of the same events on which forfeiture proceeding was based did not preclude the government from seizing and seeking forfeiture of the pickup allegedly used to transport contraband. U.S. v. One 1977 Chevrolet Pickup VIN No. CKL 147J107642, Its Tools and Appurtenances, D.C.Colo.1980, 503 F.Supp. 1027.

6a. Quantity as factor determining forfeiture

Application of this section is not dependent on the quantity of the controlled narcotic substance found. U.S. v. One 1977 Chevrolet Pickup VIN

UNITED STATES CODE ANNOTATED

May 1986

Pamphlet Number 1

Supplementing
1986 Pocket Parts

LAWS

January 30, 1986 to February 18, 1986
Public Laws 99–241 to 99–249

Executive Orders
Rules and Regulations

Tables and Index

LATER LAWS
and
LEGISLATIVE HISTORY

Consult
1986 U. S. Code
Congressional and Administrative News

ST. PAUL, MINN.
WEST PUBLISHING CO.

EXPLANATION

This Pamphlet contains the laws, classified to the United States Code, of a general and permanent nature passed by the 99th Congress, Second Session, which were approved from January 30, 1986 to February 18, 1986, Public Law 99–241 through Public Law 99–249.

Executive Orders, Court Rules and Administrative Regulations have been included to March 1, 1986. For Congressional enactments of the 99th Congress, Second Session, subsequent to February 18, 1986, see the current pamphlets of the U. S. Code Congressional and Administrative News.

Under the same classification will be found the annotations from the decisions of State and Federal courts, the Comptroller General, and the United States Merit Systems Protection Board, and the opinions of the Attorney General construing the laws closing with cases reported in:

Supreme Court Reporter .... 106 S.Ct. 874
United States Reports................................. 466 U.S. (part)
Federal Reporter, Second Series 780 F.2d 1033
U.S. Court of Appeals,
   Dist. of Columbia ....251 U.S.App.D.C.
Federal Supplement .... 623 F.Supp. 636
Federal Rules Decisions ....108 F.R.D. 235
Atlantic Reporter, Second Series...............................502 A.2d 359
California Reporter .... 222 Cal.Rptr. 404
New York Supplement, Second Series 496 N.Y.S.2d 968
North Eastern Reporter, Second Series 487 N.E.2d 598
North Western Reporter, Second Series 379 N.W.2d 346
Pacific Reporter, Second Series 711 P.2d 1155
South Eastern Reporter, Second Series 338 S.E.2d 425
Southern Reporter, Second Series 480 So.2d 1170
South Western Reporter, Second Series 701 S.W.2d 704
Opinions Attorney General ....43 Op.Atty.Gen. (part)
Decisions Comptroller General ....64 Comp.Gen. (part)
United States Merit Systems Protection
   Board Reporter ....29 M.S.P.R. 554
Claims Court Reporter................................. 9 Cl.Ct. 310
Court of International Trade .... 10 C.I.T. (part)
United States Tax Court................................ 85 Tax Ct. (part)
Military Justice Reporter .... 21 M.J.
                                              #8 Mil.App. p. 258
                                              #8 Mil.Rev. p. 761
Bankruptcy Reporter ....55 B.R. 769
Other Standard Reports

For subsequent judicial constructions, pending the publication of the next supplementary service, see Table of Statutes Construed in the later permanent volumes and weekly Advance Sheets of the Reporters listed above.

This Pamphlet supplements the 1986 Pocket Parts.

preponderance of evidence did not violate due process. U.S. v. Towers, C.A.7 (Ind.) 1985, 775 F.2d 184.

10a. Double jeopardy

Imposition of enhanced sentence for drug violation upon determination that defendant is special dangerous drug offender, based upon same evidence used to convict defendant at trial, does not violate double jeopardy; special dangerous drug offender statute does not create separate criminal charge, but merely allows sentencing judge to impose criminal penalty appropri-

ate to circumstances of offense and to history and character of defendant. U.S. v. Towers, C.A.7 (Ind.) 1985, 775 F.2d 184.

13. Ex parte communications

Statute [21 U.S.C.A. § 849] authorizing court, in extraordinary cases, to withhold material contained in defendant's presentence report does not provide for ex parte submission of material to the court by the prosecution. U.S. v. Reese, C.A.9 (Cal.) 1985, 775 F.2d 1066.

§ 853. Criminal forfeitures

Law Review Commentaries

Forfeiture of attorneys' fees under the 1984 Comprehensive Crime Control Act. Howard Jarrett Weintraub, 22 Ga.S.B.J. 67 (1985).

Notes of Decisions

Attorney fees 1
Due process 2

2. Due process

Statutory forfeiture provisions [21 U.S.C.A. § 853(e, n)] did not satisfy due process, where there was no hearing on imposition of restraining order on defendant's property and neither defendant nor third party could challenge restraining order unless and until defendant was convicted. U.S. v. Crozier, C.A.9 (Ariz.) 1985, 777 F.2d 1376.

§ 879. Search warrants

Notes of Decisions

15. Border search

Customs boarding and search was justifiable as border search, where customs officials had received tip from confidential reliable informant that motor vessel was going to Jamaica to pick up load of marijuana and bring it back to United States, officials noticed that boat had vanished from place it was being stored,

and had returned sometime thereafter, and officials were informed that captain of vessel had been at sea for some length of time and where, although boat was brand new and had no apparent need of repair, it had been hauled out of water. U.S. v. One (1) 1984 No. 1 Boat Mfg. Lobster Vessel Known as M/V Sea Power Official Documentation No. 675336, D.C.Fla.1985, 617 F.Supp. 672.

§ 881. Forfeitures

Notes of Decisions

Stay of discovery 27c

6. Transportation, concealment, etc. as grounds for forfeiture

Use of airplane or other vehicle or vessel in drug transaction, either to transport controlled substances or to transport conspirators to exchange site, establishes "substantial connection" between conveyance and criminal activity sufficient to justify order of forfeiture. U.S. v. 1966 Beechcraft Aircraft Model King Air A90 Cream with Burg & Gold Stripes SN:LJ–129, FAA REG:–333GG, Equipt, C.A.4 (S.C.) 1985, 777 F.2d 947.

15. Probable cause—Generally

Probable cause to support a forfeiture under the Comprehensive Drug Abuse Prevention and Control Act must be judged not with clinical detachment but with a common sense view of the realities of normal life; court can take into account common experience considerations such as fact that the property seized is connected to a known center for drug-smuggling and money-laundering; however, nationality of the couriers and amount of money involved cannot alone give rise to a finding of probable cause. U.S. v. $319,820.00 In U.S. Currency, D.C.Ga.1985, 620 F.Supp. 1474.

16. —— Particular cases

Government established probable cause that houseboats were purchased with funds traceable to illegal narcotics transactions, and thus subject to forfeiture

unless claimant could establish by preponderance of evidence that houseboats were not traceable to narcotics transactions; hearsay testimony, as corroborated by claimant's documented cocaine dealings, established that houseboats were purchased with money received from selling narcotics, and claimant himself had stated that all of his possessions resulted from narcotics dealings. U.S. v. 1982 Yukon Delta Houseboat, C.A.9 (Nev.) 1985, 774 F.2d 1432.

Seizure of $319,820 was supported by probable cause to believe that the currency had been used or was intended to be used in violation of federal drug laws; of particular significance was the manner in which the currency was carried, method by which the currency was banded together, denomination of the bills, and ties to Colombia and Miami. U.S. v. $319,820.00 In U.S. Currency, D.C.Ga.1985, 620 F.Supp. 1474.

27c. Stay of discovery

The Government was not entitled to stay of discovery in forfeiture proceeding pending entry of verdict or plea in criminal case and resolution of pending criminal investigation where Government offered only conclusory and insufficient allegations of how it would be prejudiced or hampered, scope and duration of requested stay was indefinite, and banks which held money sought to be forfeited were allegedly suffering injury to reputation and loss of customers and business that would continue. U.S. v. Banco Cafetero Intern., D.C.N.Y.1985, 107 F.R.D. 361.

34. —— Innocent ownership

Operator of airplane repair facility was not "innocent owner" of airplane used to transport illegal drugs, and thus, airplane was not exempt from forfeiture; operator permitted drug conspirator to use airplane on number of occasions in area where drug trafficking flourished without any inquiry as to where conspirator was flying, what he was carrying, when he was returning, who he was flying with, or for what purpose he was borrowing airplane. U.S. v. 1966 Beechcraft Aircraft Model King Air A90 Cream with

Burg & Gold Stripes SN:LJ–129, FAA REG:–333GG, Equipt, C.A.4 (S.C.) 1985, 777 F.2d 947.

Owner of motor vessel, who denied any knowledge of vessel's alleged illegal activities, failed to establish defense of innocence by preponderance of the evidence in forfeiture action, where owner knew of secret compartment built into vessel, and compartment smelled like marijuana and had been freshly painted. U.S. v. One (1) 1984 No. 1 Boat Mfg. Lobster Vessel Known as M/V Sea Power Official Documentation No. 675336, D.C.Fla.1985, 617 F.Supp. 672.

§ 881a. Production control of controlled substances

Library References

Agriculture ⚭3.5(1).
C.J.S. Agriculture §§ 26, 30.

§ 952. Importation of controlled substances

Notes of Decisions

9. Importation

Transportation of controlled substances from one point in the United States to another through international waters constituted "importation" within meaning of 21 U.S.C.A. § 952, governing offense of importation of controlled substances. U.S. v. Perez, C.A.9 (Guam) 1985, 776 F.2d 797.

§ 955a. Manufacture, distribution, or possession with intent to manufacture or distribute controlled substances on board vessels

Notes of Decisions

Custom waters 21
Elements of offense 24
Ex post facto 22
Treaty as consent 20
Vagueness 23

3. Jurisdiction

Defendant who was arrested on Panamanian vessel could not challenge jurisdiction of United States over that vessel under 21 U.S.C.A. § 955a(a), extending jurisdiction to persons on board vessel subject to jurisdiction of United States if such person possesses a controlled substance, where defendant was tried and convicted of violating 21 U.S.C.A. § 955a(c) governing persons on board any vessel within customs waters of United States. U.S. v. Bent-Santana, C.A.11 (Fla.) 1985, 774 F.2d 1545.

8. Weight and sufficiency of evidence

Defendant's "mere presence" on boat found to contain marijuana was sufficient to support conviction of knowing and intentional possession of marijuana with intent to distribute, where boat lacked equipment necessary for lobster fishing and was not in fishing area and Coast Guard officers found small amount of marijuana on deck, and strong smell of fiberglass resin along with fiberglass and resin supplies in storage compartment supported inference that marijuana was concealed shortly before ship was apprehended. U.S. v. Gonzalez-Torres, C.A.11 (Fla.) 1986, 779 F.2d 626.

16. Search and seizure

Panamanian vessel was within "customs waters" of United States within meaning of 19 U.S.C.A. § 1401(j), and thus was subject to search and seizure by United States authorities under 21 U.S.C.A. § 955a(c), where Panamanian government communicated its assent to search and seizure of the vessel to United States officials. U.S. v. Bent-Santana, C.A.11 (Fla.) 1985, 774 F.2d 1545.

19. Due process

Designating "customs waters" around a specific vessel on the high seas, thereby subjecting persons on board to United States prosecution, does not violate due process. U.S. v. Gonzalez, C.A.11 (Fla.) 1985, 776 F.2d 931.

20. Treaty as consent

Telephonic relay of consent by the Honduran government to Coast Guard's boarding, search, seizure, and prosecution of crew members of vessel pursuant to the Marijuana on the High Seas Act [21 U.S.C.A. § 955a(c)] constituted a "treaty or other arrangement" necessary to extend customs waters beyond 12 miles. U.S. v. Gonzalez, C.A.11 (Fla.) 1985, 776 F.2d 931.

21. Custom waters

When Congress adopted the same definition of "customs waters" for purposes of the Marijuana on the High Seas Act [21 U.S.C.A. § 955a(c)] as it had adopted for the Anti-Smuggling Act [19 U.S.C.A. § 1709(c)], it authorized enforcement beyond 12 miles both in waters designated by treaties and pursuant to arrangements concerning specific vessels. U.S. v. Gonzalez, C.A.11 (Fla.) 1985, 776 F.2d 931.

22. Ex post facto

Marijuana on the High Seas Act [21 U.S.C.A. § 955a(c)] is not an ex post facto law. U.S. v. Gonzalez, C.A.11 (Fla.) 1985, 776 F.2d 931.

23. Vagueness

Marijuana on the High Seas Act [21 U.S.C.A. § 955a(c)] is not unconstitutionally vague. U.S. v. Gonzalez, C.A.11 (Fla.) 1985, 776 F.2d 931.

24. Elements of offense

Consent of foreign nation to boarding of its vessel in United States "customs waters" and prosecution of crew members for drug offenses is not an element of an offense under the Marijuana on the High Seas Act [21 U.S.C.A. § 955a(c)]; rather, it is a diplomatic

5 U.S. Code Congressional & Administrative News

U.S. Code Congressional & Administrative News

U.S. Code Congressional & Administrative News

U.S. Code Congressional & Administrative News is frequently used to update research done in U.S.C.A. For example, you can find if there has been a recent change in the law affecting the federal statute you are researching. It also has the full text to newly enacted laws, congressional and administrative highlights and various cross referencing tables. This section is for illustration only.

No. 4   June 1986

UNITED STATES CODE CONGRESSIONAL AND ADMINISTRATIVE NEWS

99th Congress—Second Session

Members and Committees

Public Laws

99–273 to 99–290

Legislative History

Proclamations

Executive Orders

President's Messages

Administrative Regulations

· Court Rules

Tables

Index

West Publishing Co.
50 West Kellogg Blvd., P.O. Box 64526
St. Paul, MN 55164–0526

COPYRIGHT © 1986 WEST PUBLISHING CO.

Copyright is not claimed as to any part of the original work prepared by a United States Government officer or employee as part of that person's official duties.

All rights reserved. No part of this publication may be reproduced, stored in a retrieval system, or transmitted, in any form or by any means, electronic, mechanical, photocopying, recording, or otherwise, without the prior written permission of the publisher.

UNITED STATES CODE CONGRESSIONAL AND ADMINISTRATIVE NEWS is a trademark of West Publishing Co.

Congressional and Administrative Highlights

WASHINGTON, D.C.
June, 1986

Both Houses of Congress reconvened on April 8, 1986 following the Easter Holiday. These are major actions taken by Congress during the four following weeks:

The Senate agreed to S.Con.Res. 120, a proposed Congressional Resolution on the Budget for Fiscal Year 1987. It would project revenues of $642,212,000,000 during fiscal year 1987; outlays of $805,724,000,000; for a budget deficit of $163,582,000,000 (sic). The resolution would increase revenues by $13,212,000,000; defense outlays would be $281,962,273,000. It would authorize up to $1,800,000,000 for general revenue sharing during fiscal year 1987, subject to the enactment of authorizing legislation by the Committee on Finance.

The Senate Committee on Finance is considering H.R. 3838, a proposed Tax Reform Act of 1985. The draft bill presently being considered would reduce the maximum tax rate for individuals to 27 percent and 33 percent for corporations. The reduced tax brackets would be financed by eliminating many of the deductions in existing law, including the exclusion for capital gains income and the deduction for a contribution to an individual retirement account.

The House Committee on Ways and Means reported a bill, as yet unnumbered, entitled the Comprehensive Trade Policy Reform Act of 1986. The bill would require the President to retaliate against countries that violate

**A copyrighted Feature of the U. S. Code Congressional and
Administrative News**

i

CONTENTS

CONTENTS

CUMULATIVE INDEX

IV

The Congress

Laws of the 99th Congress
Second Session

HEALTH SERVICES AMENDMENTS ACT OF 1986

For Legislative History of Act see Report for P.L. 99–280
in Legislative History Section, post.

An Act to amend the Public Health Service Act to revise and extend the programs of assistance for primary health care.

Be it enacted by the Senate and House of Representatives of the United States of America in Congress assembled,

Health Services
Amendments
Act of 1986.

SECTION 1. SHORT TITLE: REFERENCE TO ACT.

(a) SHORT TITLE.—This Act may be cited as the "Health Services Amendments Act of 1986".

42 USC 201 note.

(b) REFERENCE TO ACT.—Whenever in this Act an amendment or repeal is expressed in terms of an amendment to, or a repeal of, a section or other provision, the reference shall be considered to be made to a section or other provision of the Public Health Service Act.

42 USC 201 note.

SEC. 2. MEDICALLY UNDERSERVED POPULATIONS.

Section 330(b) (42 U.S.C. 254c(b)) is amended—

(1) by striking out the second, third, fourth, and fifth sentences of paragraph (3); and

(2) by adding at the end thereof the following:

"(4) In carrying out paragraph (3), the Secretary shall by regulation prescribe criteria for determining the specific shortages of personal health services of an area or population group. Such criteria shall—

Regulations.

"(A) take into account comments received by the Secretary from the chief executive officer of a State and local officials in a State; and

State and local
governments.

"(B) include infant mortality in an area or population group, other factors indicative of the health status of a population group or residents of an area, the ability of the residents of an area or of a population group to pay for health services and their accessibility to them, and the availability of health professionals to residents of an area or to a population group.

Children and
youth.

"(5) The Secretary may not designate a medically underserved population in a State or terminate the designation of such a population unless, prior to such designation or termination, the Secretary provides reasonable notice and opportunity for comment and consults with—

Prohibition.
State and local
governments.

"(A) the chief executive officer of such State;

"(B) local officials in such State; and

"(C) the State organization, if any, which represents a majority of community health centers in such State.

"(6) The Secretary may designate a medically underserved population that does not meet the criteria established under paragraph (4) if the chief executive officer of the State in which such population is located and local officials of such State recommend the designation of such population based on unusual local conditions which are a barrier to access to or the availability of personal health services.".

State and local
governments.

100 STAT. 399

CUMULATIVE
TABLES IN THIS PAMPHLET

Table

[2]

Table 2

U.S. CODE

AND

U.S. CODE ANNOTATED
CLASSIFICATIONS

99th CONGRESS—2nd SESSION

The pagination of the Public Laws of this Session contained in the 1986 U.S. Code Congressional and Administrative News is identical with Volume 100 U.S. Statutes at Large. In this table a page reference to "8", for example, will be paged as "100 STAT. 8" in this service and in Volume 100 U.S. Statutes at Large.

Abbreviations

App.	Appendix	prec.	Preceding
Elim.	Eliminated	Rep.	Repealed
nt.	Note	Rev.T.	Revised Title
nts.	Notes	Sec.	Section
P.L.	Public Law	Tit.	Title

		1986–99th Cong.–100 Stat.			USCA		
Jan.	P.L.	Sec.	Page	Tit.	Sec.		Status
30	99–241	1	3	7	1314c		
		2	3	7	1314e		
Feb.							
12	99–247	1(a)	9	22	2753		
		1(b), (c)	9	22	2776		
		1(d)	9	22	2796b		
27	99–250	1	13	16	119a		
		2	13	16	119a	nt	
	99–251	1	14	5	8901	nt	
		101	14	5	8909		
		102	14	5	8903		
		103	14	5	8905		
		104(a)	14	5	8905		
		104(b)	15	5	8905	nt	
		105(a)	15	5	8901		
		105(b)	15	5	8902		
		105(c)	15	5	8901	nt	
		106(a)(1)	16	5	8902	nt	
		106(a)(2)	16	5	8902	nt	
		106(a)(3)	16	5	8902		
		106(b)	16	5	8902	nt	
		107	16	5	8904	nt	
		110	17	5	7901	nt	
		111	19	5	8903		
		112	19	5	8909	nt	
		201(a)	20	5	8341	nt	
		201(b)	22	5	8341	nt	
		201(c)	22	5	8341	nt	

[4]

Table 3

U.S. CODE
AND
U.S. CODE ANNOTATED SECTIONS
AMENDED, REPEALED, NEW, ETC.

99th CONGRESS—2nd SESSION

The pagination of the Public Laws of this Session contained in the 1986 U.S. Code Congressional and Administrative News is identical with Volume 100 U.S. Statutes at Large. In this table a page reference to "8", for example, will be paged as "100 STAT. 8" in this service and in Volume 100 U.S. Statutes at Large.

Title	Sec.	Page	Title	Sec.	Page
2	902 note	39	5 (Cont'd)	8341(e)(2)	25
5	1103(a)(7)	26		8341(e)(3)	25
	1103(a)(8)	26		8341(h)(1)	25
	1103(a)(9)	26		8341(h)(4)(A)	25
	1103(b)(4)	26		8341 notes	20, 22, 23
	3502(a)(C)	27		8342(j)(1)(B)	25
	5305 note	332		8345(f)	26
	5312	49		8345 note	27
	5334(e)	27		8901(9)	15
	5343 note	332		8901(10)	15
	5504(b)	334		8901(11)	15
	5504(b)(1)	334		8901 notes	14, 15
	5504 note	334		8902(k)(1)	15
	5924(2)(A)	26		8902(k)(2)	15
	6312	27		8902(k)(3)	15
	7901 note	17		8902(m)(2)(A)	16
	8332(j)(1)	23		8902 notes	16
	8339(j)(3)	23		8903(4)(A)	14
	8339(j)(5)(B)	23		8903(4)(C)	19
	8339(j)(5)(C)(v)	24		8904 note	16
	8339(j)(5)(C)(vi)	24		8905(b)	14
	8339(k)(1)	24		8905(f)	14
	8339(k)(2)(B)(i)	24		8905 note	15
	8339(k)(2)(B)(ii)	25		8906(g)(1)	334
	8339(k)(2)(D)	25		8906(g)(2)	334
	8339(o)	28, 334		8909(b)	14
	8339 notes	25, 29, 335		8909 notes	19, 333
	8340(c)(1)	25	7	259(a)	54
	8341(b)(1)	335		259(b)	54
	8341(d)	335		511d	99
	8341(e)(1)	25		608c note	51

[18]

6 Special Types of Research

Special Types of Research

To this point, you have used words and word indexes to find caselaw. There are times when other techniques are desirable. The following pages show several different methods used for special circumstances:

1. You have the name of a federal act and need its U.S. Code section.
2. You have the name of a case and need its citation.
3. You need a legal definition.

The final part of this chapter demonstrates the **Topic Method**, an alternate to the use of the descriptive-word indexes.

6   Special Types of Research

Popular Name Table

If you know only the popular name of a federal law you can find its corresponding U.S. Code title number and section number in the U.S.C.A.'s Popular Name Table.

Problem

You know the name of a federal law is "Contraband Seizure Act". Find the U.S. Code title and section number under which it is classified.

POPULAR NAME TABLE

For

ACTS OF CONGRESS

To January 2, 1985

The references within the parentheses indicate the classifications of Acts of Congress to the United States Code by Code title and section. The word "See", set out preceding the Code title and section, indicates that the Act Congress has been repealed (in whole or in part) and that certain provisions thereof have been restated in that Code title and section specified. In some instances, Code classifications may not be indicated for Acts of Congress that have been repealed or superseded or are obsolete. See Table II—Revised Statutes 1878 and Table III—Statutes at Large for complete chronological listing of Acts of Congress that have been classified to the Code together with their Code classifications and current status.

AAA Farm Relief and Inflation Act
  May 12, 1933, ch. 25, 48 Stat. 31 (Title 7, §§ 601–604, 607–620; Title 12, §§ 347, 462b, 636, 723, 771, 781, 810, 823 note, 992, 993, 1016–1019; See Title 31, §§ 5301, 5304)

Abacá Production Act of 1950
  Aug. 10, 1950, ch. 673, 64 Stat. 435 (Title 50, §§ 541–546)

Abandoned Military Reservations Acts
  July 5, 1884, ch. 214, 23 Stat. 103 (Title 43, § 1073 et seq.)
  Aug. 23, 1894, ch. 314, 28 Stat. 491
  July 3, 1916, ch. 217, 39 Stat. 342

Abandoned Property Collection Act
  Mar. 12, 1863, ch. 120, 12 Stat. 820

Able Seamen Act
  July 8, 1941, ch. 279, 55 Stat. 579 (Title 46, § 672–2)

Abolition of Slavery Acts (District of Columbia)
  Apr. 16, 1862, ch. 54, 12 Stat. 376
  July 12, 1862, ch. 155, 12 Stat. 538

Abolition of Slavery Act (Territories)
  June 19, 1862, ch. 112, 12 Stat. 432

Abraham Lincoln Birthplace National Historic Site Acts
  July 17, 1916, ch. 247, 39 Stat. 385 (Title 16, §§ 211–214)
  Feb. 11, 1929, ch. 176, 45 Stat. 1162 (Title 16, §§ 215, 216)
  Mar. 2, 1934, ch. 38, 48 Stat. 389 (Title 16, § 214)
  Aug. 11, 1939, ch. 686, 53 Stat. 1405 (Title 16, § 217)
  May 27, 1949, ch. 149, 63 Stat. 140 (Title 16, § 218)
  Sept. 8, 1959, Pub. L. 86–231, 73 Stat. 466 (Title 16, § 217a)

Acadia National Park Acts
  Feb. 26, 1919, ch. 45, 40 Stat. 1178 (Title 16, §§ 341, 342, 343)
  Jan. 19, 1929, ch. 77, 45 Stat. 1083 (Title 16, §§ 342a, 342b)
  May 23, 1930, ch. 315, 46 Stat. 377 (Title 16, § 343a)
  Dec. 22, 1944, ch. 674, 58 Stat. 914 (Title 16, § 343b)
  Sept. 7, 1949, ch. 541, 63 Stat. 691 (Title 16, § 343c)

707

Consumer Product Safety Act

Pub. L. 92–573, Oct. 27, 1972, 86 Stat. 1207 (Title 5, §§ 5314, 5315; Title 15, §§ 2051–2081)

Pub. L. 94–273, § 31, Apr. 21, 1976, 90 Stat. 380 (Title 15, § 2076)

Pub. L. 94–284, §§ 2, 3(b), (d), (f), 4–16, 17(d), May 11, 1976, 90 Stat. 503–510, 514 (Title 15, §§ 2052, 2053, 2056, 2058, 2059, 2060, 2064, 2068, 2069, 2071, 2072, 2073, 2075, 2076, 2079, 2081)

Pub. L. 95–319, § 3, July 11, 1978, 92 Stat. 386 (Title 15, §§ 2068, 2082)

Pub. L. 95–631, §§ 1–6, 11, Nov. 10, 1978, 92 Stat. 3742–3745, 3748 (Title 15, §§ 2053, 2056, 2058, 2067, 2068, 2069, 2076, 2081)

Pub. L. 96–373, Oct. 3, 1980, 94 Stat. 1366 (Title 15, § 2053)

Pub. L. 96–486, § 3, Dec. 1, 1980, 94 Stat. 2369 (Title 15, § 2072)

Pub. L. 97–35, title XII, §§ 1202, 1203(a), (c), 1204, 1205(a), 1206, 1207(a), (b), 1208–1210, 1211(a)–(d), (h), 1213–1215, Aug. 13, 1981, 95 Stat. 703, 704, 713, 716, 718, 720, 721, 723, 724 (Title 15, §§ 2052, 2054–2062, 2064, 2069, 2072, 2073, 2076, 2077, 2081, 2083)

Pub. L. 97–414, § 9(j), Jan. 4, 1983, 96 Stat. 2064 (Title 15, §§ 2055, 2060, 2064, 2068, 2080)

Consumer Product Safety Amendments of 1981

Pub. L. 97–35, title XII, §§ 1201–1214, Aug. 13, 1981, 95 Stat. 703–724 (Title 7, § 135; Title 12, § 24; Title 15, §§ 1193, 1201, 1204, 1262, 1263, 1274, 1276, 1471 note, 1475, 1476, 2051 note, 2052, 2054, 2055, 2056, 2057, 2058, 2059, 2060, 2061, 2062, 2064, 2069, 2072, 2073, 2076, 2077, 2080, 2081, 2083; Title 21, §§ 343, 352, 353, 362)

Consumer Product Safety Commission Improvements Act of 1976

Pub. L. 94–284, May 11, 1976, 90 Stat. 503 (Title 15, §§ 1193, 1203, 1204, 1261, 1471, 1476, 2051 note, 2052, 2053, 2056, 2058, 2059, 2060, 2064, 2068, 2069, 2071, 2072, 2073, 2075, 2076, 2078, 2079, 2080 note, 2081)

Consumer-Patient Radiation Health and Safety Act of 1981

Pub. L. 97–35, title IX, §§ 975–983, Aug. 13, 1981, 95 Stat. 598–601 (Title 42, §§ 10001–10008)

Contraband Seizure Act

Aug. 9, 1939, ch. 618, §§ 1–8, 53 Stat. 1291 (Title 49, §§ 781–788)

Aug. 1, 1956, ch. 852, § 22, 70 Stat. 911 (Title 49, § 789)

Contract Disputes Act of 1978

Pub. L. 95–563, Nov. 1, 1978, 92 Stat. 2383 (Title 5, § 5108; Title 28, §§ 1346, 1491, 2401, 2414, 2510, 2517; See Title 31, § 1304; Title 41, §§ 601–613)

Pub. L. 97–164, title I, §§ 156, 157, 160(15), 161(10), Apr. 2, 1982, 96 Stat. 47–49 (Title 41, §§ 607, 609)

Contract Labor Laws

See Alien Contract Labor Laws

Contract Services for Drug Dependent Federal Offenders Act of 1978

Pub. L. 95–537, Oct. 27, 1978, 92 Stat. 2038 (Title 18, §§ 3651, 4255)

Pub.L. 98–236, § 2, Mar. 20, 1984, 98 Stat. 66 (Title 18, § 4255 note)

Contract Services for Drug Dependent Federal Offenders Authorization Act of 1983

Pub.L. 98–236, Mar. 20, 1984, 98 Stat. 66 (Title 18, § 4255 note)

Contract Settlement Act of 1944

July 1, 1944, ch. 358, 58 Stat. 649 (See Title 18, § 3287; Title 41, § 101 et seq.)

July 28, 1953, ch. 253, 67 Stat. 226 (Title 41, § 114)

June 28, 1954, ch. 403, § 1, 68 Stat. 300 (Title 41, § 117)

Apr. 2, 1982, Pub. L. 97–164, title I, § 160(a)(14), 96 Stat. 48 (Title 41, §§ 113, 114)

Contract Work Hours Standards Act

See Contract Work Hours and Safety Standards Act

Contract Work Hours and Safety Standards Act

Pub. L. 87–581, title I, Aug. 13, 1962, 76 Stat. 357 (Title 40, §§ 327–332)

Pub. L. 91–54, § 1, Aug. 9, 1969, 83 Stat. 96 (Title 40, § 333)

Pub. L. 97–164, title I, § 160(a)(13), Apr. 2, 1982, 96 Stat. 48 (Title 40, § 330)

Control of Paperwork Amendments of 1978

Pub. L. 95–561, title XII, §§ 1211–1213, Nov. 1, 1978, 92 Stat. 2338–2342 (Title 20, §§ 1221–3, 1221e–1, 1231g)

Controlled Substance Registrant Protection Act of 1984

Pub.L. 98–305, May 31, 1984, 98 Stat. 221 (Title 18, § 2118; Title 28, § 522 note)

6 Special Types of Research

WESTLAW and West Books

Table of Cases

West digests have tables of cases which alphabetically list names of cases included in that digest. If you know only the name of the case you can consult the digest to get the case cite and look it up in the case reporter.

WESTLAW Title Search

WESTLAW can be used in a similar fashion. Given only the name of a case, you can restrict your WESTLAW search to just the title of the document, find the case and read it.

Problems

Table of cases—Find a 1985 case McBride v. Carleton in the General Digest and locate its' citation.
WESTLAW—Find the same case in WESTLAW.

TABLE OF CASES

References are to Digest Topics and Key Numbers

Lojuk v. Johnson, CA7 (Ill), 770 F2d 619.—Armed S 102; Fed Cts 572, 574, 584; U S 50.

Lombardi v. Lombardi, ConnApp, 497 A2d 52, 5 ConnApp 147.—Divorce 252.-3(1), 252.5(1), 252.5(3), 286(8).

Lomnitz v. 61 East 86th Street Equities Group, NYSup, 492 NYS2d 915.—Ex & Ad 39, 75, 91, 134, 288, 458; Land & Ten 94½, 127, 200.15.

Lones, In re, BkrtcyKy, 50 BR 801.—Bankr 421(1), 434, 436(1).

Long v. Adams, GaApp, 333 SE2d 852, 175 GaApp 538.—Courts 12(2.25); Neglig 1, 136(14); Torts 1, 18.

Long v. Hendricks, Idaho App, 705 P2d 78.—App & E 437, 970(4); Costs 172, 206, 208; Damag 133, 187, 222; Evid 555.10; Judges 24; Judgm 897; Trial 68(1), 388(1).

Long v. Wainwright, FlaApp 1 Dist, 474 So2d 7.—Hab Corp 25.1(4).

Long Island Pen Corp. v. Shatsky Metal Stamping Co., Inc., NYAD 2 Dept, 492 NYS2d 791.—Action 57(3); Impl & C C 81.

Long Island Pen Corp. v. Warshavsky, NYAD 2 Dept, 492 NYS2d 792.—Judgm 588.

Longo v. Longo, LaApp 4 Cir, 474 So2d 500.—Hus & W 248½, 258, 272(1), 272(4), 272(5).

Longwell v. State, Wyo, 705 P2d 336.—Crim Law 982.9(1).

Looney v. Gibraltar Sav. Ass'n, TexApp 7 Dist, 695 SW2d 336.—App & E 758.1, 1175(5); Pretrial Proc 698.

Loonsten, Inc. v. Mullin, BkrtcyInd, 51 BR 377. See Mullin, In re.

Lopez v. I.R.S., DCNY, 614 FSupp 1332. —Int Rev 4551, 4638, 4649, 4993.

Lopez v. Scully, DCNY, 614 FSupp 1135.—Crim Law 622.2(7); Hab Corp 45.2(7), 45.3(1.30), 45.3(1.40), 45.3(9).

Lorie v. Standard Oil Co., GaApp, 333 SE2d 110, 175 GaApp 308.—Joint Adv 1.15; Judgm 185.3(13); Mast & S 301(4).

Lorimar Productions, Inc. v. N.L.R.B., CA9, 771 F2d 1294. See N.L.R.B. v. Lorimar Productions, Inc.

Los Angeles County v. Thompson, CalApp 2 Dist, 218 CalRptr 101, 172 CA3d 18.—App & E 113(1); Child 64; Const Law 43(1); Judgm 73.

Losser v. Atlanta Intern. Ins. Co., DC-Utah, 615 FSupp 58.—Insurance 512(2), 514.6(2), 602.8.

Lott v. State, TexApp 13 Dist, 695 SW2d 237.—Crim Law 145, 369.1, 369.2(2), 369.2(4), 371(12), 730(13), 1169.1(1), 1169.2(1), 1169.11; Homic 309(3).

Lotus Maru, M/T, DCNY, 615 FSupp 78. See Uni-Petrol Gesellschaft Fur Mineraloel Producte M.B.H. v. M/T Lotus Maru.

Loud v. Dixie Metal Co., Inc., LaApp 2 Cir, 475 So2d 122.—Work Comp 847, 1277, 1279.

Louisiana Business College v. Crump, LaApp 2 Cir, 474 So2d 1366.—Action 53(1), 53(3); App & E 714(5), 1050.-1(11), 1060.1(2); Bills & N 476(2); Colleges 9.20(1), 9.25(2); Evid 370(4); Judgm 540, 951(1), 951(2), 956(1), 958(1).

Louisiana-Pacific Corp. v. Lumber and Sawmill Workers, Local No. 2949, Or, 704 P2d 104.—Labor 923, 961.

Louisiana Tax Collections, Inc. v. Bear Creek Storage Co., LaApp 2 Cir, 474 So2d 1337.—Action 13; Plead 228.12, 228.17; Schools 106.13.

Louis N. Picciano and Son v. Olympic Const. Co., Inc., NYAD 3 Dept, 492 NYS2d 476.—Contracts 9(2), 54(1),

303(5); Damag 36, 62(4), 190; Interest 31.

Louisville Cooperage v. Knoppe, KyApp, 695 SW2d 440.—Work Comp 1038, 1644, 1738.

Loutsion, In re Estate of, PaSuper, 496 A2d 1205.—Ex & Ad 490; Trusts 315(2); Wills 487(1).

Love v. Alabama Institute for Deaf and Blind, DCAla, 613 FSupp 436.—Civil R 43, 44(1), 44(5).

Love v. State, Ga, 334 SE2d 173.—Crim Law 394.6(4), 1134(3), 1158(4); Drugs & N 183; Searches 3.3(7).

Loveall v. American Honda Motor Co., Inc., Tenn, 694 SW2d 937.—App & E 961; Const Law 90.1(3); Pretrial Proc 36, 41.

Loveless v. Conner, Ga, 333 SE2d 586, 254 Ga 663.—Courts 481; Judgm 435, 440.

Lovell v. Com., KyApp, 695 SW2d 429. —Brib 1(1), 11; Crim Law 438.1, 1158(4), 1169.1(9).

Lowe v. Lowe, MinnApp, 372 NW2d 65. —Divorce 252.3(1); Evid 574.

Lowes v. Sayad, DCMo, 614 FSupp 1206. —Const Law 238.5; Mun Corp 184(1).

Lowey Leasing v. Kelly, BkrtcyOhio, 51 BR 707. See Kelly, In re.

Lowrie v. People, Colo, 703 P2d 1274. See Benson v. People.

Lowry v. Parole and Probation Com'n, Fla, 473 So2d 1248.—Mand 3(4); Pardon 51; Statut 181(1), 220.

Lozaro v. Com., Unemployment Compensation Bd. of Review, PaCmwlth, 497 A2d 680.—Social S 420, 424, 589.

L.R., In re, Vt, 497 A2d 753.—Const Law 255(5); Mental H 32, 36, 41, 51.

L.R.B., Matter of Welfare of, MinnApp, 373 NW2d 334.—Crim Law 412.2(5); Infants 174, 243, 252.

Lubben v. Lubben, IllApp 1 Dist, 90 Ill-Dec 56, 481 NE2d 856, 135 IllApp3d 302.—App & E 428(1), 430(1), 436; Divorce 254(1), 255.

Lucas v. State, OklCr, 704 P2d 1141.—Arrest 63.5(6); Crim Law 394.1(3), 394.4(12); Searches 3.3(1), 7(5).

Lucy v. State Farm Ins. Co., LaApp 2 Cir, 475 So2d 88.—Costs 260(4); Death 77, 101; Judgm 713(2).

Luczynski v. Temple, NJSuperCh, 497 A2d 211.—Const Law 228.2, 278.2(1); Zoning 5, 21, 21.5, 27, 83, 672, 682.

Luddie v. Foremost Ins. Co., ConnApp, 497 A2d 435, 5 ConnApp 193.—Work Comp 615, 666, 721, 725, 734, 1939.1, 1939.7.

Lukens, Inc. v. W.C.A.B. (Hasiey) PaCmwlth, 496 A2d 895.—Work Comp 571, 1536, 1912, 1939.6.

Lumara Foods of America, Inc., Matter of, BkrtcyOhio, 50 BR 809.—Bankr 314(6), 347; Statut 214.

Lussier v. Barrup, BkrtcyVt, 51 BR 321. See Barrup, In re.

Lutich v. Puett, TexApp 11 Dist, 694 SW2d 452.—Parties 75(6); Plead 252(2), 290(1).

Luttrell v. Department of Corrections, MichApp, 373 NW2d 168. See Edmond v. Department of Corrections.

Lutwin v. City of New York, DCNY, 106 FRD 502.—Fed Civ Proc 1935, 2443, 2444, 2446, 2450.

Luu v. U.S., Dept. of Agriculture, Food and Nutrition Service, DCMo, 614 FSupp 541.—Agric 2.6(3).

Lynch v. Andrew, MassApp, 481 NE2d 1383.—Damag 79(1), 80(1), 80(3); Ven & Pur 79.

Lynch v. Jackson, BkrtcyAppCal, 51 BR 600. See Fitzsimmons v. Jackson.

Lynch v. Urban Redevelopment Authority of Pittsburgh, PaCmwlth, 496 A2d 1331.—Admin Law 754, 763; Const Law 90.3; Covenants 49, 51(1); Zoning 384, 745, 746.

Lyon v. Continental Trading Co., NCApp, 333 SE2d 774.—Evid 543(4); Wareh 34(4), 34(7).

Lyons v. McCotter, CA5 (Tex), 770 F2d 529.—Crim Law 641.13(6), 1166.11(5).

M

M., In Interest of, IllApp 5 Dist, 90 Ill-Dec 83, 481 NE2d 883, 135 IllApp3d 145. See C.K.M., In Interest of.

M., Matter of, Mont, 704 P2d 1037. See J.M., Matter of.

M., Matter of, OklCr, 704 P2d 88. See L.G.M., Matter of.

M., Matter of Welfare of, MinnApp, 372 NW2d 431. See L.M.M., Matter of Welfare of.

M., Petition of, ColoApp, 703 P2d 1330. See D.L.M., Petition of.

Mabrey, In re, BkrtcyOhio, 51 BR 383.—Exemp 49.

McAllen State Bank v. Linbeck Const. Corp., TexApp 13 Dist, 695 SW2d 10. —App & E 213, 215(1), 1052(5), 1070(2); Cons Prot 2, 5, 32, 40; Contracts 324(1), 352(1); Damag 123, 177, 189, 191, 221(8); Evid 174(1), 373(1), 543(2); Subrog 33(1), 33(3); Trial 105(4), 350.4(1).

McAndrews, Appeal of, PaSuper, 496 A2d 1237. See Sellers, Estate of.

McBarron v. S & T Industries, Inc., CA6 (Ky), 771 F2d 94.—Mast & S 78.-1(1), 78.1(5), 78.1(6), 78.1(8); Statut 188.

McBride v. Carleton, Ala, 473 So2d 1009.—Judgm 181(33).

McBride v. Merrell Dow and Pharmaceuticals, Inc., DCDC, 613 FSupp 1349.—Libel 28, 48(1), 51(5), 112(2), 123(8).

McBroom, In re, BkrtcyVa, 51 BR 953. —Bankr 310(1), 1109(4).

McCallister v. Board of Trustees of Judges Retirement System, Ill, 89 Ill-Dec 855, 481 NE2d 698, 107 Ill2d 158. See Felt v. Board of Trustees of Judges Retirement System.

McCann v. State, TexApp 6 Dist, 695 SW2d 791.—Crim Law 494; Infants 13.

McCarthy v. McCarthy, ArizApp, 704 P2d 1352.—Divorce 235, 252.3(4), 253(2), 286(3).

McCarthy v. U.S., DCOhio, 613 FSupp 67.—Int Rev 3229, 3236, 3334.

McCay Corp. v. Mount Laurel Tp. Council, NJSuperL, 497 A2d 570, 203 NJSuper 550.—Mun Corp 236, 244(2); Statut 184, 219(1), 219(4).

McClain v. State, AlaCrApp, 473 So2d 612.—Crim Law 398(2), 700(5), 829(3); Forg 5, 14, 34(2), 35, 38.

McClellan Mortg. Co. v. Storey, ArizApp, 704 P2d 826.—Guar 3, 4; Princ & S 10, 12, 74, 83.

McCollum v. Friendly Hills Travel Center, CalApp 2 Dist, 217 CalRptr 919, 172 CA3d 83.—App & E 863; Contracts 205; Neglig 10; Princ & A 23(5), 48.

McConnell v. Town Clerk of Tipton, Okl, 704 P2d 479.—Const Law 70.-1(12); Mand 27, 28, 87; Mun Corp 63.1(6), 122(3), 621.

McCottrell v. City of Chicago, IllApp 1 Dist, 90 IllDec 258, 481 NE2d 1058,

```
WALT                          WESTLAW         ONLINE
_____

   TITLE(McBride & Carleton)



   THE CURRENT DATABASE IS  AL-CS
   PLEASE ENTER YOUR QUERY.

   The standard WESTLAW options are AGE, NOPROMPTS.
   To select other options, type them in and press ENTER.
   For more information regarding the WESTLAW options, enter OPTIONS.
   COPR.  ®  WEST 1986 NO CLAIM TO ORIG. U.S. GOVT. WORKS
```

This is the WESTLAW query used to locate McBride v. Carleton in the Alabama case law database.

```
WALT                        WESTLAW       ONLINE
_____

Citation                  Rank(R)        Page(P)       Database  Mode
473 So.2d 1009            R 1 OF 1        P 1 OF 9      AL-CS     T

    Gladys McBRIDE, personal representative and administratrix of the Estate of
                        Sidney Love, Sr., deceased
                                     v.
                          Mrs. George CARLETON.
                                  83-342.
                          Supreme Court of Alabama.
                              May 10, 1985.
                       Rehearing Denied July 3, 1985.
     In wrongful death action, plaintiff appealed from adverse summary judgment
  rendered by the Circuit Court, Clarke County, J.R. Pearson, J.  The Supreme
  Court, Embry, J., held that material fact issues existed in the action, which
  arose out of death of worker on defendant's premises when a tree limb, damaged
  some months earlier by hurricane, struck worker, concerning, inter alia, duty
  of care owed worker and respective negligent conduct of the parties, thus
  precluding summary judgment.
     Reversed and remanded.
     Torbert, C.J., concurred specially and filed opinion.
  COPR. (C) WEST 1986 NO CLAIM TO ORIG. U.S. GOVT. WORKS
```

Above is the first page of that case on WESTLAW.

Black's Law Dictionary

Words and Phrases

Legal Definitions

Occasionally, the answer to your problem depends on the legal meaning of a word or phrase. Black's Law Dictionary gives you general legal definitions. It is a good place to start if you are unfamiliar with a term. Words and Phrases gives you definitions as construed by judges in case law. It is a good source to find how a word or phrase is defined in a specific factual context.

6 Special Types of Research

Black's Law Problem

What is the doctrine of "res ipsa loquitur"?

Words and Phrases Problem

Find cases defining the doctrine "res ipsa loquitur" as it applies to the consumption of beverages, food or candy.

BLACK'S
LAW DICTIONARY

Definitions of the Terms and Phrases of
American and English Jurisprudence,
Ancient and Modern

By

HENRY CAMPBELL BLACK, M. A.

Author of Treatises on Judgments, Tax Titles, Intoxicating Liquors,
Bankruptcy, Mortgages, Constitutional Law, Interpretation
of Laws, Rescission and Cancellation of Contracts, Etc.

FIFTH EDITION

By

THE PUBLISHER'S EDITORIAL STAFF

Contributing Authors

~~~~~

JOSEPH R. NOLAN
Associate Justice, Massachusetts Supreme Judicial Court
and
M. J. CONNOLLY
Associate Professor of Linguistics
and Eastern Languages, Boston College

ST. PAUL MINN.
WEST PUBLISHING CO.
1979

things not fungible *(fungibles vel non fungibiles);* and (7) *res singulæ (i.e.,* individual objects) and *universitates rerum (i.e.,* aggregates of things). Also persons are for some purposes and in certain respects regarded as things.

Res accessoria /ríyz æksəsór(i)yə/. In the civil law, an accessory thing; that which belongs to a principal thing, or is in connection with it.

Res adiratæ /ríyz ædəréydiy/. The gist of the old action for *res adiratæ* was the fact that the plaintiff had lost his goods, that they had come into the hands of the defendant, and that the defendant, on request, refused to give them up.

Res adjudicata /ríyz æjùwdəkéydə/. A less common spelling of *res judicata.* The term designates a point or question or subject-matter which was in controversy or dispute and has been authoritatively and finally settled by the decision of a court; that issuable fact once legally determined is conclusive as between parties in same action or subsequent proceeding. Tiffany Production of California v. Superior Court of California for Los Angeles County, 131 Cal. App. 729, 22 P.2d 275. See *Res judicata, infra.*

Res caduca /ríyz kəd(y)úwkə/. In the civil law, a fallen or escheated thing; an escheat.

Res communes /ríyz kəmyúwniyz/. In the civil law, things common to all; that is, those things which are used and enjoyed by every one, even in single parts, but can never be exclusively acquired as a whole, *e.g.,* light and air.

Res controversa /ríyz kòntrəvə́rsə/. In the civil law, a matter controverted; a matter in controversy; a point in question; a question for determination.

Res coronæ /ríyz kərówniy/. In old English law, things of the crown; such as ancient manors, homages of the king, liberties, etc.

Res corporales /ríyz kòrpəréyliyz/. In the civil law, corporeal things; things which can be touched, or are perceptible to the senses.

Res derelicta /ríyz dèhrəlíktə/. Abandoned property; property thrown away or forsaken by the owner, so as to become open to the acquisition of the first taker or occupant.

Res fungibiles /ríyz fənjíbəliyz/°fə́njəbliyz/. In the civil law, fungible things, things of such a nature that they can be replaced by equal quantities and qualities when returning a loan or delivering goods purchased, for example, so many bushels of wheat or so many dollars; but a particular horse or a particular jewel would not be of this character.

Res gestæ /ríyz jéstiy/. Things done. McClory v. Schneider, Tex.Civ.App., 51 S.W.2d 738, 741. The "res gestæ" rule is that where a remark is made spontaneously and concurrently with an affray, collision or the like, it carries with it inherently a degree of credibility and will be admissible because of its spontaneous nature. Carroll v. Guffey, 20 Ill.App.2d 470, 156 N.E.2d 267, 270. "Res gestæ" means literally things or things happened and therefore, to be admissible as exception to hearsay rule, words spoken, thoughts expressed, and gestures made, must all be so closely connected to occurrence or event in both time and substance as to be a part of the happening. McCandless v. Inland Northwest Film Service, Inc., 64 Wash.2d 523, 392 P.2d 613, 618. Those circumstances which are the automatic and undesigned incidents of a particular litigated act, which may be separated from act by lapse of time more or less appreciable, and which are admissible when illustrative of such act. The whole of the transaction under investigation and every part of it. Res gestæ is considered as an exception to the hearsay rule. In its operation it renders acts and declarations which constitute a part of the things done and said admissible in evidence, even though they would otherwise come within the rule excluding hearsay evidence or self-serving declarations. The rule is extended to include, not only declarations by the parties to the suit, but includes statements made by bystanders and strangers, under certain circumstances. See Fed.Evid.Rule 803(3).

A spontaneous declaration made by a person immediately after an event and before the mind has an opportunity to conjure a falsehood. It represents an exception to the hearsay rule and should be referred to as a spontaneous exclamation rather than res gestæ.

Res habiles /ríyz hǽbəliyz/. In the civil law, things which are prescriptible; things to which a lawful title may be acquired by ordinary prescription.

Res immobiles /ríyz imówbəliyz/. In the civil law, immovable things; including land and that which is connected therewith, either by nature or art, such as trees and buildings.

Res incorporales /ríyz inkòrpəréyliyz/. In the civil law, incorporeal things; things which cannot be touched; such as those things which consist in right. Such things as the mind alone can perceive.

Res integra /ríyz íntəgrə/°əntégrə/. A whole thing; a new or unopened thing. The term is applied to those points of law which have not been decided, which are untouched by *dictum* or decision.

Res inter alios acta /ríyz ìntər éyl(i)yows ǽktə/. See **Res inter alios acta.**

Res ipsa loquitur /ríyz ípsə lówkwədər/. The thing speaks for itself. Rebuttable presumption or inference that defendant was negligent, which arises upon proof that instrumentality causing injury was in defendant's exclusive control, and that the accident was one which ordinarily does not happen in absence of negligence. Res ipsa loquitur is rule of evidence whereby negligence of alleged wrongdoer may be inferred from mere fact that accident happened provided character of accident and circumstances attending it lead reasonably to belief that in absence of negligence it would not have occurred and that thing which caused injury is shown to have been under management and control of alleged wrongdoer. Hillen v. Hooker Const. Co., Tex.Civ.App., 484 S.W.2d 113, 115. Under doctrine of "res ipsa loquitur" the happening of an injury permits an inference of negligence where plaintiff produces substantial evidence that injury was caused by an agency or instrumentality under exclusive control and management of defendant, and that the occurrence was such that in the ordinary course of things would not happen if reasonable care had been used.

WORDS AND PHRASES

PERMANENT EDITION

1658 TO DATE

Volume 37
Repay — Res Judicata

All Judicial Constructions and Definitions of Words and
Phrases by the State and Federal Courts From
the Earliest Times, Alphabetically
Arranged and Indexed

Kept to Date by Cumulative Annual Pocket Parts

ST. PAUL, MINN.
WEST PUBLISHING CO.

RES IPSA LOQUITUR—Cont'd

RES IPSA LOQUITUR—Cont'd

Cross References

Presumption of Negligence

In general

The rule of "res ipsa loquitur" is that where the thing is shown to be under the management of the defendant or his agent, and where an accident in the ordinary course of events does not happen when the business is properly conducted, the accident itself raises a presumption of negligence in the absence of any explanation. Scott v. Wingenberg, 29 O.C.D. 479, 481, 26 Cir.Ct.R., N.S., 1.

Applicable where truck was permitted to operate without driver. Savery v. Kist, 11 N. W.2d 23, 25, 234 Iowa 98.

"Res ipsa loquitur" doctrine defined. Alford v. Beaird, 192 S.W.2d 180, 181, 301 Ky. 512; Reibert v. Thompson, 194 S.W.2d 974, 975, 302 Ky. 688; Schon v. James, La.App., 28 So.2d 531, 532; Montgomery Ward & Co. v. Scharrenbeck, Tex.Civ.App., 199 S.W.2d 830, 836.

"Res ipsa loquitur" does not apply to injuries from slipping or falling on waxed or oiled floor. Harris v. Montgomery Ward & Co., 53 S.E.2d 536, 538, 230 N.C. 485.

The applicability of the doctrine of "res ipsa loquitur" depends on whether it can be said, in the light of common experience, that the accident was more likely than not the

Injuries from breaking or explosion of bottle—Cont'd

v. Garrett, Tex.Civ.App., 143 S.W.2d 1020, 1022, 1023.

In action for injuries sustained by plaintiff, who was engaged in cold drink business, when bottled soft drink exploded and piece of glass bottle struck plaintiff, even if "res ipsa loquitur doctrine" was applicable, plaintiff was not entitled to judgment simply because jury found that plaintiff suffered damages in a given sum, where defendant's evidence was sufficient to make jury question of defendant's negligence, since the finding of extent of plaintiff's injuries was not a finding of negligence by defendant. Alagood v. Coca Cola Bottling Co., Tex.Civ.App., 135 S.W.2d 1056, 1060, 1061.

Where plaintiff, who operated a restaurant, was injured when a bottle of carbonated beverage manufactured and bottled by defendant exploded while plaintiff was putting bottle in an icebox after a case of beverage had been brought to restaurant by defendant's employee, the doctrine of "res ipsa loquitur" was applicable, and doctrine of "unavoidable accident" did not apply to relieve defendant from liability for injuries, notwithstanding that bottle was in plaintiff's possession and control at time of explosion. Bradley v. Conway Springs Bottling Co., 118 P.2d 601, 603, 605, 154 Kan. 282.

Where plaintiff in action for injuries against manufacturer of bottled beverages proved that plaintiff was taking a bottle of beverage from an ice box furnished plaintiff by manufacturer and had pulled bottle a few inches above top of water in box when bottle exploded causing fragments of glass to strike plaintiff and that bottle was purchased from manufacturer on day preceding explosion and was not frozen or knocked against other bottles or sides of box as it was being pulled from water before explosion, the doctrine of "res ipsa loquitur" was applicable, and plaintiff established a "prima facie case" of negligence against manufacturer. Lanza v. De Ridder Coca Cola Bottling Co., La.App., 3 So.2d 217, 218.

Where doctrine of "res ipsa loquitur" was otherwise applicable in action against manufacturer of beverages for injuries sustained when a bottle of beverage exploded, application of doctrine was not excluded or limited because plaintiff failed to produce bottle for examination by manufacturer, especially where bottle had burst into fragments and there was no evidence that plain-

Injuries from breaking or explosion of bottle—Cont'd

tiff willfully failed to preserve and produce remains thereof. Lanza v. De Ridder Coca Cola Bottling Co., La.App., 3 So.2d 217, 218.

Injuries from consumption of beverage, food or candy, etc.

"Res ipsa loquitur" doctrine was not applicable to sustain recovery against manufacturer and bottler for injuries sustained in explosion of bottle of beer which was not within bottler's exclusive control for several days preceding explosion, in absence of evidence of reasonably discoverable defect in bottle, where proof of any such defect by means of fragments of bottle in his possession was available to person injured. Curley v. Ruppert, 71 N.Y.S.2d 578, 580.

In action against bottler for injuries caused by explosion of bottle of carbonated water, evidence not showing that bottle between time it left possession of bottler and when it came into possession of plaintiff who bought it in a store, that it was not subjected to any condition that would tend to bring about the explosion was insufficient to warrant verdict for plaintiff under "res ipsa loquitur doctrine". Kees v. Canada Dry Ginger Ale, 199 S.W.2d 76, 77, 79, 239 Mo.App. 1080.

Doctrine applicable where abnormal condition of soft drink was due to fermentation, caused by defective sealing of bottle. White v. Coca-Cola Bottling Co., La.App., 16 So.2d 579, 582.

In action against dairy company for injuries allegedly sustained from paint in milk, doctrine of "res ipsa loquitur" was applicable. Welter v. Bowman Dairy Co., 47 N.E.2d 739, 762, 318 Ill.App. 305.

In an action for damages for personal injuries resulting from consumption of a bottled beverage, the plaintiff may not rely on doctrine of "res ipsa loquitur." Tickle v. Hobgood, 4 S.E.2d 444, 445, 216 N.C. 221.

In action against a bottling company to recover for damages allegedly resulting from drinking bottled beverage containing noxious substance, the doctrine of "res ipsa loquitur" is inapplicable. Evans v. Charlotte Pepsi-Cola Bottling Co., 6 S.E.2d 510, 511, 216 N.C. 716.

In action by consumer against manufacturer for injuries allegedly caused by a fish

WORDS AND PHRASES

PERMANENT EDITION

Volume 37

Repay — Res Judicata

1985

Cumulative

Annual Pocket Part

Insert this Pocket Part in back of volume
It replaces prior pocket parts

For Use In 1985–1986

ST. PAUL, MINN.

WEST PUBLISHING CO.

37 Words & Phrases—1
1985 P.P.

73

Cite by Word or Phrase

Thus

Words and Phrases, "Accretion"

Closing with Cases Reported in

COPYRIGHT © 1951 through 1985 WEST PUBLISHING CO.

COPYRIGHT © 1985
By
WEST PUBLISHING CO.

37 Words & Phrases
1985 P.P.

In general

"Res ipsa loquitur" means the thing speaks for itself. Lanza v. Poretti, D.C.Pa., 537 F.Supp. 777, 786.

"Res ipsa loquitur" means that the thing or trans- action speaks for itself. Royal Furniture Co. v. City of Morgantown, W.Va., 263 S.E.2d 878, 881.

The doctrine of "res ipsa loquitur" applies when direct evidence of negligence is unavailable to plain- tiff due to unusual circumstances of injuring inci- dent. Benigno v. Cypress Community Hospital, Inc., Fla.App., 386 So.2d 1303, 1304.

Before "res ipsa loquitur" doctrine can be applied: event must be one which would ordinarily not occur in the absence of someone's negligence; event must be caused by an agency or instrumentality within the exclusive control of the defendant; event must not have been due to any voluntary action or contribu-

tion on the part of the plaintiff; and evidence as to true explanation of event must be more readily accessible to the defendant than to the plaintiff. Adams v. Leidholdt, 563 P.2d 15, 18, 19, 38 Colo. App. 463.

The doctrine of "res ipsa loquitur" contemplates that whenever a thing which has caused injury is shown to have been under control and management of defendants charged with negligence, and occur- rence is such as in ordinary course of events does not happen if due care has been exercised, fact of acci- dent itself is deemed to afford sufficient evidence to support recovery in absence of any explanation by defendant tending to show that injury was not due to his want of care. Fleege v. Cimpl, S.D., 305 N.W.2d 409, 412.

Term "res ipsa loquitur" means the thing speaks for itself. Dayton Tire & Rubber Co. v. Davis, Fla.App., 348 So.2d 575, 583.

"Res ipsa loquitur" means the thing speaks for itself. Sloan v. Atlantic Richfield Co., Alaska, 541 P.2d 717, 728.

"Res ipsa loquitur" is a rule of evidence which permits, but does not compel, an inference that defendant was negligent. Fosselman v. Waterloo Community School Dist. in Black Hawk County, Iowa, 229 N.W.2d 280, 283.

Doctrine of "res ipsa loquitur" is not a rule of law, but rather is an evidentiary principle which normally is determined at conclusion of trial. Id.

Under doctrine of "res ipsa loquitur" the happen- ing of an injury permits an inference of negligence where plaintiff produces substantial evidence that injury was caused by an agency or instrumentality under exclusive control and management of defend- ant, and that the occurrence was such that in the ordinary course of things would not happen if rea- sonable care had been used. Id.

"Res ipsa loquitur" merely permits trier of fact to find negligence and liability from a given set of facts; it does not compel the finder of facts to do so. Browning Ferris Industries of St. Louis, Mo., Inc. v. Baden Tire Center, Inc., Mo.App., 536 S.W.2d 203, 206.

Doctrine of "res ipsa loquitur" applies when oc- currence resulting in injury was such as does not ordinarily happen if party in charge uses ordinary care; the instrumentality involved was under management and control of defendant; and defend- ant possesses superior knowledge or means of infor- mation as to cause of occurrence. Lent v. Lent, Mo.App., 543 S.W.2d 312, 313.

Doctrine of "res ipsa loquitur" is available in products liability cases, and may be used when (1) the instrumentality involved was within the exclusive control of defendant at the time of the act of negli- gence, both as to operation and inspection; (2) the injury was not the result of any voluntary action or contribution on the part of plaintiff; and (3) the accident ordinarily would not have occurred had the defendant used due care. Auto Specialities Manu- facturing Co. v. Boutwell, Fla.App., 335 So.2d 291, 292.

In order for the doctrine of "res ipsa loquitur" to apply, the accident must be of a kind which ordinari- ly does not occur in the absence of someone's negli- gence, the accident must be caused by an agency or

RES IPSA LOQUITUR

gence when doctrine is applied. Stalter v. Coca-Cola Bottling Co. of Arkansas, 669 S.W.2d 460, 462, 282 Ark. 443.

"Res ipsa loquitur" is a Latin phrase meaning "the thing speaks for itself" and is a rule which creates an allowable inference of the defendant's want of due care if it is shown that the occurrence itself ordinarily bespeaks negligence, that the instrumentality causing the injury was within the defendant's exclusive control, and that there was no indication in the circumstances that the injury was the result of the plaintiff's own voluntary act or neglect. Brown v. Racquet Club of Bricktown, 471 A.2d 25, 29, 95 N.J. 280.

Inference permitted but not compelled

Facts of "res ipsa loquitur" case warrant but do not compel inference of negligence. Hanff v. St. Louis Public Service Co., Mo., 355 S.W.2d 922, 927.

"Res ipsa loquitur" means that the facts of the occurrence warrant the inference of negligence, not that they compel such an inference, and where the thing that causes the plaintiff's injury is shown to be under control of the defendant and the accident is of such nature that it does not ordinarily happen in the absence of negligence by the controlling defendant, it affords an inference of negligence ordinarily sufficient to make out a prima facie case for plaintiff and casts upon defendant burden of going forward with the evidence. Bergley v. Mann's, N.D., 99 N.W.2d 849, 852.

"Res ipsa loquitur" means that the facts of the occurrence warrant the inference of negligence, and not that they compel such an inference, and means that the facts of the occurrence make a case to be decided by the jury, not that they forestall the verdict. Giannone v. U.S. Steel Corp., C.A.Pa., 238 F.2d 544, 546.

Establishing an inference of negligence by evidentiary rule of res ipsa loquitur may be sufficient for jury to find a verdict for plaintiff, but it is never required to do so, and a directed verdict for defendant is not warranted, even though defendant at peril of an adverse verdict offers no testimony. Rutherford v. Huntington Coca-Cola Bottling Co., 97 S.E.2d 803, 806, 142 W.Va. 681.

In action for death of one riding in automobile driven by defendant, who had only a learner's permit, because statute required her to have a licensed driver with her for purpose of giving directions and exercising control of automobile if occasion required, as result of automobile striking a tree, res ipsa loquitur doctrine was inapplicable, as defendant did not have exclusive control of automobile. Id.

The doctrine of "res ipsa loquitur" which is a rule of evidence, permits, but does not require, the trier of fact to draw an inference of negligence from the happening of the accident, and it does not relieve a plaintiff of his burden of establishing that the defendant was negligent and does not shift the burden of proof to defendant nor compel defendant to offer an explanation. Calhoun v. Northeast Airlines, Inc., D.C.N.Y., 180 F.Supp. 532, 533.

Doctrine of "res ipsa loquitur" is that whenever a thing, act, instrument, or object which produced an injury is shown to have been under the sole control and management of defendant charged and concerned, and occurrence is such as in the ordinary course of events does not happen if due care has been exercised, fact of injury itself will, as to a party who is himself exercising ordinary care, be deemed to afford prima facie evidence to support a recovery in absence of any explanation by defendant tending to show that injury was not due to his want of care, and presumption or inference of negligence raised by application of doctrine is not absolute or conclusive but rebuttable. Roberts v. City of Sterling, 161 N.E.2d 138, 142, 22 Ill.App.2d 337.

Injuries

Under circumstances proper to its application, doctrine of "res ipsa loquitur" generally applies to physicians and hospitals. Ze Barth v. Swedish Hospital Medical Center, 499 P.2d 1, 6, 81 Wash.2d 12, 52 A.L.R.3d 1067.

Doctrine of "res ipsa loquitur" did not apply to case involving injuries to hair and scalp of plaintiff allegedly caused by use of defendant manufacturer's hair straightener product where manufacturer proved that there was an equal probability that the injury may have resulted from causes other than manufacturer's negligence. Quiroz v. Max Factor, Inc., La.App., 264 So.2d 263, 266.

Injuries from breaking or explosion of bottle

"Res ipsa loquitur" doctrine held not applicable in action against manufacturer for injuries sustained when top part of syphon bottle was suddenly expelled, striking plaintiff in the face, in view of evidence leaving only the inference that accident was caused by the manner in which plaintiff himself prepared contents of syphon and assembled its parts. Levy v. Kidde Mfg. Co., 80 A.2d 629, 632, 13 N.J.Super. 439.

Injuries from consumption of beverage, food or candy, etc.

In action for injuries allegedly sustained by plaintiff when she drank a bottled beverage containing glass particles, evidence was sufficient for the jury under the rule of res ipsa loquitur. Rutherford v. Huntington Coca-Cola Bottling Co., 97 S.E.2d 803, 806, 142 W.Va. 681.

In action for injuries allegedly sustained from drinking a bottled beverage containing glass particles, under rule of res ipsa loquitur, instructing that the jury should find for the plaintiff unless they believed that the defendant had overcome by competent evidence the inference of negligence, was error. Rutherford v. Huntington Coca-Cola Bottling Co., 97 S.E.2d 803, 806, 142 W.Va. 681.

"Res ipsa loquitur" doctrine may be invoked in action against packer or bottler for damage resulting from presence of foreign substance in sealed package or bottle of food. Southwest Ice & Dairy Products Co. v. Faulkenberry, 220 P.2d 257, 260, 203 Okl. 279, 17 A.L.R.2d 1373.

Injuries from escalator

Evidence that escalator under exclusive control of store proprietor suddenly jerked causing customer to fall backward made out a prima facie case for jury on question of negligence of proprietor under "res ipsa loquitur" doctrine. Mattox v. C. R. Anthony Co., Tex.Civ.App., 326 S.W.2d 740, 744.

In action for injuries sustained by customer when she fell backward while riding on escalator from basement to street floor of defendant's store, trial

6 Special Types of Research

Federal Practice Digest 3d

Topic Method

The Topic Method is an alternate method to the use of Descriptive Word Indexes. To use the Topic Method, you typically consult the "Outline of the Law" to find a particular topic or topics where your legal issue might be discussed. Next you consult the breakdown of the specific topic or topics (e.g. Negligence) for a key number where you might find your issue discussed. Finally, you go to that key number in digests to find cases on point. The Topic Method is normally used most efficiently by persons who have a great deal of experience doing research and are an expert in a particular area of law.

6　Special Types of Research

Topic Method Problem

Your client, an illegal alien from Central America, faces deportation proceedings. She says she fears persecution because of the widespread violence affecting all people in her home country. She wants to stop the deportation process claiming political asylum. Is she likely to prevail?

WEST'S
FEDERAL PRACTICE
DIGEST 3d

Volume 2

ADOPTION — ARMED SERVICES

ST. PAUL, MINN.

WEST PUBLISHING CO.

PREFACE

The continuing rapid growth of Federal case law reflects the increase in the volume of litigation in the Federal Courts.

To insure that the Federal Digest remains a functional indexing service to Federal case law all of the material accumulated since publication of Federal Digest 2d has been recompiled into a set of convenient, uniform bound volumes.

These new volumes will comprise Federal Digest 3d. Federal Digest 2d will continue to provide coverage of Federal case law from 1961 to November, 1975. Case law subsequent to November, 1975 is indexed in Federal Digest 3d.

The Modern Federal Practice Digest remains the reference work for Federal cases reported from 1939 to 1961.

The Federal Digest is the reference index for reported cases prior to 1939.

In the third edition are found updated and expanded topic headings, revised topics and expanded key lines within topics. These will enhance research of today's Federal case law.

THE PUBLISHER

January, 1984

*

OUTLINE OF THE LAW

Digest Topics arranged for your convenience by Seven Main Divisions of Law
For complete alphabetical list of Digest Topics, see Page XIII

---

1. **PERSONS**
2. **PROPERTY**
3. **CONTRACTS**
4. **TORTS**
5. **CRIMES**
6. **REMEDIES**
7. **GOVERNMENT**

1. PERSONS

RELATING TO NATURAL PERSONS IN GENERAL

Civil Rights
Dead Bodies
Death
Domicile
Drugs and Narcotics
Food
Health and Environment
Holidays
Intoxicating Liquors
Names
Poisons
Seals
Signatures
Sunday
Time
Weapons

PARTICULAR CLASSES OF NATURAL PERSONS

Absentees
Aliens
Chemical Dependents
Children Out-of-Wedlock
Citizens
Convicts
Indians
Infants
Mental Health
Paupers
Slaves
Spendthrifts

PERSONAL RELATIONS

Adoption
Attorney and Client
Employers' Liability
Executors and Administrators
Guardian and Ward
Husband and Wife
Labor Relations
Marriage
Master and Servant
Parent and Child
Principal and Agent
Workers' Compensation

ASSOCIATED AND ARTIFICIAL PERSONS

Associations
Beneficial Associations
Building and Loan Associations
Clubs
Colleges and Universities
Corporations
Exchanges
Joint-Stock Companies and Business
    Trusts
Partnership
Religious Societies

PARTICULAR OCCUPATIONS

Accountants
Agriculture
Auctions and Auctioneers
Aviation
Banks and Banking
Bridges

OUTLINE OF THE LAW

1. PERSONS—Cont'd

PARTICULAR OCCUPATIONS
—Cont'd

Brokers
Canals
Carriers
Commerce
Consumer Credit
Consumer Protection
Credit Reporting Agencies
Detectives
Electricity
Explosives
Factors
Ferries
Gas
Hawkers and Peddlers
Innkeepers
Insurance
Licenses
Manufactures
Monopolies
Physicians and Surgeons
Pilots
Railroads
Seamen
Shipping
Steam
Telecommunications
Theaters and Shows
Towage
Turnpikes and Toll Roads
Urban Railroads
Warehousemen
Wharves

2. PROPERTY

NATURE, SUBJECTS, AND INCIDENTS OF OWNERSHIP IN GENERAL

Abandoned and Lost Property
Accession
Adjoining Landowners
Confusion of Goods
Improvements
Property

PARTICULAR SUBJECTS AND INCIDENTS OF OWNERSHIP

Animals
Annuities
Automobiles
Boundaries
Cemeteries
Common Lands
Copyrights and Intellectual Property
Crops
Fences
Fish
Fixtures
Franchises
Game
Good Will
Logs and Logging
Mines and Minerals
Navigable Waters
Party Walls
Patents
Public Lands
Trade Regulation
Waters and Water Courses
Woods and Forests

PARTICULAR CLASSES OF ESTATES OR INTERESTS IN PROPERTY

Charities
Condominium
Dower and Curtesy
Easements
Estates in Property
Joint Tenancy
Landlord and Tenant
Life Estates
Perpetuities
Powers
Remainders
Reversions
Tenancy in Common
Trusts

PARTICULAR MODES OF ACQUIRING OR TRANS-FERRING PROPERTY

Abstracts of Title
Adverse Possession
Alteration of Instruments
Assignments
Chattel Mortgages
Conversion
Dedication
Deeds
Descent and Distribution
Escheat
Fraudulent Conveyances

VIII

1—2

IX

1—3

5. CRIMES—Cont'd

False Pretenses
Fires
Forgery
Fornication
Homicide
Incest
Insurrection and Sedition
Kidnapping
Larceny
Lewdness
Malicious Mischief
Mayhem
Miscegenation
Neutrality Laws
Obscenity
Obstructing Justice
Perjury
Piracy
Prize Fighting
Prostitution
Rape
Receiving Stolen Goods
Rescue
Riot
Robbery
Sodomy
Suicide
Treason
Unlawful Assembly
Vagrancy

6. REMEDIES

REMEDIES BY ACT OR AGREEMENT OF PARTIES

Accord and Satisfaction
Arbitration
Submission of Controversy

REMEDIES BY POSSESSION OR NOTICE

Liens
Lis Pendens
Maritime Liens
Mechanics' Liens
Notice
Salvage

MEANS AND METHODS OF PROOF

Acknowledgment
Affidavits
Estoppel
Evidence
Oath
Records
Witnesses

CIVIL ACTIONS IN GENERAL

Action
Declaratory Judgment
Election of Remedies
Limitation of Actions
Parties
Set-Off and Counterclaim
Venue

PARTICULAR PROCEEDINGS IN CIVIL ACTIONS

Abatement and Revival
Appearance
Costs
Damages
Execution
Exemptions
Homestead
Judgment
Jury
Motions
Pleading
Process
Reference
Stipulations
Trial

PARTICULAR REMEDIES INCIDENT TO CIVIL ACTIONS

Arrest
Assistance, Writ of
Attachment
Bail
Deposits in Court
Garnishment
Injunction
Judicial Sales
Ne Exeat
Pretrial Procedure
Receivers
Recognizances
Sequestration
Undertakings

X

1—4

6. REMEDIES—Cont'd

PARTICULAR MODES OF REVIEW IN CIVIL ACTIONS

Appeal and Error
Audita Querela
Certiorari
Exceptions, Bill of
New Trial
Review

ACTIONS TO ESTABLISH OWNERSHIP OR RECOVER POSSESSION OF SPECIFIC PROPERTY

Detinue
Ejectment
Entry, Writ of
Interpleader
Possessory Warrant
Quieting Title
Real Actions
Replevin
Trespass to Try Title

FORMS OF ACTIONS FOR DEBTS OR DAMAGES

Account, Action on
Action on the Case
Assumpsit, Action of
Covenant, Action of
Debt, Action of

ACTIONS FOR PARTICULAR FORMS OR SPECIAL RELIEF

Account
Cancellation of Instruments
Debtor and Creditor
Divorce
Partition
Reformation of Instruments
Specific Performance

CIVIL PROCEEDINGS OTHER THAN ACTIONS

Habeas Corpus
Mandamus
Prohibition
Quo Warranto
Scire Facias
Supersedeas

SPECIAL CIVIL JURISDICTIONS AND PROCEDURE THEREIN

Admiralty
Bankruptcy
Equity
Federal Civil Procedure

PROCEEDINGS PECULIAR TO CRIMINAL CASES

Extradition and Detainers
Fines
Forfeitures
Grand Jury
Indictment and Information
Pardon and Parole
Penalties
Searches and Seizures

7. GOVERNMENT

POLITICAL BODIES AND DIVISIONS

Counties
District of Columbia
Municipal Corporations
States
Territories
Towns
United States

SYSTEMS AND SOURCES OF LAW

Administrative Law and Procedure
Common Law
Constitutional Law
International Law
Parliamentary Law
Statutes
Treaties

LEGISLATIVE AND EXECUTIVE POWERS AND FUNCTIONS

Bounties
Census
Customs Duties
Drains
Eminent Domain
Highways
Inspection
Internal Revenue
Levees and Flood Control

XI

1—5

OUTLINE OF THE LAW

7. GOVERNMENT—Cont'd

LEGISLATIVE AND EXECUTIVE POWERS AND FUNCTIONS—Cont'd

Pensions
Post Office
Private Roads
Public Contracts
Public Utilities
Schools
Securities Regulation
Social Security and Public Welfare
Taxation
Weights and Measures
Zoning and Planning

JUDICIAL POWERS AND FUNCTIONS, AND COURTS AND THEIR OFFICERS

Amicus Curiae
Clerks of Courts
Contempt
Court Commissioners
Courts
Federal Courts
Judges
Justices of the Peace
Removal of Cases
Reports
United States Magistrates

CIVIL SERVICE, OFFICERS, AND INSTITUTIONS

Ambassadors and Consuls
Asylums
Attorney General
Coroners
District and Prosecuting Attorneys
Elections
Hospitals
Newspapers
Notaries
Officers and Public Employees
Prisons
Reformatories
Registers of Deeds
Sheriffs and Constables
United States Marshals

MILITARY AND NAVAL SERVICE AND WAR

Armed Services
Military Justice
Militia
War and National Emergency

1—6

DIGEST TOPICS

See, also, Outline of the Law by Seven Main Divisions of Law, Page VII

Abandoned and Lost
  Property
Abatement and Revival
Abduction
Abortion and Birth Control
Absentees
Abstracts of Title
Accession
Accord and Satisfaction
Account
Account, Action on
Account Stated
Accountants
Acknowledgment
Action
Action on the Case
Adjoining Landowners
Administrative Law and
  Procedure
Admiralty
Adoption
Adulteration
Adultery
Adverse Possession
Affidavits
Affray
Agriculture
Aliens
Alteration of Instruments
Ambassadors and Consuls
Amicus Curiae
Animals
Annuities
Appeal and Error
Appearance
Arbitration
Armed Services
Arrest
Arson
Assault and Battery
Assignments
Assistance, Writ of
Associations
Assumpsit, Action of
Asylums
Attachment

Attorney and Client
Attorney General
Auctions and Auctioneers
Audita Querela
Automobiles
Aviation
Bail
Bailment
Bankruptcy
Banks and Banking
Beneficial Associations
Bigamy
Bills and Notes
Blasphemy
Bonds
Boundaries
Bounties
Breach of Marriage Promise
Breach of the Peace
Bribery
Bridges
Brokers
Building and Loan
  Associations
Burglary
Canals
Cancellation of Instruments
Carriers
Cemeteries
Census
Certiorari
Champerty and Maintenance
Charities
Chattel Mortgages
Chemical Dependents
Children Out-of-Wedlock
Citizens
Civil Rights
Clerks of Courts
Clubs
Colleges and Universities
Collision
Commerce
Common Lands
Common Law
Common Scold

Compounding Offenses
Compromise and Settlement
Condominium
Confusion of Goods
Conspiracy
Constitutional Law
Consumer Credit
Consumer Protection
Contempt
Contracts
Contribution
Conversion
Convicts
Copyrights and Intellectual
  Property
Coroners
Corporations
Costs
Counterfeiting
Counties
Court Commissioners
Courts
Covenant, Action of
Covenants
Credit Reporting Agencies
Criminal Law
Crops
Customs and Usages
Customs Duties
Damages
Dead Bodies
Death
Debt, Action of
Debtor and Creditor
Declaratory Judgment
Dedication
Deeds
Deposits and Escrows
Deposits in Court
Descent and Distribution
Detectives
Detinue
Disorderly Conduct
Disorderly House
District and Prosecuting
  Attorneys

DIGEST TOPICS

Patents
Paupers
Payment
Penalties
Pensions
Perjury
Perpetuities
Physicians and Surgeons
Pilots
Piracy
Pleading
Pledges
Poisons
Possessory Warrant
Post Office
Powers
Pretrial Procedure
Principal and Agent
Principal and Surety
Prisons
Private Roads
Prize Fighting
Process
Products Liability
Prohibition
Property
Prostitution
Public Contracts
Public Lands
Public Utilities
Quieting Title
Quo Warranto
Railroads
Rape
Real Actions
Receivers
Receiving Stolen Goods
Recognizances
Records
Reference
Reformation of Instruments
Reformatories
Registers of Deeds

Release
Religious Societies
Remainders
Removal of Cases
Replevin
Reports
Rescue
Reversions
Review
Rewards
Riot
Robbery
Sales
Salvage
Schools
Scire Facias
Seals
Seamen
Searches and Seizures
Secured Transactions
Securities Regulation
Seduction
Sequestration
Set-Off and Counterclaim
Sheriffs and Constables
Shipping
Signatures
Slaves
Social Security and Public
  Welfare
Sodomy
Specific Performance
Spendthrifts
States
Statutes
Steam
Stipulations
Submission of Controversy
Subrogation
Subscriptions
Suicide
Sunday

Supersedeas
Taxation
Telecommunications
Tenancy in Common
Tender
Territories
Theaters and Shows
Time
Torts
Towage
Towns
Trade Regulation
Treason
Treaties
Trespass
Trepass to Try Title
Trial
Trover and Conversion
Trusts
Turnpikes and Toll Roads
Undertakings
United States
United States Magistrates
United States Marshals
Unlawful Assembly
Urban Railroads
Usury
Vagrancy
Vendor and Purchaser
Venue
War and National Emergency
Warehousemen
Waste
Waters and Water Courses
Weapons
Weights and Measures
Wharves
Wills
Witnesses
Woods and Forests
Workers' Compensation
Zoning and Planning

ALIENS

SUBJECTS INCLUDED

Persons of foreign allegiance; their rights and disabilities in general

Exclusion or expulsion from the country

Regulation and restriction of immigration

Admission to citizenship

SUBJECTS EXCLUDED AND COVERED BY OTHER TOPICS

Alien enemies, see WAR AND NATIONAL EMERGENCY

Domicile, application of law of, see titles of particular subjects involved

Escheat proceedings, see ESCHEAT

Federal courts, jurisdiction and venue, see FEDERAL COURTS

Particular kinds of property or particular remedies, rights and liabilities in respect of, see MINES AND MINERALS, SHIPPING, PATENTS, COPYRIGHTS AND INTELLECTUAL PROPERTY, TRADE REGULATION and other specific topics

Workmen's compensation acts, rights under, see WORKERS' COMPENSATION

Wrongful death, right of action for, see DEATH

For detailed references to other topics, see Descriptive-Word Index

---

Analysis

---

to two-year home residence requirement before applying for permanent residence in United States. Immigration and Nationality Act, § 212(e) as amended 8 U.S.C.A. § 1182(e).
Nayak v. Vance, 463 F.Supp. 244.

Constitutional rights of exchange alien's son who was born in United States would not be violated if exchange alien was required to return to native country for two years prior to applying for permanent residence in United States. Immigration and Nationality Act, § 212(e) as amended 8 U.S.C.A. § 1182(e).
Nayak v. Vance, 463 F.Supp. 244.

⬿53.10(3). Hardship cases; refugees and displaced persons.

U.S. 1981. In respect to provision of the Immigration and Nationality Act stating that the Attorney General may suspend deportation and adjust the status of an otherwise deportable alien who has been present in the United States for at least seven years, has good moral character, and is a person whose deportation would result in extreme hardship to himself or certain of his relatives, the Attorney General and his delegates have the authority to construe "extreme hardship" narrowly should they deem it wise to do so; such a narrow interpretation is consistent with the "extreme hardship" language, which itself indicates the exceptional nature of the suspension remedy. Immigration and Nationality Act, § 244 as amended 8 U.S.C.A. § 1254.
Immigration and Naturalization Service v. Jong Ha Wang, 101 S.Ct. 1027, 450 U.S. 139, 67 L.Ed.2d 123, rehearing denied 101 S.Ct. 2027.

C.A.1 1983. Immigration and Naturalization Service has considerable discretion to decide what constitutes "extreme hardship" under statute which allows suspension of deportation for extreme hardship, and to decide whether or not to reopen. Immigration and Nationality Act, § 244(a)(1), 8 U.S.C.A. § 1254(a)(1).
Luna v. I.N.S., 709 F.2d 126.

C.A.1 1983. Determination of "extreme hardship" within meaning of statute which allows suspension of deportation is committed to sound discretion of Attorney General. Immigration and Nationality Act, § 244(a)(1), 8 U.S.C.A. § 1254(a)(1).
Antoine-Dorcelli v. I.N.S., 703 F.2d 19.

Although Board of Immigration Appeals may construe extreme hardship under suspension of deportation statute narrowly, Board's failure to consider, along with economic hardships, that deportation would separate Haitian national from family that she had considered herself, and had been considered, a member of for 30 years was abuse of discretion, even though national was not related to family.

Immigration and Nationality Act, § 244(a)(1), 8 U.S.C.A. § 1254(a)(1).
Antoine-Dorcelli v. I.N.S., 703 F.2d 19.

C.A.1 1981. Fact that petitioner seeking suspension of deportation would suffer economic hardship by being deported and was eligible for suspension of deportation did not require exercise of discretion by Board of Immigration Appeals in petitioner's favor. Immigration and Nationality Act, §§ 241(a)(2), 244(a)(1), 8 U.S.C.A. §§ 1251(a)(2), 1254(a)(1).
Vaughn v. Immigration and Naturalization Service, 643 F.2d 35.

In view of fact that alien had chosen to rely on public assistance for her entire support although she was relatively young woman in good health, fact that she satisfied requirement of seven years' presence only by virtue of her two separate abuses of the privilege of voluntary departure and fact that her children, on whom she relied to establish hardship, were born while she was in this country illegally militated against suspension of deportation, and Board of Immigration Appeals was not shown to have abused its discretion in denying suspension of deportation. Immigration and Nationality Act, §§ 241(a)(2), 244(a)(1), 8 U.S.C.A. §§ 1251(a)(2), 1254(a)(1).
Vaughn v. Immigration and Naturalization Service, 643 F.2d 35.

C.A.1 1977. Board of Immigration Appeals did not abuse its discretion in ruling that petitioner, a Philippine national who had entered country as a nonimmigrant exchange visitor, did not make a sufficient showing of extreme hardship so as to avoid deportation. Immigration and Nationality Act, §§ 212(e), 244, 244(a)(1), (f), 8 U.S.C.A. §§ 1182(e), 1254, 1254(a)(1), (f).
Bonsukan v. U. S. Immigration and Naturalization Service, 554 F.2d 2, certiorari denied 98 S.Ct. 118, 434 U.S. 833, 54 L.Ed.2d 93.

Board of immigration appeals did not abuse its discretion in refusing to credit claim of Philippine national that she would be subject to political persecution if deported to the Philippines. Immigration and Nationality Act, § 106(a)(4), 8 U.S.C.A. § 1105a(a)(4); 28 U.S.C.A. § 1927.
Bonsukan v. U. S. Immigration and Naturalization Service, 554 F.2d 2, certiorari denied 98 S.Ct. 118, 434 U.S. 833, 54 L.Ed.2d 93.

C.A.2 1980. Although alien seeking to avoid deportation and to have her status adjusted to that of alien lawfully admitted for permanent residence did show that her child would suffer some dislocation and disruption if he accompanied his mother to St. Vincent, such was not sufficient to establish "extreme hardship" warranting suspension of deporta-

see United States Code Annotated

tion. Immigration and Nationality Act, § 244 as amended 8 U.S.C.A. § 1254.

> Brathwaite v. Immigration and Naturalization Service, 633 F.2d 657.

C.A.2 1980. Twenty-six-year-old married son did not qualify as a "child" nor could his father be deemed a "parent" under section permitting discretionary relief from deportation upon a demonstration that petitioner's expulsion will result in extreme hardship to certain immediate family relations, spouse, parent or child who are citizens or resident aliens, and any hardship visited upon son by virtue of his father's expulsion from the United States was not cognizable for this purpose. Immigration and Nationality Act, §§ 101(b)(1, 2), 212(h), 244, 244(a)(1), 8 U.S.C.A. §§ 1101(b)(1, 2), 1182(h), 1254, 1254(a)(1).

> Chiaramonte v. Immigration and Naturalization Service, 626 F.2d 1093.

C.A.2 1976. Where deportable alien, seeking change of status to that of a lawful permanent resident on ground that deportation would cause extreme hardship to her spouse, did not even know the present whereabouts of her citizen-husband, she could not properly claim that her deportation would cause him extreme hardship. Immigration and Nationality Act, § 244(a)(1), 8 U.S.C.A. § 1254(a)(1).

> Acevedo v. Immigration and Naturalization Service, 538 F.2d 918.

C.A.2 1976. Although in giving its views on whether nation of prospective deportation engages in persecution on account of race, religion, or political opinion, the Department of State should not apply such knowledge to the particular case, absent the alien's consent, it would be helpful if the Immigration and Naturalization Service would furnish the Department with the names of aliens whose stay applications have been denied and if the Department would endeavor to follow up on what occurred so as to make the Department's analysis of conditions in various countries current and realistic. Immigration and Nationality Act, § 243(h), 8 U.S.C.A. § 1253(h).

> Zamora v. Immigration and Naturalization Service, 534 F.2d 1055.

C.A.3 1983. The "well founded fear" standard for determining claims of political asylum equates with the "clear probability of persecution" standard formerly used and Board of Immigration Appeals did not err in requiring alien to demonstrate a clear probability of persecution. Immigration and Nationality Act, § 243(h), as amended, 8 U.S.C.A. § 1253(h).

> Marroquin-Manriquez v. I.N.S., 699 F.2d 129.

C.A.3 1982. Generalized, undocumented fears of persecution or political upheaval which affect a country's general populace are insufficient bases for withholding deportation.

Immigration and Nationality Act, § 243(h) as amended 8 U.S.C.A. § 1253(h).

> Rejaie v. I. N. S., 691 F.2d 139.

In considering Iranian's request for political asylum, Board of Immigration Appeals properly required him to prove a clear probability of persecution, a formulation that the Immigration and Naturalization Service equated with a well-founded fear of persecution. Immigration and Nationality Act, § 243(h) as amended 8 U.S.C.A. § 1253(h).

> Rejaie v. I. N. S., 691 F.2d 139.

Where petitioner, an Iranian who came to this country in 1978 to attend school for ten months, did not demonstrate by objective evidence a realistic likelihood that he would be persecuted in his native land, the Board of Immigration Appeals properly denied request for political asylum and did not err in denying motions to reopen deportation proceedings. Immigration and Nationality Act, § 243(h) as amended 8 U.S.C.A. § 1253(h).

> Rejaie v. I. N. S., 691 F.2d 139.

C.A.3 1980. Language of suspension provision evinces a legislative purpose to protect immediate members of an alien family from hardship attending deportation. Immigration and Nationality Act, § 244(a), 8 U.S.C.A. § 1254(a).

> Tovar v. Immigration and Naturalization Service, 612 F.2d 794.

Suspension provision permits Immigration and Naturalization Service to suspend deportation of an illegal alien after evaluating hardship that would result to a spouse, parent or child, if resulting hardship would be extreme. Immigration and Nationality Act, § 244(a), 8 U.S.C.A. § 1254(a).

> Tovar v. Immigration and Naturalization Service, 612 F.2d 794.

Hardship to grandchild from deportation of alien should have been considered in determining whether alien was eligible for stay of deportation where alien's relationship to grandchild closely resembled that of a parent to a child. Immigration and Nationality Act, § 244(a), 8 U.S.C.A. § 1254(a).

> Tovar v. Immigration and Naturalization Service, 612 F.2d 794.

Same privilege that suspension provision affords to the nuclear family should be extended to a grandmother-headed family. Immigration and Nationality Act, § 244(a), 8 U.S.C.A. § 1254(a).

> Tovar v. Immigration and Naturalization Service, 612 F.2d 794.

Immigration and Naturalization Service should make a fresh determination with knowledge that hardship to alien's grandchild was legally relevant to deportation, where less

For cited U.S.C.A. sections and legislative history

of deportation, including noneconomic hardship to aliens themselves or to their American-born children, the asserted hardship to parents of one of aliens, and failure to consider cumulatively hardship factors pertaining to each member of statutory class, amounted to a denial of consideration which aliens were entitled to have Board give to their claims and was an abuse of discretion. Immigration and Nationality Act, § 244(a)(1), 8 U.S.C.A. § 1254(a)(1).

Ramos v. I.N.S., 695 F.2d 181.

C.A.5 1982. Immigration and Nationality Act's forgiveness provision, forgiving fraud in obtaining an immigration visa to those who now have the requisite family ties in the United States, does not apply to a fraudulent marriage which was used to avoid the requirement of obtaining a labor certificate. Immigration and Nationality Act, §§ 212(a)(14), 241(f), 8 U.S.C.A. §§ 1182(a)(14), 1251(f).

Morales-Cruz v. U. S., 666 F.2d 289.

Purpose of the Immigration and Nationality Act's forgiveness provision is to protect family interests when the sole ground for deportability is the fraudulent submission of documents; it was not meant to forgive fraudulent documentation used to circumvent policies forbidding admission, for example, to those with criminal records or mental illnesses, nor to circumvent the important policy established by the labor certification requirement. Immigration and Nationality Act, §§ 212(a)(14), 241(f), 8 U.S.C.A. §§ 1182(a)(14), 1251(f).

Morales-Cruz v. U. S., 666 F.2d 289.

C.A.5 1979. Economic detriment, including loss of investment, does not compel a finding of "extreme hardship" for purposes of warranting suspension of deportation. Immigration and Nationality Act, § 244(a)(1), 8 U.S.C.A. § 1254(a)(1).

Chokloikaew v. Immigration and Naturalization Service, 601 F.2d 216.

There was no abuse of discretion in denying suspension of deportation to alien on grounds that he had significant investment in business which he would be forced to liquidate if deported, that he had been in the United States nearly his entire adult life, a period in excess of ten years, and that he faced possible imprisonment upon return to Thailand for having violated Thai military conscription law, where he had been granted ample time to arrange sale of business assets, had been without valid, unexpired visa for all but first four years of time in United States, had lived in Thailand, where his family presently lived, until he was 21, and draft violation problems were essentially self-imposed. Immigration

and Nationality Act, §§ 241(a)(2), 244(a)(1), 8 U.S.C.A. §§ 1251(a)(2), 1254(a)(1).

Chokloikaew v. Immigration and Naturalization Service, 601 F.2d 216.

C.A.5 1978. Burden of proving that deportation will lead to persecution rests with the alien. Immigration and Nationality Act, § 243(h), 8 U.S.C.A. § 1253(h).

Fleurinor v. Immigration and Naturalization Service, 585 F.2d 129.

Legal options open to deportable aliens who seek to remain in the United States are to apply for asylum with the district director having jurisdiction over their place of residence or the port of entry or to petition for withholding of deportation. Immigration and Nationality Act, § 243(h), 8 U.S.C.A. § 1253(h).

Fleurinor v. Immigration and Naturalization Service, 585 F.2d 129.

A "feared persecution" claim under the section of the Immigration and Nationality Act relating to petitions for withholding of deportation is entirely different from an "asylum claim" in that the former is part and parcel of the deportation proceeding while an asylum claim can obviate the need for any deportation proceeding. Immigration and Nationality Act, § 243(h), 8 U.S.C.A. § 1253(h).

Fleurinor v. Immigration and Naturalization Service, 585 F.2d 129.

C.A.7 1983. Immigration and Naturalization Service must consider all relevant factors in a proceeding to suspend deportation on ground of extreme hardship. Immigration and Nationality Act, § 244, 8 U.S.C.A. § 1254.

Diaz-Salazar v. I.N.S., 700 F.2d 1156, certiorari denied 103 S.Ct. 3112.

It was not abuse of discretion to deny motion to reopen deportation order, on ground of extreme hardship, notwithstanding that petitioner, a Mexican illegally in the country, had an American born wife and two children under age of three and had a good job and that due to lack of formal education and current economic conditions in Mexico he would have a difficult time finding similar employment there. Immigration and Nationality Act, § 244, 8 U.S.C.A. § 1254.

Diaz-Salazar v. I.N.S., 700 F.2d 1156, certiorari denied 103 S.Ct. 3112.

By itself, economic hardship does not constitute "extreme hardship" for purpose of suspending deportation. Immigration and Nationality Act, § 244, 8 U.S.C.A. § 1254.

Diaz-Salazar v. I.N.S., 700 F.2d 1156, certiorari denied 103 S.Ct. 3112.

Economic conditions in an alien's homeland are not a dispositive factor in a proceeding to suspend deportation on ground of ex-

For cited U.S.C.A. sections and legislative history

West's
FEDERAL PRACTICE
DIGEST 3d

Vol. 2

Adoption — Armed Services

1985
Cumulative Annual Pocket Part

THE WEST DIGEST TOPIC NUMBERS WHICH CAN BE
USED FOR WESTLAW SEARCHES ARE LISTED ON
PAGE III OF THIS POCKET PART.

*All Federal Case Law of
The Modern Era*

**Up-Dated Weekly by West's
Federal Reporter Advance Sheets**

The ☞ symbol, WEST's, and Federal Practice Digest are registered trademarks of West
Publishing Co.   Registered in U.S. Patent and Trademark Office.

ST. PAUL, MINN.
WEST PUBLISHING CO.

Closing with Cases Reported in

COPYRIGHT © 1983, 1984 WEST PUBLISHING CO.

_____

COPYRIGHT © 1985
By
WEST PUBLISHING CO.

2 West's Fed.Pract.Dig.3d
1985 P.P.

§§ 1101(a)(15)(J), 1182(e).—Sheku-Kamara v. Karn, 581 F.Supp. 582.

☞53.10(3). Hardship cases; refugees and displaced persons.

U.S. 1984. The "continuous physical presence" requirement in statute authorizing suspension of deportation is not to be construed as requiring yet a further assessment of hardship. Immigration and Nationality Act, §§ 101(a)(13), 244(a)(1), as amended, 8 U.S.C.A. §§ 1101(a)(13), 1254(a)(1).—I.N.S. v. Phinpathya, 104 S.Ct. 584.

C.A.1 1984. That an alien and alien's citizen children may find economic or educational circumstances more difficult outside United States does not require Immigration and Naturalization Service to find "extreme hardship," within meaning of statute providing that Attorney General may suspend deportation if it would result in extreme hardship. Immigration and Nationality Act, § 244(a)(1), 8 U.S.C.A. § 1254 (a)(1).—Holley v. I.N.S., 727 F.2d 189.

C.A.1 1983. Claims of loss of job, home, and other assets, deprivation of educational opportunities for children, and difficulty of children in adjusting to life in another country, along with deprivation for therapy for depression caused by deportation and his wife's apparent infidelity did not show extreme hardship on the part of alien seeking suspension of deportation. Immigration and Nationality Act, § 244(a)(1), 8 U.S.C.A. § 1254(a)(1).—Moore v. I.N.S., 715 F.2d 13.

C.A.2 1974. Reid v. Immigration and Naturalization Service, 492 F.2d 251, affirmed 95 S.Ct. 1164, 420 U.S. 619, 43 L.Ed.2d 501.

C.A.3 1985. Board of Immigration Appeals, in denying applications for asylum, did not abuse its discretion in equating statutory of "well-founded fear" of persecution with a "clear probability," "good reason," or "realistic likelihood," as opposed to a "reasonable possibility" standard. Immigration and Nationality Act, §§ 208, 243(h), as amended, 8 U.S.C.A. §§ 1158, 1253(h).—Sankar v. I.N.S., 757 F.2d 532.

C.A.3 1983. Marroquin-Manriquez v. I.N.S., 699 F.2d 129, certiorari denied 104 S.Ct. 3553.

C.A.5 1984. Adverse economic impact of deportation alone is insufficient to justify finding of extreme hardship warranting suspension of deportation. Immigration and Nationality Act, § 244, as amended, 8 U.S.C.A. § 1254.—Zamora-Garcia v. U.S. Dept. of Justice I.N.S., 737 F.2d 488.

In context of determining issue of whether deportation would impose an extreme hardship upon alien, it is unrealistic as well as unjust to adopt such a rigid view of family unit as to find that only blood relations may constitute "family." Immigration and Nationality Act, § 244, as amended, 8 U.S.C.A. § 1254.—Id.

Board of Immigration Appeals need not consider hardship to unrelated children, cared for over a period of 14 years by alien employed by children's parents, posed by possibility of alien's deportation when determining issue of whether deportation would cause extreme hardship to alien. Immigration and Nationality Act, § 244, as amended, 8 U.S.C.A. § 1254.—Id.

When determining whether deportation of alien would cause extreme hardship to alien, thus warranting suspension of deportation, Board of Immigration Appeals must consider hardship to alien posed by possibility of separation from unrelated family with which alien had lived and which had employed her for 14 years. Immigration and Nationality Act, § 244, as amended, 8 U.S.C.A. § 1254.—Id.

C.A.6 1985. Citizen of Iraq whose education in United States was being paid for by Iraqi government, who had never opposed Iraqi government, and who had never been mistreated or threatened with mistreatment by that government failed to establish clear probability of persecution in support of claim for withholding of deportation, or well-founded fear of persecution in support of petition for asylum, where there was no showing that he would be singled out by Iraqi government for persecution upon return to Iraq. Immigration and Nationality Act, §§ 208, 243(h), as amended, 8 U.S.C.A. §§ 1158, 1253(h).—Moosa v. I.N.S., 760 F.2d 715.

C.A.6 1984. Petitioners, citizens of Iraq who remained beyond the authorized limits of their stay, failed to establish that the Board of Immigration Appeals abused its discretion in denying their applications for asylum. Immigration and Nationality Act, §§ 208, 243(h), as amended, 8 U.S.C.A. §§ 1158, 1253(h).—Youkhanna v. I.N.S., 749 F.2d 360.

C.A.6 1984. Clear probability of persecution test for avoiding deportation requires at least that an alien show that it is more likely than not that he as an individual will be subject to persecution if forced to return to his native land. Immigration and Nationality Act, § 243(h), as amended, 8 U.S.C.A. § 1253(h).—Dally v. I.N.S., 744 F.2d 1191.

A clear probability of persecution so as to avoid deportation is more than a matter of alien's own conjecture; an alien must show that he will be singled out for persecution or some other special circumstances before relief can be granted. Immigration and Nationality Act, § 243(h), as amended, 8 U.S.C.A. § 1253(h).—Id.

C.A.6 1984. Requests by alien for asylum made after institution of deportation proceedings are also to be considered as requests for withholding exclusion or deportation pursuant to the Immigration and Nationality Act. Immigration and Nationality Act, §§ 208, 241(a)(2), 243(h), as amended, 8 U.S.C.A. §§ 1158, 1251(a)(2), 1253(h).—Nasser v. I.N.S., 744 F.2d 542.

C.A.7 1984. Alien is required to show clear probability of persecution to be entitled to withholding of deportation. Immigration and Nationality Act, § 243(h), as amended, 8 U.S.C.A. § 1253(h).—Carvajal-Munoz v. I.N.S., 743 F.2d 562.

Applicant for asylum must present specific facts establishing that he or she has actually been victim of persecution or has some other good reason to fear that he or she will be singled out for persecution on account of race, religion, nationality, membership in a particular social group, or political opinion. Immigration and Nationality Act, § 208, as amended, 8 U.S.C.A. § 1158.—Id.

C.A.8 1984. Bureau of Immigration Appeals may construe the extreme hardship which would warrant suspension of deportation narrowly but the BIA must consider all factors relevant to the hardship determination. Immigration and Nationality Act, § 244(a)(1), 8 U.S.C.A. § 1254(a)(1).—Carrete-Michel v. I.N.S., 749 F.2d 490.

It was error for Board of Immigration Appeals to characterize as mere "economic hardship" alien's claim that he would be completely unable to find work in Mexico if suspension of deportation were not granted where alien was relatively poor, uneducated, unskilled laborer who had been in the United States for 11 years and who had nine children living in the country. Immigration and Nationality Act, § 244(a)(1), 8 U.S.C.A. § 1254(a)(1).—Id.

Economic hardship, by itself, could not be the basis for suspending deportation. Immigration and Nationality Act, § 244(a)(1), 8 U.S.C.A. § 1254(a)(1).—Id.

Board of Immigration Appeals could not consider the effect of deportation on alien's Mexican citizen spouse and children. Immigration and Nationality Act, § 244(a)(1), 8 U.S.C.A. § 1254(a)(1).—Id.

In determining whether alien seeking suspension of deportation was faced with extreme hardship, Board of Immigration Appeals gave inadequate consideration to personal and emotional hardship to alien due to the division of his family and his inability to visit his brother and cousins in this country. Immigration and Nationality Act, § 244(a)(1), 8 U.S.C.A. § 1254(a)(1).—Id.

Board of Immigration Appeals abused its discretion in determining that, even if alien established that he would suffer extreme hardship if deported, suspension of deportation was warranted because he deceived the government and gave mendacious testimony to the immigration judge; those issues went to whether he established good moral character and BIA was required to make the latter determination. Immigration and Nationality Act, § 244(a)(1), 8 U.S.C.A. § 1254(a)(1).—Id.

C.A.8 1983. Resident alien who was found to be deportable on grounds that he had been convicted of a crime involving moral turpitude and had been sentenced to a term of confinement of one year or more sufficiently apprised Board of Immigration Appeals of his claims for hardship relief where he argued to BIA that his deportation would result in de facto deportation of his wife and daughter, American citizens, and thus on remand BIA had to review and evaluate alien's hardship claims. Immigration and Nationality Act, §§ 212(c), 244(a, e), as amended 8 U.S.C.A. §§ 1182(c), 1254(a, e).—Okoroha v. I.N.S., 715 F.2d 380.

C.A.9 1985. Board of Immigration Appeals has discretion to construe extreme hardship narrowly, but exercise of its discretion must not be arbitrary, irrational, or contrary to law. Immigration and Nationality Act, § 244(a)(1), 8 U.S.C.A. § 1254(a)(1).—Saldana v. I.N.S., 762 F.2d 824.

Fact that alien married permanent resident when both were aware of possibility of his deportation should not have been considered in alien's claim that deportation would cause extreme hardship to his wife and their step-children in absence of evidence that marriage was a sham or fraudulent from its inception. Immigration and Nationality Act, § 244(a), 8 U.S.C.A. § 1254(a).—Id.

C.A.9 1985. Withholding of deportation is no longer discretionary; alien has a right to the withholding of deportation if he presents sufficient evidence to show a likelihood of persecution. Immigration and Nationality Act, § 243(h), 8 U.S.C.A. § 1253(h).—Duran v. I.N.S., 756 F.2d 1338.

In moving to reopen to apply for suspension of deportation, alien must present new evidence and make a prima facie showing of continuous presence in the United States for seven years, of good moral character, and that deportation would cause extreme hardship to the alien or to alien's family members who are United States citizens or permanent residents. Immigration and Nationality Act, § 244(a)(1), as amended, 8 U.S.C.A. § 1254(a)(1).—Id.

C.A.9 1985. In order to be eligible for asylum, alien must meet statutory definition of refugee. Immigration and Nationality Act, §§ 101(a)(42)(A), 208(a), as amended, 8 U.S.C.A. §§ 1101(a)(42)(A), 1158(a).—Espinoza-Martinez v. I.N.S., 754 F.2d 1536.

Decision whether or not to grant alien an application for asylum, once alien has met refugee definition, rests in discretion of Attorney General. Immigration and Nationality Act, §§ 101(a)(42)(A), 208(a), as amended, 8 U.S.C.A. §§ 1101(a)(42)(A), 1158(a).—Id.

Clear probability standard for determining alien's eligibility for withholding of deportation means that it is more likely than not that alien would be subject to persecution if returned to his country. Immigration and Nationality Act, § 243(h), as amended, 8 U.S.C.A. § 1253(h).—Id.

C.A.9 1984. Alien must show clear probability of persecution to invoke statutory bar to deportation. Immigration and Nationality Act, §§ 208(a),

243(h), as amended, 8 U.S.C.A. §§ 1158(a), 1253(h).—Bolanos-Hernandez v. I.N.S., 749 F.2d 1316.

Evaluation of whether alien has well-founded fear of political persecution, and thus is eligible for discretionary grant of asylum, includes consideration of applicant's state of mind as well as evaluation of conditions in country of origin, its laws, and experiences of others. Immigration and Nationality Act, § 208(a), as amended, 8 U.S.C.A. § 1158(a).—Id.

In order to invoke statutory bar to deportation on ground that alien's life or freedom would be threatened on account of political opinion, alien must show likelihood of persecution, persecution by government or by group which government is unable to control, persecution resulting from alien's political beliefs, and that alien is not danger or security risk to United States. Immigration and Nationality Act, § 243(h), as amended, 8 U.S.C.A. § 1253(h).—Id.

In denying alien's application for withholding of deportation and political asylum, Board of Immigration Appeals erred in treating specific threat against alien's life as representative of general conditions in alien's home country of El Salvador; significance of specific threat to alien's life or freedom is not lessened by fact that the alien resides in a country where lives and freedom of a large number of persons are threatened. Immigration and Nationality Act, § 243(h), as amended, 8 U.S.C.A. § 1253(h).—Id.

Mere fact that threat was made may not be sufficient to establish clear probability of persecution to justify invocation of statutory bar to deportation; whether it is more likely than not that alien would be subject to persecution may depend on whether threat is a serious one—whether there is reason to take the threat seriously. Immigration and Nationality Act, § 243(h), as amended, 8 U.S.C.A. § 1253(h).—Id.

Under statutory bar to deportation available to aliens who fear persecution in their native country for their political opinions, remaining neutral is no less political decision than is choosing to affiliate with particular political faction, and thus alien who chose to remain neutral could claim benefits of the bar. Immigration and Nationality Act, § 243(h), as amended, 8 U.S.C.A. § 1253(h).—Id.

Reasons underlying individual's political choice are of no significance for purposes of withholding deportation and granting political asylum and government may not inquire into them. Immigration and Nationality Act, §§ 208(a), 243(h), as amended, 8 U.S.C.A. §§ 1158(a), 1253(h).—Id.

Native of El Salvador whose life was threatened by guerrillas after refusing to join them was entitled to benefit of statute barring deportation upon showing of probability of political persecution. Immigration and Nationality Act, § 243(h), as amended, 8 U.S.C.A. § 1253(h).—Id.

C.A.9 1984. Board of Immigration Appeals must consider all relevant factors in determining whether alien established extreme hardship and BIA must demonstrate that it has done so. Immigration and Nationality Act, § 244(a)(1), as amended, 8 U.S.C.A. § 1254(a)(1).—Patel v. I.N.S., 741 F.2d 1134.

Evidence that alien was under treatment for mild to moderate hypertension and that continued treatment was recommended did not show extreme hardship resulting from deportation so as to warrant adjustment of status. Immigration and Nationality Act, § 244(a)(1), as amended, 8 U.S.C.A. § 1254(a)(1).—Id.

C.A.9 1984. In order to obtain withholding of deportation, an alien must prove: a likelihood of persecution, i.e., a threat to life or freedom, persecution by government or by a group which government is unable to control; persecution resulting from alien's political beliefs; and that alien is not a danger or security risk to the United States. Immigration and Nationality Act, § 243(h), as amended, 8 U.S.C.A. § 1253(h).— Zepeda-Melendez v. I.N.S., 741 F.2d 285.

Contentions of El Salvadorian alien that, if deported, he would be persecuted both by El Salvadorian government and local guerillas because his mother owned a house in a strategic location and because he himself was a male of military age who had sworn allegiance to neither faction were insufficient to demonstrate a clear probability of persecution to require withholding of deportation. Immigration and Nationality Act, § 243(h), as amended, 8 U.S.C.A. § 1253(h).—Id.

C.A.9 1984. Board of Immigration Appeals, in denying application for suspension of deportation, failed to consider all relevant factors presented by Salvadorian on issue of hardship, including ability to find work in El Salvador, and friendships and attachments she had formed during her 15 years in this country, and BIA abused its discretion in denying her hardship claim. Immigration and Nationality Act, § 244(a), as amended, 8 U.S.C.A. § 1254(a).—Zavala-Bonilla v. I.N.S., 730 F.2d 562.

C.A.9 1984. Conclusion of Board of Immigrations appeal that citizen of El Salvador had failed to make a prima facie showing that he was eligible for asylum based on political persecution was not an abuse of discretion. Immigration and Nationality Act, § 243(h), 8 U.S.C.A. § 1253(h).— Chavez v. I.N.S., 723 F.2d 1431.

There must be some special circumstances present before political asylum can be granted.— Id.

Tragic and widespread danger of violence affecting all Salvadorians was not "persecution" sufficient to support showing required for political asylum. Immigration and Nationality Act, § 243(h), 8 U.S.C.A. § 1253(h).—Id.

C.A.9 1981. Phinpathya v. Immigration and Naturalization Service, 673 F.2d 1013, certiorari granted 103 S.Ct. 291, 459 U.S. 965, 74 L.Ed.2d 275, reversed 104 S.Ct. 584, 464 U.S. 183, 78 L.Ed.2d 401, on remand 758 F.2d 656.

C.A.11 1984. Asylum applicant's assertions that conditions had changed in Nicaragua and that advisory opinion of the State Department to the contrary was faulty and outdated did not provide any basis for relief from dismissal by the Board of Immigration Appeals of appeal from determination that applicant had failed to establish reasonable fear of persecution if returned to Nicaragua. Immigration and Nationality Act, § 208, as amended, 8 U.S.C.A. § 1158.—Chavarria v. U.S. Dept. of Justice, 722 F.2d 666.

Applicant for withholding of deportation must establish that he specifically will be subject to persecution in event of deportation. Immigration and Nationality Act, §§ 208, 243(h), (h)(1), as amended, 8 U.S.C.A. §§ 1158, 1253(h), (h)(1).—Id.

C.A.Fla. 1984. Refugee Act does not create an entitlement to asylum, and carries with it no guarantee of securing the substantive relief sought, and thus the grant of asylum does not create interest protected by due process clause. Immigration and Nationality Act, § 208(a), as amended, 8 U.S.C.A. § 1158(a); U.S.C.A. Const. Amends. 5, 14.—Jean v. Nelson, 727 F.2d 957, rehearing denied 733 F.2d 908.

Notice of opportunity of alien to apply for asylum before district director is not clearly mandated by terms of the Refugee Act, and no right to notice derives a fortiori from establishment of asylum procedure, and thus although aliens have protected statutory and regulatory right to petition for asylum, Immigration and Nationality Service is not required to inform all potential applicants of their right to seek asylum. Immigration and Nationality Act, § 243(h), as amended, 8 U.S.C.A. § 1253(h); U.S.C.A. Const.Amends. 1, 5.—Id.

C.A.Fla. 1975. Geisser v. U.S., 513 F.2d 862, on remand Petition of Geisser, 414 F.Supp. 49, vacated and remanded 554 F.2d 698, appeal after remand 627 F.2d 745, certiorari denied Bauer v. U.S., 101 S.Ct. 1741, 450 U.S. 1031, 68 L.Ed.2d 226, rehearing denied 101 S.Ct. 3023, 451 U.S. 1032, 69 L.Ed.2d 401.

C.A.5 (La.) 1985. Under either "clear probability" standard or possibly more liberal "well-founded fear" standard, the fact finder was justified in concluding that alien failed to demonstrate that he would be persecuted on account of his political opinions if he was returned to Guatemala, where alien himself never engaged in political activities in Guatemala, and his fear of political persecution stemmed from his son's political activity.—Young v. U.S. Dept. of Justice, I.N.S., 759 F.2d 450.

C.A.La. 1975. Pelaez v. Immigration and Naturalization Service, 513 F.2d 303, certiorari denied 96 S.Ct. 190, 423 U.S. 892, 46 L.Ed.2d 124.

C.A.N.Y. 1984. Statute prohibiting Attorney General from deporting or returning alien to country in which his life or freedom would be jeopardized creates substantive entitlement to relief from deportation or return to such country. U.S.C.A. Const.Amend. 5; Immigration and Nationality Act, § 243(h), as amended, 8 U.S.C.A. § 1253(h).—Augustin v. Sava, 735 F.2d 32.

C.A.N.Y. 1982. Stevic v. Sava, 678 F.2d 401, certiorari granted I. N. S. v. Stevic, 103 S.Ct. 1249, 460 U.S. 1010, 75 L.Ed.2d 479, reversed 104 S.Ct. 2489.

C.A.5 (Tex.) 1985. Factors which the Board of Immigration Appeals must consider in determining whether alien is to be required to leave the United States include length of residence in the United States, community ties in the United States, possibility of obtaining a visa, financial burden of alien having to go abroad to obtain a visa, and health and age of the alien.—Sanchez v. U.S. I.N.S., 755 F.2d 1158.

In ordering that alien be deported to Mexico, Board of Immigration Appeals did not fail to accord sufficient consideration to relevant hardship factors, either individually or cumulatively, including, inter alia, facts that alien had been in the United States, illegally, since 1970, he had various personal community ties in the United States, and he would likely have difficulty finding employment if he were returned to Mexico. Immigration and Nationality Act, § 244(a), 8 U.S. C.A. § 1254(a).—Id.

D.C.D.C. 1983. Non-immigrant exchange visitor who was in this country to receive graduate medical education established the "exceptional hardship" on his spouse which justified waiving requirement that an exchange visitor return to his native land for two years before he is eligible to apply for permanent residence in this country, in that spouse's departure to nonimmigrant visitor's home would disrupt her professional career, move to nonimmigrant visitor's home would have serious economic consequences for visitor and his spouse, and American vice-consul in Toronto, Canada had assured exchange visitor that he would not have to depart from the United States for two years. Immigration and Nationality Act, §§ 101(a)(15)(J), 212(e), 8 U.S.C.A. §§ 1101(a)(15)(J), 1182(e).—Slyper v. Attorney General, 576 F.Supp. 559.

Consideration in isolation by district director of the Immigration and Naturalization Service of each factor allegedly qualifying as exceptional hardship on alien's spouse or child to support waiver of foreign residence requirement was in itself error. Immigration and Nationality Act, §§ 101(a)(15)(J), 212(e), 8 U.S.C.A. §§ 1101(a)(15)(J), 1182(e).—Id.

D.C.D.C. 1975. Chinese Am. Civic Council v. Attorney General, 396 F.Supp. 1250, affirmed 566 F.2d 321, 185 U.S.App.D.C. 1.

Federal Supplement. Part of West's
National Reporter System

West Reporter Features

The following pages are included to illustrate added features in
many West case law reporters.

They include in order:
1. Map of Federal Judicial Circuits
2. Judges of Federal Courts with appointment dates
3. Table of cases reported in this volume
4. Table of cases arranged by court subdivision
5. Table of statutes/rules indicating what cases in the same
   volume cite statutes or rules
6. Words and Phrases section—an alphabetical list of words
   defined in cases in this volume
7. Key Number Digest—Digest paragraphs from cases in this
   volume
8. Judicial Highlights—Current decisions of interest (in the
   Advance Sheets)

FEDERAL

SUPPLEMENT

Volume 617

Cases Argued and Determined

in the

UNITED STATES DISTRICT COURTS

UNITED STATES COURT OF INTERNATIONAL TRADE

SPECIAL COURT, REGIONAL RAIL REORGANIZATION ACT

and Rulings of the

JUDICIAL PANEL ON MULTIDISTRICT LITIGATION

The above symbol and Federal Supplement are registered trademarks of West Publishing Co. Registered in U.S. Patent and Trademark Office.

ST. PAUL, MINN.

WEST PUBLISHING CO.

1986

The Thirteen Federal Judicial Circuits

See 28 U.S.C.A. § 41

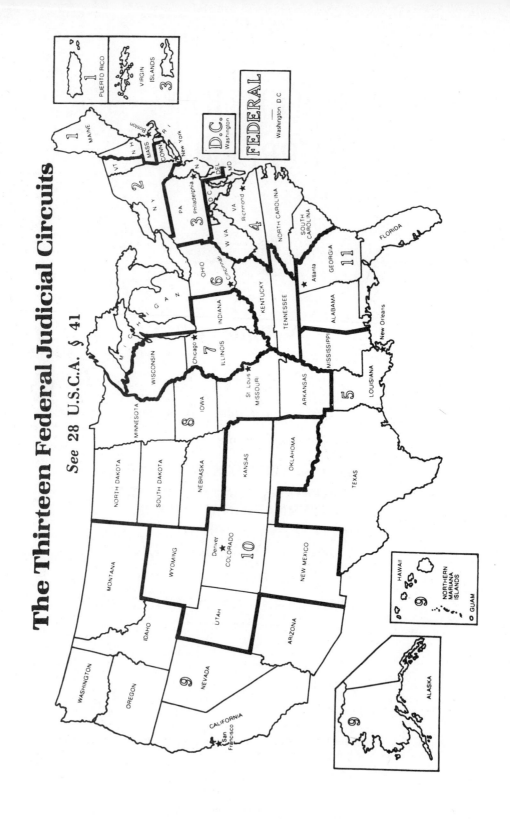

JUDGES
OF THE
FEDERAL COURTS

With Date of Appointment

DISTRICT OF COLUMBIA CIRCUIT

WARREN E. BURGER,
Circuit Justice .... 6–23–69 .... Washington, D. C.

CIRCUIT JUDGES

SPOTTSWOOD W. ROBINSON, III,
C. J.* .... 11– 3–66 .... Washington
J. SKELLY WRIGHT* .... 3–30–62 .... Washington
PATRICIA M. WALD .... 7–26–79 .... Washington
ABNER J. MIKVA .... 9–26–79 .... Washington
HARRY T. EDWARDS .... 2–20–80 .... Washington
RUTH BADER GINSBURG .... 6–18–80 .... Washington
ROBERT H. BORK .... 2–12–82 .... Washington
ANTONIN SCALIA .... 8–17–82 .... Washington
KENNETH W. STARR .... 9–20–83 .... Washington
LAURENCE H. SILBERMAN .... 10–28–85 .... Washington

SENIOR CIRCUIT JUDGES

DAVID L. BAZELON .... 2–10–50 .... Washington
JOHN A. DANAHER .... 3–31–54 .... West Hartford, Conn.
CARL MCGOWAN .... 3–27–63 .... Washington
GEORGE E. MACKINNON .... 5– 6–69 .... Washington
ROGER ROBB .... 5– 6–69 .... Washington
MALCOLM RICHARD WILKEY .... 2–25–70 .... Washington

DISTRICT JUDGES

AUBREY E. ROBINSON, Jr., C. J. 11– 3–66 .... Washington
GERHARD A. GESELL .... 12– 7–67 .... Washington
JOHN H. PRATT .... 6– 7–68 .... Washington
BARRINGTON D. PARKER .... 12–19–69 .... Washington
CHARLES R. RICHEY .... 5– 5–71 .... Washington
LOUIS F. OBERDORFER .... 11– 1–77 .... Washington
HAROLD H. GREENE .... 5–19–78 .... Washington
JOHN GARRETT PENN .... 3–23–79 .... Washington
JOYCE HENS GREEN .... 5–11–79 .... Washington
NORMA HOLLOWAY JOHNSON ...... 5–12–80 .... Washington

* Former U. S. District Judge.

CASES REPORTED

CASES REPORTED

ARRANGED UNDER THEIR RESPECTIVE CIRCUITS

DISTRICT OF COLUMBIA CIRCUIT

FIRST CIRCUIT

STATUTES AND RULES

For later citations, see same Table in current Advance Sheets

---

STATUTES

UNITED STATES CODE CONGRESSIONAL AND ADMINISTRATIVE NEWS

1984, p. 2734—617 F.Supp. 33
1984, p. 2773—617 F.Supp. 33
1984, p. 2974—617 F.Supp. 858
1984, p. 3037—617 F.Supp. 858
1984, p. 3038—617 F.Supp. 841
1984, p. 3039—617 F.Supp. 841
1984, p. 3182—617 F.Supp. 292
1984, p. 3486—617 F.Supp. 292
1984, p. 3487—617 F.Supp. 292
1984, p. 3491—617 F.Supp. 292
1984, p. 5576—617 F.Supp. 1531
1984, p. 5649—617 F.Supp. 1531
1984, p. 5689—617 F.Supp. 1531
1982, p. 2431—617 F.Supp. 920
1982, p. 2487—617 F.Supp. 920
1982, p. 2488—617 F.Supp. 920
1982, p. 2496—617 F.Supp. 920
1982, p. 2497—617 F.Supp. 920
1982, p. 3367—483 N.E.2d 1102
1980, p. 236—617 F.Supp. 1204
1980, p. 254—617 F.Supp. 1304
1980, p. 255—617 F.Supp. 1304
1980, p. 2283—706 P.2d 825
1980, p. 2296—706 P.2d 825
1980, p. 4007—617 F.Supp. 190
1980, p. 4015—617 F.Supp. 190
1978, p. 2211—617 F.Supp. 96
1978, p. 2242—617 F.Supp. 96
1978, p. 2243—617 F.Supp. 96
1978, p. 2723—617 F.Supp. 365
1978, p. 2831—617 F.Supp. 365
1978, p. 2891—617 F.Supp. 365
1978, p. 5787—706 P.2d 611
1978, p. 5865—706 P.2d 611
1978, p. 5963—706 P.2d 611
1978, p. 6320—706 P.2d 611
1978, p. 6321—706 P.2d 611
1977, p. 4503—617 F.Supp. 480
1977, p. 4525—617 F.Supp. 480
1977, p. 4526—617 F.Supp. 480
1976, p. 2183—617 F.Supp. 825
1976, p. 5659—617 F.Supp. 619
1976, p. 5700—617 F.Supp. 1021
1976, p. 5701—617 F.Supp. 1021

1976, p. 5779—617 F.Supp. 619
1976, p. 5816—617 F.Supp. 1021
1976, p. 5908—617 F.Supp. 619
1976, p. 5912—617 F.Supp. 619
1976, p. 6604—617 F.Supp. 311
1976, p. 6604—617 F.Supp. 351
1976, p. 6609—617 F.Supp. 351
1976, p. 6619—617 F.Supp. 311
1972, p. 3730—617 F.Supp. 1190
1972, p. 3745—617 F.Supp. 1190
1972, p. 3746—617 F.Supp. 1190
1972, p. 3747—617 F.Supp. 1190
1972, p. 4573—374 N.W.2d 690
1972, p. 4596—374 N.W.2d 690
1972, pp. 4647–4650—374 N.W.2d 690
1972, p. 4650—374 N.W.2d 690
1970, p. 460—498 A.2d 210
1970, p. 461—498 A.2d 210
1970, p. 559—498 A.2d 210
1968, p. 1794—617 F.Supp. 244
1966, p. 2397—617 F.Supp. 1399
1966, p. 2398—617 F.Supp. 1399
1965, p. 1113—617 F.Supp. 365
1965, p. 1115—617 F.Supp. 365
1965, p. 2020—493 N.Y.S.2d 784
1965, p. 3824—617 F.Supp. 365
1954, p. 4344—617 F.Supp. 575
1954, p. 4995—617 F.Supp. 575

UNITED STATES CODE CONGRESSIONAL SERVICE

1949, p. 1328—617 F.Supp. 229

UNITED STATES CODE ANNOTATED

5 U.S.C.A.—Government Organization and Employees

Sec.
551—617 F.Supp. 365
551(2)—617 F.Supp. 279
551(4)—374 N.W.2d 690
551 et seq.—617 F.Supp. 359
551 et seq.—617 F.Supp. 365
552—617 F.Supp. 101
552—617 F.Supp. 258
552—617 F.Supp. 280
552—617 F.Supp. 602

617 F.Supp.   LI

RULES

ADMIRALTY RULES

SUPPLEMENTAL RULES

Rule

C(6) 774 F.2d 1432

FEDERAL RULES OF CIVIL PROCEDURE

Supplementing

Wright and Miller, Federal Practice and Procedure: Civil

WORDS AND PHRASES

For other definitions of Words and Phrases listed below, see
publication WORDS AND PHRASES, comprising judicial definitions of Words and Phrases by the Courts, State and Federal, in paragraph form.

ACCOUNT STATED,
   Navimex S.A. De C.V. v. S/S Northern Ice, D.C.N.Y., 617 F.Supp. 103, 105.

ACTUAL CONTROVERSY,
   Electro Medical Systems S.A. v. Cooper Lasersonics, Inc., D.C.Ill., 617 F.Supp. 1036, 1038.

BUILDINGS,
   Foremost Ins. Co. v. Lowery, D.C.Miss., 617 F.Supp. 521, 524.

CONFIDENTIAL,
   Burnside-Ott Aviation Training Center, Inc. v. U.S., D.C.Fla., 617 F.Supp. 279, 286.

CONSPICUOUS,
   Agristor Leasing v. Guggisberg, D.C.Minn., 617 F.Supp. 902, 909.

CONSTRUCTIVE NOTICE,
   Amjems, Inc. v. F.R. Orr Const. Co., Inc., D.C.Fla., 617 F.Supp. 273, 278.

CRIME OF VIOLENCE,
   U.S. v. Bushey, D.C.Vt., 617 F.Supp. 292, 300.

DELIVERED,
   Sprague & Rhodes Commodity Corp. v. M/V Procer Fulgencio Yegros, D.C.N.Y., 617 F.Supp. 911, 912.

DOMICILIARY INSURER,
   Sears, Roebuck & Co. v. Northumberland General Ins. Co., D.C.Ill., 617 F.Supp. 88, 89.

DOMICILIARY STATE,
   Sears, Roebuck & Co. v. Northumberland General Ins. Co., D.C.Ill., 617 F.Supp. 88, 89.

EMPLOYEE,
   Thomas v. Brock, D.C.N.C., 617 F.Supp. 526, 534.

EMPLOYER,
   Beckwith v. International Mill Services, Inc., D.C.Pa., 617 F.Supp. 187, 189.

EMPLOYERS,
   Brock v. Hutto, D.C.Ala., 617 F.Supp. 623, 627.

ENTERPRISE,
   Brock v. Hutto, D.C.Ala., 617 F.Supp. 623, 626.

FRONT PAY,
   Endres v. Helms, D.C.D.C., 617 F.Supp. 1260, 1268.

FUNCTIONAL,
   Porter v. Farmers Supply Service, Inc., D.C.Del., 617 F.Supp. 1175, 1189.

GOVERNMENT CONTACTS,
   Chase v. Pan-Pacific Broadcasting, Inc., D.C.D.C., 617 F.Supp. 1414, 1425.

INCOME,
   Lapin v. U.S., D.C.D.C., 617 F.Supp. 167, 169.

INEQUITABLE CONDUCT,
   A.B. Dick Co. v. Burroughs Corp., D.C.Ill., 617 F.Supp. 1382, 1395.

JUDGMENT NUNC PRO TUNC,
   Middleton v. Dan River, Inc., D.C.Ala., 617 F.Supp. 1206, 1221.

LODESTAR,
   Daggett v. Kimmelman, D.C.N.J., 617 F.Supp. 1269, 1280.

KEY NUMBER DIGEST

ABANDONED AND LOST PROPERTY

I. ABANDONMENT.

1. Nature and elements.

D.C.Idaho 1985. For abandonment to occur there must be present intent to abandon, and physical acts evidencing clear intent to relinquish the property interest.—State of Idaho v. Oregon Short Line R. Co., 617 F.Supp. 213.

ACCOUNT STATED

1. Nature and subject-matter in general.

D.C.N.Y. 1984. An "account stated" is an agreement, express or implied, that a statement of account has been asserted, and has been accepted as correct; both parties must express assent to the account as correct; assent may be inferred by silence when an account rendered remains unquestioned a reasonable time after receipt.—Navimex S.A. De C.V. v. S/S Northern Ice, 617 F.Supp. 103.

5. Assent of parties in general.

D.C.N.Y. 1984. Supplementary statement of account did not constitute an account stated, where there was an underlying dispute between parties as evidenced by objection, thereby precluding finding of consent to statement.—Navimex S.A. De C.V. v. S/S Northern Ice, 617 F.Supp. 103.

6(2). Retention without objection in general.

D.C.N.Y. 1984. Defendants' failure to object for five months to plaintiffs' summary statement of account was unreasonable, and converted statement into an account stated, considering course of conduct between parties who operated under an agreement for two and a half years during which time they were in frequent communication.—Navimex S.A. De C.V. v. S/S Northern Ice, 617 F.Supp. 103.

8. Conclusiveness.

D.C.N.Y. 1984. In spite of defendants' previous assent to account stated, they could attack balance shown in account by evidence of errors; however, defendants had burden of showing where account was incorrect.—Navimex S.A. De C.V. v. S/S Northern Ice, 617 F.Supp. 103.

19(1). Presumptions and burden of proof.

D.C.N.Y. 1984. In spite of defendants' previous assent to account stated, they could attack balance shown in account by evidence of errors; however, defendants had burden of showing where account was incorrect.—Navimex S.A. De C.V. v. S/S Northern Ice, 617 F.Supp. 103.

19(3). Weight and sufficiency.

D.C.N.Y. 1984. Defendants who claimed that there were errors in account stated because of accounting method used did not meet their burden of showing that account was incorrect, considering that accounting method which defendants attacked was method which they used throughout relationship between the parties, and defendants acquiesced in method not only during the relationship, but also by assenting through their silence to the statement of account, converting it into an account stated.—Navimex S.A. De C.V. v. S/S Northern Ice, 617 F.Supp. 103.

Defendants in action on account stated met burden of establishing that plaintiffs incorrectly included in the account double commissions totaling $14,180.02, considering joint venture agreement providing that either plaintiff but not both was to receive a 2.5% commission.—Id.

ACTION

I. GROUNDS AND CONDITIONS PRECEDENT.

6. Moot, hypothetical or abstract questions.

CIT 1985. Mexican exporter's claim alleging a change in headnote to tariff schedules brought its merchandise within an item number subject to embargo was rendered moot by agreement between United States and Mexico regulating imports of the product, regardless of a pending antidumping order determination, since scope of such orders is made without regard to tariff classifications. Tariff Act of 1930, § 516A(a)(2), as amended, 19 U.S.C.A. § 1516a(a)(2); 28 U.S.C.A. § 1581(c); Tariff Schedules, GSP Items 310.5015, 310.5049.—Acrilicos v. Regan, 617 F.Supp. 1082.

ADMINISTRATIVE LAW AND PROCEDURE

II. ADMINISTRATIVE AGENCIES, OFFICERS AND AGENTS.

124. Meetings in general.

D.C.D.C. 1985. In seeking to close a meeting, agency bears burden under Sunshine Act [5 U.S. C.A. § 552b(c)] of establishing that its meeting is subject to at least one of ten statutorily defined grounds for closure.—Shurberg Broadcasting of Hartford, Inc. v. F.C.C., 617 F.Supp. 825.

Even if one or more exemptions justify closure of a portion of a particular meeting under Sunshine Act [5 U.S.C.A. § 552b], agency must attempt to segregate non-exempt from exempt portions, and close only those portions of meeting involving exempt topics, unless, after making such efforts, agency can persuade court that segregation of exempt and non-exempt topics would make a coherent discussion impossible.—Id.

(1)

Current Decisions of Interest

May 1986

ATTORNEYS—Fees. An award of attorney fees exceeding $1.7 million has been approved in a Clayton Act case. The lodestar was calculated with reference to hourly rates from 1979 through 1985. That amount was enhanced by one-third because of the uncertainty that the attorneys, who necessarily advanced over $120,000 for the cost of the action, would receive any payment. The attorneys had represented service station operators against a major oil company, claiming price discrimination, and the case involved two trials and an appeal. Hasbrouk v. Texaco, Inc., March 21, 1986 (E.D.Wash.) (Opinion by District Judge Justin L. Quackenbush).

An award of attorney fees of $1.5 million to special counsel who successfully represented a bankruptcy estate before an international claims tribunal was not excessive. Counsel secured an award of $4.6 million and compensation was in accordance with a contingent fee agreement with the bankruptcy trustee. The special counsel's prior experience with the debtor enabled him to reconstruct the claim after the debtor was put out of business, and his previous experience in international law prepared him for the presentation of the claim. In re International Technical Products Corp., 58 B.R. 33 (Bkrtcy.S.D.Fla. 1986) (Opinion by Bankruptcy Judge Thomas C. Britton).

BANKRUPTCY—Good Faith. A Bankruptcy Court should have applied the good-faith test to dismiss a joint Chapter 13 petition. The petition had been filed by a financially secure husband and wife for the sole purpose of rejecting an option agreement which they felt was not as profitable as could be. The Eleventh Circuit concluded that the plan was proposed in a bad-faith attempt to use and abuse Chapter 13 for a greedy and unworthy purpose. The Court noted that there was little legislative history as to the construction of the good-faith provision of 11 U.S.C.A.

A Special Copyrighted Feature of West Publishing Co. Reporters

1

8 West Hornbooks

Hornbook shown with
WESTLAW terminal

West Hornbooks

The Hornbook is a one-volume treatise on a specific area of law. In this example, the area of law is TORTS.

The enclosed sample pages illustrate a discussion of TRUTH as a DEFENSE to a suit for DEFAMATION. Recent editions of many Hornbooks include WESTLAW references with suggested queries for WESTLAW research.

Prosser and Keeton
on
THE LAW OF TORTS

W. Page Keeton

General Editor

W. Page Keeton

Holder of W. Page Keeton Chair in Tort Law
University of Texas at Austin

Dan B. Dobbs

Rosenstiel Professor of Law, University of Arizona

Robert E. Keeton

Langdell Professor Emeritus, Harvard Law School

David G. Owen

Professor of Law, University of South Carolina

FIFTH EDITION
HORNBOOK SERIES
LAWYER'S EDITION

St. Paul, Minn.
WEST PUBLISHING CO.
1984

The Hornbook

Dr. Johnson described the hornbook as "the first book of children, covered with horn to keep it unsoiled." Pardon's *New General English Dictionary* (1758) defined it as "A leaf of written or printed paper pasted on a board, and covered with horn, for children to learn their letters by, and to prevent their being torn and daubed."

It was used throughout Europe and America between the late 1400s and the middle 1700s.

Shaped like an old-fashioned butter paddle, the first hornbooks were made of wood. The paper lesson the child was to learn was fastened to the wooden paddle and covered with a piece of horn. The transparent strip of horn was made by soaking a cow's horn in

hot water and peeling it away at the thickness of a piece of celluloid. The horn was necessary to protect the lesson from the damp and perhaps grubby hands of the child. Hornbooks commonly contained the alphabet, the vowels, and the Lord's Prayer. Later hornbooks were made of various materials: brass, copper, silver, ivory, bronze, leather, and stone.

As the art of printing advanced, the hornbook was supplanted by the primer in the book form we know today. Subsequently West Publishing Company developed its "Hornbook Series", a series of scholarly and well-respected one volume treatises on particular areas of law. Today they are widely used by law students, lawyers and judges.

WESTLAW Introduction

Prosser and Keeton on the Law of Torts offers a detailed and comprehensive treatment of the basic rules and principles of tort law. However, lawyers frequently need to find additional authority. In an effort to assist with comprehensive research of the law of torts, preformulated WESTLAW references are included after each section of the text in this edition of the hornbook. The WESTLAW references are designed for use with the WESTLAW computer-assisted legal research service. By joining this publication with the extensive WESTLAW databases, the reader is able to move straight from the hornbook into WESTLAW with great speed and convenience.

Some readers may desire to use only the information supplied within the printed pages of this hornbook. Others, however, will encounter issues in tort law that require further information. Accordingly, those who opt to go beyond the material contained in the textual format into WESTLAW can rapidly and easily access WESTLAW, an electronic law library that possesses extraordinary currency and magnitude.

Appendix B gives concise, step-by-step instruction on how to coordinate WESTLAW research with this hornbook.

THE PUBLISHER

*

xiii

ing. The mere fact that the publication was not privileged because it was inaccurately and negligently made does not mean of course that under present law the plaintiff would recover. The plaintiff, as a public official, or public figure, or private person, would have to establish the kind of fault on the part of the defendant with respect to the truth or falsity of the alleged defamatory imputation made about the plaintiff in the proceeding as is constitutionally required.

WESTLAW REFERENCES

digest(qualified /5 privilege* immunity /s defam! slander! libel!)

qualified /5 privilege* immunity /p defam! slander! libel! /p constitution! unconstitution!

Interest of Publisher
topic(237) /p selfdefense selfprotection 237k46

Interest of Others
restatement /s torts +5 603

libel! slander! defam! /p limited qualified /5 privilege /s profession**

restatement /s torts /5 595 596

Common Interest
digest(defam! libel! slander! /p "common interest*") 237k51(4)

Communications of One Who May Act in the Public Interest
libel! slander! defam! /p "public interest" /s qualified /s immunity privilege 237k51(5)

digest(libel! slander! defam! /p public /p "fair comment")

Abuse of Qualified Privilege Regarding Private Publication of Private Matters
opinion(abus! misus! /s qualified conditional /s privilege immunity)

"private defamation"

Burden of Proof—Court and Jury
digest(defam! slander! libel! /p "burden of proof")

defam! slander! libel! /p burden /4 proof proving /s defense privilege* immunity

Report of Public Proceedings—A Special Type of Privilege
defam! slander! libel! /p public legislative executive council committee /7 proceeding* meeting* /s report!

fair** accurate** correct** /s report! /s public legislative executive council committee /s proceeding* meeting* /p libel! slander! defam!

The Constitution Privilege
negligen! /s publish! publication! /p defam! libel! slander! /p constitution! unconstitution!

§ 116. Truth and Other Defenses

Truth or Justification

To create liability for defamation, there must be publication of matter that is both defamatory and false.[1] The well-settled common law rule prior to decisions by the United States Supreme Court related to the constitutional privilege to defame was that truth is an affirmative defense which the defendant must plead and prove. Thus, under the common law rule, the defamatory statement is regarded as false unless the defendant proves truth. It has been said that meeting the constitutional requirements regarding the necessity for proof of at least negligence with respect to the truth or falsity of a defamatory statement makes it necessary for the plaintiff to allege and prove the falsity of the communication.[2] The basis for this position is that the Supreme Court of the United States, in holding that the plaintiff must establish some kind of fault with respect to the issue of truth or falsity, has by implication allocated the issue of falsity to the plaintiff. But there can be two answers to this. In the first place, the constitutional privilege to defame may not extend to defamatory utterances privately made about private persons.[3] In the second place, there is no inconsistency in assuming falsity until defendant publisher proves otherwise and requiring the plaintiff to prove negligence or recklessness with respect to the truth or falsity of the imputation. There is, in other words, nothing inconsistent about requiring the defendant to prove truth if absolute protection is to be provided for a

---

§ 116

1. Second Restatement of Torts, § 581A, Comment a.

2. See, Second Restatement of Torts, § 613, Comment j; Eldredge, The Law of Defamation, 1978, Sec. 63; Morris on Torts, Second edition, 1980, p. 350.

3. See § 113.

the defense of truth, and formerly these rules were carried to ridiculous extremes,[28] but it is now generally agreed that it is not necessary to prove the literal truth of the accusation in every detail, and that it is sufficient to show that the imputation is substantially true,[29] or, as it is often put, to justify the "gist," the "sting," or the "substantial truth" of the defamation.[30] Thus an accusation that the mayor of a town has wasted $80,000 of the taxpayers' money has been held to be justified by proof that he wasted $17,500, since there is no more opprobrium attached to the greater amount.[31] If, however, the defendant adds to the facts stated an opinion or comment of his own, the comment must be justified as a proper one in the light of the facts proved.[32]

The defense of truth frequently is a hazardous venture for the defendant, since if he fails to sustain it the jury may be permitted to find that he has reiterated the defamation, and to consider the fact in aggravation of the damages.[33] The modern cases, however, have tended quite properly to recog-

nize that the defendant is entitled to present an honest defense without being penalized, and have limited such aggravation to cases where it appears that the defense was entered in bad faith, without evidence to support it.[34]

WESTLAW REFERENCES

Truth or Justification

digest(defam! libel! slander! /s truth /s defense)
defam! libel! slander! /p commonlaw /p burden /5 proof proving

Truth

justification /s libel! slander! defam!
truth /s justification /s libel! slander! defam!

§ 116A. Damages and Matters in Mitigation

Damages which may be recovered in an action for defamation are: (1) compensatory or actual, which may be either (a) general or (b) special; (2) punitive or exemplary; and (3) nominal.[1]

Downs v. Hawley, 1873, 112 Mass. 237; Sun Printing & Publishing Association v. Schenck, 2d Cir. 1900, 98 F. 925; Kilian v. Doubleday & Co., 1951, 367 Pa. 117, 79 A.2d 657.

27.   Gardner v. Self, 1852, 15 Mo. 480; Buckner v. Spaulding, 1891, 127 Ind. 229, 26 N.E. 792; Pallet v. Sargent, 1858, 36 N.H. 496; Haddock v. Naughton, 1893, 74 Hun 390, 26 N.Y.S. 455. Cf. Stewart v. Enterprise Co., Tex.Civ.App.1965, 393 S.W.2d 372, refused n.r.e., appeal after remand 439 S.W.2d 674, refused n.r.e. (two accusations, truth of only one proved).

28.   See for example Swann v. Rary, Ind.1833, 3 Blackf. 298 (two hogs and one); Sharpe v. Stephenson, 1851, 34 N.C. (12 Ired.) 348 (time and place); cf. Coffin v. Brown, 1901, 94 Md. 190, 50 A. 567 (time and place). See Courtney, Absurdities of the Law of Slander and Libel, 1902, 36 Am.L.Rev. 552, 561–564.

29.   Alexander v. North Eastern R. Co., 1865, 6 B. & S. 340, 122 Eng.Rep. 1221; Zoll v. Allen, S.D.N.Y.1950, 93 F.Supp. 95; Florida Publishing Co. v. Lee, 1918, 76 Fla. 405, 80 So. 245; McGuire v. Vaughan, 1896, 106 Mich. 280, 64 N.W. 44; Skrocki v. Stahl, 1910, 14 Cal. App. 1, 110 P. 957.

30.   Edwards v. Bell, 1824, 1 Bing. 403, 130 Eng. Rep. 162; Bell Publishing Co. v. Garrett Engineering Co., Tex.Civ.App.1941, 154 S.W.2d 885, affirmed 141 Tex. 51, 170 S.W.2d 197.

31.   Fort Worth Press Co. v. Davis, Tex.Civ.App. 1936, 96 S.W.2d 416. Cf. Smith v. Byrd, 1955, 225 Miss. 331, 83 So.2d 172 (statement that sheriff shot a

man justified by proof that sheriff was acting in concert with deputy who shot him).

32.   Cooper v. Lawson, 1838, 8 Ad. & El. 746, 112 Eng.Rep. 1020; Commercial Publishing Co. v. Smith, 6th Cir. 1907, 149 F. 704; cf. Morrison v. Harmer, 1837, 3 Bing.N.C. 759, 132 Eng.Rep. 603.

33.   Will v. Press Publishing Co., 1932, 309 Pa. 539, 164 A. 621; Coffin v. Brown, 1901, 94 Md. 190, 50 A. 567; Krulic v. Petcoff, 1913, 122 Minn. 517, 142 N.W. 897; Hall v. Edwards, 1942, 138 Me. 231, 23 A.2d 889 (with other evidence of malice). See Note, 1958, 56 Mich.L.Rev. 659.

In Domchick v. Greenbelt Consumer Services, 1952, 200 Md. 36, 87 A.2d 831, it was held that pleading truth makes a prima facie case as to malice. In Shumate v. Johnson Publishing Co., 1956, 139 Cal.App.2d 121, 293 P.2d 531, a publisher who verified a pleading of truth was held subject to punitive damages, although he was out of the state and took no other part.

34.   Webb v. Gray, 1913, 181 Ala. 408, 62 So. 194; Fodor v. Fuchs, 1910, 79 N.J.L. 529, 76 A. 1081; Willard v. Press Publishing Co., 1900, 52 App.Div. 448, 65 N.Y.S. 73; Las Vegas Sun, Inc. v. Franklin, 1958, 74 Nev. 282, 329 P.2d 867; Snyder v. Fatherly, 1930, 153 Va. 762, 151 S.E. 149.

§ 116A

1.   See, Stidham v. Wachtel, Del.1941, 2 Terry 327, 21 A.2d 282; Dobbs, Remedies, 1973, Sec. 7.2, pp. 513–523.

WESTLAW with Federal Reporter 2d

Case Illustration

This section illustrates a case (U.S. v. Shovea) as reported in the Federal Reporter 2d series and part of the same case as it appears on WESTLAW.

We reverse the district court finding/conclusion that it does not have jurisdiction to entertain the summary, *ex parte*, IRS application for administrative search warrants. We remand for further proceedings consistent with this opinion relative to the sufficiency of the affidavit to establish that degree of "probable cause" deemed necessary to satisfy the commands of the Fourth Amendment in the context of the administrative enforcement of the federal tax laws.

UNITED STATES of America,
Plaintiff-Appellee,

v.

Scott Andrew SHOVEA, Gebbie Hugh
Robba, Stephen Howard Gaias, Jr.,
Defendants-Appellants.

Nos. 77–1078, 77–1079 and 77–1184.

United States Court of Appeals,
Tenth Circuit.

Submitted May 8, 1978.

Decided July 27, 1978.

Rehearing Denied in No. 77–1078
Sept. 13, 1978.

Defendants were convicted in the United States District Court for the District of Colorado, Fred M. Winner, Chief Judge, of conspiracy to manufacture and possess with intent to distribute methamphetamine, a scheduled II controlled substance, and they appealed. The Court of Appeals, Barrett, Circuit Judge, held that: (1) one defendant did not have standing to challenge X-ray search of suitcase; (2) federal agents had sufficient probable cause to attach electronic tracking device to defendant's car without first acquiring court order and did not violate defendant's Fourth Amendment right in so doing; (3) evidence sustained

convictions and (4) trial court did not err in failing to grant defense motion to strike testimony of DEA agent, even though all of agent's investigatory notes had been destroyed after being turned over to another agent who incorporated the notes into a report.

Affirmed.

1. Searches and Seizures ⊸7(26)

Defendant did not have standing to challenge X-ray search of suitcase, where the search was directed at another person. U.S.C.A.Const. Amend. 4.

2. Searches and Seizures ⊸3.6(2)

Reference to X-ray search in affidavit executed in support of search warrant did not vitiate affidavit's efficacy nor taint validity of subsequent search and seizure, where suitcase was not opened, X-ray established only that suitcase contained four bottles, no direct evidence of search was offered by Government, and one defendant's purchase of chemical, a primary precursor of methamphetamine, his elusive trip to airport while carrying suitcase, and his subsequent flight to another city combined with strong odors emanating from residence to which the suitcase was brought, generated sufficient independent probable cause for issuance of warrant. 18 U.S.C.A. § 2; Comprehensive Drug Abuse Prevention and Control Act of 1970, § 401(a)(1), 21 U.S.C.A. § 841(a)(1); U.S.C.A.Const. Amend. 4.

3. Searches and Seizures ⊸7(10)

Utilization of electronic tracking device, without prior court approval, may be justified by probable cause and exigent circumstances. U.S.C.A.Const. Amend. 4.

4. Searches and Seizures ⊸7(10)

Federal agents had sufficient probable cause to attach electronic tracking device to defendant's car without first acquiring court order and did not violate defendant's Fourth Amendment rights in so doing, where agents knew that codefendant had purchased chemicals, a primary precursor of methamphetamine, and agents observed co-defendant leave residence, carrying suitcase in careful manner, drive to airport in elusive manner, fly to another city where he was met by defendant and drive to defendant's residence. 18 U.S.C.A. § 2; Comprehensive Drug Abuse Prevention and Control Act of 1970, § 401(a)(1), 21 U.S.C.A. § 841(a)(1); U.S.C.A.Const. Amend. 4.

5. Criminal Law ⏎1144.13(3, 5)

On appeal from jury conviction, Court of Appeals must view evidence, both direct and circumstantial, and all reasonable inferences to be drawn therefrom in light most favorable to Government in determining its sufficiency.

6. Conspiracy ⏎47(12)

Evidence supported conviction of conspiracy to manufacture and possess with intent to distribute methamphetamine, a schedule II controlled substance. 18 U.S.C.A. § 2; Comprehensive Drug Abuse Prevention and Control Act of 1970, § 401(a)(1), 21 U.S.C.A. § 841(a)(1).

7. Criminal Law ⏎696(1)

Trial court did not err in failing to grant defense motion to strike testimony of DEA agent, although all of agent's investigatory notes had been destroyed after being turned over to another agent who incorporated the notes into a report.

8. Criminal Law ⏎1171.3

Although evidence did not support assistant United States attorney's closing argument that it was possibility that defendant had given another the idea to use fictitious name of defendant's employer in ordering chemical used to make controlled substance, since defendant's participation in conspiracy to manufacture was substantial, error, if present, was harmless. 18 U.S.C.A. § 2; Comprehensive Drug Abuse Prevention and Control Act of 1970, § 401(a)(1), 21 U.S.C.A. § 841(a)(1).

9. Criminal Law ⏎728(2)

Where defense was aware that comment unsupported by evidence was made in prosecution's closing argument, but defense

attorney opted, as trial tactic, not to move court for corrective action at that time and the comment was relatively harmless, trial court properly refused to grant defendant's motion for mistrial.

Jonathan L. Olom, Denver, Colo. (Stanley H. Marks, Denver, Colo., on brief) for appellant Shovea.

Edward L. Kirkwood, Asst. Federal Public Defender, Denver, Colo. (Daniel J. Sears, Federal Public Defender, Denver, Colo., on brief) for appellants Robba and Gaias.

Edward W. Nottingham, Asst. U. S. Atty., Denver, Colo., for appellee (Joseph F. Dolan, U. S. Atty., Denver, Colo., with him on brief for Shovea and Robba, Cathlin Donnell, U. S. Atty., Denver, Colo. (Interim) with him on brief for Gaias).

Before BARRETT, and McKAY, Circuit Judges, and BRATTON, District Judge.[*]

BARRETT, Circuit Judge.

Scott Shovea (Shovea), Gebbie Robba (Robba) and Stephen Gaias (Gaias) appeal their jury convictions of conspiracy to manufacture and possess with intent to distribute methamphetamine, a schedule II controlled substance, in violation of 18 U.S.C.A. § 2 and 21 U.S.C.A. § 841(a)(1).

Appellants were originally indicted with Geoffrey Hungerford (Hungerford). At the commencement of the trial, the Government dismissed its charges against Hungerford. Thereafter, a mistrial was declared as to Gaias. The trial proceeded as to Shovea and Robba. They were convicted. Subsequent thereto, Gaias was tried individually and convicted. A detailed recitation of the pertinent facts should facilitate our review.

Gaias originally ordered a chemical, phenyl–2–proponone (p–2–p), a primary precursor of methamphetamine, from a New York chemical company under the name of "Jay Edwards." The order was submitted on behalf of "Royce International, 315

---

[*] Of the District of New Mexico, sitting by designation.

Broadway, Port Jefferson, New York." Thereafter federal agents set up a controlled delivery for the chemical.

On September 17, 1976, Gaias was observed by the agents picking up the chemical, after which he was followed to 315 Broadway, a house in a residential area. Shortly thereafter, Gaias was observed exiting the house carrying a suitcase very carefully. He held the suitcase flat, rather than by the handle. Two agents then followed Gaias to an airport. While en route, Gaias drove in excess of the posted speed limits in an elusive manner. Once at the airport, Gaias boarded a plane which flew to Denver. The agents flew to Denver on the same plane. They kept Gaias under surveillance at all times. Gaias arrived in Denver during the early morning hours of September 18, 1976. He was met there by Robba. Gaias and Robba drove from the airport to a residence located at 3352 West Gill Place. Agents followed them to the residence. After Robba and Gaias entered the house, the agents placed an electronic tracking device on Robba's car. Sporadic surveillance of the residence continued September 18 through September 20, 1976.

Gaias' suitcase did not arrive on his incoming flight but it did arrive in Denver later that morning. Prior to its arrival, Gaias filled out a lost luggage claim wherein he listed Robba's name and requested that the suitcase be delivered to 3352 West Gill Place upon its arrival. The suitcase was X-rayed following its arrival at the Denver airport. The X-rays revealed that four bottles were in the suitcase. The agents did not open the suitcase. Pursuant to Gaias' request, the suitcase was delivered to 3352 West Gill Place.

Shortly after the suitcase was delivered, Gaias and Robba were observed by the agents leaving the residence and proceeding to Royce International where they, together with Shovea, loaded and unloaded boxes from their vehicles. Robba and Shovea were both employed at Royce International at that time. Investigation had established that someone allegedly associated with Royce International had, within the prior

four months, ordered various chemicals and glassware from a scientific company, all of which could be utilized in the manufacture of methamphetamine.

On the evening of September 20, 1976 agents detected a strong odor of ether emanating from the 3352 West Gill Place residence. Shovea was observed leaving the residence, walking down the street, looking in all directions, and then returning to the residence. The agents, based on their prior experience, associated the strong odor of ether and Shovea's suspicious movements with the clandestine manufacturing of methamphetamine. Accordingly, when all of the defendants were observed leaving the residence carrying boxes which they loaded into Hungerford's car, the three agents arrested them.

After the arrests were effected, the cars and the residence were secured while a search warrant was obtained. The affidavit in support of the requested warrant stated in part: "Fellow agent Larry Lamberson stated that he checked with the airport authorities and found that the suitcase carried by Gaias was X-rayed and 4 bottles were seen inside." [R., Vol. IV, at 8.] The warrant was issued. A subsequent search of the cars and residence disclosed concentrated liquid methamphetamine and numerous articles used in its manufacture.

Prior to trial, a hearing was held on defendants' motions to suppress evidence allegedly seized as a result of the X-ray search of the suitcase as well as the evidence seized by searching the cars and the residence. The trial court ruled that the X-ray search of the suitcase constituted an unlawful search violative of Gaias' Fourth Amendment rights. A mistrial was granted as to Gaias. The trial court ruled, however, that the evidence of the airport X-ray search was admissible against Shovea and Robba; that evidence seized by search of the cars and the residence was admissible against all of the defendants; and that the search of the cars and residence was not tainted by reference in the affidavit alluding to the X-ray search of the suitcase which disclosed the four bottles.

After the court had ruled on the various motions to suppress, Shovea and Robba proceeded to trial. In the course of their trial, the Government developed the conspiracy in detail. A forensic chemist testified for the Government. He identified the chemical seized as methamphetamine and stated that the volume seized would produce approximately 100,000 doses. At the close of the Government's case, Shovea and Robba elected not to present any evidence. Verdicts of guilty were subsequently returned against them.

Thereafter, Gaias was tried. Prior to trial, the court ruled that the *Wong Sun* doctrine did not preclude admission of the evidence obtained via issuance of the search warrant inasmuch as the information relative to the X-ray of the suitcase contributed little to the search of the residence, and that the Government "could easily have established probable cause for the search of the house had there been no search at the airport." [R., Vol. I, p. 10.] At the conclusion of the Government's case, Gaias moved for acquittal. The motion was denied. Thereafter, the defense rested without introducing any evidence. Gaias was convicted.

I.

Robba contends that the trial court erred (1) by allowing the Government to introduce evidence obtained by exploitation of the X-ray search of the suitcase, and (2) by allowing the admission of evidence obtained by exploitation of the illegal surveillance precipitated by the use of an electronic tracking device placed on his vehicle.

(a)

Robba claims that the trial court erred in allowing the Government to introduce testimony and exhibits obtained by exploitation of the illegal X-ray search of the suitcase and by ruling that he did not have standing to challenge the X-ray search. Robba argues, in part based upon an affidavit which was not admitted in evidence, that he provided Gaias funds to purchase p–2–p in New York, that he was the owner of the p–2–p purchased, that the p–2–p was purchased in the name of Royce International where he was employed and that the lost luggage claim filled out by Gaias set forth his (Robba's) name and residence for purposes of identity and delivery of the suitcase. Robba contends that under these circumstances he had standing to challenge the X-ray search. Robba declares that the X-ray search was illegal and that the illegality thereof was compounded when the Government exploited the X-ray results in order to obtain the search warrant. Under the totality of these circumstances, Robba concludes that the "fruit of the poisonous tree" doctrine as enunciated in *Wong Sun v. United States,* 371 U.S. 471, 83 S.Ct. 407, 9 L.Ed.2d 441 (1963) precluded admission of all "the incriminating evidence which the government developed after they searched Robba's residence and the two vehicles adjacent thereto." We hold that the trial court did not err in finding that Robba lacked standing to challenge the X-ray search or in admitting in evidence the testimony and certain exhibits derived from the search.

[1] Robba failed to establish standing to challenge the search. In *United States v. Galvez,* 465 F.2d 681 (10th Cir. 1972), we said:

> Our conclusion that the two defendants in the instant case have no standing to contest the legality of the seizure of the package containing hashish from Karen's automobile in Walsenburg is supported by our understanding of such cases as *Jones v. United States,* 362 U.S. 257, 80 S.Ct. 725, 4 L.Ed.2d 697 (1960); *Wong Sun v. United States,* 371 U.S. 471, 83 S.Ct. 407, 9 L.Ed.2d 441 (1963); and *Alderman v. United States,* 394 U.S. 165, 89 S.Ct. 961, 22 L.Ed.2d 176 (1969), as well as by numerous cases from this circuit.

In *Jones,* the Supreme Court declared as follows:

> "In order to qualify as a 'person aggrieved by an unlawful search and seizure' one must have been a victim of a search or seizure, one against whom the search was directed, as distinguished

from one who claims prejudice only through the use of evidence gathered as a consequence of a search or seizure directed at someone else. * * *

"Ordinarily, then, it is entirely proper to require of one who seeks to challenge the legality of a search as the basis for suppressing relevant evidence that he allege, and if the allegation be disputed that he establish, that he himself was the victim of an invasion of privacy. * * *"

In *Wong Sun,* it was held that heroin unlawfully taken from another was nonetheless admissible in evidence against Wong Sun because the "seizure of this heroin invaded no right of privacy of person or premises which would entitle Wong Sun to object to its use at his trial." So, here, the seizure of the hashish from Karen invaded no right of privacy of person or premises which would entitle Donald or Veronica Galvez to object to its use at their trial.

And in *Alderman,* the Supreme Court "adhered" to such cases as *Jones* and *Wong Sun,* and to the general rule "that Fourth Amendment rights are personal rights which, like some other constitutional rights, may not be vicariously asserted."

Cases from this circuit which hold that to be a "person aggrieved" within Fed.R. Crim.P. 41, the person moving to suppress must himself have been the victim of any unlawful invasion of his own privacy, are: *United States v. Humphrey,* 409 F.2d 1055 (10th Cir. 1969); *Cochran v. United States,* 389 F.2d 326 (10th Cir. 1968), cert. denied, 391 U.S. 913, 88 S.Ct. 1808, 20 L.Ed.2d 653 (1968), reh. denied, 393 U.S. 899, 89 S.Ct. 70, 21 L.Ed.2d 187 (1968); *Sumrall v. United States,* 382 F.2d 651 (10th Cir. 1967), cert. denied, 389. U.S. 1055, 88 S.Ct. 806, 19 L.Ed.2d 853 (1968), and *Elbel v. United States,* 364 F.2d 127 (10th Cir. 1966), cert. denied, 385 U.S. 1014, 87 S.Ct. 726, 17 L.Ed.2d 550 (1967), reh. denied, 386 U.S. 939, 87 S.Ct. 959, 17 L.Ed.2d 812 (1967). . . .
465 F.2d, at 684–685.

Inasmuch as the X-ray search was directed at Gaias and not Robba, and since Robba "claims prejudice only through the use of evidence gathered as a consequence of a search or seizure directed at someone else," he has not attained standing to challenge the X-ray search.

Even assuming, *arguendo,* that Robba did have standing, the reference to the X-ray search in the affidavit executed in support of the search warrant did not vitiate its efficacy nor did it "taint" the validity of the subsequent search and seizure. The affidavit clearly contained adequate factual basis establishing probable cause without reference to or reliance on the X-ray search. The affidavit stated, *inter alia*: Gaias was observed purchasing p–2–p in New York in the name of Royce International and thereafter flying to Denver; odors emanating from the 3352 West Gill Place residence on September 20, 1976, were identical to those which the experienced agents had smelled on numerous prior occasions while investigating the clandestine manufacture of amphetamines; and the agents were aware that Royce International, where Robba and Shovea were employed, had recently received chemicals and equipment normally used in the manufacture of amphetamines.

The adequacy of the affidavit, aside from any reference to the X-ray search, was recognized by the trial court:

If the evidence had been what I understood it to be, that there would not have been any search of the house had it not been for the X-ray at the airport, then I would say you are within the *Wong Sun* rule, but that record is pretty strong that the airport search contributed very, very little to the search at the house. And as I analyze the evidence, beyond any shadow of a doubt, the agency and the government could easily have established probable cause for the search of the house had there been no search at the airport. And indeed, as I look at the search warrant affidavit, the probable cause, I think, is clearly there absent the airport search.

Now, if you want to put on more testimony, you may. But on the basis of the record made, I do not think that the *Wong Sun* rule includes any evidence of taint at the house in the course of the search there made. I just do not think it goes that far.

And I realize that at this point, I am contradicting, in a sense, what I have said before, and what I have said in a written order to the effect that it was, the airport search was a major part of the reason for the search of the house. I am just plain wrong; it was not. The appellate courts get to read it and think about it; we have to just listen to it.

[R., Vol. I, at 10–11.]

Furthermore, even assuming that Gaias was actually purchasing the p–2–p for Royce International, Robba would nevertheless have no standing as an individual to challenge the search. *See: United States v. Curtis,* 537 F.2d 1091 (10th Cir. 1976), *cert. denied,* 429 U.S. 962, 97 S.Ct. 389, 50 L.Ed.2d 330 (1976), and cases cited therein.

[2] In the final analysis, the reference to the X-ray search in the affidavit did not give rise to error, particularly when, as here: the suitcase was simply X-rayed, and not opened; the X-ray established that the suitcase contained four bottles, but it did not in anywise establish the *content* of the bottles; no direct evidence of the X-ray search was offered by the Government; and Gaias' purchase of the p–2–p, his elusive trip to the airport and his subsequent flight to Denver, combined with the strong odors emanating from the residence, generated sufficient independent probable cause for issuance of the warrant.

(b)

Robba contends that the trial court erred in allowing the Government to introduce testimony and exhibits obtained by reason of the exploitation of an illegal surveillance of his vehicle by the use of an electronic tracking device. As noted, *supra,* when Gaias arrived at the airport in Denver, he was met by Robba and the pair then proceeded to Robba's residence in his car. After the parties entered the residence, agents placed an electronic tracking device on Robba's car.

Later the same day, Robba and Gaias were observed leaving the residence in Robba's car. Several agents followed the car. While en route, the agents following the car lost visual contact. Thereafter, by utilizing the tracking device, the agents were able to trace Robba and Gaias to Royce International where they were observed, together with Shovea, loading and unloading boxes from their respective vehicles.

[3] The utilization of an electronic tracking device, without prior court approval, may be justified by probable cause and exigent circumstances. The following observations in *United States v. Frazier,* 538 F.2d 1322 (8th Cir. 1976), *cert. denied,* 429 U.S. 1046, 97 S.Ct. 751, 50 L.Ed.2d 759 (1977) are applicable here:

Whether the installation of an electronic tracking device on a motor vehicle is a search or seizure within the protection of the Fourth Amendment is a difficult question. At a minimum, the attachment of such a device, without consent or judicial authorization, is an actual trespass. Although only a limited intrusion, it is one which raises a concern that the government could plant a tracking device on a person's car and follow its movements whenever and wherever it is being driven. *See United States v. Martyniuk, supra* [D.C.], 395 F.Supp. [42] at 44–45. In contrast, it is at least questionable whether a person has a reasonable expectation of privacy with regard to his movements on public roads. *See Cardwell v. Lewis,* 417 U.S. 583, 588–92, 94 S.Ct. 2464, 41 L.Ed.2d 325 (1974); *United States v. Carpenter, supra* [D.C.], 403 F.Supp. [361] at 364–65. *Cf. Katz v. United States,* 389 U.S. 347, 350–59, 88 S.Ct. 507, 19 L.Ed.2d 576 (1967). In any event, the issue need not be resolved in this appeal since we are convinced the intrusion committed in the instant case, assuming arguendo that it is a search or seizure within the ambit of the Fourth Amendment, was justified by probable cause and exigent circumstances.

The search of a motor vehicle, especially its exterior, is less intrusive and implicates a lesser expectation of privacy than otherwise applies under the general warrant requirement. *See Cardwell v. Lewis,* 417 U.S. 583, 589–91, 94 S.Ct. 2464, 41 L.Ed.2d 325 (1974); *Almeida-Sanchez v. United States,* 413 U.S. 266, 279, 93 S.Ct. 2535, 37 L.Ed.2d 596 (1973) (Powell, J., concurring). If there is probable cause, an automobile, because of its mobility, may be searched without a warrant in circumstances that would not justify a warrantless search of a house or office. *Chambers v. Maroney,* 399 U.S. 42, 48–51, 90 S.Ct. 1975, 26 L.Ed.2d 419 (1970); *Carroll v. United States,* 267 U.S. 132, 158–59, 45 S.Ct. 280, 69 L.Ed. 543 (1925); *United States v. Brown,* 535 F.2d 424 (8th Cir. 1976). Probable cause exists when the facts and circumstances within a police officer's knowledge would " 'warrant a man of reasonable caution in the belief that' an offense has been or is being committed." 538 F.2d at p. 1324.

See also: United States v. Moore, 562 F.2d 106 (1st Cir. 1977) and *United States v. Hufford,* 539 F.2d 32 (9th Cir. 1976), *cert. denied,* 429 U.S. 1002, 97 S.Ct. 533, 50 L.Ed.2d 614 (1976).

[4] Applying these standards we hold that the agents had sufficient probable cause to attach the electronic tracking device to Robba's car without first acquiring a court order, and that such an installation herein was not violative of Robba's Fourth Amendment rights.

Prior to attaching the device to Robba's car the agents knew that Gaias had recently purchased p–2–p, a primary precursor of methamphetamine, and that he had made the purchase in the name of Royce International; after purchasing the p–2–p Gaias was observed leaving his residence carrying a suitcase in a flat, careful manner; Gaias was observed driving to a New York airport in an elusive manner and thereafter flying to Denver where he was met by Robba during the early morning hours after which the pair proceeded to Robba's residence.

Furthermore, as in *Frazier, supra,* "[t]hese same facts also suggest the existence of exigent circumstances justifying the limited intrusion (installation of a beeper) conducted in the instant case." Gaias was followed directly from New York to Denver and thence to Robba's residence, arriving in the early morning hours. Surveillance was initiated shortly thereafter at a time when no magistrates were available, and at a time when the agents had no idea if Robba and Gaias would remain in the residence for a few minutes, a few hours, or for a few days.

Although the agents were therefore fully justified in attaching the electronic tracking device to Robba's car, without first securing a court order, we note the device did little more than assist the agents in following Robba and Gaias to Royce International. Once at Royce International, Robba and Gaias were observed, along with Shovea, in loading and unloading boxes into their respective vehicles. This evidence was not dispositive nor crucial and its exclusion would not have affected the outcome reached.

II.

Shovea contends: (1) the evidence was insufficient to convict; (2) the trial court erred in refusing to strike Agent Barker's testimony; (3) his motion for mistrial should have been granted after the United States Attorney made improper rebuttal argument; (4) the trial court erred in not suppressing the evidence obtained via execution of the search warrant; (5) the jury was improperly instructed relative to possession; and (6) Government witnesses were allowed to testify as experts in an area in which they were not properly qualified.

(a)

[5, 6] Shovea contends that the evidence was insufficient to support the verdicts of guilty returned against him for conspiracy, manufacture and possession with intent to distribute methamphetamine, and aiding and abetting. On appeal from a jury con-

viction, we must view the evidence, both direct and circumstantial, and all reasonable inferences to be drawn therefrom in the light most favorable to the Government in determining its sufficiency. *United States v. Walton,* 552 F.2d 1354 (10th Cir. 1977), *cert. denied,* 431 U.S. 959, 97 S.Ct. 2685, 53 L.Ed.2d 277 (1977); *United States v. Brown,* 540 F.2d 1048 (10th Cir. 1976), *cert. denied,* 429 U.S. 1100, 97 S.Ct. 1122, 51 L.Ed.2d 549 (1977). Applying this standard to the facts in this record, we hold that the evidence is sufficient to sustain the Shovea conviction.

Aside from the fact that Shovea was observed at his place of employment, Royce International, on September 18, 1976, together with Robba and Gaias moving objects between a warehouse and his vehicle which "brief vignette . . . [Shovea alleges] . . . connects up in no way with the subsequent facts of the case," Shovea was observed exiting and reentering the residence in question on the evening of the arrest looking about carefully, at a time when methamphetamine was being manufactured in the residence and from which a strong odor of ether emanated. He was thereafter observed shortly prior to his arrest, carrying boxes and a barrel from the house which contained methamphetamine. These facts established sufficient evidence upon which the jury could convict Shovea. *See: United States v. Stricklin,* 534 F.2d 1386 (10th Cir. 1976), *cert. denied,* 429 U.S. 831, 97 S.Ct. 92, 50 L.Ed.2d 95 (1976).

(b)

[7] Shovea contends the trial court erred in failing to grant his motion to strike the testimony of DEA Agent Barker following revelation that all of the agent's investigatory notes relative to the events herein had been destroyed. Agent Barker's notes taken during the investigation, were turned over to Agent Moren. Thereafter, Agent Moren incorporated Barker's notes into a report, after which Barker's notes were destroyed pursuant to established policy.

An *in camera* hearing was held on Shovea's motions to dismiss based on the destruction of the notes or in the alternative to strike:

THE COURT: But I'm not aware of any substantial body of law which supports a motion to strike or any other type of motion based upon the destruction of notes in the absence of a showing that the destruction was with malice or evil motive or intent.

I'm not aware of any body of law which says that the motion is good, whereas here the destruction I gather was in accordance with recently established investigative practices in the— within the rules and regulations of this particular agency at that time.

I find absolutely nothing in the evidence to suggest that there was any evil motive in destruction. I find absolutely nothing in the evidence to suggest possible prejudice to the defendant. If you can show me either evil motive or real prejudice to the defendant, that's something else again, but I'm not going to grant your motion in the absence of that.

MR. MARKS: Your Honor, I understand what the criteria are that the Court is setting out. I would submit that I think it would be extremely difficult for any attorney to show prejudice when the document is no longer in existence. And, of course, I don't have any way of advising the Court of what was contained therein.

THE COURT: That's entirely true, but the cross-examination in the area was pretty limited. I think if you'd really thought there was any evil motive or prejudice, knowing your abilities as a cross-examiner, you would have gone a lot farther and a lot harder. I would have.

MR. MARKS: Frankly, I would, too. I don't know of any evil motives and I doubt there were evil motives.

THE COURT: So do I.

[R., Suppl. Vol. II, pp. 322–323.]

In *United States v. Covello,* 410 F.2d 536 (2d Cir. 1969), *cert. denied,* 396 U.S. 879, 90

S.Ct. 150, 24 L.Ed.2d 136 (1969), the Court opined:

> Appellant next claims that the good faith destruction of handwritten interview notes deprived him of his rights at trial under the Jencks Act. At the close of the direct examination of each of the Government's main witnesses defendant requested and received FBI reports regarding FBI interviews with each of the witnesses. Defendant claims, however, that under 18 U.S.C. § 3500 he was also entitled to the original handwritten interview notes of the FBI agents from which the reports were made. At a voir dire examination the agents testified that, pursuant to the practice they customarily follow, they destroyed their notes in good faith after incorporating them into typewritten reports. Under the circumstances, we find no violation of § 3500. The case law amply supports our ruling. Absent an indication that the notes were destroyed for an improper purpose or that the handwritten data was not preserved in the formal reports the reports satisfy the requirements of § 3500. . .
>
> (Citations omitted.)

410 F.2d, at p. 545.

See also: United States v. Lane, 574 F.2d 1019 (10th Cir. 1978), where this court said in pertinent part:

> We think it would be a judicial invasion into proper law enforcement to *require* the preservation of such notes (DEA agents' investigatory notes) and are convinced that to reverse this case as appellant urges at this late date would thwart justice. *See generally, United States v. Smaldone,* 10 Cir., 484 F.2d 311–18, *cert. denied,* 415 U.S. 915, 94 S.Ct. 1411, 39 L.Ed.2d 469.

P. 1022.

Applying this standard, we hold that the trial court did not err in refusing to strike Agent Barker's testimony.

(c)

Shovea contends the court erred in refusing to grant his motion for a mistrial made subsequent to rebuttal argument presented by the Government. In closing his argument the Assistant United States Attorney stated:

> And they'd have you believe, well, the reason Mr. Shovea was out at Royce International is because he worked there. Well, I'll concede that he did work there, ladies and gentlemen, but an interesting thing about that, Mr. Shovea—it came out in testimony that he worked there at Royce International. Well, I'm just wondering, perhaps, if he was the one that gave Mr. Gaias the idea to use the fictitious name in New York of Royce International to order the phenyl–2–proponone that was used to make the metamphetamine. It's a possibility. And it's something I would like you to consider in your deliberations.
>
> Thank you for your time and patience.

[R., Suppl. Vol. II, pp. 359–360.]

Shovea argues that "no evidence whatsoever was ever introduced which could lead to the supposition or inference that Mr. Shovea gave Mr. Gaias the idea to use the name in New York of Royce International with which to order the phenyl–2–proponone." Shovea did not object to the statement when made but he did move for a mistrial thereafter:

> MR. MARKS: Based upon Mr. Fanning's last comments in his closing statement, his comments as far as his surmise as to what may have happened, were not supported by the evidence.
>
> THE COURT: Had you objected at the time, I would have corrected it, but I'm not going to give you a mistrial.
>
> MR. MARKS: Well, I didn't want to object at that time. I thought that would bring more attention.
>
> THE COURT: You could have corrected it. Do you want time tomorrow. No, I'll deny your motion for mistrial.

[R., Suppl. Vol. IV, p. 384.]

[8] In light of the fact that Shovea did not object to the prosecutor's statement when made, we must determine if the statement gave rise to clear error. In *United States v. Stevens,* 452 F.2d 633 (10th Cir. 1972), we observed:

In determining whether the "clear error" rule should be invoked, the entire record must be reviewed and considered. *Adams v. United States,* 375 F.2d 635 (10th Cir. 1967), cert. denied, 389 U.S. 880, 88 S.Ct. 117, 19 L.Ed.2d 173 (1967); *Jennings v. United States,* 364 F.2d 513 (10th Cir. 1966), *cert. denied,* 385 U.S. 1030, 87 S.Ct. 760, 17 L.Ed.2d 677 (1967). And in weighing whether there was a clear error the most significant factor to be considered is the strength of the case against the defendant. *United States v. Williams,* 445 F.2d 421 (10th Cir. 1971). The evidence against Stevens is substantial; the testimony concerning other stolen vehicles could not have had a significant effect in influencing the jury verdict. *Kotteakos v. United States,* 328 U.S. 750, 66 S.Ct. 1239, 90 L.Ed. 1557 (1946).

452 F.2d, at p. 635.

We hold that the prosecutor's comment did not give rise to clear error. Shovea's participation in the conspiracy was substantial. Error, if present, was harmless. In *United States v. Guerrero,* 517 F.2d 528 (10th Cir. 1975), we stated:

We recently noted in *Young v. Anderson,* 513 F.2d 969 (10th Cir. 1975), citing to *Donnelly v. DeChristoforo,* 416 U.S. 637, 94 S.Ct. 1868, 40 L.Ed.2d 431 (1974):

. . . not every trial error or infirmity which might call for application of supervisory powers correspondingly constitutes a "failure to observe that fundamental fairness essential to the every concept of justice." *Lisenba v. California,* 314 U.S. 219, 236 [62 S.Ct. 280, 290, 86 L.Ed. 166] (1941).

416 U.S. 637, at 642, 94 S.Ct. 1868, at 1871, 40 L.Ed.2d 431.

517 F.2d, at p. 531.

See also: United States v. Hall, 536 F.2d 313 (10th Cir. 1976), *cert. denied,* 429 U.S. 919, 97 S.Ct. 313, 50 L.Ed.2d 285 (1976); *Sanchez v. Heggie,* 531 F.2d 964 (10th Cir. 1976); *cert. denied,* 429 U.S. 849, 97 S.Ct. 135, 50 L.Ed.2d 122 (1976).

[9] Shovea's trial attorney was aware that the comment was made. He opted, as a matter of trial tactic, not to move the court for corrective action at that time. Under these circumstances and in view of the relative harmless nature of the comment, the trial court properly refused to grant Shovea's motion for mistrial.

(d), (e) and (f)

Shovea's remaining allegations of error do not merit further detailed discussion. The evidence obtained by the search following execution of the search warrant was proper, as discussed under Robba, *supra;* the trial court's instructions relating to possession were proper; and the Government's experts were properly qualified.

III.

Gaias' sole allegation of error is that the trial court erred in allowing in evidence that which the Government obtained by search and seizure at 3352 West Gill Place following the execution of the search warrant, since "that search warrant was substantially based upon a previous unconstitutional search of . . . [his] . . . suitcase." This contention is without merit. *See* Robba (a), *supra.*

WE AFFIRM.

Citation   Rank(R)   Page(P)   Database   Mode
580 F.2d 1382   R 1 OF 1   P 1 OF 35   CTA   T

UNITED STATES of America, Plaintiff-Appellee,
v.
Scott Andrew SHOVEA, Gebbie Hugh Robba, Stephen Howard Gaias, Jr.,
Defendants-Appellants.
Nos. 77-1078, 77-1079 and 77-1184.
United States Court of Appeals,
Tenth Circuit.
Submitted May 8, 1978.
Decided July 27, 1978.
Rehearing Denied in No. 77-1078 Sept. 13, 1978.
Defendants were convicted in the United States District Court for the District
of Colorado, Fred M. Winner, Chief Judge, of conspiracy to manufacture and
possess with intent to distribute methamphetamine, a scheduled II controlled
substance, and they appealed. The Court of Appeals, Barrett, Circuit Judge,
held that: (1) one defendant did not have standing to challenge X-ray search of
suitcase; (2) federal agents had sufficient probable cause to attach electronic
tracking device to defendant's car without first acquiring court order and did
not violate defendant's Fourth Amendment right in so doing; (3) evidence
sustained convictions and (4) trial court did not err in failing to grant
defense motion to strike testimony of DEA agent, even though all of agent's
COPR. (C) WEST 1986 NO CLAIM TO ORIG. U.S. GOVT. WORKS

580 F.2d 1382   R 1 OF 1   P 5 OF 35   CTA   P

349K7(10)
SEARCHES AND SEIZURES
K. Persons, places, and possessions protected from searches and seizures
without warrant.
C.A.Colo. 1978.
Utilization of electronic tracking device, without prior court approval, may be
justified by probable cause and exigent circumstances. U.S.C.A.Const. Amend.
4.
U. S. v. Shovea
580 F.2d 1382
COPR. (C) WEST 1986 NO CLAIM TO ORIG. U.S. GOVT. WORKS

349K7(10)
SEARCHES AND SEIZURES
K. Persons, places, and possessions protected from searches and seizures without warrant.
C.A.Colo. 1978.
Federal agents had sufficient probable cause to attach electronic tracking device to defendant's car without first acquiring court order and did not violate defendant's Fourth Amendment rights in so doing, where agents knew that codefendant had purchased chemicals, a primary precursor of methamphetamine, and agents observed codefendant leave residence, carrying suitcase in careful manner, drive to airport in elusive manner, fly to another city where he was met by defendant and drive to defendant's residence. 18 U.S.C.A. s 2; Comprehensive Drug Abuse Prevention and Control Act of 1970, s 401(a)(1), 21 U.S.C.A. s 841(a)(1); U.S.C.A.Const. Amend. 4.
U. S. v. Shovea
580 F.2d 1382
COPR. (C) WEST 1986 NO CLAIM TO ORIG. U.S. GOVT. WORKS

   Jonathan L. Olom, Denver, Colo. (Stanley H. Marks, Denver, Colo., on brief) for appellant Shovea.
   Edward L. Kirkwood, Asst. Federal Public Defender, Denver, Colo. (Daniel J. Sears, Federal Public Defender, Denver, Colo., on brief) for appellants Robba and Gaias.
   Edward W. Nottingham, Asst. U. S. Atty., Denver, Colo., for appellee (Joseph F. Dolan, U. S. Atty., Denver, Colo., with him on brief for Shovea and Robba, Cathlin Donnell, U. S. Atty., Denver, Colo. (Interim) with him on brief for Gaias).

   Before BARRETT, and McKAY, Circuit Judges, and BRATTON, District Judge.[FN*]

     FN* Of the District of New Mexico, sitting by designation.

   BARRETT, Circuit Judge.
   Scott Shovea (Shovea), Gebbie Robba (Robba) and Stephen Gaias (Gaias) appeal their jury convictions of conspiracy to manufacture and possess with intent to distribute methamphetamine, a schedule II controlled substance, in violation of 18 U.S.C.A. s 2 and 21 U.S.C.A. s 841(a)(1).
   Appellants were originally indicted with Geoffrey Hungerford (Hungerford). At the commencement of the trial, the Government dismissed its charges against
COPR. (C) WEST 1986 NO CLAIM TO ORIG. U.S. GOVT. WORKS

Hungerford. Thereafter, a mistrial was declared as to Gaias. The trial
proceeded as to Shovea and Robba. They were convicted. Subsequent thereto,
Gaias was tried individually and convicted. A detailed recitation of the
pertinent facts should facilitate our review.

 Gaias originally ordered a chemical, phenyl-2-proponone (p-2-p), a primary
precursor of methamphetamine, from a New York chemical company under the name
of "Jay Edwards." The order was submitted on behalf of "Royce International,
315 Broadway, Port Jefferson, New York." Thereafter federal agents set up a
controlled delivery for the chemical.

 On September 17, 1976, Gaias was observed by the agents picking up the
chemical, after which he was followed to 315 Broadway, a house in a residential
area. Shortly thereafter, Gaias was observed exiting the house carrying a
suitcase very carefully. He held the suitcase flat, rather than by the
handle. Two agents then followed Gaias to an airport. While en route, Gaias
drove in excess of the posted speed limits in an elusive manner. Once at the
airport, Gaias boarded a plane which flew to Denver. The agents flew to Denver
on the same plane. They kept Gaias under surveillance at all times. Gaias
arrived in Denver during the early morning hours of September 18, 1976. He was
met there by Robba. Gaias and Robba drove from the airport to a residence
located at 3352 West Gill Place. Agents followed them to the residence. After
Robba and Gaias entered the house, the agents placed an electronic tracking

COPR. (C) WEST 1986 NO CLAIM TO ORIG. U.S. GOVT. WORKS

device on Robba's car. Sporadic surveillance of the residence continued
September 18 through September 20, 1976.

 Gaias' suitcase did not arrive on his incoming flight but it did arrive in
Denver later that morning. Prior to its arrival, Gaias filled out a lost
luggage claim wherein he listed Robba's name and requested that the suitcase be
delivered to 3352 West Gill Place upon its arrival. The suitcase was X-rayed
following its arrival at the Denver airport. The X-rays revealed that four
bottles were in the suitcase. The agents did not open the suitcase. Pursuant
to Gaias' request, the suitcase was delivered to 3352 West Gill Place.

 Shortly after the suitcase was delivered, Gaias and Robba were observed by the
agents leaving the residence and proceeding to Royce International where they,
together with Shovea, loaded and unloaded boxes from their vehicles. Robba and
Shovea were both employed at Royce International at that time. Investigation
had established that someone allegedly associated with Royce International had,
within the prior four months, ordered various chemicals and glassware from a
scientific company, all of which could be utilized in the manufacture of
methamphetamine.

 On the evening of September 20, 1976 agents detected a strong odor of ether
emanating from the 3352 West Gill Place residence. Shovea was observed leaving
the residence, walking down the street, looking in all directions, and then
returning to the residence. The agents, based on their prior experience,

COPR. (C) WEST 1986 NO CLAIM TO ORIG. U.S. GOVT. WORKS

WEST NUTSHELL SERIES

ACCURATE, BRIEF, CONVENIENT

PRICED FOR STUDENT BUDGETS

Accounting and Law—Faris
Administrative Law, 2nd Ed.—Gellhorn & Boyer
Admiralty, 2nd Ed.—Maraist
Agency-Partnership—Steffen
American Indian Law, 2nd Ed.—Canby
Antitrust Law & Economics, 3rd Ed.—Gellhorn
Appellate Advocacy—Hornstein
Art Law—Duboff
Banking & Financial Institutions, 2nd Ed.—Lovett
Civil Procedure, 2nd Ed.—Kane
Civil Rights—Vieira
Commercial Paper, 3rd Ed.—Weber & Speidel
Community Property, 2nd Ed.—Mennell & Boykoff
Comparative Legal Traditions—Glendon, Gordon & Osakwe
Conflicts—Siegel
Constitutional Analysis—Williams
Constitutional Federalism, 2nd Ed.—Engdahl
Constitutional Law—Barron & Dienes
Consumer Law, 2nd Ed.—Epstein & Nickles
Contract Remedies—Friedman
Contracts, 2nd Ed.—Schaber & Rohwer
Corporations, 2nd Ed.—Hamilton
Corrections & Prisoners' Rights, 3rd Ed.—Krantz
Criminal Law, 2nd Ed.—Loewy
Criminal Procedure, Constitutional Limitations, 4th Ed.—Israel & LaFave
Debtor-Creditor Relations, 3rd Ed.—Epstein
Employment Discrimination, Federal Law of, 2nd Ed.—Player
Environmental Law, 2nd Ed.—Findley & Farber
Estate Planning, Introduction to, 3rd Ed.—Lynn
Evidence, Federal Rules of, 2nd Ed.—Graham
Evidence, State and Federal Rules, 2nd Ed.—Rothstein
Family Law, 2nd Ed.—Krause
Federal Estate & Gift Taxation, 4th Ed.—McNulty
Federal Income Taxation of Corporations & Stock-holders, 3rd Ed.—Sobeloff & Weidenbruch
Federal Income Taxation of Individuals, 4th Ed.—McNulty
Federal Jurisdiction, 2nd Ed.—Currie
First Trial—Goldberg
Future Interests—Waggoner
Governmental Contracts—Keyes
Health Care Law and Bioethics—Hall & Ellman
Historical Introduction to Anglo-American Law, 2nd Ed.—Kempin
Immigration Law & Procedure—Weissbrodt
Injunctions—Dobbyn
Insurance Law, 2nd Ed.—Dobbyn
Intellectual Property—Patents, Trademarks & Copy-right—Miller & Davis
International Business Transactions, 3rd Ed.—Fol-som, Gordon & Spanogle

International Human Rights—Buergenthal
International Law, Public, 2nd Ed.—Buergenthal & Maier
International Taxation—Doernberg
Introduction to the Study and Practice of Law—Hegland
Judicial Process—Reynolds
Juvenile Courts, 3rd Ed.—Fox
Labor Arbitration Law & Practice—Nolan
Labor Law, 2nd Ed.—Leslie
Land Use, 2nd Ed.—Wright & Wright
Landlord & Tenant, 2nd Ed.—Hill
Law Study & Law Examinations, Introduction to—Kinyon
Legal Interviewing & Counseling, 2nd Ed.—Shaffer and Elkins
Legal Research, 4th Ed.—Cohen
Legal Writing—Squires & Rombauer
Legislative Law & Process, 2nd Ed.—Davis
Local Government Law, 2nd Ed.—McCarthy
Mass Communication Law, 3rd Ed.—Zuckman, Gaynes, Carter & Dee
Medical Malpractice, 2nd Ed.—King
Military Law—Shanor & Terrell
Oil and Gas, 2nd Ed.—Lowe
Personal Property—Burke
Post Conviction Remedies—Popper
Products Liability, 3rd Ed.—Phillips
Professional Responsibility—Aronson & Weckstein
Real Estate Finance, 2nd Ed.—Bruce
Real Property, 2nd Ed.—Bernhardt
Regulated Industries, 2nd Ed.—Gellhorn & Pierce
Remedies, 2nd Ed.—O'Connell
Sales, 2nd Ed.—Stockton
Schools, Students & Teachers—Alexander & Alexander
Sea, Law of the—Sohn & Gustafson
Secured Transactions, 3rd Ed.—Bailey & Hagedorn
Securities Regulation, 3rd Ed.—Ratner
Sex Discrimination—Thomas
State and Local Taxation and Finance—Gelfand and Salsich, 1986
State Constitutional Law—Marks & Cooper
Torts: Injuries to Persons & Property—Kionka
Torts: Injuries to Relations—Malone
Trial Advocacy, 2nd Ed.—Bergman
Trial & Practice Skills—Hegland
Unfair Trade Practices, 2nd Ed.—McManis
Uniform Commercial Code, 3rd Ed.—Stone
Uniform Probate Code, 2nd Ed.—Averill
Water Law—Getches
Welfare Law: Structure & Entitlement—LaFrance
Wills & Trusts—Mennell
Workers' Compensation & Employee Protection—Hood & Hardy

P7-AIT-062

0-314-32019-9